SO-ATF-021

THE WORLD OF WORK

CAREERS AND THE FUTURE

**Edited by
Howard F. Didsbury, Jr.**

WORLD FUTURE SOCIETY
Bethesda, MD ● U.S.A.

Editor: Howard F. Didsbury, Jr.

Editorial Review Board: Deirdre H. Banks, James J. Crider, Howard F. Didsbury, Jr. (Chairman), Theodore J. Maziarski, Andrew A. Spekke, Stephen H. Van Dyke

Staff Editors: Edward Cornish, Jerry Richardson

Production Manager: Jefferson Cornish

Editorial Coordinator: Sarah Warner

Editorial Consultants: David G. Cox, Mary Ann Madison, Veronica Perry, Michael Warner

Cover Art: Cynthia Fowler

Typesetting: Harper Graphics

Published by:
World Future Society
4916 St. Elmo Avenue
Bethesda, Maryland 20814-5089 ● U.S.A.

Library of Congress Catalog Number: 83-50328

International Standard Book Number: 0-930242-21-1

Printed in the United States of America

Contents

INNOVATION AND ECONOMIC STRATEGY

INCENTIVES AND MOTIVATION

CAREERS AND WORK TRENDS

EDUCATION: WHAT DO WE DO?

WORK, LIFE-STYLE, AND LEISURE

ADDITIONAL READING

Note

This volume was prepared in conjunction with the World Future Society's special conference, "Working Now and in the Future," held in Washington, D.C., August 11 and 12, 1983. Kenneth W. Hunter served as general chairman of the conference. The staff coordinator was David A. Smith.

The papers presented here were selected from the very large number submitted to the Editorial Review Committee. The committee regrets that space limitations permitted only a small number of papers to be published in this volume. In addition, many papers had to be cut substantially. Footnotes and other scholarly paraphernalia were minimized, so that as wide a selection of thoughts as possible could be presented.

Preface

The papers in this volume offer insights into the problems associated with work and careers, employment and unemployment in a world that is being rapidly transformed by accelerating technological innovations. The authors examine, from a wide variety of perspectives, the likely impacts of the multi-faceted changes now under way. As is the usual case with a volume in which there are a large number of contributors, a sharp delineation of topics is difficult, if not impossible.

We hope the arrangement that has been adopted will be helpful to the reader. The introduction, "Finding Solutions to the Real Problems," is designed to serve as a general orientation. Following this, the book is organized into eight sections. These sections are: Structural Changes in the Economy; Managing Technological Change; Innovation and Economic Strategy; Incentives and Motivation; Careers and Work Trends; Education: What Do We Do?; Work, Life-style, and Leisure; and Additional Reading.

Two additional brief comments:

The reader will find that the section entitled "Education: What Do We Do?" offers a number of radically different views of the role and need for education in the emerging electronic age. Some views appear to be contradictory. Confronted with such contradictory assertions, one can sympathize with policy-makers' dilemmas.

Lastly, the eighth section consists of a brief, selective bibliography of additional sources for further reading.

Introduction

Finding Solutions to the Real Problems

by

Howard F. Didsbury, Jr.

The United States—once without peer—faces serious and far-reaching economic and technological challenges of both international and national consequence. On this there is general agreement.

In retrospect, the *Pax Americana*, the United States Century, was accelerated and compressed into the period of 1945 to 1975 or thereabouts. The first Arab oil embargo occurred in the fall of 1973; 1975 marked the end of the Vietnamese War. Massive United States productivity, economic growth, general prosperity (albeit with periodic recessions), and rising expectations charactērized those years when both the vanquished and victorious of World War II recuperated and rebuilt. In terms of sheer geopolitical and military power, two giants stood astride the globe, the United States and the Soviet Union.

Today these two giants find themselves handicapped—perhaps profoundly—by their own enormous destructive technology. As the twenty-first century approaches, there is every indication that it will be characterized by an even greater tendency toward polycentrism, that is, a multipolar political world. In addition, it is reasonable to anticipate many new members joining the ranks of the advanced and technologically sophisticated nations. The economic and political implications of humanity's novel state of affairs are immense.

Is such an eventuality a cause for alarm, fear, or despair? Sober reflection suggests that it is not. The vast economic and technological transformation in which more and more nations are involved means that the United States may no longer be the first of two great powers. From here on, we and the Soviet Union—excluding nuclear madness, of course—will be but two of an increasing number of advanced technological nations. This newly emerging arrangement may, in fact, foreshadow the evolution of a planetary system only vaguely perceived at this time. Such a development should not be alien to Americans. The Great Seal of the United States itself announces the expectation of *"Novus Ordo Seclorum,"* the advent of "New Order for the Ages."

Howard F. Didsbury, Jr., is professor of history and executive director, Program for the Study of the Future, Kean College of New Jersey, Union, New Jersey. He is also director of media projects for the World Future Society.

ix

Consider the national dimension of the economic and technological challenges we face. One hears much about the lack of worker incentive and morale, productivity decline, excessive taxation, governmental meddling and regulations, etc., as the causes (one or all in concert) of the national economic malaise. Such myths and misconceptions tend to cloud our thinking and distract us from a pursuit of the truly novel insights required for imaginative, effective planning.

Is excessive taxation destroying initiative and discouraging investment? The United States has lower tax rates than 16 other industrialized nations. We hear that the power of unionized labor inhibits economic progress. But U.S. workers are the least unionized of advanced industrial nations. According to the Bureau of Labor Statistics of the U.S. Department of Labor, in 1980 only 20.8% of the U.S. labor force was unionized. American workers, it is asserted, have too much time off, yet German workers as well as others have more holidays. Another notion alleges U.S. workers to be overly concerned with job security. This may well be—and for very good reason. The American worker can be fired more easily than a worker in most other industrial nations—job insecurity is a reality. Do inordinate social-service expenditures hobble investment and drag the economy down? Other industrial nations spend more proportionately on such services. In fact, "Alone of all industrial countries, the U.S. lacks a national health insurance system."[1]

Governmental interference and regulations, especially environmental regulations, are also cited as causes of poor economic performance. Yet, other industrial nations, such as West Germany and Japan, have much more governmental interference and more stringent environmental regulations. Finally, "Few truisms are so firmly implanted in the American consciousness as the notion that our economy is a private-enterprise one. The fact is that it is not. It is private and public, profit-making and not-for-profit: a pluralistic economy." "The important distinction is between the private, profit-seeking sector and the total not-for-profit sector."[2] The not-for-profit sector employs one worker out of three. The structural changes taking place in our economy become clearer when such myths are dispelled, and solutions to genuine problems can then be sought.

The transformation of the economy was described by Eli Ginzberg and George J. Vojta in a recent article:

> Four mutually reinforcing changes—the displacement of goods by services at the cutting edge of economic growth, the growth of the not-for-profit sector, the increasing importance of human capital and the internationalization of the business system—have transformed the U.S. economy over the past 30 years.[3]

Are we not an information economy when one-half of the gross national product is concerned with the production, processing, and handling of information? When one-half of the U.S. labor force is so employed? We must not assume these fundamental changes to be mere departures or aberrations from the "normal" course of events. To do so would be folly.

A microelectronics revolution is occurring and we can forecast some of its likely effects. Changes in the twentieth century, especially in the latter half, appear to be accelerating. Technological innovation and application, encompassing robotics, is everywhere evident. With such changes, technological unemployment and underemployment may well prove to be a permanent, nontransitional phenomenon. As refutation, past historical examples of such fears and their final banishment with the creation of greater employment could be cited. It is the fable of the boy crying wolf, we are reminded. But in the fable the wolf finally appears. Can we be sure that this wolf, permanent unemployment, has not at last arrived?

In a provocative book review article in two parts entitled "Management and the Microelectronic Revolution,"[4] Brian C. Twiss discussed a growing consensus among experts that microelectronics would eliminate more jobs than it created. They foresee a decline in the number of skilled workers because of the computer's speed, accuracy, memory capacity, and processing capability. Before long, robots will combine decision-making with manual dexterity. "Whereas previous technologies such as the car industry created multiplier effects which stimulated the growth of new labour employing activities, for example car repair and garage[s] . . . the reverse is the case with microelectronics. Amongst the reasons for this are the long life, reliability, small size, low material usage, low power consumption and high speed of operation of microelectronic circuits." These experts feel that microelectronics will decimate office jobs. Overall, improved production techniques will allow marked increases in productivity without corresponding increases in the work force in the microelectronics industry. Such effects weaken the view that the microelectronics revolution is just another technological revolution. Ultimately, workers may become superfluous by "design." The objective is to increase productivity and cut costs. Why redesign a job in order to "enrich" it for the worker if the worker himself can be eliminated by redesign?

In the past, it is true, a new technology led to increased employment—ultimately. It should be noted, though all too frequently it is not, that that "ultimately" signified considerable interim anxiety, hardship, and tragedy for many people. Whenever someone glibly declares that things will be fine in the long run, one is reminded of a remark attributed to John Maynard Keynes to the effect that in the long run we are all dead. It all depends upon how long the run is, and who is forced to do the running. What is to be done with the many while they await the happy day of new employment alternatives?

The previous historical trend may not be duplicated. The new jobs created may not be greater than the number eliminated. Equally important, though often obscured by all the talk of the need for increased levels of education and training and retraining, will the new jobs be more challenging or less challenging than the jobs being eliminated? For all? For whom?

A dark side of the glamorous picture of the need for "advanced" education and/or retraining lies in the fact that much of the new technology demands great mental powers for its creation, but for its operation or, more properly, "tending," it requires much lower mental abilities than the tasks it replaces or eliminates. In other words, the creators of the systems will be immensely stimulated; the "tenders" of the systems immensely bored.

Another problem is women in the work force today and tomorrow. In the course of the development of industrial civilization, few thinkers ever contemplated women permanently in the work force seeking their own personal career and talent development. Full employment, when discussed, was assumed to mean full *male* employment.

Technological unemployment and women permanently in the work force are factors in the crucial question: Will there be jobs for all who want jobs? This question posed today means something very different than it did when posed 30 or 40 years ago. Today, it must be considered in a totally new cultural milieu. Failure to do so may lead to great social unrest.

In a world of pervasive mass communication media that create and perpetuate insatiable wants and extravagant life expectations, who will take jobs that are dull or unpleasant, however euphemistically they may be described? If the financial rewards for doing such tasks are raised dramatically to attract takers, the incentive on the part of employers to substitute robots, etc., becomes increasingly attractive, if not compelling for economic survival.

Unwillingness to accept just any job on the part of the jobless, though widely denounced in terms approaching moral condemnation, is a logical result of people living immersed in a world of communication media that inculcate an ethos of personal gratification and individual self-fulfillment. There is little, if any, esteem for the performance of dull or unpleasant jobs. We are victims of our own success. We have succeeded remarkably in communicating the easy, selfish, hedonistic life-style so well that few will accept anything less. Time and again, in discussions of jobs, there seems to be a failure to appreciate sufficiently the cultural milieu created by the media and how this milieu affects attitudes toward work and worker expectations. One wonders how long the misery and suffering associated with the rise of industrial civilization would have been quietly endured if mass communication media had existed at the time. Not long, one suspects.

Contrary to a widespread current view that sees a lessening role for government in the future as a desired goal or inevitable trend, the complexity, interrelatedness, and extensiveness of such problems as the structural transformation of the economy and the microelectronics revolution suggest that such a view may be illusory. Does it seem likely that the private, for-profit sector can possibly respond adequately to the multiplicity of complex challenges that must be dealt with simultaneously? The private sector cannot meet these momentous challenges—not because of ignorance or indifference but from incapacity.

The challenges we face and the passage of time will make it clear that extravagant faith in the dynamics of untrammelled self-interest is becoming increasingly unproductive, if not positively detrimental to national survival. There is beginning to appear a recognition of the limitations of the "adversarial syndrome" that has been so characteristic of the United States. More and more, people are discovering the necessity of having a genuine sense of cooperation among industry, labor, and government. Effective, productive cooperation will be the result of responsible leadership, vision, and dedication on the part of each.

Notes

1. Ira C. Magaziner and Robert B. Reich, *Minding America's Business: The Decline and Rise of the American Economy.* New York: Harcourt Brace Jovanovich, 1982, p. 19. See chapter 1 (The American Standard of Living, pp. 11–27) and chapter 3 (Common Explanations for the Productivity Decline in the United States, pp. 41–59).

2. Eli Ginzberg, "The Pluralistic Economy of the U.S." in *Scientific American,* December 1976, Vol. 235, No. 6, p. 25.

3. "The Service Sector of the U.S. Economy" in *Scientific American,* March 1981, Vol. 244, No. 3, pp. 52–53.

4. "Management and the Microelectronics Revolution—Part I—Book Review Article," *Long Range Planning,* 1981, Vol. 14, No. 5, pp. 101–105. "Management and the Microelectronics Revolution—Part II—Book Review Article," *Long Range Planning,* 1981, Vol. 14, No. 6, pp. 83–89.

Structural Changes
in the Economy

Changes in the World of Work: Some Implications for the Future

by

David Macarov

There are certain changes in society that can be likened to an incoming tide—slowly, inexorably, and quietly they make their way over a long period of time until one day the results become clearly discernible. There are other changes that are more like a tidal wave—suddenly, within a relatively short time, immense changes take place. There are still other changes that are like underground water—unless and until searched for, they remain mostly invisible. In this paper, three changes in the world of work and some of their implications for the future will be discussed: the ongoing shift from industrial to service employment; the impact of technology; and changing worker attitudes, each of which is a change of a different kind. Each of these changes influences the others, and is, in turn, influenced by them. They are discussed separately here purely for heuristic purposes.

There are, to be sure, important changes taking place in the world of work in addition to these three, such as the entry of more women into the workplace; the role of minority groups; the use of migrant and immigrant labor; the aging of work populations; higher levels of education among workers; and others. However, the three changes mentioned above seem more overarching, affecting more societal aspects, and of greater portent than any others, and hence make up the subject of this article.

The data and trends used herein are mainly taken from American sources, unless otherwise noted. The time-frame, forward and backward, is middle-range—about 50 years. Work is used to mean that which people do to acquire the material necessities and luxuries of life and the services that they need and want.

The Shift to Service Employment

The shift from manufacturing or industrial employment to employment in the services can best be likened to an incoming tide. It has been growing slowly but continually for at least the last 50 years—so slowly that the implications of this basic shift in one of the most important bases of

David Macarov is associate professor, Paul Baerwald School of Social Work, The Hebrew University of Jerusalem, Mt. Scopus, Jerusalem, Israel.

society has not yet resulted in the public attention, the research, the adoption of new policies, and modifications in attitudes that the magnitude of the shift requires.

In 1929, 40% of the jobs in the United States were in the service sector (Gershuny and Rosengren). In 1950, the United States moved into that which has been termed "the service society," with 51% of the jobs in the services (Gershuny and Rosengren; Gartner and Reissman). This grew to 55% in 1967, and by 1980 was estimated at 80% (Thurow). In fact, of all the new jobs created between 1973 and 1980, 70% were in the services (Bolan), and almost 50% of total job growth in the 1970s came from the white collar and service sectors (Leon). In addition, two-thirds of the self-employed in the United States produce services (Newland). And there are forecasts that service employment will constitute 95% of all employment by the end of this century (Stellman), and even that it will reach 97% as early as 1990 (Best).

Most of the studies and projections listed above simply distinguish between people who create or change physical objects, and those who do not. However, an understanding of the extent of the shift and its implications demands more precise definitions. Unfortunately, it is not easy to arrive at a satisfactory definition of the services. A Bureau of Labor report on productivity in the services says: "There are severe conceptual as well as data problems in measuring productivity in such industries as education and social services, and in the important field of medical services" (Mark). Some of these difficulties can be understood when it is recognized that in Britain, for example, half of the people who are said to be engaged in services perform functions that are in direct support of production activities (Gershuny). Or, looked at another way, about a third of the people who work in goods-producing activities have service jobs (Newland). These are the people who type the letters, move the goods, keep the books, solicit sales, prepare advertising, and clean the offices and plants. Without them, production would be neither possible nor useful; without production, these workers would have no function. In these cases, the relationship between services and production is symbiotic.

There is no generally accepted way of defining services. Definitions tend to be operational, i.e., depending on the purpose of the research or the thrust of the article. For example, the Bureau of Labor Statistics distinguished between four categories of white-collar workers; four categories of blue-collar workers; service workers; and farm workers. Howe would add "pink-collar" workers, and discussants of robots sometimes refer to them as "steel-collar" workers. The Occupation Code used by the InterUniversity Consortium for Political Research (Robinson, et al.) lists social workers as professional and technical, as are accountants and funeral directors, whereas army officers are listed as service workers. Other studies use other bases for grouping jobs (Morris and Murphy; Roe; Super). Some equate social class with types of jobs (Freeman and Lambert), and even the term "working class" is defined differently in many investigations (Miller, 1964).

The definitional differences *within* the services are no less formidable.

Miller (1978), for example, divides services between those that contribute to labor power and those that contribute to well-being. However, between these two (and ignoring the overlap among them) there are services that contribute to well-being directly and indirectly; personally and anonymously; greatly or marginally; by performing a service or by delivering a service; and even by making it possible for the person to serve himself or herself.

For example, nurses generally perform services directly for patients, while the fruits of medical researchers' work is an indirect service. The social worker may deal with an individual on a personal and caring basis, whereas the ticket-seller at the theatre neither knows nor cares about the purchaser as an individual. The policeman who thwarts a crime contributes greatly to the well-being of the intended victim, while the giving of parking tickets contributes only marginally to the well-being of most people. Similarly, peacetime soldiers are rarely seen as performing as direct a personal service as are firemen fighting a blaze. The hairdresser, the plumber, the electrician may be seen as performing a service, while the fastfood counter person, the bank teller, or the postman may be seen as delivering a service. Finally, the person who installs the vending machine or the bankomat makes it possible for the client to serve himself or herself. Even within the so-called "human services," usually thought of as consisting of education, nursing, and social work, but actually including institutional care, probation officers, guidance counselors, etc., there are those who distinguish between "general" and "personal" services (Kamerman and Kahn), and—within the personal services—between working with individuals, families, groups, neighborhoods, and communities.

These definitional and taxonomic distinctions and confusions are not simply pedantic—they mask real differences in the demands and rewards of various jobs, and must be taken into account when attempting to understand patterns, attitudes, and trends in the world of work. Unfortunately, the differences between productive and service jobs, no matter how fuzzily defined, and the differences between various types of service jobs are rarely taken into consideration in research on or discussions of work and workers. Indeed, the great bulk of research done in, and attention paid to, the world of work continues to take place within the manufacturing sector and among industrial workers, despite the fact that only a small minority of jobs are actually goods-producing today.

And yet the service society in which we live may be different from the industrial society of the past in many ways, with differences between the various types of services equally great. In light of the research-lag that exists—and even the lack of an adequate taxonomy of services—some of these differences can only be identified through tangential evidence, and others through anecdotal, impressionistic, and logical means. Some of these changes, and their implications, follow.

Prestige. In the past, working in the services has generally been considered more prestigeful than engaging in factory work (Caplow), when the level and conditions of the job are held constant. Under the same circumstances, women were found to prefer clerical work to factory work, even when the former paid less (Caplow). Among all service workers, performing personal services under the aegis of an organization was preferred to doing the same work for an individual. These findings, however, are now 30 years old. Beaumont, among others, feels that service jobs—or, more precisely, public service jobs—have fallen into comparative disrepute in the intervening period, due to increased personal financial security, the difficulty of measuring results in the services, increasing affluence, and budget-cutting measures that posit public services as "fat" that can be reduced without damaging anyone. There is also the possibility that services in many areas, having been taken over by new immigrants, are no longer seen as prestigious. It is equally possible that such jobs have been relegated to new immigrants precisely because they lack status. In any case, the extent to which working in the services—or in certain services—is seen as more or less prestigious may have growing implications for the recruitment and retention of workers in such positions.

Salaries and productivity. It is difficult to find aggregate figures that compare salaries in industry with those in service, due to the definitional problems mentioned previously. However, if one accepts the Bureau of Labor Statistics' taxonomy, then it is clear that the services—widely defined—pay less than other sectors. In 1980 the average gross weekly wage in the private sector of the United States, excluding agriculture as an area and supervisory/managerial personnel as a category, was $235. Workers in mining, construction, manufacturing, transportation, and public utilities earned more than the average; persons in wholesale and retail trade, finance, insurance, real estate, and the services earned less. For example, mine workers earned $396; wholesale and retail workers, $176; and service workers, $190. How the addition of supervisory and managerial services in the various sectors would affect these relationships is not clear, but to the extent that these figures affect reality on the nonmanagerial level, then the shift from manufacturing to service occupations will result in lower incomes from most workers, unless the wage structure is adjusted to match the new reality.

A continuing problem in the determination of wages in the service sector is the measurement of productivity (Miller). Even if one considers units of service, instead of individuals, there is general agreement that results are difficult to measure, as are the problems in simply determining costs. A Steelcase-sponsored study called the measurement of white-collar productivity "the most perplexing and troublesome issue" in the area (*World of Work Report*, January, 1983).

Because of such difficulties—and adding to them—most measures of productivity in the services use the methods and instruments of industry, and thus tend toward the quantitative. In a productivity drive in the New York City social welfare department, for example, results were cited in the number of cases cut from the rolls. There was no attempt to measure the quality of the service, or even the number of people entitled to services and not receiving them (Katzell). Amitai Etzioni has pointed out the service implications of such measurements—when there is an emphasis on counting, there is a tendency to do the things most easily counted, regardless

6

of their effectiveness. It is for this reason that Peter Drucker holds that service organizations cannot perform: since there is no "bottom line" indicating profit or loss, they have no real criterion for success. Services for the aged, for example, suffer in comparison with rehabilitation services, for the former are clearly an expense, while the latter can be seen as an investment (Black).

The inability to measure the productivity of the services, particularly in qualitative terms, has obvious implications for the growth of the service society. Less obvious is the fact that salaries thus become based on seniority, if not longevity, with raises coming automatically rather than on merit. The meaning of this factor for the quality of services has not yet been explored in any meaningful way.

Education and training. Among the many instruments of socialization that prepare people for the world of work, the educational system is among the most important. The toddler on the see-saw in nursery school is taught to sing that when Jack gets a new master, he shall get but a penny a day because he can't work any faster. Caplow points out that the potato race in kindergarten is conducted along more competitive lines than is the insurance business. Official British reports criticize the educational system as not preparing people sufficiently for work (Anthony), while an official American report says that "the market value of education has driven out its other values" (*Work in America.*) Such socialization, however, usually views work within the industrial context, and the qualities that it seeks to implant arise from that sector. Emphasis is usually on punctuality, behavior, and following the rules; on competition, precision, and seeking pragmatic or measurable results.

It is possible, however, that successful work in the service sector requires different emphases—on creativity, feelings, creating good relationships, cooperation, neighborliness, and (that oft-misunderstood word) empathy. That the socialization undergone in the educational system is still based on industrial rather than service employment is understandable, given the lag between the recognition of a need and its incorporation into formal educational structures, which—according to Marland—may be as great as 50 years.

Another aspect of the educational area has to do with training and retraining courses. Many of these are given in order to make possible a job transition from no-longer-available jobs to new, or other, jobs. Again, most of this training is for industrial or, at best, indirect-service jobs. This may explain, in part, the poor track record of many such training programs. The number of people who do not complete such programs is high, while— as Somers found—drop-outs have a higher job-placement rate than do those who complete such courses. Those who do graduate tend to find jobs in areas other than those for which they were trained (Goldstein). In Israel, only 44% of lightly injured employees who underwent training courses got work in the fields for which they were trained (*Rehabilitation of the Work Injured*). When they get jobs in the field for which they were trained, the job or the pay is usually not as good as in the previous job. Finally, it is not at all clear the extent to which, or in what areas, training

7

or experience in industrial settings is directly transferable to service job needs.

Personal characteristics. It seems entirely possible, if not prima facie evident, that the personal characteristics necessary to succeed in service jobs, and particularly in the so-called "hands-on" services, may be different from those necessary in the industrial world. Neff, for one, has called attention to the possibility of a "work personality"—a relatively enduring set of characteristics, derived from lifelong socialization, that marks the attitude of the individual toward work. Others have sought the developmental factors that lead to differential attitudes toward work (Macarov, 1982). There are also some studies that attempt to correlate personality characteristics with attitudes toward work, but these, inevitably, are done only within the industrial sector.

What is not clear is the extent to which certain personality characteristics are necessary for, or contribute to success in, service jobs. Levinson and associates, discussing service workers, say "These people needed to be loved. And they were loved. That's what giving service gets you." But beyond this, do service workers need to be flexible rather than rigid; outgoing, not introverted? And would these differences be equally important on a production line, for example? Professional schools do sometimes seek evidence of certain characteristics among candidates. In Israel, the desire for medical students who would become family doctors rather than specialists led, at one time, to a search for tests for altruism. Schools of social work sometimes interview candidates for their emotional characteristics as much as for their intellectual level. There are calls for altruism (Lubove), empathy (Keefe), and self-awareness (Brill), among other characteristics. To work successfully in the human services, one may need to be able to live comfortably with uncertainty, since in few services are the results immediately observable and in many of them even the action indicated is a choice among equals. Further, Shamir has pointed out the necessity for social workers to live with the constant role strain of being between "service and servility." Others have discussed "burn-out" in the services in terms of the constant "giving" of oneself that is inherent in the helping professions (Cherviss). There is also the frustration present in not being able to do the job for which one has trained due to lack of resources, lack of time, inadequate arrangements, and bureaucratic regulations (Fisch). An unpublished report of the Ministry of Work and Welfare in Israel speaks of the tendency of experienced social workers to develop hostility toward their clients, due to the abovementioned strains. Consequently, many professional schools, including nursing and social work, either seek empathic candidates, or attempt to teach/instill empathy in students, despite many questions concerning the concept itself (Macarov, 1978). Pearson even questions whether unskilled male workers, presently unemployed, are suitable recruits for the service sector or the new technologies.

Satisfactions. The sources of satisfaction in the services may be quite different from those in industry. In Herzberg's well-known studies, in which sources of satisfaction and dissatisfaction were found to be dissimilar, relationships with others was considered an aspect of work conditions, rather than the work itself, and therefore a dissatisfier. In a study conducted in an Israeli kibbutz, interpersonal relationships were almost evenly divided between satisfiers and dissatisfiers. Further examination revealed that this study included child-care workers and teachers, for whom, in general, relations with pupils resulted in satisfactions, while relations with students' parents had the opposite effect (Macarov, 1971). Thus, satisfactions at work within the services might contain different and/or additional items than satisfaction in industry.

This possibility is fraught with immense importance. Although 50 years of searching has begun to result in the conclusion that there is no reliable, replicable, generalizable relationship between satisfactions and work patterns in industry (Strauss; Locke; Lawler and Porter), the possible influence of workers' feelings on the services they render has hardly been examined. Dyer and Schwab say that "During the (past) decade . . . researchers continued to find no consistent causal or correlational relationship between satisfaction and performance." However, although an assembly-line worker who is highly dissatisfied with some aspect of his or her job might not be inclined or able to vent these feelings on the product—or might be able to do so in a visible, and therefore repairable, manner—the quality of the service worker's "product," be it nursing, social work, or teaching, might suffer in a manner that is not immediately discernible, but which might be counter-indicated, or even damaging. On the other hand, satisfactions from contact with others might be so helpful that they lead to absence of alienation, stress, absenteeism, and the other ills to which job malaise in industry is related.

Again, there is little research in this area, but there is logic in believing that sources of worker satisfaction are different in the services, and that there is a possibility that this has a differential impact on productivity, however measured.

Societal implications. In addition to these differences in individuals that might demarcate the services from industry, there are also societal implications. Self-help groups of various kinds, from recreational to substance-abusers, long presaged the new Quality Circles and similar phenomena in industry, in which meeting together in search of satisfaction and results are of the essence. Many of these groups provide members with services of various kinds, and are characteristic of what Riessman terms the "self-help ethos." He identifies 15 million people in half-a-million such groups. In addition, there is the entire volunteer network in society, which operates almost entirely outside the industrial complex. Gidron indicates that one out of every four Americans over the age of 14 is doing some form of volunteer work, and that the dollar value of this contribution to society is somewhere between $34 billion and $68 billion annually. Indeed, such groups may even reduce the need for service workers. Gershuny postulates that the do-it-yourself movement, as well as those appliances that take the place of workers or service-providers— washing machines, dryers, dishwashers, rug-shampooers, adhesive-backed wallpaper, and similar devices—will lead to the "self-service" society, in which the need for outside services will be minimized. Glazer sees the same general result from the decentralization of services now taking place.

Further, the societal implications of the shift to services should include the fact that the service sector has proved more recession-proof than has the industrial sector, in terms of jobs maintained and created (Urquhart), a fact that also has great implications for the future as society becomes increasingly service-oriented.

Shifting from industry to services. Finally, a word needs to be said about the much-discussed manpower shortage in the services, which the fallout from industry is postulated as filling in. On the one hand, the so-called need is rarely viewed in terms of needing more persons in the indirect services—more ticket sellers, night watchmen, or insurance salesmen, for example—but rather in the human services. Here, too, the need is not seen for more highly trained technicians in the medical field, or even for more teachers. In most cases, there are enough people available, or ready to become available. The shortage is in jobs; or, more precisely, in jobs that will attract workers through good conditions, which Rubin lists as pay, permanence, and perquisites, but which also include status, hours, and the actual work performed. It is doubtful, for example, if there is an actual shortage of nurses in the United States, despite understaffed institutions. One-third of the nurses in the United States are not working in their profession, while another third work only part-time (Rowland). The problems are shift-work, night work, low pay, and little opportunity for advancement. In Israel, where it is officially estimated that another 8,000 nurses are needed, 41% of those trained work only part-time (Handless). Shortages in hospitals are described as lack of job-slots, not of personnel. Training more people, who will also not work or work only part-time, is not an answer.

The actual shortage of service personnel, although rarely defined so openly, is for the lowest levels of the occupations—those who will push the wheelchairs, empty the bedpans, change the linens, do the laundry, serve the food, clean the floors—in short, that which Gans has called the dirty, dead-end jobs of society. In addition to undertaking these tasks, such personnel are called upon to hold the client's hand; listen to complaints, histories, and stories (perhaps many times over); be supportive, cheerful, warm, and helpful; and to maintain high morale among themselves and clients. In return, they will receive the lowest wages, the least job security, the worst conditions, and the lowest status. Mildred Rein points out that only a quarter to a third of the AFDC caseload has employment potential—and then only if the jobs pay more than the minimum wage, and have stability and good fringe benefits. In short, the jobs that society expects the unemployed to take are those that can be filled only through absolute absence of alternatives. To get those jobs filled requires a punitive attitude on the part of society regarding unemployment compensation, social welfare, or other means of sustenance. As McKinlay points out, one should not overestimate the extent to which the service sector can absorb workers who are otherwise unable to find employment. The shift from skilled, semi-skilled, or even unskilled industrial jobs will not ensure enlargement of this area of the service sector.

The Impact of Technology

Whereas the shift to services has been going on for a relatively long time without being given the attention it deserves, the impact of technology on many phases of human life is constantly in the news and often in the headlines. The changes that are taking place are constant, visible, and meaningful—in short, a tidal wave. Technology has a major impact on productivity, production, jobs, and social systems, among other things.

Productivity. Despite fluctuations from year to year, and from country to country, the long-term and middle-term effect of technology on productivity—person/hours output—has been constantly upwards for at least the last 50 years or so. From 1956 to 1964, productivity rose by 41%; from 1966 to 1975, another 27%. According to the International Labor Office, productivity increases, on the average, about 2.7% per year. Since each year's increase is measured by the previous year, there is a compounding effect; in 10 years, individual worker productivity grows by almost 35%.

Although many factors contribute to changes in productivity, the most important factor is that of technological progress, which is often considered a function of investment in research and development. Wilson points out that technology accounted for 54.5% of growth in national income per employed person from 1948 through 1969. As a factor in the postwar growth of the American economy, technology was four times greater than business capital investment; 2.8 times greater than investment in education, and 3.8 times higher than the improvements from more efficient use of resources. "Without technology the growth rate of the postwar economy would have been cut in half" (Wilson).

The role of technology in increasing productivity becomes more evident when compared to human work. Rosow estimates that only 10–25% of the changes in productivity are caused by human labor. In other words, reliance on people working harder, longer, or better as a method of increasing productivity may be badly misplaced. If the goal is productivity, rather than keeping people busy or in income, then efforts to change human work patterns may be very inefficient. The major changes in productivity come about through new methods, new machines, and new materials, including energy. The assembly line and interchangeable parts are examples of new methods; robots and microprocessors are today's new machines; and new materials range from synthetics to tailor-made metals to the results of genetic splicing. Indeed, the constant rise in productivity, over long periods, is hardly attributable to human effort at all—very few people today work as long or as hard as their grandparents did.

In the eighteenth century, a bill was offered in the British House of Parliament to abolish the patent office, since everything possible had already been invented. There is no more probability that technology will cease to advance today than there was then. Indeed, in many respects modern technology is autonomous, each change or invention calling for, making possible, and involving still further inventions. Mensch points out that oversupply of some types of technology results in even stronger demands for technology. The growth of technology and its concomitant, productivity, must have great influence not only on the production of more goods and services at cheaper prices, and on the development of new goods and services, but on other fundamental aspects of society as well.

Work and non-work patterns. The constant growth in productivity has made possible a proliferation of various kinds of material goods. Indeed, there is hardly an item in the Western world that is in short supply due to production difficulties. Most goods are produced in expectation of consumer demand, and could be made available in much greater quantities without straining production capacities. Increased productivity has also made possible the invention and introduction of new items, as well as an expansion in services and the invention of (and requirement for) new services. In fact, the above-mentioned shift from production to services is almost completely a function of growing technology.

Three important changes that have been brought about by technology include the impact on work times, on the number of jobs available, and on the content of the jobs.

Work times. One overall figure typifies the situation: In 1900, the average workweek in the United States was 53 hours; in 1980, 35.5 hours. In addition, vacations are longer, there are more workless holidays, entry into the work force is later, and retirement is earlier. These figures, which are from the International Labour Organization, include part-time workers and take into account overtime work. Insofar as workers holding second jobs is concerned, this has been constant at about 5% of the work force for many years (Michelotti: Rees; Taylor and Sekscenski). There are many predictions that work times will continue to decrease, and there is no reason to believe that the trend will cease or reverse itself. On the contrary, Bell predicts a 30-hour week and 13 weeks of vacation a year by the year 2000. Emery foresees a week of four 8-hour days, with summer and winter vacations, while Albus predicts a 10-hour week. Others use different figures and different time-frames, but no one predicts stabilization of hours at present levels, much less a return to longer work hours.

This is not to say, however, that within these hours people work hard, or to their full capacity. Increasing productivity, which can be translated into less demand for human labor, runs head-on into society's need to provide members with income via jobs, as well as societal values that equate working with worth. Hence, many jobs continue to be maintained despite the fact that changes in machines or methods could eliminate many, if not almost all, the human workers. And in some cases, the jobs are maintained together with the introduction of machinery that makes the job all but useless. Thus, as in the case of the *New York Times* change in printing methods in 1974, 630 people were given lifetime contracts for work that only required 350 people (Zimbalist). Seen on a large scale, the introduction of labor-saving machinery almost always results in some unnecessary jobs being maintained as the cost of labor peace.

Not only as a result of such Luddism, but as a consequence of increasing productivity, most people with jobs that are not at the upper levels of the organizational hierarchy are not called upon to use all their energy, or their full potential. Walbank found that people use about 44% of their ability in their jobs, and Berg and Associates found that 54% of the people could work harder than they do. In this author's research, when kibbutz members were asked why they did not work to their full ability, the response almost invariably was that the job did not require it (Macarov, 1971).

As a consequence of holding jobs that do not require working at full capacity, the phenomenon known scientifically as "unproductive work time," and more familiarly as "loafing" (Schrank), seems to be growing (Kendrick). In addition to anecdotal material of workers gossiping, hanging around, making personal phone calls, and leaving the worksite for personal errands, Cherrington reports tracking workers on a construction job for over two years, finding that only 49% of the time used was related to the job. A study of managers' time use found that only 55% of the time was used for managing (*World of Work Report*, June, 1982). That this is a general phenomenon is supported by a report from Moscow that shop hours in the Soviet Union are being changed to keep workers from "slipping away from their jobs to shop and run errands," and that raiding parties visit bars, restaurants, barber shops, and stores looking for workers who have "ducked out of the office" (*Jerusalem Post*, January 16, 1983).

As technology continues to make inroads on the areas that once required human labor, work times will continue to decrease, but since that decrease will lag behind the actual needed changes, the amount of unproductive time on the job will probably continue to grow.

Impact on the number of jobs. In addition to impacting on the content of jobs, technology will also affect the number of jobs available. The extent of this change, and even its direction, are still hotly debated, in terms of whether technology creates new industries and thus new jobs; whether it replaces old industries with new ones, and thus has a negligible effect; or whether it wipes out more jobs than it creates. Hull and associates hold that technology decreases jobs in manufacturing by about 3% a year, but whether this is made up by increases in service jobs is not clear. One must look at the aggregate figures for employment, while holding constant many other factors such as the price of energy, to arrive at a reasonably educated guess.

What does seem to be clear, however, is that, except for times of war, no industrialized country has had full employment, whether this is defined simply as more jobs than workers available; or jobs of some kind for everyone who wants one; or decent jobs, paying a living wage, offering a good or a service that is socially desirable, through a process that does not damage the ecology. Official unemployment rates throughout the West have been generally rising since World War II, with the "acceptable" rate of unemployment having risen from 4% after the War to 6–7% today—rates that have not been achieved. And the official rate must be seen as one-half to one-third of the actual rate, due to definitional artifacts (Field) and hidden unemployment in terms of part-time jobs, discouraged workers, persons on training stipends, etc. (Macarov, 1980). Together with the classic definitions of frictional, structural, and cyclic unemployment, there seems to exist in most countries that which can best be described as "permanent" unemployment—a situation that training programs, job creation, public service employment, subsidies, and so forth seem unable to eliminate (Taggart; Rein). Indeed, intensified technological competition is the reason for many bankruptcies (Mensch), which adds to unemployment.

It would be a mistake to assume that the impact of technology is confined to the industrial sector. Despite the previously-mentioned difficulties in defining and measuring productivity in the services, such efforts continue (Carnes; Carey and Otto; Carnes and Band) and indicate a growth not less than that in maufacturing—about 2.5% annually. It has been estimated, for example, that automation in offices could easily result in 15% more productivity within five years (*World of Work Report*, November 1980). Even at present, over 30% of middle-management positions in banks could be eliminated without any appreciable effect on service (*World of Work Report*, June 1982). In short, the service sector is no less vulnerable to the inroads of automation than is the manufacturing sector.

Constantly reduced work times, maintenance of unneeded jobs, growing unproductive work time, and increasing unemployment may arise from reasons other than the advance of technology, but the latter has certainly been an important component in the mixture, and one whose impact must be taken into account by all social planners.

Job content. As in other areas of the technology discussion, there is no agreement as to whether technology turns interesting jobs into dull, routine ones ("gauge guarding"); or whether it tends to take over the latter. Insofar as robots are concerned, it seems reasonably clear that they are first introduced to do the difficult, dangerous, undesirable jobs— welding hard-to-get-at spots, spraying paint, etc. As they have become more sophisticated, overriding humanlike shapes, only two arms, and such restrictions, they have moved further and further into tasks that require discrimination, decisions, and the use of humanlike senses. With these advances, a number of researchers have concluded that robots tend to wipe out the dirty, difficult, disagreeable jobs (Glenn and Fielding; Zimbalist; Kraft), thus making life better for workers. On the other hand, there are those who see technology as removing the interesting aspects of work, thereby increasing worker alienation (Richardson). Gable and Meers studied mechanization in a bank setting, and found that one-quarter of the workers seemed to have limited capabilities and/or ambition, and were neutral regarding the change; one-quarter were unsatisfied by the content of their work, but compensated by other elements; and fully one-half of the workers wanted more enriching work.

Regardless of their effect on work or workers, robots seem destined to play an increasingly large role in the future of work. Cassier-Lotto points out that a robot costing $45,000, amortized over eight years, will cost $5 an hour as compared to $15 an hour now paid a human worker in industry. Schrank half-facetiously suggests that it would be well for workers to buy robots to do their own jobs and then lease them to the employers, while living on the differential. Albus seriously discusses changes that will be needed to avoid societal dysfunctions, and dislocations in the event of broadened use of robots, and suggest, inter alia, "if all humans could own the equivalent of one or two robots, they would be financially independent regardless of whether they were employed or not." In any case, much of Japan's successful competition with other industrial countries has been attributed to the policy of using robots in place of humans wherever possible (*New York Times*, March 21, 1982).

It is possible that technology actually polarizes the job situation, removing whatever interest there was in low-level jobs, in terms of interpersonal contacts, control, and interest; while adding interest to upper-level jobs through ability to get more done, to do new things, to solve problems, etc. However, even at this level, there is evidence of an erosion of interest as technology takes over. Computer programmers, for example, who were once thought to have been awarded interesting careers, are now being phased out by computers that program themselves.

Again, changes in the content of jobs are not confined to the industrial sector. The nurse who monitors a computer screen indicating the condition of each patient on the ward may be more efficient than one who makes regular rounds, but may miss the contact, the excitement, and even the exercise. An Israeli study of nurses' satisfactions, for example, indicated that satisfactions from contact with patients far outweighed satisfactions from contact with other nurses, charge nurses, or doctors (Handless). Heller's study of automated office equipment indicated a number of physical and emotional problems as a result. Baim says that growing numbers of service or clerical workers experience the same feelings of alienation as do factory workers.

System changes. Technological changes should not be viewed only within the context of specific machines taking over certain human tasks. The more pervasive impact of technology is on total systems. Gabor, for example, writing in 1964, foresaw wide advances for technology, but confessed that he could not conceive of a machine that would deliver milk to his porch every morning. In the relatively short period since, milkmen have become extinct, because the method of distributing and buying milk, involving supermarkets, cars, deep freezers, throw-away containers, etc., has changed completely. Similarly, if flexitime and flexiplace continue to grow, making it possible to do one's work at home at one's own convenience, this will not only have enormous implications for physical planning, architecture, traffic, and pollution control, but will also impact heavily on the services. The changes possible in child-care patterns and services for the elderly alone are staggering, since many of the current facilities for such people arise due to inability of parents or adult children to be home with the person needing care, due to work commitments. Although, as the Solomons point out, there are people who prefer not to be home with their dependents, or not to be home at all, there are undoubtedly many parents and adult children who would prefer home care for their dependents rather than institutionalization. The same magnitude of change, based on new systems, can be anticipated in leisure-time patterns, among others.

Rate and possibilities of change. Although technological change probably started before the invention of the wheel, the essential difference today is in the rate of change, which seems to be accelerating greatly. Insofar as information is concerned, an Organization for Economic and

Cultural Development report says that information processing capacity is increasing tenfold in capability per unit cost every five years, and this makes information technology qualitatively different from past technical changes (*Science and Technology Policy for the 1980s*).

Insofar as knowledge, as distinct from information, is concerned, by the time the child born today graduates from college, the amount of knowledge in the world will be four times as great. By the time that same child is 50 years old, it will be 32 times as great, and 97% of everything known in the world will have been learned since the child was born (Hillard). In general, there have been more profound changes in the past four decades than there were in the previous six centuries (Shane and Sojka). Mensch holds that 80% of the industrial products and processes now sold in the markets will be phased out by 1990 and replaced by some alternatives; further, about 60% of the present industrial produce will be replaced during this decade by something still to be developed or to be specified. He predicts that the next new cluster of basic innovations will arrive about 1989. On a more piquant note, of the 136 inventions foreseen by George Orwell over 30 years ago, over a hundred are now practical—and 1984 has not yet arrived (Rada).

Of course, such progress is uneven. Airplane travel and automobiles have hardly improved over the last 50 years. Except for some increase in speed, the former is less convenient and more expensive now than in the past; and the latter have only changed cosmetically. As compared to developments in computers, for example, planes and cars have practically stood still. If automobiles had developed at the same rate and distance as computers, you could buy a Rolls Royce for $2.75, get 3 million miles to the gallon, and have enough power to drive the Queen Elizabeth II (Evans).

Finally, a word must be said about the "wolf" theory; that is, that immense changes have been predicted for the progress of technology and have not—as in the case of a workless world—come to pass. First, many of the changes have actually outdistanced previous predictions. Secondly, it is salutary to remember the end of the story of the boy who cried, "Wolf!" The wolf actually came (and the society was unprepared). Rada points out that to hold that because something has not happened it will never happen is analogous to saying that a natural resource cannot be depleted because it has not yet become so. Indeed, one can imagine one dinosaur reassuring another that there is nothing to worry about—there have always been predictions of their extinction, and they continue to exist.

Changing Attitudes

If the shift to services is like a tide, and the growth in productivity like a tidal wave, then changing attitudes toward work are like underground water—rarely seen, unless searched for with the proper instruments. In examining this area, one must distinguish between attitudes actually held, attitudes expressed, and attitudes assumed by others.

It is possible that attitudes toward work have always been negative, else there would have been no need for the admonitions, demands, fables, proverbs, and parables used to coerce people into working since Biblical times, at least. Diocletian had to require youngsters to continue in their fathers' occupations, since they were found to be looking for easier work (Kranzberg and Gies). Certainly in ancient agricultural societies there was no profit to be gained from producing a surplus, which would only rot (Macarov and Fradkin). Indeed, the desire to make work easier was the beginning of all technology, and the desire to work less the root of many social reforms.

Luther's postulation that one served God by working hard placed a religious value on what had been an instrumental activity. Adam Smith's "invisible hand," which required each person to compete with all others in order to arrive at high quality and low prices for all, made non-working, or not working hard, an injury to one's fellows, and thus non-neighborly. Mercantilist philosophy, which put national wealth ahead of individual welfare, made working a patriotic duty. Finally, Freud's prescription for happiness—to love and to work—added an element of mental normality to the reasons for working. In every case, the belief that people should work hard arose from those other than the workers themselves. The socialization that ensued involved all the power of the family, the educational system, the church, the welfare system (Macarov, 1980), and—of course—the economic system. Hence, people have been taught (and often really believe) that not to work is to be immoral, a bad neighbor, unpatriotic, and somehow mentally disturbed.

Consequently, it is no surprise that much survey research finds people reporting themselves as satisfied with their work—90% in Quinn and Staines' study, for example. But both Gutek and Haavio-Mannila warn that, in surveys, most people report themselves as satisfied with every aspect of their lives, even when subsequent probing or behavior indicate that this is probably not true. Deeper probing has led a number of researchers to the conclusion that attitudes toward work are best described as "resigned acceptance" or "fatalistic contentment" (Lasson), arrived at by a surrender process (Robinson), in which expectations from work are lowered. Gardell finds that "the psychological rewards of work, in the form of fellowship and self-realization . . . can be considered satisfactory for no more than a minority of people." Bargal and Shamir, attempting to increase workers' satisfactions through the provision of occupational welfare workers, conclude that in many production and service organizations technological and economic considerations simply do not enable the levels of autonomy, variety, meaningfulness and significance of jobs to be enhanced.

Workers' behavior supports the thesis of growing dissatisfaction at work. Although the reduced work time discussed above does not spring simply from workers's desires, it has certainly not come about over their objections. With the exception of some workaholics (Macholowitz), no one works more than they are paid for. In addition, about five million American workers are absent every working day (Bain; Leon). Finally, given the choice of three additional years of pay and full benefits if they retire at age 65, over 70% of American workers opt for retirement at 62, on 70% benefits (*Social Security Bulletin*). This behavior does not add up to happiness at or with work.

Efforts to humanize work (Macarov, 1981), as typified in the quality of Working Life movement, succeed at most in removing dissatisfactions (Bar-Gal), which—as Herzberg has pointed out— is not the same thing as adding satisfactions. Schrank has pointed out that most job redesign programs usually mean that the worker takes on additional tasks or responsibilities without additional compensation—a dubious method of increasing satisfactions. Even Maslow's highest order motivation—self-actualization—has been called into question insofar as work is concerned (Macarov, 1976) and Fein holds that "It is only because *workers choose not to find fulfillment in their work* that they are able to function as healthy human beings . . . By rejecting involvement in work which cannot be fulfilling, workers save their sanity."

Insofar as changing attitudes are concerned, there is both survey and behavioral evidence that workers are beginning to view their work as mainly instrumental, and no longer as moral, religious, patriotic, nor enriching. Yankelovich, who has been tracking worker attitudes for years, speaks of a "new breed" of worker, who demands intrinsic satisfactions. The Lordstown strike is often considered typical of young workers' rejection of purely banal work. The student riots in Paris in 1964 included a poster reading: "Work makes you ugly." A T-shirt seen on an Atlanta street reads: "I've been working hard all my life, but somehow it seems longer." Numerous bumper stickers proclaim, "I'd rather be fishing (or golfing, skiing, or whatever)." Lefkowitz has written about people who simply decided to stop working. The Institute for Social Research found that, between 1973 and 1977, reported work satisfactions dropped by large percentages—ranging from 11.3% to 43%—in all occupational groups studied. The National Opinion Research Center reports that during the past 20 years employee satisfaction in general has been decreasing. In addition, there has been a significant drop in the satisfaction of managers, once the most satisfied of all groups. Among managers, clerical employees, and hourly workers, job satisfaction had declined to its lowest point ever. In a number of current studies of work patterns, younger workers do not work as hard as older workers do (Macarov, 1982). Finally, there is the growing amount of loafing on the job mentioned previously, which indicates that the work ethic is more often a statement of belief than a code of behavior.

Cotter attributes changes in work attitudes to 12 sources, including rising expectations as encouraged by the media; distrust of those in power; the weakening of traditional institutions; and changing values, among others.

Most of the research on worker satisfactions and their changes has been done in industrial settings, however. Very little is yet known concerning satisfactions in the services generally, or in specific services. Similarly, there has not yet been very much research on changes in satisfaction brought about by the introduction of technology, except concerning initial resistance to new methods, and worker/union reactions to methods of mechanization (Emspak). It is possible, as noted above, that contact with customers, clients, or patients might have a considerable impact on satisfactions in either direction. Similarly, technology might make some jobs more interesting, while wiping out the interesting features of others, both in industry and in services.

Much more research is needed in this whole area, including its wider implications. Varga, for example, found that amounts of free time are positively correlated with marital cohesion, while Solomon found that working at home, a lá flexiplace, results in more intra-family tensions. Such areas of present attitudes and attitude changes require much more investigation.

Changes in the World of Work

The three changes in the world of work discussed here—the shift to services, the impact of technology, and changing attitudes—interact with each other, and with other changes, in a dynamic and unceasing manner. Each change reverberates throughout the others, resulting in further changes. Unfortunately, the implications of such changes, not only for the world of work, but for society as a whole, have not yet been given the study and emphasis that they deserve.

As these trends continue—and there is little reason to believe that they will not—they will call for sweeping changes in both the value system and the structure of present society. Insofar as jobs continue to be necessary or important, they will have to be accommodated more and more to the demands of nonwork activities in contrast to the past when nonwork activities were subordinated to the demands of work (Jamal, et al.). Insofar as human labor becomes unimportant and increasingly redundant, Western society will enter a transition period containing pain and grief for individuals, families, communities, and regions, if they are not managed with foresight and judgement (Coates). As Hart says, "We must find a way to shift from the economy of the past to the economy of the future with as little pain and as much excitement as possible." This is the most compelling problem before social planners, economists, and everyone else concerned with the future of human society.

References

Albus, J.S., "Robots in the Workplace: The Key to a Prosperous Future," *The Futurist,* 17 (February, 1983):22–27.

Anthony, P.D., *The Ideology of Work.* London: Tavistock, 1978.

Baim, J.I., *Work Alienation and Its Impact on Political Life: Case Study of District Council 27 Workers.* New York: CUNY, 1981 (unpublished Ph.D. dissertation).

Bar-Gal, D., "Domains of Work and Methods of Work of Occupational Welfare Officers: An Exploratory Study of an Emerging Role," *Journal of Social Service Research* (in press).

Bar-Gal, D., and B. Shamir, "Occupational Welfare as an Aspect of Working Life," in G. Mensch and R.J. Niehaus (eds.), *Work, Organizations, and Technological Change.* New York: Plenum, 1982.

Beaumont, P., and D. Macarov, *The Retreat from Public Service Employment* (in press).

Bell, I., "The Future That Never Was," *Public Interest,* 51(1978): 35–73.

Berg, I., M. Freedman, and M. Freeman, *Managers and Work Reform: A Limited Engagement*. New York: Free Press, 1978.

Best, F., *Preparing California's Workforce for the Jobs of the Future*. Unpublished paper prepared for meeting of California Commission on Industrial Innovation, 1982.

Black, B.J., "Vocational Rehabilitation," in Encyclopedia of *Social Work*. New York: National Association of Social Workers, 1965.

Bolan, R.S., "Social Planning and Social Welfare in the 1980s," *The Urban and Social Change Review*, 14(1981)"4–11.

Brill, N.I., *Working With People: The Helping Process*. Philadelphia: Lippincott, 1973.

Caplow, T., *The Sociology of Work*. New York: McGraw-Hill, 1954.

Carey, J.L., and P.F. Otto, "Output per Unit of Labor Input in the Retail Food Store Industry," *Monthly Labor Review*, 100 (January, 1977):42–47.

Carnes, R.B., "Laundry and Cleaning Services Pressed to Post Productivity Gains," *Monthly Labor Review*, 101(1978):38–42.

Carnes, R.B., and H. Band. "Productivity and New Technology in Eating and Drinking Places," *Monthly Labor Review*, 100(September 1977):9–15.

Casner-Lotto, J., "Robots Expected to Boost Productivity: Labor Unions Accept Use with Caution, Insist on Job Security as Condition," *World of Work Report*, 5(March 1981):17.

Cherrington, D.J., *The Work Ethic: Working Values and Values That Work*. New York: Amacom, 1980.

Cherviss, C., *Professional Burnout in Human Service Organizations*. New York: Praeger, 1980.

Coates, V.T., "The Potential Impacts of Robotics," *The Futurist*, 17(February 1983):28–32.

Cotter, J.J., "Ethics and Justice in the World of Work: Improving the Quality of Working Life," *Review of Social Economy*, 40(December, 1982):393–406.

Drucker, P.F., *Management: Tasks, Responsibilities, Practices* New York: Harper and Row, 1973.

Dyer, L., and D.P. Schwab, "Personnel/Human Resource Management Research," in Kochan, T.A., D.J.B. Mitchell, and L. Dyer, *Industrial Relations Research in the 1970s: Review and Appraisal*. Madison: IRRA, 1982.

Emery, F., *Futures We Are In*. Leiden: Martinus Nijhoff Social Sciences Division, 1977.

Emspak, F., *The New Technology: Who Pays?* Paper delivered at Expert's Consultation on the Future of Work, Adelphi University, Garden City, New York, 1982.

Etzioni, A., *Modern Organizations*. Englewood Cliffs: Prentice-Hall, 1964.

Evans, C., *The Micro Millennium*. New York: Washington Square Press, 1979.

Fein, M., "Motivation to Work," in R. Dubin (ed.), *Handbook of Work, Organization, and Society*. Chicago: Rand McNally, 1976.

Field, F., *The Conscript Army*. London: Routledge and Kegan Paul, 1977.

Fish, D.H., *A Study of the Turnover and Separation of Social Workers in Public Welfare Agencies*. Ramat Gan, Israel: Bar-Ilan University School of Social Work, 1976.

Freeman, H.E., and C. Lambert, Jr., "The Identification of 'Lower-Class' Families in an Urban Community," in A.B. Shostak and W. Gomberg (eds), *Blue-Collar World: Studies of the American Worker*. Englewood Cliffs: Prentice-Hall, 1965.

Gabor, D., *Inventing the Future*. New York: Knopf, 1971.

Gans, H., "Income Grants and 'Dirty Work'," *Public Interest*, 6(1967):110.

Gardell, B., "Reactions at Work and Their Influence on Nonwork Activities: An Analysis of a Sociopolitical Problem in Affluent Societies." *Human Relations*, 29(1976):885–904.

Gartner, A., and F. Riessman, *The Service Society and the Consumer Vanguard*. New York: Harper and Row, 1974.

Gershuny, J., *After Industrial Society: The Emerging Self-Service Economy*. London: Macmillan, 1978.

Gersuny, C., and W.R. Rosengren, *The Service Society*. Cambridge, MA: Schenkman, 1973.

Gidron, B., "Volunteer Workers: A Labour Economy Perspective," *Labour and Society*, 5(October, 1980)355–365.

Glazer, N., "Towards a Self-Service Society?" *The Public Interest*, 70(1983):66–90.

Glenn, E.N., and F.L. Feldberg, "Proleterianizing Clerical Work: Technology and Organizational Control in the Office," in A. Zimbalist (ed.), *Case Studies on the Labor Process*. New York: Monthly Review Press, 1979.

Gobel, R., and A. Meers, "Impact of Two Successive Mechanization Projects on Motivation and Work Organization in a Bank," in G. Mensch and R.J. Niehaus (eds.), *Work, Organizations, and Technological Change*. New York: Plenum, 1982.

Goldstein, J.H., *The Effectiveness of Manpower Training Programs: A Review of Research on the Impact on the Poor*. Washington: Government Printing Office, 1972.

Gross, A.M., "Appropriate Cost Reporting: An Indispensable Link to Accountability," *Administration in Social Work*, 4(1980):308–339.

Gutek, B., "The Relative Importance of Intrapsychic Determinants of Job Satisfaction," in K.D. Duncan, M.M. Gruneburg and D. Wallis, *Changes in Working Life*. Chichester: Wiley, 1980.

Haavio-Mannila, E., "Satisfaction with Family, Work, Leisure and Life Among Men and Women," *Human Relations*, 24(1971):585–601.

Handless, Y., L. Appel and M. Sagin, *Satisfactions of Nurses at Work*. Tel Aviv: General Federation of Labour in Eretz Israel, 1982.

Hart, G., "Investing in People for the Information age," *The Futurist*, 17(February 1983):10–14.

Heller, J., *The Video Display Terminal in the Office*. Baltimore: Johns Hopkins University, 1981.

Herzberg, F., *Work and the Nature of Man*. Cleveland: World, 1966.

Herzberg, F., B. Mausner, and B.B. Snyderman. *The Motivation to Work*. New York: John Wiley, 1959.

Hillard, R., quoted in W. Abbott, "Work in the Year 2001," in E. Cornish (ed.), *1999: The World of Tomorrow*. Washington: World Future Society, 1978.

Howe, L.K., *Pink Collar Workers*. New York: Putnam, 1977.

Hull, F.M., N.S. Friedman, and T.F. Rogers, "The Effect of Technology on Alienation from Work," *Work and Occupations*, 9(1982):31–57.

Jamal, M., V.V. Baba and F.F. Mitchell, "The Nature of Structure in Nonwork," *Relations Industrielles*, 37(1982):618–633. *Jerusalem Post*, January 16, 1983. p. 4.

Kamerman, S.B., and A.J. Kahn, *Social Services in the United States: Policies and Programs*. Philadelphia: Temple University, 1976.

Katzell, R.A., P. Bienstock, and P.H. Faerstein. *A Guide to Worker Productivity Experiments in the United States 1971–1975*. New York: New York University Press, 1977.

Keefe, T., "Empathy: The Critical Skill," *Social Work*, 21(1976):10–14.

Kendrick, J.W., "Productivity Trends and the Recent Slowdown," in W.E. Fellner (ed.), *Contemporary Economic Problems*. Washington: American Enterprise Institute, 1979.

Kraft, P., "The Industrialization of Computer Programming: From Programming to 'Software Revolution'," in A. Zimbalist (ed.), *Case Studies in the Labor Process*. New York: Monthly Review Press, 1979.

21

Kranzberg, M., and J. Gies, *By the Sweat of Thy Brow*. New York: Putnam, 1975.

Lasson, K., *The Workers*. New York: Grossman, 1971.

Lawler, E.E. III, and L.W. Porter, "The Effect of Performance on Job Satisfaction," in G.A. Yukl and K.N. Wexley (eds.), *Readings in Organizational and Industrial Psychology*. New York: Oxford University Press, 1971.

Lefkowitz, B., *Breaktime: Living Without Working in a Nine-to-Five World*. Harmondsworth: Penguin, 1979.

Leon, C.B., "Occupational Winners and Losers: Who They Were During 1970–80," *Monthly Labor Review*, 105(June 1982):18–23

Levinson, H., C.R. Price, K.J. Munden, H.J. Mandl and C.M. Solley, *Men, Management and Mental Health*. Cambridge: Harvard, 1962.

Locke, E.A., "The Nature and Causes of Job Satisfaction," in M.D. Dunnette (ed.), *Handbook of Industrial and Organizational Psychology*. Chicago: Rand McNally, 1976.

Lubove, R., *The Professional Altruist*. New York: Atheneum, 1973.

Macarov, D., *Work Incentives in an Israeli Kibbutz*. Jerusalem: Hebrew University, 1971 (Hebrew).

Macarov, D., "Work Without Pay: Work Incentives and Patterns in a Salaryless Environment," *International Journal of Social Economics*, 2(Summer, 1975):106–114.

Macarov, D., "Reciprocity between Self-Actualisation and Hard Work," *International Journal of Social Economics*, 3(1976):39–44.

Macarov, D., "Empathy: The Charismatic Chimera," *Journal of Education for Social Work*, 14(1978):86–92.

Macarov, D., *Work and Welfare: The Unholy Alliance*. Beverly Hills: Sage, 1980.

Macarov, D., "Humanizing the Workplace as Squaring the Circle," *International Journal of Manpower*. 2(1981):6–14.

Macarov, D., *Worker Productivity: Myths and Reality*. Beverly Hills: Sage, 1982.

Macarov, D., "Pursuing Leisure as a Moral Imperative," *Leisure Information Newsletter*, 9(Winter, 1983):6–7.

Macarov, D., and G. Fradkin, *The Short Course in Development Training*. Ramat Gan: Massada, 1973.

Machlowitz, M.M., *Workaholics: Living With Them, Working With Them*. New York: Mentor, 1981.

Mckinlay, J.B., "The Limits of Human Service," *Social Policy*, 8(1978):29–34.

Mark, J.A., "Measuring Productivity in Service Industries," *Monthly Labor Review*, 105(June 1982):3–8.

Marland, S.P., Jr., *Career Education: A Proposal for Reform*. New York: McGraw-Hill, 1974.

Mensch, G.O., "The Co-Evolution of Technology and Work Organization," in G. Mensch and R.J. Niehaus (eds.), *Work, Organizations and Technological Change*. New York: Plenum, 1982.

Michelotti, K., "Multiple Jobholding Rate Remained Unchanged in 1976," *Monthly Labor Review*, 100(June 1977):44–48.

Miller, S.M., "The American Lower Classes: A Typological Approach," in A.B. Shostak and W. Gomberg, *Blue-Collar World: Studies of the American Worker*. Englewood Cliffs: Prentice Hall, 1964.

Miller, S.M., "Productivity and the Paradox of Service in a Profit Economy," *Social Policy*, 9(1978):4–6.

Morris, R., and R. Murphy, "The Situs Dimension in Occupational Literature," *American Sociological Review*, 23(1959):231–239.

Neff, W.S., *Work and Human Behavior*, New York: Atherton, 1968.

Newland, K., *Productivity: The New Economic Context*. Washington Worldwatch Institute, 1982.

New York Times, March 21, 1982, p. 26F.

Pearson, R., "Personnel Planning: The Importance of the Labour Market," in G. Mensch and R.J. Niehaus (eds.), *Work, Organizations and Technological Change*. New York: Plenum, 1982.

Quinn, R.P., and G.L. Staines, *The 1977 Quality of Employment Survey*. Ann Arbor: University of Michigan, 1979.

Rada, J., *The Impact of Micro-Electronics*. Geneva: International Labour Office, 1980.

Rees, A., *The Economics of Work and Pay*. New York: Harper and Row, 1979.

Rehabilitation of the Work Injured. Jerusalem: National Insurance Institute, 1974. (Hebrew)

Rein, M., "Work in Welfare: Past Failures and Future Strategies," *Social Servicie Review*, 56(June 1982):211–229.

Richardson, V., "Social Change in Perceptions of Work Relations," *Social Service Review*, 56(1982):438–447.

Riessman, F., *The Self-Help Ethos*. Paper delivered at the Experts' Invitational Consultation on the Future of Work, Adelphi University, Garden City, New York, June 1982.

Robinson, J.P., "Occupational Norms and Differences in Job Satisfaction: A Summary of Survey Research Evidence," in J.P. Robinson, R. Athanasiou and K.B. Head, *Measures of Occupational Attitudes and Occupational Characteristics*. Ann Arbor: University of Michigan, 1969.

Roe, A., *The Psychology of Occupations*. New York: Wiley, 1956.

Rosow, J.M., "Productivity and People," in J.M. Rosow (ed.), *Productivity: Prospects for Growth*. New York: Van Nostrand Reinhold, 1981.

Rowland, H.S., *The Nurses' Almanac*. Germantown, Md.: Aspen, 1978.

Rubin, L.B., *Worlds of Pain: Life in the Working Class Family*. New York: Basic Books, 1976.

Salomon, I., and M. Salomon, "Telecommuting—The Employee's Perspective," *Technological Forecasting and Social Change* (in press).

Schrank, R., *Ten Thousand Working Days*. Cambridge, Mass: MIT Press, 1979.

Schrank, R., "Horse-Collar Blue-Collar Blues," *Harvard Business Review*, (May/June 1981):133–138.

Science and Technology Policy for the 1980s. Paris: OECD, 1981.

Shamir, B., "Between Service and Servility: Role Conflict in Subordinate Service Roles," *Human Relations*, 33(1980):741–756.

Shane, H.G. and G.A. Sojka, "John Elfreth Watkins, Jr.: Forgotten Genius of Forecasting," *The Futurist*, 16(February 1982):9–12.

Social Security Bulletin, Annual Statistical Supplement, Washington: Department of Health and Human Services, 1980, p. 113.

Somers, G.G., "Retraining the Unemployed: A Preliminary Survey," in S. Lebergott (ed.), *Men Without Work: The Economics of Unemployment*. Englewood Cliffs: Prentice-Hall, 1964.

Stellman, J., *Human and Public Health Aspects of Telecommunications*. Paper delivered at Fourth General Assembly, World Future Society, Washington, 1982.

Strauss, G., "Job Satisfaction, Motivation, and Job Redesign," in *Organizational Behavior: Research and Issues*. Madison: Industrial Relations Research Association, 1974.

Super, D., *The Psychology of Careers*. New York: Harper, 1957.

Taggart, R., *Job Creation: What Works?* Salt Lake City: Olympus, 1977.

Taylor, D.E., and E.S. Sekscenski, "Workers on Long Schedules, Single and Multiple Jobholders," *Monthly Labor Review*, 105(May 1982):47–53.

Thurow, L.C., *The Zero-Sum Society: Distribution and the Possibilities for Economic Change*. Harmondsworth: Penquin, 1981.

23

Urquhart, M., "The Services Industry: Is It Recession-Proof?" *Monthly Labor Review*, 104(October, 1981):12–18.

Varga, K., "Marital Cohesion as Reflected in Time-Budgets," in A. Szalai (ed.), *The Use of Time*. The Hague: Mouton, 1972.

Walbank, M., "Effort in Motivated Work Behavior," in K.D. Duncan, M.M. Gruneberg and D. Wallis (eds.), *Changes in Working Life*. Chichester: Wiley, 1980.

Wilson, J.O., *After Affluence: Economics to Meet Human Needs*. New York: Harper and Row, 1980.

Work in America. Cambridge: Mass.: MIT Press, 1973.

World of Work Report. Scarsdale: Work in America Institute, various issues.

Yankelovich, D. *New Rules: Searching for Fulfillment in a World Turned Upside Down*. New York: Random House, 1981.

Yearbook of Labor Statistics: Sixteenth Edition: Twenty-Sixth Edition: Thirty-Sixth Edition. Geneva: International Labour Organization, 1956, 1966, 1976, 1978.

Zimbalist, A., "Technology and the Labor Process in the Printing Industry," in A. Zimbalist (ed.), *Case Studies on the Labor Process*. New York: Monthly Review Press, 1979.

The Changing Nature of Work

by

Joseph F. Coates

"What are you going to be when you grow up?" must stand high on the list of dumb questions asked of a child. The child cannot answer, for the three bases of a stable national pattern of work—technology, the work force, and social conditions—are all in flux.

Information has become the dominant commodity in American society, making telecommunications and computer technologies the primary physical instruments of fundamental social change. Since the changing technological base drives the economy, it is the most unequivocally radicalizing element in the future of work. Today roughly 55% of the work force is in the business of generating, producing, storing, handling, transmitting, or regurgitating knowledge and information. Those involved include everyone from researchers to clerks, from school teachers to white-collar workers, from lawyers, architects, or medical specialists to key-punch operators and word-processing technicians.

Preparation for work in the information society must be different from what has gone before, for the new information technologies are not mere analogs of the carpenter's plane and the mechanic's wrench. The new vocations will not be limited to the physical manipulation of natural and synthetic substances, but will extend to the manipulation of man's own creations—of data, theory, and knowledge. The work world will change accordingly.

The physical requirements of the workplace are already changing as we become captivated and even captured by electronic devices. We are finding, for instance, that people who work all day with CRTs (cathode ray tubes) may experience unpleasant side effects. Adapting the workplace to the worker needs more attention than it did in the industrial area. Work is moving to smaller locations, suburban locations, even to the home. Robotics and automation make it practical for a worker to move from the office to the factory floor and back.

Robotics and automation are creating new occupations and new jobs in

Joseph F. Coates is president of J.F. Coates, Inc., a futures research and policy analysis group located in Washington, D.C. This article was originally published in VocED, *the journal of the American Vocational Association, and is reprinted here with their permission.*

maintenance and manufacturing, but are eliminating many at the same time. Supply and demand imbalances are occurring in industries affected by telecommunications, increasing the need for training, retraining, and on-the-job training of the work force. These imbalances will also be felt in other sectors of the economy as the applications of new technologies spread.

For the rise of telecommunications is not the only major technological upheaval shaping our future. New biotechnology and accommodations to the irreversible increase in the cost of petroleum will affect the when, where, and who of industrial processes, mining, and manufacturing. There will be new occupations in the fields of energy, materials, and genetics, altering the credentials and qualifications required of the work force.

The biotechnological revolution springs from fundamental new understanding of the genetic code that determines the inherited characteristics of microorganisms, plants, animals, and people. We are rapidly developing the technology for manipulating genes. While the most obvious and urgent short-term effects of the genetic revolution will be in human health and disease, applied genetics will eventually transform forestry and agriculture and make substantial inroads into the manufacturing of chemicals and foods.

There are already factories producing tens of thousands of tons of so-called "single-cell protein," which compares well in nutritive value with soybean and fish meal. The industrialization of microorganisms promises to produce many widely used industrial chemicals under milder conditions, with less waste and fewer dangerous by-products, and opens up the pos-

U.S. Labor Force in the Information Sector

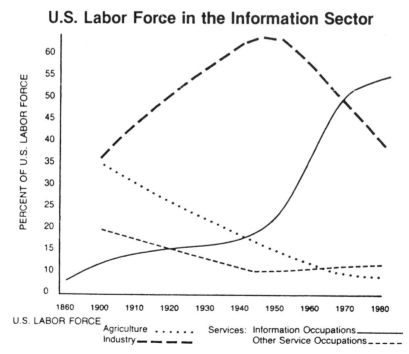

U.S. LABOR FORCE
Agriculture . . . . . .   Services: Information Occupations_____
Industry — — — —   Other Service Occupations _ _ _ _ _

26

sibility of new bases for the chemical industry. Raw material could very well shift from petroleum to wood or other biomass. Such changes could alter the physical and chemical characteristics and hence the industrial handling of plastics, dyes, resins, and the myriad organic chemicals that are so central to the commerce of our civilization.

Great change is also likely to occur in energy technology. The movement toward conservation is already having a wide and visible impact on the work force, with innovation in insulation and the application of passive solar energy. We can expect to see continuing development of modifications in the design and operation of structures, instruments, devices, household goods, and all other things in our society that consume energy.

Another broad flow of innovation will accompany the exploiting of new and unconventional energy sources. Getting usable energy from the wind and the sun, the oceans and the tides is, without question, workable. However, the extent to which the technology becomes practical and dots our countryside and coastlines with mechanisms to capture and use solar energy remains to be seen. Less speculative are vast new open-pit mines, coal gasification, and synthetic crude oil facilities. These changes in the fuel of our social metabolism are going to create new demands on and for skilled and professional workers, stimulate growth in many regions of the country, and create a wave of innovation only rivaled in history during the last quarter of the nineteenth century.

Demography—the study of births, deaths, marriages, divorces, and other vital statistics—gives us additional valuable clues to the future of work. Such information reflects forces operating in society that will be felt throughout the economy, such as the size of the work force in a given decade. The baby-boom cohort is now contributing to the relative scarcity of available entry-level jobs. By the year 2000, however, as the baby-bust cohort grows up, there will be a shortage of entry-level workers. Meanwhile, the baby-boom cohort will be caught in an upward crush in middle management. There will be a surfeit of workers with the skills to move ahead who are thwarted by limited opportunities.

This dark prospect assumes no change in the industrial and organizational structure of work. But other social factors are of equal or greater salience. It appears that the inexorable tide of population changes will be accompanied by other tides of change that affect labor supply.

Women's entry into the labor force on a parity with men—not as mere sources of secondary income, as ancillary workers or casual respondents to the shifts in the labor market—will increasingly change the makeup of the work force and materially alter our social ambience and expectations about work. Women are, of course, joined by blacks, browns, and the handicapped in a major workplace revolution—equality of access. That movement will be reinforced by robotization and the use of computers and telecommunications, all of which are indifferent to race, religion, national origin, or any other personal attributes. To an unprecedented degree, egalitarianism will enter the work site.

Other changes in attitude will occur in response to the steady supply of new workers provided by immigration, which now accounts for 25% of the net population growth. Because the new immigrants are by and large from non-European cultures, we can expect to see new expectations about work and new mores where people work.

An unprecedented degree of independence among workers will be stimulated by the rise of the dual-income family. This independence will show up in pressure for improved quality of work life, worksite amenities, shifting work schedules, different management styles, and wider worker participation in decisions. The prevalence of the dual-income family will promote job-sharing and off-and-on work. It may tend to stabilize population in cities and reduce migration. With greater discretionary income and less time, the dual-income family will demand more services or technological solutions to service needs. Children in such families will become more valuable commodities simply by being fewer in number, and will be members of smaller, more prosperous households. (On the other hand, the increasing numbers of single-parent families will be economically and socially stressed. Business and industry will have to respond to these stresses.)

The continuing flow of survey research on work and workers suggests two things of central importance. First, the desire to work is not dying, fading, or in any sense being rejected. Second, workers' aspirations are shifting. The growth of participation, the need for autonomy, the interest of labor and management in higher quality, the search for satisfaction in work—these are symptoms of a deep-seated change in public attitudes throughout American society.

In 1979, a Gallup poll found some 61% of male workers reporting that they would continue to work even if they did not have to, although 21% would only work part-time. Only 10% of the male workers surveyed said they would stop working if they could. Of equal interest, 81% said they would prefer a difficult job to an unchallenging job. The Gallup polls and many other sources show that new workers want interesting jobs, they want opportunity, they want fair treatment, and they want their work to fit a total life pattern. According to one survey, 68% of workers want interesting jobs, 45% want higher salaries, 42% want security, and 20% want work with a sense of social mission.

Michael Maccoby, in a ground-breaking work on the value system in corporate America, has highlighted the likelihood that workers of the future will demand of business and industry jobs that not only lead to career advancement, but provide work that is personally satisfying. Lester Thurow, an economist at the Massachusetts Institute of Technology, devastatingly analyzes and deplores today's commonly accepted value system, which sees work as a series of challenges oriented around a zero-sum mentality—I win, you lose; you win, I lose. Other thinkers, among them Clare Graves, have pointed out that new values in American society are creating legions of workers who reject the materialistic, independent, conquest model of the world and tend to focus on love, affection, community, and cooperation. A smaller but perhaps more important group in the long run is concerned with understanding the world, with existence, and with acceptance.

These indications of changing values interact with our changing technological base. Recent research on why people buy microcomputers for use at home shows that they do so for reasons that have surprisingly little relationship to keeping bank records and kitchen recipes. People buy microcomputers to achieve a sense of autonomy and control. They want this same sense at work.

The American worker is striving to increase opportunities for personal autonomy and work-related decision-making. One sees this in the attempt of many companies to introduce the quality circle and the work team. It is also visible in the growth of the "appropriate technology" movement, which favors simple technologies that employ human labor rather than capital equipment. Technological advance is taking place in concert with these new developments and with the lively current interest in social independence and local governance. One consequence is that traditional social and work-related distinctions are rapidly blurring. Among these are the distinctions between work and leisure, between white-collar and blue-collar workers, between vocational and non-vocational education, and between professional and sub-professional work.

We are witnessing a rapid technological transformation that contributes to the growing complexity of society at large. With literally tens of thousands of discrete occupations possible, youth coming on the work scene can have only an extremely limited perception of what work is like. The new terms sound like magic; they have few connotations. What does it mean to work as a fiber optics technician, a robot attendant, an electromyography technician, or a gene splicer? Surely few children today can specify what they are going to be when they grow up.

The dominant message of the changing nature of work is that an increasingly greater percentage of Americans will, over a lifetime, hold a succession of different jobs, even different careers, many flowing one into the other, but others involving substantial disruption and change. Old technologies will become obsolete and new ones will have to be mastered. Old skills will be dropped and new ones learned. Old attitudes will yield to new ones.

Resources

Bell, Daniel. *The Coming of Post-Industrial Society: A Venture in Social Forecasting.* New York: Basic Books, 1973.

Graves, Clare W. "Human Nature Prepares for a Momentous Leap." THE FUTURIST (April 1974), pp. 72–85.

Maccoby, Michael. *The Gamesman: The New Corporate Leaders.* New York: Simon and Schuster, 1976.

Thurow, Lester C. *The Zero-Sum Society: Distribution and the Possibilities for Economic Change.* New York: Penguin, 1981.

Robots and the Future of Work

by

Edmund Byrne

The Automation Revolution, prophesied from the outset of the Industrial Revolution[1] and prematurely announced following development of the computer after World War II,[2] is now on the verge of realization, thanks to the discovery and inexpensive mass production of compact and versatile microprocessors that make possible so-called "smart" robots and other components of automated assembly systems. First exploited by the Japanese, robotization is likely to be (perhaps along with biotechnology) the single most significant characteristic of technological history in the 1980s. And when the decade is over, the configuration of human work will have been radically transformed, along with the technology that undergirds and now increasingly is replacing it.

In a word, many humans are going to lose their jobs. Whether they will find others that need doing or that they are qualified to do is a very hard question to answer. But it is one that society will be required to answer; and the answer that society comes up with will determine in a very fundamental way the future of the human condition.[3] As of now, however, there is no adequate plan for a social equivalent of Isaac Asimov's third law of robotics, namely, that a robot should never harm a human. Robots will harm humans. They are doing so already. Not by crudely striking a blow to the head, but just by being able to do better what humans have been doing poorly by default. In the process, of course, robots will be sparing humans a lot of pain, but the pain associated with sweat on the brow is as nothing compared to the pain of being unemployed and unemployable. And that, quite clearly, is just what lies ahead for people in all parts of the world, especially in developed nations.

Questions to be considered, then, are the following. What is a robot? What can robots do? What impact will robots have on human work? And what, if anything, should humans do about "keeping robots in their place"?

What Is a Robot

There are three definitions of the word *robot*, only two of which are

---

Edmund Byrne is professor and chairman of the Department of Philosophy, Indiana University, Indianapolis, Indiana.

relevant here. The most common (in popular usage as well as in science fiction) is that of a manufactured apparatus that has a humanoid appearance and exercises humanlike functions well enough to be considered human in a given context. There are, in fact, robots of this type in use, e.g., to direct pedestrian and/or vehicular traffic.[4] But the presence or absence of humanlike features is of no importance in the discussion that follows.

A second definition of the word *robot* is a programmable manipulator of versatile automation components. This is the usage generally accepted by industry people. A third and considerably narrower definition, favored by research and development people, is an artificial intelligence machine with humanlike functions. Programmable automation manipulators have been around for decades. "AI" machines are only now beginning to make their appearance but are expected to mushroom in the decade ahead. It is important but not always easy to determine which definition is being invoked by a writer or speaker on the subject, especially when one is trying to count the number of robots in a plant or industry, in a particular country (e.g., Japan), or in the world. Unless noted otherwise, I shall take "robot" in the broader sense as including all programmable automation manipulators.

Robots are distinguishable with regard to degrees of freedom, method of articulation, control of motion, or method of actuation. Three degrees of freedom are required to position an object in space, three more to orient the object in any direction (a minimum for a "general-purpose manipulator"). Robot joints may swivel ("polar"), slide ("cartesian"), or combine these two methods ("cylindrical"). Only a terminal point is specified in point-to-point control; the precise path and the velocity of the entire movement are determined by continuous-path control. Pneumatic actuation of a robot is cheap and simple but adequate only for point-to-point operations. Electric actuation is simple to install and easy to maintain; a hydraulic system yields better dynamic performance and power-to-weight ratio.

Jasia Reichardt identifies nine levels of automation (she calls them "stages, or degrees"), with robots entering the scene on the fifth level. If the task to be performed is bending a pipe and some tool is employed in the process, the pre-robotic tool might be (1) a hand tool, (2) a power tool, (3) power machinery under human control, (4) powered machinery executing a programmed sequence of operations without variation. A robotic tool bending a pipe might be (5) pre-programmed only for that task as to sequence of and length of time between operations; (6) provided with several programs stored and selected automatically (a variable sequence robot), (7) controlled by means of programs stored in a large memory device and subject to change automatically (continuous-path robots with servomechanisms), (8) a computer-aided manufacturing system that activates the motors of numerically controlled robots by means of programs stored on punched paper tape, or (9) "blue collar" or "smart" or "intelligent" robots with tactile and visual capabilities. Only the latter, which utilize only recently feasible "artificial intelligence," are considered true robots by experts in this field.

According to one estimate, there are some 15,000 robots installed around the world, about half of which are in Japan and a fourth in the United States.[5] In second place is the Soviet Union, where there are now some 6–7,000 units, but most of these are technologically retarded, having only 3–4 axes of movement.[6]

Far more important for the future of work in the world are projections for the growth of robot usage in the decades ahead. In the next five years the Russians plan to add 40,000 additional units, and during the five years thereafter they will be installing sensory robots. One hundred and fifty companies in Japan produced robots (five times as many as in the United States) at a level of $400 million in 1980, and expect to be producing at a level of $2.2 billion in 1985, $4.5 billion in 1990.[7] In the United States, robot production was at a level of $50 million/year in 1981, but may expand to $250 billion over the next 20 years.[8]

The key factor in the upcoming expansion of robot production and use is not the quantity of dollars or units but the quality, that is, the capabilities, of the units to be produced. As Reichardt observes, "One has to prepare and present data in a way in which a robot can use them, which means that the cost of equipping a factory for robot operation may be ten times the cost of the robots themselves. The need exists, therefore, to design robots capable of working in moderate disorder, with some ability to recognize colors, shadows, markings, and textures."[9]

This challenge is now beginning to be met by artificial intelligence, which utilizes increasingly sophisticated microelectronic technology to solve problems heuristically. To this end, robots must have "sensory" capability, in varying degrees depending on the task, both in regard to "touch" and in regard to "vision," and both are now becoming technologically and economically feasible. A Mitsubishi robot, for example, "knows" when it has reached the correct object on a workbench by comparing images of it in two television cameras, one mounted on the robot's hand and the other overlooking the workbench. A Hitachi robot is so touch-sensitive that it can insert a piston into a cylinder with a clearance of 20 microns in three seconds. Selective choice and evaluation of parts will be coming soon. Still in the future is a "thinking" robot that when shown what to do will establish the most efficient way of doing it.[10]

What Impact Will Robots Have on the Work Force?

What impact is all this likely to have on the human work force? The answer to this question is all too simple: humans will be rendered superfluous and displaced. This much is fairly certain. All that remains uncertain is the scope of the displacement. But there are already indications that it will soon be extensive and will eventually be massive.

In the period 1990–2000, according to one projection, robots and automated systems will be producing half of all manufactured goods and, as a result, up to one-quarter of the factory work force may be dislodged.[11]

That this will come about seems an inevitable outcome of the belief common among industrialists that it will be cost effective in the long run and for that very reason is a necessary condition for staying competitive in the industries affected. Estimates vary as to just how much less expensive it may be to use robots rather than humans. As one writer puts it, a Japanese robot in automotive production can do at $5.50/hr. what a UAW worker does for $18.10/hr. (wages and fringes).[12]

Other factors, including not only OPEC but also the almost total unwillingness of U.S. auto manufacturers to deviate from 60-year-old production methods, have helped bring about the current disarray, if not imminent disappearance, of the U.S. auto industry. But robotics, if ever really taken seriously, might make a difference. At least, such is the impression of those who still believe that an old dinosaur can be taught new tricks. And this belief is quite enough to put the automotive work force on notice.

Fiat's Robogate system boosted production 15% in 1978, we are reminded, but replaced few workers. But with sensory robots the Italian manufacturer could, it is estimated, cut manpower 90% before 1990.[13] This lesson has not been lost on General Motors, which will be spending $200 million by 1983 to install 800 robots on 14 assembly lines in 7 of its plants in Italy. And by 1990, GM will have invested $1 billion in 13,000 robots to paint, load/unload machines, and assemble components, with the help of Robogate, thereby cutting labor costs by an estimated 70% and the labor force by 50% just in the next nine years.[14] However impressive these numbers may be in a vacuum, they may well be too little too late: from its present total of 450 robots, GM hopes to expand to 5,000 by 1985 and to 13,000 by 1990—but the Japanese already have 7,000 in place! And they have no more intention of yielding the lead in robotics than in electronics in general. MITI, the quasi-governmental research arm of Japanese industry, plans to spend $140 million over a seven-year period to develop smart robots to assemble an entire product, such as an automobile, beginning as early as 1983. With this new system, one could effect changeover simply by changing the system's software. By 1985, Hitachi hopes to be using robots with visual and tactile sensors for 60% of its assembly operations. And three major Japanese companies are working on a robot that will be able to position a component within four-hundredths of an inch. One of these companies, Fujitsu Fanuc Ltd., has opened a $38 million plant to produce other robots and computerized tools automatically, using robots, numerically controlled machine tools, and only one shift of 100 human workers to assemble robot-made parts (until, that is, robots start doing even that).[15]

By comparison to the Japanese commitment to robotics, American auto makers are in a technological feudal age. But even belatedly introduced technology is having an effect on the work force. Take the example of the PUMA (programmable universal machine for assembly), a $20,000 robot arm developed by GM and Unimation. By 1990, GM expects to be using 5,000 of these in assembly work and 4,000 to load/unload machines, thereby bumping 50% of assembly-line laborers.[16]

Another industry on the verge of transformation by robotics is that of consumer appliances, which in the United States is dominated by General Electric. GE had two robots in 1978, added 26 more in 1979, and may be using 1,000 by the end of this decade. The company spent over $15 million in 1980 for 47 new robots expected to save $2.6 million/year in labor and materials. So far, displaced assembly workers have been transferred, e.g., to robot maintenance, with work-force reduction being limited to attrition.[17] For example, GE's dishwasher plant in Louisville, Kentucky, is 60% automated, but workers are free to stop the line at key points to prevent defects from being built in. But the technology for full-scale automation, including a robotic "eye" and a CAD/CAM (computer-aided design and manufacture) system, has been under development.[18] And once this is in place, reduction in work force will follow. In fact, GE plans to robotize as many as half of its 37,000 assembly-line jobs to achieve 6% per year improvement in productivity.[19] Nor does the company really have much choice in the matter because of new competition from Japanese manufacturers such as Sanyo, which has opened an automated refrigerator plant on the West Coast and others in Tennessee, Arkansas, and other states.

GE's in-house robotization agenda is, however, only the tip of the iceberg. GE is now bent on supplying robots and other automation equipment to other manufacturers. To this end, the company has acquired licenses to use robotics technology developed by Italy's Digital Electronic Automation, Japan's Hitachi, and most recently, Volkswagenwerk. According to reports, the arrangement with VW will authorize GE to build five of that company's robot models and sell them worldwide. These additions will give GE a total of 12 models, including one capable of handling components weighing more than 200 pounds, which will be of interest to the automotive, aerospace, and heavy equipment industries.[20]

Nor is GE going to be lonesome in the robot marketplace. In addition to smaller companies such as Cincinnati Milacron and Unimation, which turn out $30–40 million worth of robots a year, and Automatrix, the race for what could be a $25 billion market by 1990 has been joined by such giants as Digital Equipment, IBM, and Texas Instruments. One result of this expanded interest is that the cost of a $50,000 robot is expected to drop to $10,000 by the end of the decade. And the result of all these factors may be, according to one projection, that "smart robots could displace 65% to 75% or more of today's factory work force."

Be that as it may, there are customers for robots almost literally waiting in line for delivery. A new Robotics Division at Westinghouse, for example, has a mandate to robotize "any and all manufacturing areas." And toward this end the company, like others around the country, has been doing a feasibility study (on NSF money) of automated batch-assembly of 450 different versions of eight different fractional-horsepower motors at a rate of 1 million units/year. Cybotech, a joint venture between Renault and Ransberg Corporation, an Indianapolis-based company, has been providing robots on a turnkey basis, if desired, to such diverse companies as General Motors, Jeep Corporation, Lockheed, and Caterpillar Tractor, with Renault spending $6.2 million/year on visual R&D and Cybotech $2.5 million/year on sensile/tactile technology.[21] More generally, it is estimated that U.S. industry will more than triple its 1981 automation investments to $5 billion in 1985, this amount to be divided about equally between computer-aided design (CAD) and such devices as minicomputers, numerical controls, programmable controls, and robots.[22]

34

Thanks to this new technology, especially microcomputers and so-called "friendly" (ordinary language) software, production programs can be changed right on the factory floor for customized batch production in runs of less than 50 units. And this, in turn, means perhaps a 30% decrease in use of workers, commonly by introducing an unmanned third shift—what in German is called the ghost shift (*"die Geisterschicht"*). The Japanese, however, are prepared to go this stunt one better: *flexible manufacturing complex* (FMC), a $60 million prototype of which is now in place, with the expectation that 20% of Japan's total factory output will be FMC'd by 1985. What FMC involves is five fully automatic manufacturing operations all interconnected and controlled by a hierarchy of computers, with humans on hand only as safety overseers of lasers used for treating and machining.

As these examples have suggested, the impact of the "new wave" of automation on blue-collar unions may turn out to be absolutely devastating. The United Auto Workers expect to lose 200,000 of their 1 million members between 1978 and 1990. The IUE, the International Association of Machinists, and the International Brotherhood of Electrical Workers will also be hard hit. But so also will white-collar personnel—possibly as many as 38 million of the present 50 million white-collar jobs may be affected, just as automation has already reduced employment in the U.S. Postal Service from 744,000 in 1970 to 677,000 in 1981: a 10% reduction. At racetracks, window betting is being taken over by an automated "sell-pay" system that shortens line, saves 10–50% on costs of operation, and eliminates jobs. Similarly, when U.S. air traffic controllers went on strike in 1981, their complaint about job stress was, if anything, counterproductive. For the U.S. government is engaged in a 10-year $8.5 billion project to reduce the need for technicians and controllers by one-third with an automated ATC system that would require only one rather than three humans per display screen, thus allegedly saving $6.7 billion in the 1980s and over $17 billion in the 1990s.[23]

Examples such as these could be multiplied, but the point is clear: a very significant number of jobs are on the block in the decade ahead, not only in the United States but in other countries as well. If it is any consolation, the traumas of transition are at least as likely in Western Europe.[24] And in Japan, the world's leader in automation, it may well prove to be catastrophic. In that country, workers in manufacturing dropped from 14.4 million in 1973 to 13.7 million in 1980. Six million workers in cottage industries still represent 81% of Japan's 55.4 million workers, but these are being replaced by more reliable robots. The country has need of 745,000 computer software engineers, but it now has less than 100,000. Even jobs available as robot tenders are difficult to fill because the Japanese are not accustomed to working on any but the normal daytime shift. The conclusion of a government study that the impact of microelectronics on employment is not serious is much criticized; but the government is doing little to create new jobs.[25] Nor is this a problem only in developed countries. As is well known, electronics manufacturers have in years past gone to places such as South Korea, Taiwan, Hong Kong, and Singapore for low-level assembly operations. But computer-controlled assembly in the

United States and Japan is now competitive with labor-intensive production elsewhere, and the result may be the end of an era for these developing Asian countries.

What is suggested by all these details is that, as has occurred before in history, the human cost of progress may be excruciatingly high. That there will in time be protests and demonstrations, if not worse, seems inevitable. But in this instance, unlike that of popular protest against nuclear power plants, the economics (if the "experts" can be believed) would oppose rather than support the sentiments of the protesters. However, as is commonly the case, only internal costs are being figured, not the external costs, direct and indirect, that spill over onto society in the wake of a technological upheaval of the magnitude that lies ahead. So, as our own federal government prepares to abandon CETA and other relevant and timely social service programs, and state governments do little to fill the vacuum, we in the United States are left with little reason to gloat over the plight of the Japanese worker.

What Can We Do About Displaced Workers?

What possible remedies are there for the severe dislocations that this inevitable revolution is bringing over the horizon? The obvious answer, namely, that anyone laid off should get another job, seems especially cynical at a time of high unemployment. In addition, the factor of high interest rates intensifies the trauma of relocation, if that is required. Nor can an unskilled laborer count on finding employment even if willing to move. Even those who are still at work on assembly lines may find that computers are being used to subject them to time-study; and should they decide to strike in protest, they may become the victims of what one UAW official calls "technological scabbing." A short-term solution, of course, is to find ways to pace the introduction of automation, regulate the use of time-study, and participate in decision-making with regard to new technological systems on the basis of appropriate and adequate data.

Moreover, if unions want to protect their members, they need to have more control over job skills required by the new computer-based technology, e.g., diagnosis of problems by an electrician; programming and editing of numerical control tapes, robots, and all other "programmable automation," including work on machines that are leased or under warranty; and, by way of corollary, adequate training for performance of such jobs.

Unfortunately, outside of a few countries, notably in Scandanavia, presently available retraining programs are neither adequate nor effective to deal with the anticipated impact of robotics.

Above and beyond the comparatively short-term needs for programs to assist displaced workers, there is an endemic long-term need to rethink and restructure our educational system to provide the next generation of workers with the kinds of skills they must have to find employment in the decades ahead. Not that every student needs to become adept at microelectronics or biogenetics or whatever. But the socioeconomic consequences of the coming shift in technology require us to anticipate and prepare for a radically different society that we dare not approach behind a veil of ignorance.

As we contemplate this profound challenge, we will look in vain for ethical theories that can guide our search for responsible decisions—unless one is prepared to admit that "might makes right" is an ethical theory. A duty-based search for the absolutely right course of action to pursue disintegrates in the presence of complexities beyond the reach of assertions about duty. In a word, the standard objections on the basis of competing claims and correlative duties simply apply a fortiori.

Which workers should be given preference when layoffs are required? Those with seniority or those with protected group status, e.g., women or minorities? To whom are persons on various levels of management more responsible—investors, customers, suppliers, employers, or the community or communities in which their plants are located? Or perhaps the governmental entities that have favored the company with direct or indirect subsidies? What import should or can be given to individuals who would be seriously affected by a given decision but who are represented by no organizational structure that has direct input into or on the level of the relevant decision-making process? Even assuming the existence of an effective world government, which part of the world's population should be favored, and on the basis of what considerations? Developed or developing nations? One developed nation more than another? The country with the largest percentage of unemployed, or the largest number of unemployed, or the fewest robots? Or, just to make the madness complete, might robots themselves have rights, or even rights prior to those of humans—some humans, or all humans?

What is lacking is nothing less than the Marxist ideal of an international proletariat. Language barriers aside, this sort of shared community of interest is not likely to come about until the plight of the economically dispensable electronics worker in Asia and that of the robot-replaced automotive worker in Detroit are seen to be interrelated and equally important. Avowed Communists have failed to show that such solidarity is attainable without exploitation. But non-Communists, or capitalists, have done little better. That does not mean, however, that it is an ideal beyond human capability.

Notes

1. See Langdon B. Winner, *Autonomous Technology*, Cambridge, Mass.: MIT Press, 1977; John Cohen, *Human Robots in Myth and Science*, New York: Allen & Unwin, 1967.

2. See George Terborgh, *Automation Hysteria*, New York: Norton, 1966; Henry Elsner, Jr., *Technocrats: Prophets of Automation*, New York: Syracuse Univ. Press, 1967.

3. See Alvin Toffler, *The Third Wave*, New York: Morrow, 1980; G. Harry Stine, *The Third Industrial Revolution*, New York: Putnam, 1975.

4. Jasia Reichardt, *Robots: Fact, Fiction, and Prediction*, New York: Penguin, 1978, p. 120 (see also for discussion of the definition of a robot).

5. Desmond Smith, "The Robots (Beep, Click) Are Coming," *Pan Am Clipper*, April 1981; Ed Janicki, "Is There a Robot in Your Future?" *The Indianapolis Star Magazine*, Nov. 22, 1981.

6. "Russian Robots Run to Catch Up," *Business Week*, August 17, 1981.

7. "The Push for Dominance in Robotics Gains Momentum," *Business Week*, December 14, 1981.

8. Smith, *op cit*. See also *Metalworkers and New Technology: Results of IMF Questionnaire on Industrial Robots*, Geneva, Switzerland: IMF Document 81-13, 1981, pp. 37–38.

9. Reichardt, *op cit*. p. 138.

10. "Racing to Breed the Next Generation," *Business Week*, June 9, 1980.

11. "High Technology: Wave of the future or a market flash in the pan?" *Business Week*, November 10, 1980 (chart on "The Coming Impact of Microelectronics").

12. Responding to a survey conducted by Carnegie-Mellon University graduate students, users and prospective users of robots "*overwhelmingly* ranked efforts to reduce labor cost as their main motivation for installing robots. Current trade journal articles also give this as the primary motivation." *The Impacts of Robotics on the Workforce and Workplace*, Department of Engineering and Public Policy and Department of Humanities and Social Science, Carnegie-Mellon University, Pittsburgh, Pennsylvania, 1981.

13. "Racing to Breed the Next Generation," *op. cit.*, 76.

14. "GM's Ambitious Plan to Employ Robots," *Business Week*, March 16, 1981.

15. "Fanuc Edges Closer to a Robot-Run Plant," *Business Week*, November 24, 1980. See also David Fleischer, "Robot-Built Robots," *Science Digest*, Dec. 1981.

16. GM's Ambitious Plan . . . ," *op. cit.*; Harley Shaiken, "The Brave New World of Work in Auto," *In These Times*, September 19–25, 1979.

17. "How Robots are Cutting Costs for GE," *Business Week*, June 9, 1980.

18. "General Electric: The Financial Wizards Switch Back to Technology," *Business Week*, March 16, 1981.

19. "Robots Join the Labor Force," *Business Week*, June 9, 1980.

20. "GE Is About to Take a Big Step in Robotics," *Business Week*, March 8, 1982.

21. Personal communication, Geary Soska, Director of Application Engineering, Cybotech, Indianapolis, Indiana.

22. "The Speedup in Automation," *Business Week*, August 3, 1981.

23. "Revamping Air Traffic Control," *Business Week*, January 18, 1982.

24. Habib Boulares and Francoise Hubscher, "La Technologie et Nous," *Jeune Afrique*, August 13 and 20, 1980.

25. "A Changing Work Force Poses Challenges," *Business Week* Special Issue: Japan's Strategy for the 80's, December 14, 1981.

Nine Paradoxes for the 1990s

by

Robert M. Fulmer

Futurists come in varying degrees of optimism and pessimism. One group, known as the "Neo-Malthusians," anticipates a world that is growing dirtier, drier, more crowded, and more quarrelsome. They see the stark realities of famine, poverty, totalitarianism, and terrorism becoming a daily reality for billions of people.

On the other hand, the "Super Optimists" see astonishing advances in medicine, agriculture, information technology, and space exploration that may be able to delay the aging process, forestall death, overcome cancer, provide food from the oceans, and transport large loads of passengers in space vehicles to all corners of the earth and beyond.

As the world grows in size and complexity, it becomes more and more difficult for a single individual to assimilate all of the changes that are confronting us. A natural reaction is to focus on one single mind-set and use that as a reference point for the changes that occur. The focus of this article is to suggest that managers assess both sides of contrasting trends that seem to be emerging. With particular emphasis on changes that will be affecting the world of work and workers, I will identify and discuss nine paradoxes of the 1990s.

Paradox I. The Decline of Traditional Incentives, with Increased Popularity of Financially Rewarding Careers

Many managers complain, "People just aren't willing to work as hard as they used to. The work ethic no longer exists." In reality, the incentives that have traditionally encouraged people to work hard have become less effective. These inducements include money, fear, and other techniques that don't depend on motivation for productivity. According to Daniel Yankelovich, these traditional incentives still work for 56% of the U.S. work force. They mean nothing, however, to the other (primarily younger) 44% of contemporary workers. Basically, the work force can be divided into the following groups:

- 19%—older dedicated workers who want to make a contribution.

Robert M. Fulmer is director of management programs, Graduate School of Business Administration, Emory University, Atlanta, Georgia.

- 22%—habitual workers who are older, in lower-level jobs, and who want job security.
- 15%—young, ambitious go-getters who are motivated by money and the opportunity to get ahead.
- 17%—young, middle-managers, highly educated professionals who are more interested in challenge and responsibility than traditional incentives.
- 27%—alienated, turned off, poorly educated, low-income workers who are not motivated at all. Unfortunately, this group seems to be growing.

While traditional incentives seem to be losing some of their clout, financially-oriented professions are increasing in popularity. College enrollments in liberal arts and humanities are declining dramatically. Concurrently, enrollments in business, engineering, and preprofessional programs are experiencing record growth. Since 1964, the number of MBA graduates produced annually has risen by 900%. Since 1971, the number of individuals taking the Test for Advanced Study in Management has risen from 83,915 to 212,500.

Clearly, the prospect of a financially rewarding career is a stimulus to many individuals who are currently enrolled in colleges. In some instances, these "practical-minded" students would have preferred to major in English, history, or sociology, but their assessment of the marketplace indicates that this could be a pleasant but unproductive choice. This may also suggest that the value systems of the emerging college graduate may allow for more flexibility than was true in the past. Idealism is tempered with a sense of practical reality. Challenge and responsibility will continue to be key watchwords, but money is important too. These "new workers" will be dissatisfied if financial rewards are not forthcoming; however, they will probably not stay in a dead-end job or accept arbitrary transfers unless there is more than money to lure them to new assignments.

Paradox II. Increased Competition for Promotions, But More Flexibility in Work Positions

By 1990, more than half of the labor force will be between the ages of 25 and 44. By 2000, the baby-boom generation will be between 35 and 55. This means increased competition for available promotions. In the 1960s, there were about 10 workers who competed for each middle-management position. By the end of this decade, the ratio will have doubled.

The reasons for this promotion crunch are quite simple. First and foremost is the maturing of the baby-boom group (born between 1945 and 1965) as candidates for management positions. This will be compounded by deferred retirement of present managers who will stay on their jobs longer because of a persistent inflation problem. These two factors will be further aggravated by a generally slow economic growth rate throughout this decade (probably two to three percent per year), which will limit the creation of new management positions. Roy Amara, president of the Institute for the Future, predicts that new management structures will be required to accommodate this unprecedented number of potential managers. "A flattening of organizational pyramids, creation of smaller, autonomous work groups, development of "working manager" positions, job design and restructuring . . . these are some of the ways to ease the expected crunch."

With this kind of competition for advancement, we might conclude that organizations will be less accommodating of special employee interests or demands than has been true in the past. Just the opposite will actually occur. At the lower end of the organizational pyramid, there will be a shrinking supply of entry-level workers. This group will grow during the 1980s at less than one-half the rate of the 1970s. A potential shortfall of entry-level applicants will probably begin in the late 1980s.

The impact of a rapid decline in fertility rates since the mid 1960s will be the major contributing factor. Because so many women are already working, labor-force participation among female workers will not continue to grow as dramatically. Finally, the rising expectations of entry-level workers will contribute to the need for greater flexibility. In order to meet the demand for entry-level positions, organizations will allow more workers to schedule their own hours under flextime. Many workers will probably hold two jobs or go to college on a part-time basis. Already the need for lifetime learning is a generally accepted principle. Moreover, the number of moonlighters increased almost 20% during the 1970s, and the number of women holding multiple jobs doubled.

In *The Third Wave*, Alvin Toffler describes the emerging trend of the "cottage office." Increasing numbers of people will be contracting with organizations to complete work in their own homes. It could be artwork for an advertising campaign, instructional materials for a training program, or software packages. The worker gains the advantage of flexibility and reduced commuting expenses while the company eliminates the overhead commitment, fringe benefits, and additional "extras" associated with full-time employees.

This work "decentralization" will continue to pick up momentum throughout the decade. The growth of portable computers, which can be hooked up to telephone lines and television sets to retrieve data and file reports, will hasten this move. Demand for "office space" in future houses and apartments will experience significant growth. Corporations will not eliminate their headquarters locations, but the need for them to "warehouse" large groups of workers in a single building will decline. In *Megatrends*, John Naisbitt argues that the "High Touch" corollary of High Tech will keep the electronic cottage from gaining widespread acceptance. Yet, what could be higher touch than parents being able to work in close proximity to their young children. And, of course, the stimulation of being around co-workers can be achieved by a couple of days per week in the office rather than a daily commute.

Over all, companies will become even more accommodating to eliminate the regimentation and boredom associated with entry-level positions. At the same time, increased competition for managerial promotions will be quite intense. Although these jobs will be more demanding than those at the lower levels of an organization, they will be in great demand because of their scarcity and the economic rewards associated with promotions.

Paradox III.   Increased Financial Pressures, Yet More Superaffluent Families

In the 1970s energy prices rose 165%, shelter 160%, medical care 111%, and food 115% in the United States. During the same period, median family income grew only 107%. The Labor Department reported that real hourly compensation for 1980 was at the same level as in the third quarter of 1972. Not much real progress has been made since. In summary, during the remainder of this century, real-income growth will probably exceed the 1970s, but it will not grow as fast as it did during the 1950s and 1960s. An increase of about 50% in real family income between 1980 and 2000 seems likely. In 1980, the price of the average house on today's market was $77,600. If inflation averages 10% in this decade, by 1995 the average house will cost $314,000.

Coping with inflation became a national pastime during the late 1970s. It will doubtless enjoy a comeback in popularity. The four major strategies that have been used to meet the challenge are more workers per family, lower savings, increasing debt, and home equity.

Moonlighting, exhaustion, persistent worry, and fighting over money share the spotlight that shines through the picture window of many middle-American homes. Workers dream of upper mobility, affluence, and getting ahead but, in reality, find themselves skipping their annual physical checkup, cashing in insurance policies, and quibbling with children about allowances. Epidemic advances in alcoholism, drug addiction, divorce, and early heart attack are not unrelated to financial pressures created by this desperate race to hold on to the good life.

Yet, the picture is not totally bleak. Currently, every 30 minutes, another dozen people will enter the 50% tax bracket. In 1980, over 2.3 million Americans discovered the good news and the bad news associated with qualifying for this painful honor. By 1995, approximately 40% of all families will be earning more than $32,500 in 1983 dollars; about 8% will be "superaffluent"—earning more than $65,000 per year.

As suggested above, the two-income household, along with an emphasis on fewer children, has been one of the most effective ways of preserving living standards. Demand is still high for luxury items such as expensive cars, European vacations, and costly jewelry.

In addition to the extremes of large groups of individuals struggling to make ends meet and the rapid growth of the superaffluents, there may also be an acceleration of the "rags-to-riches rollercoaster." The same individual may go through several stages of relative poverty and affluence.

For example, young people today typically come from families that are wealthier than was true a generation ago. When they leave home and establish their own independence, the high cost of housing and energy often forces them into a period of relative poverty. When they join forces to create a two-income family, both living standards rise dramatically. If that relationship fails to survive (which is the case with about 40%), both partners are reduced to another round of struggle. This struggle can also come about merely because of the high cost of educating and caring for children. Eventually, however, most people will rear their children, work out living arrangements, and enjoy advanced middle-age with a rediscovered joy of discretionary income.

Paradox IV: The Increased Importance of Family, Yet More Marriage Failures

The trends that will mark the change in the family emphasis are already apparent. During the past decade, the number of marriages increased 7.3%. The number of divorces increased 65.3%, and the number of unmarried couples living together increased 157.4%. The number of children living with one parent grew by 40.1%.

As has already been indicated, families are assuming greater importance as far as financial security is concerned. Sociologist Charles Westoff predicts an expansion of communal living as unrelated people of all age levels band together to reduce housing costs. By the year 2000, almost 75% of married people will have both parties working. By the end of this decade, women will contribute 40% of family incomes. This compares with about 30% today.

Families also play a greater role in the pressure to create more flexible working hours and working relationships, as well as day-care facilities. The impact is just beginning to surface as more individuals decline promotion opportunities because it would involve relocating a working spouse. A rapidly growing number of companies are providing job-finding assistance for spouses of transferring managers.

While families are making themselves heard as an active constituency in job-related decisions, they are also being subjected to an increasing number of pressures. Most individuals who are currently in management positions have not totally resolved their ambivalence about the changing stereotypes of sex roles. Despite the increased representation of women in the work force, most two-income families report that women are expected to assume more responsibility for meal preparation and housekeeping. Clearly, if the two-career family is to succeed, men must take a more active role in child-rearing as well as household tasks.

No one yet knows the long-range impact of the "latch-key children" approach to parenting. The Work in America Institute, Inc., a research organization based in Scarsdale, New York, estimates that more than 30 million American children have working mothers. They further estimate that at least 5 million of these children may be receiving inadequate care during their parents' working hours. The Urban Institute predicts that by 1990 there will be a 64% jump in the number of working mothers with children under 6. Almost half of the children in the country will spend part of their childhood in a single-family situation.

The divorce rate, which currently runs around 40% of the number of marriages performed in a given year, will probably remain high but not increase dramatically. Marriage is still an important institution: about 90% of U.S. citizens will eventually marry. In 1982, one-third of all weddings were a second marriage for at least one of the participants. People are, however, waiting longer before remarrying.

Paradox V. More Ability and Need to Centralize Decisions, But More Pressure to Decentralize

Computers, television, and satellites are already cutting down on the need for travel, allowing people access to information and communication from their homes or offices. By 1990, many experts believe that home computers will be in 80% of U.S. dwellings and will offer assistance with everything from office and school work to balancing the family checkbook.

A more direct involvement in the democratic process will shortly be possible via electronic referendums. Within five years, Japan will initiate voting and census taking through video centers within the home. Unfortunately, access to tremendous amounts of data does not necessarily create more information or knowledge. Electronics may be able to bring in a vast variety of entertainment and data into homes, but it will be increasingly difficult for people to comprehend what it all means. The increasing sophistication of electronics in the home may also discourage them from moving out of their "hibernated existence" at home.

Just as technology is making it possible for more individuals to have access to information and to participate in decision-making, the same kind of high-quality information is making it possible for centralized decisions to be made with more efficiency. Despite the sad record of government planning, the future offers the potential of much more efficient, intelligent approaches to predicting and controlling the future. Even the optimistic head of the Hudson Institute, Herman Kahn, admits that progress during the last fifth of this century is dependent upon a combination of "good luck and good management." It might appear that there is a greater need for efficiency in decision-making than participation. At present, the economic decisions that need to be made are extremely difficult because of political implications. Would it not be more reasonable for someone to make the decisions based on more input and better analysis than the average citizen can muster?

Regardless of the efficiency of centralized decision-making, SRI International (formerly Stanford Research Institute) has concluded that the move for more participation in decision-making will affect all aspects of life during this decade. Many of the decisions made in this manner may not be optimal, but they will benefit from the motivation associated with taking part in the process.

Paradox VI: More People Working, Yet Higher Unemployment

One of the complex issues of the 1980 U.S. presidential election was the convincing argument of the incumbent president that more Americans were at work and earning more money than had been true at any other point in the history of the country. Conversely, the challenging candidate was citing impressive figures to prove that there were more people unemployed than had ever been out of work in the past. Despite the apparent contradiction, both sets of facts were absolutely true. Moreover, both of these trends will probably continue.

Labor economists will remember the 1970s for its unprecedented growth in new workers, primarily fueled by the maturation of babies born after World War II and the rapid influx of women. During the same period, "acceptable" unemployment increased from about 4% to 6% and, of course, is even higher now.

While the work force will not continue to grow at the same rate as has been true in the past, there will probably be 16.4 million more people at work in 1990 than now. Technical areas such as computers and electronics will create increased employment opportunities along with such professions as accounting, nursing, and engineering. Certain industries such as aerospace, communication, electronics, broadcasting, health care, and energy will experience dramatic increases.

The Center for the Study of Social Policy in Menlo Park, California, portrays chronic unemployment and underemployment as fundamental concerns of the post-industrial society. This concern rests on the proposition that economic growth may not continue to generate enough jobs to accommodate even a slowly expanding work force and the quality of available jobs may not be compatible with the rising expectations associated with the higher educational levels of the population. The U.S. Chamber of Commerce believes that rising unemployment can be explained by the following three trends:

- Increased benefits offered by unemployment compensation, welfare, and food stamp programs provide less incentive for people to find jobs.
- Dramatic increases in the number of women and teenagers in the work force lead to higher unemployment since these two groups tend to quit or change jobs more often than other workers.
- Because of the existence of two full-time workers in families, if one person becomes temporarily unemployed, the other affords a buffer against hardship that was not available before.

In addition to unemployment, Herbert Greenberg, president of Marketing Survey and Research Corporation, believes that 80% of American workers are doing jobs for which they are not suited. This figure applies to "every job category . . . every educational group . . . every part of the country." It, of course, involves people who have stumbled into jobs for which they have little training or aptitude as well as individuals who are highly trained but unable to find employment in their own fields.

Of course, unemployment figures only reflect those individuals who are currently actively seeking employment. When those who no longer seek work, those who are in featherbedding or make-work situations, drop-outs, or those in holding institutions such as reform schools and mental institutions are taken into account, real unemployment may be 20 to 25% of the potential work force. We will probably have to learn to live with a large number of underemployed and unemployed workers even when there is a tight labor market for entry-level jobs.

Paradox VII. Dramatic Progress for Women, But Continued Inequality

According to the National Commission on Working Women, 80% of the working women in the United States are concentrated in the low-paying, low-status jobs. Most are in "pink-collar" jobs such as waitress, beautician, and clerical positions. Another large concentration of working women may be found in blue-collar jobs (skilled and union trades).

Surprisingly, there has been little progress in closing the gap between earnings for men and women. Since 1967, women have consistently earned about two-thirds of what their male counterparts do. Even in the female ghetto of clerical work, where salaries are extremely low, women's wages are only 63% of those paid for the few men in this field. The Labor Department reports that women who support their families earn less than half (46.9%) the amount earned by male breadwinners. The median income of female-headed families is only $10,400. In families where only the husband works, the median income is just under $21,000. When both husband and wife are employed, the family income averages almost $28,000.

There have been important areas of progress during the past 20 years. Female banking and financial officers have increased from 2,100 to 122,000. Female sales management positions have increased from 200 to 12,000. According to the *U.S. News Washington Letter*, the 1980s will see dramatic strides made by women in obtaining more equality in the U.S. work force. Within the next 20 years, females may hold the top spots in 10% of the nation's 500 largest companies. That's progress, but hardly equality.

SRI International predicts that one of the most significant changes of the 1980s will be the impact of women making key management decisions. The backhanded compliment that "you think like a man" will give way to women making decisions as women. In other words, instead of being forced into a masculine mode, women will gain more freedom to make decisions in their own way. Women do make decisions differently from men. They generally utilize the right hemisphere of their brain in thinking more than men. This means that they are more likely to be creative or intuitive than relying totally upon logic. Your reaction to the foregoing statement may be a test of your own adaptability. Some readers will view the statement that "women make decisions differently" as a sexist comment. But there are obvious, important differences between men and women. Women will have achieved a degree of progress when they are not forced to compete with men by duplicating the male behavior pattern. When they can approach problems and challenges in their own individual manner, there may be some surprising but productive approaches to organizational lives. In summary, there will be more progress than equality.

Paradox VIII. Shorter Working Hours, with Less Leisure

Time spent away from the job is generally expected to expand. Americans will probably be willing to trade some income for added leisure time—especially where people are faced with the pressures of a two-career family. The emergence of a larger number of affluent families will place a greater premium on leisure time. Labor Department projections suggest that annual work hours will drop from 1,900 today to about 1,775 in 2000. This translates to a move from 36.5 to 34.1 hours per week. William Lazer, past president of the American Marketing Association, believes that the 4½-day workweek will become quite common.

While more time that might be referred to as "discretionary" will be available, time demands for other life-style activities are also likely to expand. This will probably result in even less free time than is currently available. Lazer also estimates that "a full-time working housewife may well average over 60 hours at work, both at home and on the job." The same is probably true of a male who is actively involved in a career and family responsibilities. These time demands affect life-style, purchase behavior, and other product/service needs.

Two-career families affect the demands for such categories of needs as one-stop shopping, repair service on weekends and nights, flexible working arrangements, Sunday and evening store hours, family restaurants, fast-food chains, foods that can be prepared quickly at home, convenience items, products that require little service, summer school programs and extensive camps for children, products that stress usefulness and individualism, and any item that will help save time on household tasks. Leisure, when it is actually available, will become more important. Individuals pressured with the demands of expanded responsibilities will treasure the time that they can be away from the demands of their day-to-day responsibilities. Balancing the demands of careers, families, and self-improvement will reduce the amount of true leisure that is available, even though the number of hours that must be spent at the office will decline.

Paradox IX. The Triumph of Worker Participation, Yet a Revival of Scientific Management

I've already documented the move toward greater decentralization of decision-making. This trend will be particularly important in organizations. In business, it will be accentuated by the results of a quarter century of research in the field of human relations, as well as the example of Japanese management and the successes of a few U.S. pioneers. We can anticipate that industrial workers will be involved in autonomous work teams where they make many of their own production decisions. This "uni-management" is already occurring in a few companies as a result of agreements with the United Auto Workers in such firms as Dana Corporation, Rockwell, and Harman. At the Edgerton, Wisconsin, Dana factory, production committees of workers and supervisors elect a union-management screening committee that sifts suggestions as to how the factors of production should be organized. At Harman Industries in Bolivar, Tennessee, Worker-Supervisor Core Committees plan production within each department. Their decisions are subject to review by a plant-wide union-management work committee.

In Europe, co-determination has made rapid strides. Swedish law puts union representatives on corporate boards. In 1976, West Germany gave workers the right to elect half of the directors of firms employing over 2,000 people. Andre Thiria, international secretary of the Swedish Confederation of Trade Unions, explains, ''Demands are being raised for a better work environment and more satisfaction on the job, while at the same time mechanization and streamlining of production make it more difficult to meet these demands.'' Joint efforts by workers and management constitute one attempt to solve this dilemma.

Because of the widespread recognition of America's problem of productivity, there will be a concurrent return to some of the basics of scientific management and production efficiency. Unlike the scientific-management movement that emerged around the turn of the century, workers will no longer be viewed as minor cogs in the production process. Productivity and efficiency are two themes that will increase dramatically in their popularity during the 1980s. At the beginning of this decade, productivity growth was less than 1% per year. This compares unfavorably with countries like Japan (6.8%), West Germany (5.3%), and even Great Britain (2.5%). Already, however, improved production technology (with greater emphasis on computer-assisted manufacturing and robots), an older and more experienced work force, economic pressures on workers, *and* greater involvement of workers in decisions that affect them are leading to productivity increases.

Conclusion

The observation that ''We live in an age of transition'' may have been first spoken by Adam as he escorted Eve from the Garden of Eden. It certainly is an appropriate description of the period that lies before us. In the midst of dramatic and sometimes conflicting trends, the astute manager must be able to read the ebb and flow of tides that affect his or her operation. Ralph Waldo Emerson once said, ''A foolish consistency is the hobgoblin of little minds.'' The challenge of the 1980s is to unravel the inconsistencies and to understand the paradoxes that confront us. It will not be a time for ''little minds.''

Toward Full Unemployment

by

Robert Theobald

The goal of full employment has been put forward as the centerpiece of the good society for at least two generations. It is now so fully accepted that very few people stop to examine its changing implications given the new technologies that are developing so rapidly.

In industrial societies, jobs are essential for the survival of almost all citizens: they provide income, enable people to claim a viable position in the society, determine status. Those without a job, whether by choice or by inability to find employment, usually feel out of the mainstream. This reality is shown by the deep depression that hits those who lose their jobs and also by the often expressed feeling: "I'm just a housewife."

Movies and books have explored this trauma. It has even been suggested that people may well feel a right to rob banks and other organizations because society has failed them. To make the point clearly, the industrial-era social contract *demands* that we find jobs for everybody who wants them.

This statement may appear exaggerated because less than half of the American population is employed. However, the vast majority of those who do not hold jobs at any particular time still obtain their rights to resources through their own past job-holding or their relationship to a job-holder. The unemployed, the sick, and the retired usually have income rights because of previous employment. The young and spouses and most of the old who do not hold jobs are normally supported by those who do.

The job is the cornerstone of today's socio-economic order. The maintenance of relatively full employment for over 35 years, since the Second World War, has provided opportunities for people to enter the labor force who would previously have stayed in the home. The increase in the percentage of women employed has been dramatic and has indeed changed societal functioning in ways that are still largely misunderstood. In the United States in April 1947, 29.8% of females aged 15 and over were in the labor force; in 1977, 48% were holding jobs. In the seventies, three out of five people entering the labor force were women. Well over 50% of married women between the ages of 20 and 44, living with their

Robert Theobald is president of Participation Publishers, Wickenburg, Arizona. This paper is drawn from a forthcoming book entitled Social Economics.

husbands, were holding jobs as opposed to under a third in 1947.

Nevertheless, despite the apparent priority given to job-holding, society today discourages many people from holding jobs who would have done so in the past. Children must stay in school until they are 16 or more in most rich countries, and they are encouraged to gain even more education. Retirement is possible at 65, or even 60, when many people are still healthy and strong.

The central thesis of this paper is that the industrial-era social contract is now obsolete. It is inevitable that unemployment will rise in the eighties because of the impact of computers and robots. It is already possible to use a computer for less than the cost of the minimum wage, and costs will continue to fall. The development of the voice-actuated typewriter and computer during the eighties, to choose only one emerging example of technological change, will have a further dramatic impact on white-collar employment.

As it becomes clear that we cannot usefully employ everybody, the contradictions in our present attitudes toward employment will lead to major conflicts. If we are to avoid the most dangerous possibilities, we must look behind the current academic and political smokescreens. Before we can begin to sort out the apparent contradictions in policy and actions, we must recognize the dramatic drop in the percentage of the average individual's life spent on the job. In the mid-nineteenth century, the average male spent about 40% of his total hours of life on the job, leaving a maximum of 60% for sleep, meals, education, church, early childhood, etc. The pattern of the eighties requires the average individual to spend not more than 14% of his life on the job and the percentage is dropping.

The early industrial era had an insatiable need for hands and bodies. Machinery was, to use today's jargon, labor-intensive. Given the need for hands and bodies, societies accepted the intolerable. People were torn from rural societies, moved into towns and cities, and coerced to work outrageous hours. Cheap labor was seen as essential and the consequent social and personal costs were hidden behind sentiments such as those taken from an 1848 *Economist* article: "Suffering and evil are nature's admonitions: they cannot be got rid of and the impatient attempts of benevolence to banish them from the world by legislation, before benevolence has learned their object and their end, is more productive of evil than of good."

In the first half of the nineteenth-century, therefore, children in many mills in Britain were working 14 hours a day and were being subjected to brutal ill-treatment. Others were working in mines pulling heavy carts in place of donkeys, going underground before daybreak and emerging after the sun set. As late as 1833, it was considered a significant reform when the employment of children under 9 was prohibited in all textile mills except silk, and the working hours of a young person were limited to 12 a day and 69 a week.

Not surprisingly, workers accustomed to rural rhythms found factory conditions unacceptable. They often worked at their jobs, therefore, until they had earned enough to get drunk at the ubiquitous gin mills—only coming back when their money had run out. Trying to run efficient factories under these conditions was impossible. Efforts were therefore made, both consciously and unconsciously, to lead people to get satisfaction from their jobs.

Listen to this paean of praise for the work ethic:

"Work is a grand cure for all the maladies and miseries that ever beset mankind—honest work which you intend getting done." (Thomas Carlyle)

"Honor lies in honest toil." (Grover Cleveland)

"There is no substitute for hard work." (Thomas A. Edison)

"Any man who has a job has a chance." (Elbert Hubbard)

"Work is the inevitable condition of human life, the true source of human welfare." (Leo Tolstoy)

This cultural graft took. People came to believe that hard work was required to support their self-image. Hard work became the god of the secular society and of the church. Leaders were therefore slowly freed from a Middle-Ages personal and social framework in which change was considered threatening—and in many senses impossible—because one would be tampering with the divine will. Societies were increasingly challenged to believe that there were no limits to their capabilities. The capacity of technology, coupled with personal commitment to jobs, created a mighty engine for growth and the improvement of material conditions.

The Impact of Industrial-Era Technology

Almost as soon as the industrializing societies managed to convince people that hard work was good in and of itself, the impacts of industrial-era technology began to produce a new set of conditions. The number of hours of work required from each individual began to decline significantly.

Societies adapted. They cut out Sunday working where it existed and went to half-days on Saturdays and eventually eliminated Saturday working for many people. Vacations were lengthened. New public holidays were invented. Periods of education were lengthened. The concept of retirement was created and then ages of retirement were maintained even though life-spans got longer and longer.

These steps were not enough, even when combined with longer periods of schooling, to cope with the capacity of industrial-era systems to produce more and more goods. The thirties slump overwhelmed the effect of previously adopted measures for balancing the socio-economy. Fortunately, John Maynard Keynes provided at this time a new solution for coping with surplus. He argued that the amount of effort required from people could be maintained if people and societies were enabled to consume more, for then additional jobs would be required to produce all that people wanted to consume. A full-employment system, based on balancing ever-increasing consumption desires with ever-rising productive abilities, therefore became the norm after the Second World War.

Keynes knew, however, that this situation was temporary—even though his disciples missed this critical point. In an essay entitled "Economic Possibilities for Our Grandchildren," he argued that we would have to come to recognize for the vices they actually are those behaviors we now proclaim as the highest virtues. He saw clearly that the encouragement of consumption would move us into a profoundly new context and that we should then need to change fundamentally our life-styles and life cycles in ways that would seem surprising and shocking to many. Unfortunately, societies have ignored his insights and failed to use the last 50 years to think through the needed changes; instead, they have strengthened and maintained Keynes's temporary solution.

It is not difficult to understand why we have largely failed to perceive the new realities. Part of the resistance comes from the normal unwillingness to admit the reality of any change in conditions. In addition, we should recognize that the failure has to some extent been inevitable because those who sell ideas and make policy today have less leisure time than the typical job-holder: a total reversal of the nineteenth-century pattern. People with high-level skills usually work excessive hours—and are often workaholics. They assume—all too often—that most of the population shares their ideas and attitudes. One critical, and central, idea of Reaganomics—that most people are committed to their jobs but are discouraged from further work by high tax rates—emerges from this elitist group. This belief is untrue, as more and more surveys have shown. In reality, the job is no longer the center of life for most people.

Although most people do not value jobs themselves, they are still committed to maintaining—and, if possible, improving—their standard of living. This remains true even though there is a significant and increasing group, members of which have decided to opt for voluntary simplicity— a life-style that limits consumption to real needs. The majority of the population, however, still feels that it is justified in fighting back if its real income erodes. The general decline in levels of income in recent years—except for those people who have been able to send an additional family member out to work—has led to widespread frustration. This, in turn, is resulting in considerable tax evasion as wage-earners feel they are being deprived of their fair share of the production of the society.

Some workers evade taxes by hiding second jobs at which they earn additional income. Tax evasion can also develop within jobs. Thomas Brom, writing in the *Los Angeles Times* of November 28, 1980, states:

> Jerry is a house framer working in an exclusive suburban development near San Francisco Bay. He works under union contract, which requires a short work week as an incentive for builders to hire more carpenters. So once every two weeks, Jerry has what carpenters call a Black Friday: no work, no pay.
>
> But Jerry and his mates come to work anyway. They are paid ''off the books'' in cash, and spend much of their time hiding from the business representative of their own union. The framers don't declare the income, the contractor doesn't declare wages and, so, if the union doesn't find out, everybody but Uncle Sam is happy.

Jerry is a microcosm of the societal problem we must unravel. We are caught in a situation where jobs are the key to survival but enough jobs are not, and will not, be available. Indeed, as we have already seen, the problem is going to worsen rapidly. Fortunately, the fact that a growing number of people see jobs as a way to get income, rather than as being valuable in themselves, could provide flexibility in the culture if leaders were prepared to face reality.

There is a positive mythology around the full-employment ethic that must be broken before we can hope to make intelligent new policies. We must ask, as Keynes did, whether full employment is a desirable and effective way to mobilize the energies of human beings, and we must ask this question based on emerging communications-era realities rather than on obsolete industrial-era models. We must recognize that today's society simply cannot function without the maintenance of full employment but that we do have a choice whether we shall continue to perpetuate present socio-economic models through the eighties.

In order to understand this point, we must understand that any functioning socio-economic system must necessarily be logical and coherent so long as its basic premises are not challenged. To break out of current norms, we must re-examine the fetters imposed on us by the full-employment model in the same way as slavery was challenged in the nineteenth century. It is obvious that comparing a full-employment system to slavery will seem shocking to many, but we must recognize that the ethical contrast between slavery and employment was less clear to those involved in nineteenth-century debates than it is now. William Wilberforce, the great British anti-slavery figure, was widely criticized for his patterns of child employment, which were argued by many to be equally as inhumane as the slavery he so vigorously attacked.

Similarly, some of the more intellectual Southerners raised fundamental questions at the time of the Civil War that have been ignored since. They argued that the conflict was not, basically, a moral one but emerged rather from the fact that different styles of employment were effective for different patterns of production. They pointed out that the South needed a stable labor force and had met its needs through slavery. They argued that the North wanted a labor force that it could hire and fire according to the needs of the trade cycle because Northern industrialists could not afford to hold onto their labor in times of slump. Their arguments were shown to have considerable validity, as the great novels written by the late-nineteenth-century muckrakers made abundantly clear.

It is time to break out of the pieties that surround the job issue and face up to the real and fundamental nature of the contract between the employer and the employee, who must strike a bargain in terms of wages and conditions of work. Given a full-employment situation, the worker—particularly when supported by trade unions—can strike a decent deal. Indeed, the power of workers almost overwhelmed employers at certain points in the last 30 years.

These days, however, are gone forever. Full employment in the current sense of a job for all those who might want one will not be restored, and more and more people are aware of this reality. In these circumstances, the worker inevitably serves at the pleasure of the employer and must always worry about the impact of his or her behavior on job tenure.

Such a system destroys morale and human dignity when jobs are scarce, for the worker must increasingly pander to the prejudices of the employer to survive. Nor can labor unions be effective, given their present perceptions of their roles. They can protect some workers some of the time. But the more effective they are, in these limited activities, the worse the overall situation will become, because an ever-larger proportion of the available jobs will be monopolized and those outside the system will have even less chance of entering it.

In his book *Player Piano*, Kurt Vonnegut explores the dangers of trying to maintain the myth of a full-employment system, once the reality of unemployment becomes dominant. He shows how we shall be forced toward a serf society. The patterns of workfare, or compulsory activity required by the state in order to obtain welfare payments, which are developing already in many states, show how his fears could be easily realized in the immediate future.

It might seem that we are caught in an insoluble bind. But this is because we insist on looking at too narrow a picture. One overwhelming reality of today is the amount of work that needs to be done and that cannot be structured into jobs for which wages and salaries can be paid. Cities are run-down, human services are increasingly inadequate, education is less good than in the past. The other overwhelming reality is that people are crying out for meaningful challenges that move beyond the economic into improving personal and societal functioning.

In order to get a sense of the implications of the necessary shifts in direction, I have developed definitions of various work-related terms as they might appear in a twenty-first century dictionary:

Work: Activity that provides a sense of self-worth to the individual; previously linked to economic reward but not in present conditions.

Toil: Activity that nobody would choose to do. Greatly reduced by the microelectronic revolution, but today each person is expected to do some of the necessary toil as part of his obligations as a citizen; failure to do this toil typically incurs significant social penalties.

Job (Obsolete): An individual was paid by an employer who controlled his or her activities through fear of dismissal and prospects of promotion.

Leisure (Obsolete): The division between job and leisure was central to twentieth-century thinking: people ''bought'' pleasant activities to counteract the unsatisfactory nature of their jobs. The late-twentieth-century turbulence was caused, in part, by leisure becoming more important than the jobs that supported it.

Unemployment (Obsolete): People who could not get jobs were paid to support their idleness; meanwhile, both work and toil went undone, with a consequent worsening of the quality of life.

In this context, the words *full employment* are seen to be inadequate. It becomes clear that we need to break out of an employment and unemployment ethic into a new world in which work, prestige, and income are allocated according to totally new patterns.

With these changes in mind, then, what are the primary alterations that can be expected in patterns of work and activity? The word *primary* must be stressed, of course, because as work patterns change so will the whole pattern of the society and there is no space here to detail the full implications of such shifts.

Flexible Work and Learning Patterns

There is a dominant style to the late industrial era: People prepare for jobs, work at jobs, and retire from jobs. As the number of hours it is necessary to spend at jobs has declined, this system has begun to fray at the edges. For example, community colleges now spend much of their time teaching older students and recycling them back into the economic system in new opportunities. This pattern will continue to develop.

In the work world, there are the beginnings of job-sharing—with two people each taking half of the work and the responsibilities that would previously have been carried out by one. More and more people are being given time off to renew themselves and to develop further skills. Flextime, where people have the right to choose starting and quitting times, is becoming a conventional management tool.

The number of workers with "floating" starting and quitting times has risen substantially from 1977's three million, says Georgetown University's Stanley Nolan, according to a December 2, 1980, *Wall Street Journal* report. "New York City plans to adopt flextime to enhance productivity and expand services. More concerns extend the benefits to production or technical workers. Among them: Digital Equipment Corp., Corning Glass Works, and Sercel Industries Inc., a seismic equipment assembler."

Older workers will also spend part of their time passing on their skills to younger ones in one-on-one or one-on-many real situations. The California State Department of Education is seeking to legitimate, through legislation, the apprentice process so that it may be considered the equivalent of more formal education. If this should occur, we shall recognize that skilled older workers can usually spend years introducing young people to their crafts and to a responsible method of working. This will allow us to relate young people to old in effective and challenging patterns.

But the most profound and critical change will be in the way we think about life cycles and the way we plan our passages through life. Once we accept the reality of this change, we shall be able to perceive how much alteration there has already been from the classic industrial-era models. For example, the goal of lifetime learning is rapidly being institutionalized in our culture. One force driving this change is that people cannot function effectively with what they learned in school or college one or more decades ago. Another is that educational institutions cannot survive without finding different groups of people to attend college—and older citizens are the largest untapped market.

Another area where profound change is taking place is that more and more of the critical work in the culture demands total attention and total commitment: it cannot be accomplished in 40 hours or 5 days a week. This type of work is highly exciting and challenging and people are pleased to do it. However, individuals need to concentrate completely on this type of work and they must have all the support systems they require to be effective.

Few people can, or should, however, continue to work intensively for a lengthy period, for they lose their perspective on the overall reality of the society. Burnout occurs and people want and need to renew themselves.

This reality is already being recognized in the political arena, where we know that the mental maps of politicians often freeze soon after they enter Congress because of their overloads. Shorter terms are therefore being proposed for politicians: Indeed the concept of single nonrenewable terms for all those involved in legislation is now being proposed in order to avoid the pathologies that emerge as people look toward ensuring their re-election rather than meeting the fundamental needs of the society.

This suggestion for movement into and out of work activities rests on a key assumption: that an individual can learn to learn. In other words, many of the myths about the difficulty of learning to perform effectively in various jobs are related primarily to the desire to maintain power, prestige, and authority structures rather than to the actual problems of learning new types of activity; this is increasingly true given the development of computer knowledge systems. One of the more depressing aspects of the present culture is that the ever-rising tide of credentialization prevents us from challenging most people to use their brains more effectively.

We hear from time to time about the maverick who has failed to follow the credentializing route but has nevertheless held a variety of jobs that are believed to require very lengthy periods of education: doctors, air pilots, etc. The inevitable lesson is that skills could be effectively learned more rapidly by many, but this is prevented by the desire of the society to maintain a scarcity of qualified persons in various professions because this ensures higher incomes for them.

While we do not need untrained people in high-risk professions, the future *will* require flexibility and freedom, particularly in movement along one's chosen life-path. Unfortunately, freedom is frightening to many. We shall therefore need to preserve, for a substantial number of years, structures and jobs for those who have built cages for themselves or have been built into cages by their experiences, from which they are now unable to escape. Contrary to the normal prescriptions, we should now be encouraging most young people to find their own work so that the remaining conventional jobs can be preserved for older people who require structures because their life experience limited their capacity to deal with choices. One fascinating aspect of this change in experience patterns was expressed by a banker who said: "The most positive thing you can do for an older man is to offer him overtime. It is the most negative possibility for most younger people."

Today's real failure with the young is not our inability to provide them with jobs, for the evolution of the socio-economy makes this inevitable. Our true catastrophe is that we have not educated people to grasp opportunities *outside* the conventional job market or to make choices among the wide range of options available within the communications era.

Toil As a Responsibility for All

One primary, and urgently needed, change is for young people to recognize that the unplanned "invention" of adolescence was one of the worst mistakes made by a society. The period of schooling was extended further and further and children were deprived of the possibility of taking

56

responsibility for their decisions. This pattern was recognized as dangerous in early Greece, when Plato argued that teenagers needed to be challenged physically rather than to sit down passively and learn ideas.

Fortunately, a concept has been developed over recent years that could, with some modification, serve the needs of the young and the urgent requirements of the culture. It has been suggested that everybody should do work that would benefit the society during their teenage years. This time now needs to be placed, however, in a new developmental context.

Young people should continue to be educated within their home communities from kindergarten through eighth grade. The learning pattern would be revised, however, to encourage values learning and the development of personal responsibility within the home, the school, and the community. The timing of various types of learning would also be changed to fit what we have learned from childhood development studies.

Young people would then be encouraged to spend the next four years (largely outside their own home communities) doing the heavy challenging work that older people would rather not do, or will not do at all. Included in these activities would be the renewal of cities, care of the sick and the elderly, stoop agriculture, reforestation, and a multitude of societally necessary tasks that are today not being done or only being accomplished by coercion based on poverty and the consequent need for people to take any available job.

There would be no compulsion to engage in this type of activity, but there should be substantial rewards in terms of future educational entitlements. In addition, as this type of activity becomes built into the culture, those who choose to avoid it will inevitably find themselves disadvantaged in both obvious and subtle ways.

The most dramatic, and exciting, implication of such a shift will be a new way of getting the toil of the culture accomplished. We have always needed poverty to guarantee that dirty work is done in our type of culture. If we have a large-scale labor force available for these purposes, then we can for the first time imagine a society in which extremes of wealth and poverty are abolished.

Such a suggestion for new socialization processes, with their overtones of cultural coercion, may be rejected by those who have failed to examine the ways in which societies are held together. We shall have to recognize that freedom is only possible within synergetic societal structures. Encouraging young people to engage in activities where they will be challenged to accept responsibility is a valid way to provide them with the ability to cope with freedom later in their lives.

At the age of 18, most people will have a better sense of what they want to achieve. Some will be ready for more academic education. Some will want to move toward technical skills. Some will move into apprenticeship patterns. Some will marry and raise families.

The new society we are entering will tolerate, and indeed encourage, a far wider diversity of life-styles. But as already suggested, there will be one fairly common pattern: Many people will tend to work intensively for a period of time and then need to re-create and re-educate themselves. We shall extend rapidly the concept of sabbaticals in terms of the number of people involved, the number of occupations for which they are considered relevant, and the length of time for which people can free themselves up from responsibilities. Societies will be able to make free time available because of the impacts of computers and robots, which will limit the amount of human energy needed for industrial-era jobs.

During the industrial era, the job has been the primary way in which we have got the work of the culture done. It has also been the method of allocating income. In addition, it has been used to allocate prestige and position.

The job will not be effective for these purposes in the communications era since we can no longer afford to devalue the contributions made by parents in the home and volunteers in the community. In the communications era, we shall come to recognize parenting as a full-time paid career for as much as 20–25 years of one's life: this will be seen as one of the options for personal development. We shall also support, both socially and financially, the community volunteer.

More and more people have been attracted to these options for more than a decade. But it has been impossible to achieve the necessary changes because of our patterns of income distribution. One of the most urgent tasks is to change these in the light of the ways in which wealth is created in the communications era.

Managing Technological Change

Computer Integrated Manufacturing: The Human Factors

by

Ross Bishop

There is a good deal of discussion today about the coming transformation called the "Information Age." Futurists tend to wax poetic about approaching periods of great transformation. I am certain that every age has something to be excited about, but I have to admit that, as I look into this new age, I cannot help but be impressed by the enormity of the change that is being spread before us. It is an incredible smorgasbord. Although the Information Age will produce dramatic changes in all aspects of society, the most significant transformations may be those which occur in industry. Computer-integrated manufacturing (CIM) is the embodiment of machine intelligence in manufacturing. By creating intelligent machines and tying them into a highly sophisticated manufacturing system, man will make a quantum leap in his ability to produce goods. He will dramatically alter the economics of manufacturing and provide society with the means to grow and expand, transcending its present values and structure.

We have made enormous strides in manufacturing over the last century, but we are still dependent upon human labor to produce our goods. Most manufacturing (60%) is in batches too small to be automated at present. In addition to the obvious economic considerations, workers must be subjected to heat, noise, fumes, and the risk of injury in a boring and often mindless environment. Computer-integrated manufacturing with its robots, intelligent machines, and sophisticated information technologies will permanently change that.

Response to these new technologies has been somewhat erratic. The Japanese have embraced them eagerly and have become one of the most advanced and productive manufacturers in the world. They utilize half the world's robots and a tremendous amount of semi-robotic equipment. In the West, attitudes toward these new technologies have been much more conservative. We have been reluctant to assume the lead in CIM. Ironically, it is in the West that these technologies have been developed.

Ross Bishop is a futurist who specializes in the areas of organizational changes created by social and technological changes. He is a consultant for corporations and government agencies.

Western businessmen point to the cost and shortage of capital as the culprit restricting the use of these new technologies. Not only is this explanation simplistic, it does not speak, I believe, to the real issue. The problem goes much deeper than that. As an example, American auto makers, faced with enormous losses and significant erosion of market share, would have allocated the capital if all they had needed was some new hardware. Unfortunately, it was not that simple. The automakers were locked into a system of technology and management that was designed for another age. Even if they could have read the Japanese handwriting on the wall, I am not at all certain that there was much they could have done about it.

Any society, especially a business, must adapt its values, organization, and management style to maximize significant technological development. If not, it runs the risk of impeding its own growth and development. I do not speak of change for the sake of fashion, but rather for survival in a competitive environment. Samuel Lilley, in his profound *Men, Machines and History*, points to the necessity for this parallel development:

> ". . . at each level of technological development certain social conditions must be satisfied if the technology is to advance yet farther. And as a result, amid all the variety of history one basic pattern is repeated time and time again. Each form of society is at first well adapted to encourage technological advance. In these conditions, the technological level rises more or less rapidly, and eventually reaches a point at which yet further progress requires a different form of social organization. Then progress is slowed down—until the required social change is made."[1]

We stand at a most unique time in human history. Within our lifetimes we shall witness the end of one age and the birth of another. We are experiencing the end of a great industrial cycle—the end of the Age of Steel and the technologies and social structure associated with it; and we will bear witness to the development of the Age of Information. Computer-Integrated Manufacturing (CIM) will require a substantial restructuring of the corporate organization, both functionally and philosophically. The system will require a good deal of decentralized autonomy, accelerating the current shift from the traditional authoritarian hierarchy to more egalitarian forms of decision-making.

CIM will spark a redefinition, perhaps for the second time in man's history, of the nature of work. Blue-collar values that have been established over a century of factory labor will be transformed by the conditions of the new system. A new stratum of workers will be institutionalized between blue- and white-collar groups—I call them "grays." They are the myriad of technical support people essential to the success of the computer-integrated system. Job-security issues and new standards of compensation will present themselves for resolution as CIM evolves. Retraining, job fracturing, leapfrogging, and outsourcing will take on new importance.

There will also be mobility issues to be resolved. Manufacturing could become highly portable. Experts predict the development of general-purpose manufacturing equipment that will perform a wide range of tasks. With this programmable equipment in place, a plant could produce a wide variety of products. Thus, a firm will be able to relocate to another facility by simply transferring its software. This will exacerbate job migration, regional economies, and a host of other issues. Smaller batch breakevens and the ease of "retooling" may make contracted manufacturing the prevalent method of production. It will also bring new competitors.

It is always difficult to see transitions from the inside, "through a glass darkly," as it were. Changes of this kind are evolutionary. A little happens every day until the world is different, but often only a historical comparison illustrates the extent of the shift. Transitions of this magnitude are frequently punctuated by loud and boisterous conflicts as contending forces jostle for position. We would be naive not to expect them.

Technology

In the workplace as elsewhere, technology is the great amplifier. It expands the resources available to society by creating a reservoir of knowledge and power. Technology not only allows us to do more and do it better, but also gives us the power to use energies totally beyond the range of our natural senses. Consider that without technology you would be a subsistence farmer.

If technology did not advance, half the population would be employed as telephone operators—placing calls for the other half. "Ridiculous," you say, "we'd never do that." And you would be correct. With a static technology, we would never have allocated that much of our human resources to expand the communications system that has played such an important role in õur social and economic development. It is through the expansion of resources such as this that civilizations grow. Whether you like technology or not, the fact is that without it we would have developed little beyond feudalism. Each technological step allows fewer people to do more than before, expanding society's resource base and freeing us to pursue other goals.

The effect of an earlier technologically based social transformation is illustrated in Figure 1. Two to three million years ago, human society consisted mostly of hunters and gatherers. Then, about 10,000 years ago, a transformation occurred as man developed the technologies of agriculture. By 1500 A.D., most of human society had given up hunting for farming. Agriculture had become the dominant mode of living. Not only did agriculture allow man to live more successfully, it gave impetus to a new and much more effective social structure. Human civilization was able to transcend nomadic life and to develop civilizations and cultures that were impossible before. An anthropologist once said, "It was the success of the simplest tools that started the whole trend of human evolution and led to the civilizations of today." In response, Arthur Clarke commented, "Note the phrase, 'the whole trend of human evolution.' The old idea that we invented tools is a misleading half-truth; it would be more accurate to say that tools invented man."

Agrarian man lived on the strength of his back; his tools were simple and dictated that he focus his energies on survival. The guild craftsman was a specialist, but he was limited by his own strength, speed, and

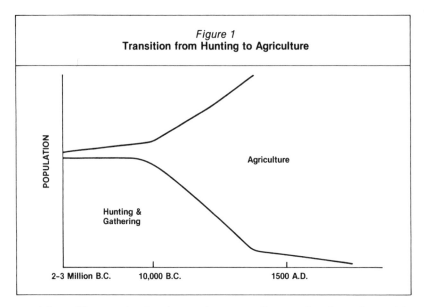

Figure 1
Transition from Hunting to Agriculture

POPULATION

Agriculture

Hunting &
Gathering

2-3 Million B.C.   10,000 B.C.   1500 A.D.

precision. The goods that he made were of exceptional workmanship, quite expensive, and produced in very limited quantities. The machines of the period were beginning to free man from the limits of his hands; they pioneered industrial society.

As we study the industrial period (Figure 2), we see an evolution very similar to the agrarian transformation thousands of years before. Remember that in 1500 we were all subsistence farmers. There was little else one could do. The industrial transformation once again expanded the pool of resources available to society and allowed the social order to completely transcend the limitations of agrarian feudalism. The growth of society during this time—absolutely in terms of population and relatively as regards social development—was simply phenomenal. Every aspect of the society was dramatically affected. Those that would not change were broken. It is not coincidental that the American and French Revolutions and a series of revolts in Britain occurred during the period.

Early industrial man still depended upon his brawn, but machines freed him from the limitations of his body. Although in the 1700s 90% of the work force of the United States was engaged in agriculture, the mechanized farmer was much more productive than his predecessor. As Figure 3 illustrates, the percentage of the work force necessary to feed the population has declined steadily since 1790. (Actual farm employment [Figure 4] did increase until just after the turn of the century when tractors and other powered implements began to appear [Figure 5]. But as the work force grew, it moved into the industrial sectors.) Although the data is from a more contemporary period, Figures 6–9 vividly illustrate the effects of technological change on farming. While farm production has simply rocketed, the amount of human resources required per unit of production has steadily declined. There are those who decry the loss of our bucolic farming society, but I have worked on farms and I am certainly glad there

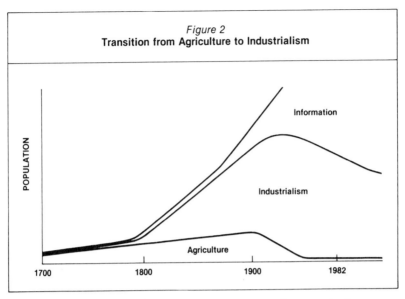

Figure 2
Transition from Agriculture to Industrialism

are other options. Incidentally, one of the reasons I use agriculture as an example is that it is one of the few industries whose products have not been completely transformed by technological development, allowing for historical comparisons.

The new technologies reduced the farming population—as, in a limited sense, robots and other intelligent machines will affect the "hands on" manufacturing work force. But the reason the farmer (or, most likely, his children) could make the transition was that there were factory jobs available. Had industrialization not occurred, the workers would simply have remained farmers and society would have continued the more limited growth of medieval agrarianism. It is important to remember that one would not have occurred without the other.

The transition from farm life to factory regimentation was not easy. It was filled with all the soul-wrenching discontinuities of rapid transition. Workers were asked to trade the values of agricultural society for those of the factory. As Charles Dickens so aptly noted, the early factories were snake pits of abuse and inhumanity. The factories' redeeming quality was that they were an improvement over the poverty, famine, misery, and disease common to rural society at the time. The social fabric was eventually reforged to accommodate and benefit from the shift to industrialization. But as with other transitions, it took time and conflict to develop a new set of social values compatible with the changes in technology.

Technology, for all its wonder and power, is nothing more than an extension of the human condition. Man is a technological creature; it is his nature. There is no dualism between man and machine. If technology brings about good, it is because man has directed it so. If it is used for evil, it is because there is also a dark side to man. It is not mere coincidence that man's greatest technological achievements have come at the same time as his greatest atrocities.

65

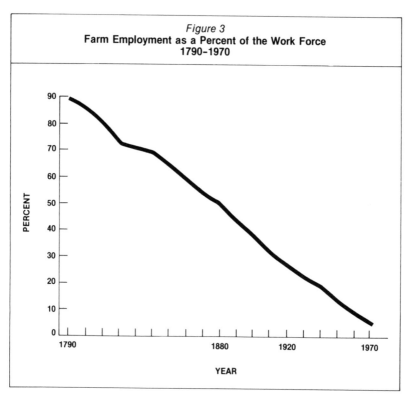

Figure 3
Farm Employment as a Percent of the Work Force
1790–1970

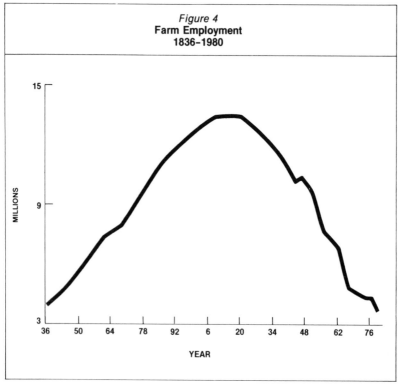

Figure 4
Farm Employment
1836–1980

66

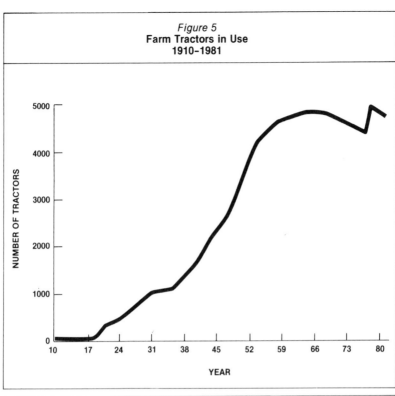

Figure 5
Farm Tractors in Use
1910–1981

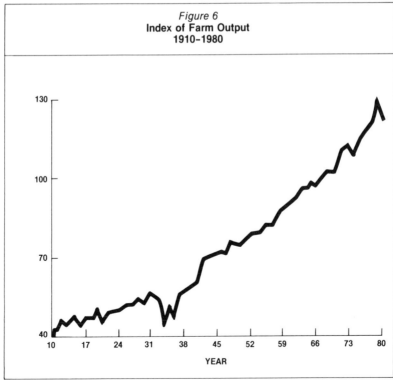

Figure 6
Index of Farm Output
1910–1980

67

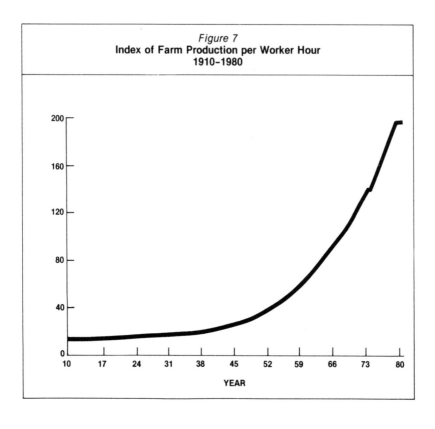

Figure 7
Index of Farm Production per Worker Hour
1910–1980

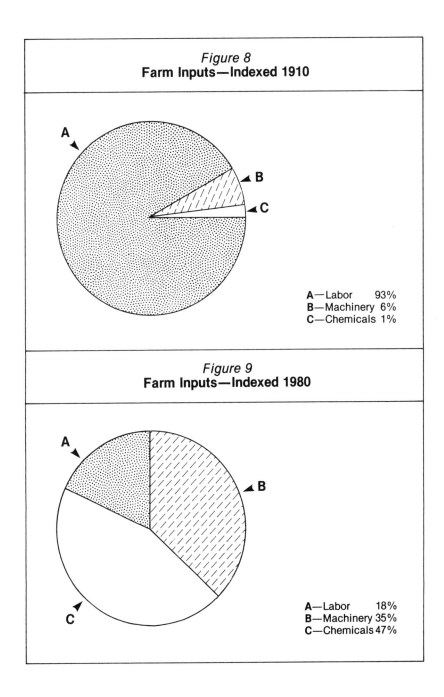

Figure 8
Farm Inputs—Indexed 1910

A—Labor   93%
B—Machinery 6%
C—Chemicals 1%

Figure 9
Farm Inputs—Indexed 1980

A—Labor   18%
B—Machinery 35%
C—Chemicals 47%

The fact that it is in man's nature to develop technology does not mitigate the concerns expressed by its critics. We have developed a great society, but have paid little attention to the human values for which it was ostensibly created. We have many things, and much anxiety. We are, as Robert Heilbroner has commented, "of high capitalism and low socialism." Our industry is not guided by codes of morality, only by laws against pollution. The anxiety of those who oppose technology is the concern that we all must share about dehumanization, pollution, the invasion of privacy, cold bureaucracy, and mass destruction.

Predictions

It would be easier if we could peer into the future and ordain what is to come, but we cannot. Seers will make predictions, but predicting is a tricky business, and prophesying technological impacts presents some special problems. As a result, technologists and their critics have a fairly poor record of accurately predicting the effects of new developments. Remember the nuclear power that was going to be too cheap to meter? Or the private airplane that would replace the family car? In 1948, Norbert Wiener predicted that we would all be unemployed in 10 years because of automation. Later, computers were going to take over management, eliminating the need for millions of white-collar workers. There is an important lesson to be learned from these experiences. Images of the future must be built by imagination. The visions created by supporters and critics, fueled by their passions, become larger than life and present a distorted image of what will likely occur. Our recent experiences should teach us to take most of these predictions with a grain, or perhaps a good deal, of salt. Personally, I'm still waiting for my picturephone.

The section that follows is a scenario of the future computer-integrated factory. I have tried to posture it so that it is within the realm of what is probable with present technology. Other developments I leave to your imagination.

Factory Scenario

The high-tech factory is not an entity, at least not yet. It is only a representation of the manufacturing system that will supersede our present production methods. Although the changes will be substantial, they may not be convulsive. Transformations of this kind tend to be evolutionary rather than revolutionary, but what they lack in speed they make up in momentum. They have enormous inertia.

The high-tech firm is an octopus with the computer at its heart. In the old industrial system, an army of people performed boring and repetitive jobs both on the line and in the office. The production line was an inhumane and unforgiving taskmaster that was much better suited to the machine. A very sophisticated computer system and intelligent manufacturing equipment have taken over many of the routine functions, freeing people to make decisions and create.

Product design and development was always an art, but now the computer performs the mundane tasks, freeing designers and engineers to make better use of their talents. Computer-aided design (CAD) has re-

70

placed the need for endless rows of drafting tables and erasers. Designers work with light pens at consoles. The computer makes detailed drawings, debugs designs, and offers alternate suggestions. It also performs stress and reliability testing, minimizing design problems and reducing lead times.

The computer is the master production organizer and coordinator. Computer-aided manufacturing (CAM) has meant tying all the various parts of the production process together to take advantage of the computer's speed and accuracy. Design and scheduling changes are quickly coordinated with the entire organization and its outside contacts. Computers facilitate coordination of the entire manufacturing matrix as has never been possible through the human planners, coordinators, managers, programmers, and other support people. The fine-tuned precision of the operation is well beyond the efficiencies of the old hard-tooled line. The high-tech factory has changed the way products are made, introducing many exotic materials and fostering the reconceptualization of virtually every product we use.

A visit to a high-tech facility is strange for people accustomed to the traditional factory. "Intelligent" machines perform most of the assembly work once done by people. Machines move and whir, products move through the assembly area, the whole thing orchestrated as if by magic. Factories run continuously, producing a variety of high-quality products at greater volume and lower cost.

The manufacturing process is organized around "cells" of general-purpose machines and support equipment. Dedicated tooling is rarely necessary or economical. Reprogrammable general-purpose equipment is made to perform a wide range of functions and is itself mass produced, drastically reducing its effective cost. It has significantly reduced batch breakeven costs. In 1980, 60% of our manufacturing was in batches too small for mass production. Now almost everything fits. This has allowed many new companies to compete successfully with established firms who were committed to the older technologies and fixed production systems.

Only infrequently does one see a human directly involved in production, an oddly soft enigma to all this hard machinery. Irrespective of all the publicity, people and robots perform very different functions. In the old days, people were the only resource available to perform the monotonous and mindless repetitive production line work. The significant advances in robotic and other production technologies have eliminated the need for people to function like well-oiled machines. Now most workers are operators, controlling sophisticated systems, using their heads instead of their hands. Operations are very decentralized, with most of the operating and planning decisions made on the shop floor.

The other workers perform an array of servicing, monitoring, and planning tasks that keep the incredible pace of the factory operating smoothly. Mental stress is higher, as an error at this pace means a lot of wasted product or some very expensive down-time. Each cell has a host of support people who attend to various units throughout the facility. Quite a few skilled trades people are employed maintaining machines, modifying the lines, and installing new equipment. The people who control and support the high-tech system comprise a new strata of "gray collar" workers. There are many data entry people, systems analysts, schedulers, computer techs of all kinds, planners, and coordinators. They are not blue-collar, but they really are not management either.

One of the lingering problems of old industrialism was the conflict between labor and management over the nature of work. The workplace was never designed for humans in the first place. Management really wanted something that didn't mind boring repetition and noise, didn't get sick, and didn't have an ego. Workers, on the other hand, sought some outlet for the basic human need to make a creative contribution, to mentally "own" what they made. Neither had a choice; the human was the best machine that management could get, and the worker needed to eat. It was an uncomfortable accommodation.

The solution came in robotics and computer-integrated machines. They operate tirelessly, with "up" time around 95%—a 20% improvement over human labor. They do not get bored, take vacations, or require pensions—and are not sensitive to heat and noise. They can easily be reprogrammed, so a line can be "retooled" quickly. Down-time is minimized and quality control held tight by the equipment's ability to monitor its own performance. It can tell if it is nearing tolerance limits and will either self-correct or notify the operator. Waste is minimized and critical shutdowns are avoided.

As we move back into today, the question most frequently asked is "When will all this happen?" The answer is that it already is happening. The industrial process is being transformed a little every day. Some industries, like some countries, are moving more quickly than others, but each trade show brings new developments in computer-integrated technology and moves us a step closer.

Jobs

It is not surprising that today's workers—already restive from massive unemployment and a sluggish economy—view the computer-integrated factory with its robots, automated manufacturing, and sophisticated information technology somewhat anxiously. Open a newspaper or magazine today and you are likely to find an article about a "revolution" called the information society or, alternately, the post-industrial society. These articles often express concern for large-scale technological unemployment as machines replace people on production lines, reviving old arguments about jobs and technology.

History teaches us that economies remain viable and that jobs are created through the development of new products and new technologies. It has also demonstrated that although the workplace gets stirred up by technological change and the social changes that accompany it, most workers remain employed. The simple fact is that during the last 150 years of enormous technological change, with only rare exceptions, 95% or more of the work force has remained employed (Figures 10–11). Certainly if technological employment were a macro problem we would have witnessed it by now.

72

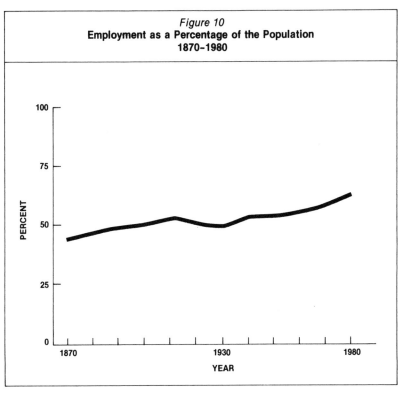

Figure 10
Employment as a Percentage of the Population
1870–1980

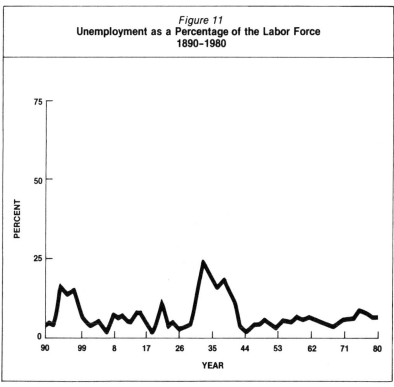

Figure 11
Unemployment as a Percentage of the Labor Force
1890–1980

73

Sizable employment discontinuities have more to do with matters economic than technological. During the 1960s there was a great deal of concern about technological unemployment. Research had exonerated technology, but so deep was the conviction (or so strong the politics) that in 1964 Congress created the National Commission on Technology, Automation, and Economic Progress to "identify and describe the impact of technological and economic change on production and employment, including the major types of worker displacement." Louis Rader noted that, "It is accurate to say that the major concern—the one most responsible for the establishment of the Commission—arose from the belief that technological change was the major source of unemployment . . ." When the Commission's report was issued in 1966, it completely absolved technology. The large-scale unemployment that many critics had predicted never materialized.[2] In fact, quite the opposite occurred. The new technologies had created millions of jobs and entire new industries.

Unemployment from technological change does not come from its presence but rather from its absence. When a firm does not invest in new technology either because of short-term management thinking or prohibitive capital markets, then it sets in motion a downward spiral from which recovery is very difficult. The company's older equipment usually means higher production costs. It is frequently unable to maintain competitive quality standards, and product improvements cannot be matched. For these and other reasons, sales begin to slip, production is cut, and unit production costs rise, eroding profits. Layoffs begin. Investment confidence slips. Plants are closed. If the new factories are overseas, so are the jobs, stranding the work force. It is not a pretty sight, nor is it a hypothetical one. Look around you.

Misunderstandings also arise from the failure to distinguish between what is technologically possible and what is economically sound. Studies of technological implementation indicate an average diffusion rate of a decade from the first industrial use to widespread adoption. The implementation of a new technology will depend upon its long-run advantages, its transitional costs and aggravations, and the ease with which it dispels its skeptics. Then, too, it will hang on such matters as politics, sociology, economics, and military strategy.[3]

Some workers do get caught in the transition between waves of technological change as the old gives way to the new. Their numbers are not large, but that does not detract from their individual pain and anxiety. We have not developed an effective mechanism to help workers with this transition. It is a condition that in the words of one research report is "pretty shameful."

Faced with the abyss of job loss and few viable alternatives, workers have fought to maintain the status quo. The fear of job losses to new technology has permeated the history of the industrial revolution. In the 1700s, French weavers threw their wooden shoes (*sabots*) into the mechanized looms that they feared would take their jobs (giving rise to the term *saboteur*). The Luddites of England (branded as anti-technologists) selectively smashed weaving looms of unscrupulous employers who were producing inferior goods or using the new technologies to circumvent existing labor agreements. In the early 1960s, Walter Reuther, president of the United Auto Workers, and Luther Hodges, U.S. Secretary of Labor, opposed automation because they believed it caused unemployment. George Meany told his AFL-CIO convention in 1963 that automation was "rapidly becoming a curse to this society."

Although history notes many worker revolts and uprisings, workers do not seem inherently opposed to new technology. They are however, opposed to losing their jobs—a very important distinction. The utilitarian attitude toward employees propogated early in the industrial revolution by Jeremy Bentham and the Fabians has endured because it gives license to short-term gain. It is little wonder that job security has been such a large issue in the history of industrial society. Someday we will learn that a good employee is worth more than the wage costs of replacement. It also illustrates why workers with secure employment, such as in Japan or at IBM, are much more receptive to new technology.

In the next few years, we are going to hear a great deal about machines replacing people at work. Journalists and science-fiction writers can dream up mechanical replacements for man, but as the people who make robots will tell you, it is a lot easier to talk about than to do. Taking nothing away from the significant advances we have made in robotic technology, we are still light years from creating the fanciful R2D2 and C3PO of "Star Wars." The human system is extremely subtle and complex; it has evolved over several million years. I am reminded of Wernher von Braun's comment about astronauts. He said, "Man is still the best computer we can put aboard a spacecraft—and the only one that can be mass produced with unskilled labor."

Nonetheless, intelligent technology is already impacting the workplace. Initially it has taken the dangerous and unpleasant jobs. As the technology improves and its costs become more competitive, it will assume the mindless and repetitive tasks. It is no longer a question of if, but when. The transfer of work from man to machine is what the industrial revolution has been all about. The transplantation of intelligence to machines will redefine, for the second time in man's history, the concept of work. In reality, the movement of work off the shop floor began long ago. In 1899, non-production workers accounted for 7% of the manufacturing work force. By 1950, they represented 18% and in 1978, 28%. The trend since 1919 is illustrated in Figure 12. Blue-collar employment leveled off in 1960 and has been on a plateau since then (Figures 13–14). In 1900, the white-collar segment was 10% of the work force. Today it is 65%. Clerical occupations alone will increase 46% between 1970 and 1985 and will represent 20% of the work force by then.[4]

There will be few jobs unaffected by the high-tech system. Work will bear little resemblance to the sweat and muscle jobs of present factories. The United States will cease to be a nation of tool workers and will become a nation of knowledge workers. Operating automated assembly equipment is a good deal different then assembling pieces by hand. You have to use your head a lot more. Brawn doesn't mean a great deal in a world where robots do most of the heavy work. Interpersonal relationships will become more important in the high-tech environment. Work will become a team

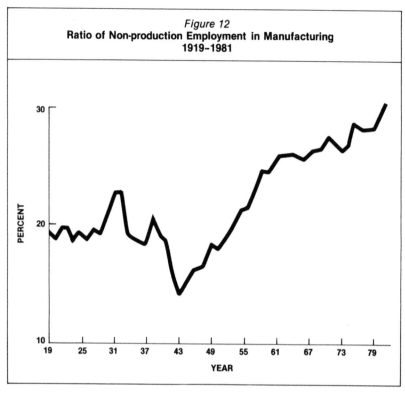

Figure 12
Ratio of Non-production Employment in Manufacturing
1919–1981

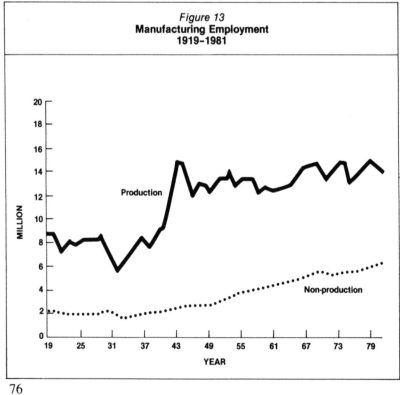

Figure 13
Manufacturing Employment
1919–1981

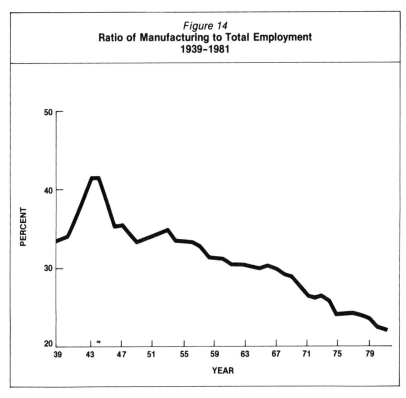

Figure 14
Ratio of Manufacturing to Total Employment
1939–1981

exercise. The old jobs discouraged thinking, but the complexity of the high-tech system will demand contribution from everyone. With expensive equipment, mistakes are costly, so job tension will be higher. Computers will provide performance data for each work station. In an environment where the worker already feels powerless, there is a high risk that "big brotherism," perceived or real, will be an issue of friction. The proximity to 1984 is somewhat ironic. The sexes will be much more equal, but the minority kids with no experience, inferior educations, and who are socially maladjusted—"the underclass"—will be at a great disadvantage.

Gray-Collar Workers

Today a gap (some would describe it as a gulf) exists between blue- and white-collar ranks. The high-tech factory will obliterate that distinction forever. This gap will be filled with clerical, scheduling, coordinating, engineering, and maintenance personnel plus computer technicians, systems analysts, programmers, and jobs we don't have names for yet. These people will be specialists—staff support for the system. They are not blue-collar and really are not management; they are the ones I call grays. In order to be successful, work groups will have to be integrated teams in which each person contributes. There will not be room for arbitrary distinctions based on rank. Work groups will not be regular. Assignments will vary with task and technical requirements, making conventional organization impractical.

Former blue-collar workers should, with retraining, be qualified for many of these new jobs. The knowledge they have gained working on the line will be invaluable. Compensation standards will change. Present jobs are paid on the basis of seniority, skill, or sweat. Workers will expect to be compensated for their contribution, not unlike salaried employees who are also required to think. The shift in values will doubtless provide some lively bargaining.

In the 1960s, the computer added a new dimension to business management. In many regards it created middle management. The high-tech system will create the gray collar and alter every job in the system. That is a great deal of change.

There will, of course, be new jobs requiring new skills and specialized training. These specialists are already in short supply. Computer programming and systems application job opportunities are growing at 25% a year. Skilled tradesmen such as electricians are in demand. Young people will migrate to these jobs. Many of them shy away from the personal sacrifices demanded by the old production line and they are more comfortable with the new technologies. There is little reason that experienced workers cannot be trained for these jobs as well. The issue, as always, is who will pay for it.

Workers will become concerned about skill obsolescence. The functions that people perform will change more frequently as the rate of technological change increases. Thus workers will need to be retrained more often. Although some jobs are "leapfrogged" and others are "fractured" as technology advances, there is little evidence that there are large dislocations. It would seem beneficial for firms to consider a more permanent work force, selected for its ability to adapt to these changes. The turnover discontinuities we presently endure will be very disruptive to a trained and integrated work group.

Increasing technological complexity does not necessarily increase worker skill requirements. In fact, it is usually just the opposite. We incorporate those complexities into our equipment and processes, making their operation, in most cases, more simple. Research conducted during the technological changes of the 1950s and 1960s determined that technological change actually lowered skill requirements. James Bright reported in 1958:

> During the several years which I spent in the field research in so-called automated plants . . . I did not find that the upgrading effect had occurred to anywhere near the extent that is often assumed . . . .

On the contrary, there was more evidence that automation had reduced the skill requirements of the operating work force, and occasionally of the entire factory force including the maintenance organization . . . .

In sum, I see little justification for the popular belief that present labor is employable in automated plants only with extensive retraining . . . .[5]

Fred Best wrote in 1973:

> The debate stems from the popular assumption during the 1950s and 1960s that technological advances would raise the skill requirements of future jobs and require the cultivation of a highly educated labor force. Today this assumption

is being challenged. It is true that new and highly complex forms of work are evolving. However, hard data gathered during the last two decades present strong arguments that with most work, skill requirements are remaining at the same level or even declining.[6]

Management and Organization

The substantial technological changes made by the computer-integrated factory will necessitate organizational and management adjustments in order to maximize its effectiveness. The most significant of these will be a reordering of the basic values and structure that have brought industrial society to its present position of power and success. The technological complexity of the new system, its sophisticated networking and overlapping functional responsibilities, in addition to its pace and need for flexibility, will be seriously crippled by a rigid decision-making hierarchy. With many interdisciplinary considerations involved in each decision, consensus-based systems are proving to be far more effective. In a system where each individual has a critical role, personal commitment and motivation become crucial to the success of the group.

The business community has survived and prospered for several centuries using an authoritarian hierarchy. Centralized authority and decision-making were manageable under the old linear production line; information theoretically flowed up and decisions and direction flowed down. Everyone did his job and did not worry a great deal about the next person. That concept has been modified, as we have realized the need for increased networking as manufacturing systems grew in complexity. The high-tech system will require a structure that is highly integrated and flexible. Each production cell will be a matrix of overlapping responsibilities as a myriad of operators, schedulers, maintenance people, programmers, etc., try to do their jobs. Each has a perspective that must be considered. This complexity, in addition to the pace of the operation, will simply not permit the one-person bottlenecks and bureaucratic barriers common in today's organizations.

Most management people want better communication, and they work hard to get it. That is why management philosophy has been evolving away from authoritarianism. Virtually every management book written in the last 20 years has extolled the virtues of non-authoritarian management and correctly pointed out that the most effective leaders are noted for their ability to create and maintain conditions of consensus. Today even theory "Y" is being succeeded by more egalitarian concepts. Although we have not changed the vestiges of authority, our operating modes have been evolving in that direction.

In an environment of rapid change, consensus organizations demonstrate greater effectiveness. A hierarchical pyramid does not adapt quickly. In fact, one of the strengths of the hierarchy is its ability to endure without changing. It can make decisions quickly, but deciding and doing are very different processes. The isolation of the decision-maker, the layers of bureaucracy, and the sheer size of organization combine to give the hierarchy enormous resistance to capricious influence. Unfortunately, they also serve to create institutional rigidity and a reluctance to change, often in the face of obvious advantage. As Bennis and Slater, in their insightful assessment of organizational democracy, point out, ". . . it is only when the society reaches a level of technological development in which survival is dependent on the institutionalization of perpetual change that democracy becomes necessary . . . .[7] Note their choice of the word *necessary*. The change from authoritarian hierarchy to an egalitarian form will not come from an idealistic desire for higher good but simply because the traditional structure, with its centralized decision-making, will be unable to remain competitive.

Geographic decentralization will further deconcentrate decision-making. Without the need for expensive retooling and immense fixed production lines, facilities can be dispersed to reduce transport costs and inventories, access labor pools, and more directly serve regional markets. This speaks to a further decentralization of responsibility. Also, the more universal nature of general-purpose manufacturing cells means that the factory travels literally with its software. It seems a bit preposterous, but "manufacturing" could take on a briefcase portability. Certainly it will be more mobile. In a very simplified sense, the geographic dispersion of manufacturing need be limited only by product and raw material transportation. There is every reason to expect that these new technologies will make it easier for our growing list of foreign competitors, and thus for the continued outflow of American manufacturing.

Another variation is the concept of contract manufacturing. Using programmable technology, independent manufacturing organizations could contract their services to marketing firms much as we do now in the computer business for private-label manufacture. This could become the operating norm for manufacturing. In any case, producers will be anxious to contract out unused production time to help amortize capital costs.

Although production may be decentralized, other functions may not. These new technologies will be expensive. The corporate conglomerate, with its ability to generate large blocks of capital, may be necessary to finance ventures of this kind. The fast pace and marketplace complexity that computer-integrated manufacturing could generate will call for some very sophisticated marketing and planning.

Smaller firms may be able to compete with the large producers by carefully selecting a range of products or markets. Most of the advantage the large firm has today is in the power of its mass production and its ability to command market share. With significantly reduced production break-even costs, a smaller firm could market regionally and be price competitive.

It will be necessary to move real decision-making "down" the organization. One of the ironies of our present management system is that we have employees with high-quality information and no authority; and bosses with little good information and all the authority. Preempted from participation, subordinates are quick to criticize an erring management and feel little compulsion to shoulder the problem. Business people talk a lot about the delegation of authority, but as long as "the buck" stops somewhere upstairs, the people on the bottom are not going to take responsibility for it. A decentralized, highly integrated system moves decision-making closer to the source of information. Managers and workers have finely tuned skills; each brings different information and a unique perspective to a problem. We need to get them together instead of erecting barriers between them. We need to learn to trust and respect our employees.

The "glue" that can hold a decentralized organization together is a firmly held common purpose. The discussion of Japanese management is becoming a cliche, but there are some things that we can learn from their success. There is probably no more powerful—or more efficient—force on earth than a group of people who hold the same goals and ideals and who are willing to work for them. In an environment of rapid change there is nothing more adaptable. The most significant task a senior management group could undertake would be the development of a corporate philosophy that would guide the entire organization in its efforts. This is the most powerful way in which a senior group can impact the organization. In ancient Japan, the *Hagakure* was the bible of the Samurai warrior. I have always been impressed by one of its basic precepts: "It is because preparation has been long that a decision may be quickly reached."

Management will be more important than it is today, but it will be different. Managing a consensus-based system requires different skills and a different approach to people than is commonly practiced in the West. I offer the following as desirable attributes for the manager of the not too distant future:

1. The patience to work in a context of complexity and pluralism.
2. The intellecfual clarity to conceptualize a workable consensus.
3. The flexibility to revise conceptions.
4. The integrity to win the trust of contending forces.
5. The sensitivity to subtle variations in human attitudes and their changes.
6. The self-confidence to risk and to be spontaneous.
7. The persuasiveness to mobilize a constituency of willing allies in pursuit of goals that are tolerable for all.[8]

The other critical management component of the future is employee commitment. The computer-integrated system makes each individual's contribution much more important. We can no longer afford the atmosphere of ambivalence, sabotage, high turnover, and distrust that so often characterizes the manufacturing climate. Surveys point to the fear and powerlessness felt by today's employees. Feelings of this kind generate low aspirations, make them hostile, cause them to behave ineffectively, and encourage them not to risk.[9] It troubles me to hear executives speak of the need for greater employee loyalty. Loyalty and allegiance are concepts whose roots originate in the obligations of a feudal vassal to his liege lord. It is this kind of power relationship that has created the barriers that exist today. The computer-integrated system needs grass-roots commitment—not just support.

Man is an animal of both passion and intellect. We need to care about the things we do, else we become robots ourselves. And yet, we have created this compartmentalized, Taylorized, impersonal business hierarchy that robs employees of any real opportunity to possess their work and to be responsible for its outcome. Mills wrote about the need for a craftsman to psychologically own his work in order to accept responsibility for its quality. This principle holds true for all of us. I recommend Frederick Herzberg's concept: "The employer's task is not to motivate his people to get them to achieve; he should provide opportunities for people to achieve, so they will become motivated."[10]

In 1980, General Motors received fewer than one suggestion per employee per year. Toyota got 18. At GM, 22% of the employee suggestions were accepted; at Toyota, 90% were put to use. There is a considerable difference between the two systems concerning respect for the individual. It is a fundamental part of the Oriental culture, and their management practices demonstrate it. It is evidenced by their product quality, low absenteeism, and low turnover. They don't have unions because they don't need them.

Management is going to have to become much more flexible in thinking as well as in organization. We often operate with what has made us successful rather than what is needed. The ability to adapt to an uncertain environment has always been important in competitive athletics and chess; it is becoming a critical necessity for business. Along with flexibility, management will have to be much more future oriented. We will have to raise our sights. Many business decisions are made today with a limited view toward year-end performance and return on investment, and the long-term consequences go unheeded. Short-term thinking is already a burden, and I believe it will become an onerous one in the future. We will have to be much more risk oriented, less hobbled by the restrictions of conservative financial management. The future rewards those who move with it, as long as they do so prudently. Prudence, however, under the limiting influence of current philosophies, is proving to be far too conservative in a highly competitive, rapidly changing environment. The West is lagging in its adoption of computer-integrated technology. If a firm does not innovate, does not take the short-term risk, it runs the greatest risk of all, i.e., that of long-term obsolescence. We have some industries that are belatedly learning that lesson, and there isn't much they can do about it now.

Conclusion

George Bernard Shaw said, "The only thing men learn from history is that men learn absolutely nothing from history." Arguments are made during each period of technological change that it differs from the others, and yet, when it is over, we find that the pattern has remained intact. The vast majority of workers remain employed and skill requirements, if anything, are reduced. There are workers who get caught between the heaving tectonic plates of technological change. Their numbers are not large, but we have not provided the assistance they need in order to develop new skills.

New technology creates jobs in numbers beyond anything previously experienced. New companies spring up utilizing the newly developed technologies and provide an economic and technological transformation to the entire economy. The social structure of the business community is rewoven to manage these new developments. Society catapults to levels of consciousness, freedom, and social development previously unattainable. Unfortunately, most of these changes are not readily discernible until they occur. There is a strong historical pattern of this societal growth, but it requires a leap of faith in humanity and a certain willingness to risk in order to accept its continuation without guarantees. The history of man's development has been far from perfect, and it is certainly open to criticism, as much contemporary literature will attest; but for all its flaws, it has been an amazingly successful process.

The new robotic and computer technologies are simply another chapter in the ancient relationship between man and machine—freeing us from the limitations of our bodies, performing the routine and precise tasks for which we are ill equipped, and permitting us the freedom to pursue our unique human nature. Man and machine make far better companions than competitors. Economist Leo Cherne has said, "The computer is incredibly fast, accurate and stupid. Man is unbelievably slow, inaccurate and brilliant. The marriage of the two is a force beyond calculation."

Notes

1. Samuel Lilley, *Men, Machines, and History*, (New York: International Publishing, 1965), pp. 320–322.

2. Louis T. Rader, "Automation Over The Years," *Vital Speeches*, No. 6, Vol. XLVII, 1981.

3. Charles E. Silberman & The Editors of Fortune, *The Myths of Automation*, (N.Y.: Harper & Row, 1966); Richard Nelson, Merton J. Peck, and Edward D. Kalachek, *Technology, Economic Growth, and Public Policy*, (The Brookings Institution, 1967), pp. 99–100; John L. Enos, "Invention and Innovation in the Petroleum Refining Industry," in *The Rate and Direction of Inventive Activity*, (Princeton: Univ. Press, 1962).

4. U.S. Department of Labor, Bureau of Labor Statistics.

5. James R. Bright, "Does Automation Raise Skill Requirements?" Harvard Business Review, (July/Aug. 1958).

6. Fred Best, *The Future of Work* (NY: Prentice-Hall, 1973), p. 101.

7. Warren Bennis and Phillip Slater, "Organizational Democracy: Towards Work by Consent of the Employed," in Fred Best, *The Future of Work* (New York: Prentice-Hall, 1973), pp. 73–85.

8. Adapted from a letter from John Gardner to Joseph Slater, 3/23/78.

9. Rosabeth Moss Kanter, *Men and Women of the Corporation*, (NY: Basic Books, 1977).

10. Frederick Herzberg, "Putting People Back Together," *Industry Week* (July 24, 1979), p. 49.

The Future of Management

by

William Exton, Jr.

No aspects of the future can be of greater importance than the nature of and the requirements for management. As that class or form of behavior which affects, in one way or another, the interests and lives of all of us— as well as the utilization of most of the resources upon which we all depend—it must continue to play a critical part in determining the character and patterns of work; the kind and availability and distribution of goods and services; and the nature of the tangible and intangible incentives that motivate contribution to the general economy.

Only governments, natural or man-made catastrophes, or major alterations in the environment can exert more potent effects than does—and will—the practice of management: the performance of those who manage others—at any level, and for any purpose.

All organizations may be regarded as in some degree productive of goods and/or services; but it is logical to regard management as classifiable according to whether it operates in an economically oriented environment, or within some form of governmental activity, or in a "non-profit" organization. Such distinctions may be blurred under conditions other than those fostering or permitting "free enterprise"; but the managers in socialist environments are still constrained to apply generally recognized principles of management, so far as feasible, to the extent that their goals parallel those of the managers of and in organizations operating for the usual capitalist objectives of maximizing productivity and optimizing profit through market-oriented strategies and policies.

This paper considers the future of management in terms of the probable adaptation and development of currently effective practices in view of known or detectable trends, and of the anticipated effects of the current or predictable availability of new or imminent technological resources. It does not consider the possible effects of major political or sociological change, or of basic modifications in the organization of the economy as a whole.

Management has been changing in so many different ways, and in

William Exton, Jr., is the principal of William Exton, Jr., and Associates, Management Consultants, in New York City.

response to so many different conditions, factors, and influences, that any responsible attempt at prediction must aim at presenting the *resultant* of many diverse forces. Even such an extremely complex undertaking is further complicated by such considerations as these:
- The functions of management are increasingly numerous and complex.
- There are many "theories" of management.
- The size, scope, and actual or potential geographical dispersion of many organizations impose new or extended managerial requirements.
- The diversity of products, services and markets makes special demands on the management of many companies.
- The acceleration of technological innovation imposes a growing need for creativity, alertness, sophistication of competition, and efficient conduct and exploitation of research and development.
- Persistent enlargement of scale and great—even exponential—increments in complexity and diversity affect most considerations confronting management.

One way to organize an attempt to project management into the future is to consider—more or less separately, though they are functionally interrelated—what are generally regarded as major functions of management. These are commonly listed as planning, organizing, leading (co-ordinating), and controlling. Let us then look at what the future holds for these basic managerial functions.

Planning

It is easy to foresee that the planning function of management will involve increasing exploitation of computer capabilities. The two primary effects will be the increase in and approved availability of information; and a quantum advance in the techniques of and resources for mathematical modeling.

These areas of progress will be further enhanced by ever more helpful computer graphics, both for the more effective display of information, and for visual demonstration of—and, often, replacing the need to calculate—the effects of various factors on mathematically modeled situations.

None of this, of course, will totally eliminate the necessity for the application of personal values and judgment and for the making of many decisions. And it will require greatly increased capabilities for the creation of ever more sophisticated software and programming. It will also demand a very high degree of sophistication and perceptiveness on the part of the users of such resources and techniques, especially to identify, recognize, and allow for the dissimilarities between models and reality.

There *are* those who are troubled by the assumption that "everything is quantifiable" and who believe that intangibles and unrecognized, un-allowed-for variables will continue to assert themselves in the real world—confounding and frustrating those who rely too completely on the rigidities often characteristic of the so-called "management sciences." To the degree that mathematical models fail to parallel, significantly and relevantly, the reality they are intended to represent, the results and derivatives of such modeling must also diverge from reality—possibly, even, to a much greater degree.

As for the fundamental dimension of all planning—time—it is likely that the future will see progress in several directions, each of which will involve changes (adjustment, adaptation, or basically different evaluations) in the perception of time and of its effect on planning and on activities planned for. In these developments, a certain paradox will appear as many activities and operations, now quite time consuming, will be accomplished with far greater rapidity—many of them virtually instantaneously. And some functions that have had to be exercised sequentially or alternatively will be carried out simultaneously—and also integratedly, if appropriate.

At the same time, planning will be based on broader and longer perspectives. Despite the generally accelerating rate of change, computer-based analyses working on greatly expanded data banks—and with programming that represents both factually detected trends, anticipated developments, and/or meticulously delineated potential contingencies—will provide more valid projections over longer ranges. And these, processed against carefully defined assumptions, will contribute to the formulation of strategies, policies, programs, project designs, and many other products of managerial functioning.

Organizing

The nature of all organizations, and perhaps especially of business organizations, will change in the future as the result of both technological and sociological change—and probably also as the nature of work, specific tasks, and working relationships also change.

1. Technological change will have many different kinds of effects. Among them:

• Larger capital investment in facilities, per individual worker.

• Closer integration of work and working relationships—especially vertically (between higher and lower levels) and horizontally (between remote and differentiated but interacting functions) as a result of ever more elaborate electronic interconnections and computer tie-ins, and extended systematization.

• Shared experience in training for and utilization of advanced equipment, even when functions and responsibilities differ and participants may be some levels apart.

• Shift of worker evaluation from previously valued attributes to those applicable to tasks of the future—primarily utilization of computers, robots, and related equipment.

2. Sociological changes will also affect personnel in many ways.

• Impersonality of many working and selling relationships will result increasingly from greater use of electronic interfacing, teleconferencing, elaborated telephonic capabilities, electronic mail, etc.

• Individuals will increasingly identify with the elaborate equipment that makes their functioning possible. They will tend to feel lost, powerless, and inadequate without it. This will be enhanced when "cause and effect" are not as obviously related, in the working situation, as they are now with most mechanical and even most electrically operated equipment.

• Organizational structure will change, adapting to the processes and systems developed to exploit technological advances. Organizations will have fewer hierarchical levels, though perhaps more horizontally functioning components with differentiated functions. Intermediate and directly supervisory levels will need greater appreciation of overall organizational functioning; they will have to evaluate the effectiveness of integration of their contributions in relation to the organization as a whole, rather than merely conform to the standards imposed on their output. "Span of control" potentials will be enlarged.

• In many situations, qualifying for specific positions will be subject to exacting tests. Such considerations as seniority will tend to become obsolete, as age and sex become irrelevant; and demonstrated capability (innate, or acquired by special education, or by training and/or experience), adaptability, and motivation will become the governing criteria for personnel selection and assignment.

• The prospective (and incipient) changes in working hours (decreases, flexibility) and in place of work (own home, etc.) will also require organizational changes—especially in delegation, in the nature and authority of supervision, and in the evaluation and the control of work performed.

• Meanwhile, the innovative trends toward work redesign, team production, and the involvement of worker initiatives in the enhancement of productivity and quality will exert substantial, and probably synergistic, effects on organizational character.

Leading

This term is such a "high-order abstraction" that it symbolizes many quite different forms of activity—from personal command of troops in battle to the creation of exemplary (or popular, commercially successful) works of art.

In the future it is likely that, in the context of management, the term "leadership" will be applied to:

• Effective, successful innovation in hardware, software, applications, techniques, design, services, or other aspects of high-technology operations.

• Predominance in any significant field—as signified by size, sales volume, profitability, "style," "class," "status," distinctive marketing, or other characteristics of a favorable organizational "image."

• Individuals, groups, or firms that manifest (in the context of contribution to or management of high technology) the "old-fashioned virtues" that traditionally won the accolade of "leadership." Such leadership will be increasingly difficult to assert and make apparent, in the impersonal context of electronically interconnected working relationships.

It was easy—though risky—for King Henry of Navarre to demonstrate leadership directly and personally, by inviting his retainers to follow the white plume on his helmet into the thickest of the fight. And his demonstration of courage in daring that risk, as well as his potent fighting ability, set an example that so motivated his men—and so intimidated his enemies—as to ensure his victory. But it is difficult to find a real parallel for such direct, personal, and dramatic leadership by example in business—past, present, or future.

The growing impersonality of electronically mediated interaction and the context of tasks focused on electronic or electronically controlled processes will minimize the opportunity for the exercise of leadership above that required for appropriate but routine management. However, in that same context, the manifestation of admirable personal characteristics, the demonstration of competence to meet emergencies and to relate constructively to subordinates and leaders, will all amount to the kind of leadership that can exert positive, optimizing effects upon the operations involved.

Furthermore, it is foreseeable that most workers will be performing their duties in a relatively dull, symbol-dominated, remote-from-the-action environment. The display of attractive, interesting, and admirable personal characteristics in such an environment—so long as it is not distracting, disturbing, or disruptive—may be an important psychological "plus" for the routine-ridden workers. The "humanizing" of management may well become a major requirement for success in many future activities and operations.

Coordination has generally been regarded as a major aspect of leadership, and coordination will be increasingly required by the increasing complexity of operations and activities to be foreseen. But computers, programs, and perhaps mathematical modeling can greatly facilitate at least the specification (and—usually—the execution) of who, what, where, when, how, with what, etc.

Communication is the most essential tool of management—and there can be no leadership without it. Future managements will have far superior high-technology facilities for communication. The future may also reveal the extent to which and the ways in which management can satisfactorily supersede the unique and natural face-to-face mode of communication without a serious—if intangible—loss.

Controlling

The term "control" has been grossly abused. At one extreme—that of corporate cost controllers, accountants, and financial executives—it refers to the availability of data purportedly representative of certain quantitative aspects of ongoing activities and of corporate operations generally. But such "controls" are mere numerical symbols—cues for action, but not, by themselves, capable of effecting change, or of any other initiative.

At the other extreme, "control" denotes actual exertion of the capability to direct and to change an ongoing situation (being "in control"—whether or not this involves the use of or reference to data).

And, in between, the same term refers to the physical means or the intermediary agencies whereby or through which direction and change are effectuated.

In the future, management will benefit by important advances in all three of these aspects of control.

Advances in computerization are already providing the means for recording, storing, processing, and retrieving data essential to knowledge of ongoing operations and significant situations—and can do so on a current, "real time" basis. Advances in the means of communication and in the interconnection of communication facilities and systems will render the input and reporting of data ever more timely. Advances in the production and transmission of graphics (process generated, operator guided, or combinations of these) will make transmissions increasingly meaningful and more easily and rapidly evaluated.

Improved instrumentation and the further development of automatically functioning control mechanisms—with applications not now feasible, and with the potential for reacting to phenomena, conditions, or computerized interventions not now feasible—will relieve managers (as well as nonmanagerial operations) of more and more elements of their responsibilities, leaving only those diminishing but ultimately irreducible matters involving value judgments and discretionary decisions.

And, finally, the specific exertions of control by managerial intervention will be far better informed—not only as to relevant current detail, but also via projections of alternative courses—based on far more elaborate and complex models, and more probably programmed modifications thereof, than any available today.

The composite result of this threefold advance will be to provide greatly enhanced assurance that plans will be carried out far more faithfully than at present. But this advantage should necessitate not only the fullest and most detailed care in planning but also the recognition that the planners must rely less on adaptation, adjustment, trial-and-error, and other modifications in the implementation of plans, since it will be easier to automate controlling factors than to provide the evaluative and discretionary sensitivity necessary to maintain the flexibility now both usual and essential.

Another way to organize the development of ideas about the future of management is to consider the various theories of management and the related sciences, disciplines, or fields of knowledge associated with them.

Harold Koontz in "The Managerial Jungle Revisited" (*Academy of Management Review*) identifies and comments on 13 differentiated theories of management (including one, Operational, which purports to combine all others). Certain academic disciplines—more or less well-defined fields of knowledge, scholarship, and research—are associated with these theories. And it is reasonable to assume that the theories of management will gain or lose influence—and consequent effect upon the performance of managers—as the related disciplines develop or regress and as they are determined to be more or less relevant to and supportive of actual managerial processes.

Accordingly, some indications of the future of management can probably be gained by projecting the future of these several identified academic disciplines, and deducing from such projections the effects upon management—or at least on the current theories of management, and thus upon the exercise of management guided by such theories.

Here is a listing (derived from Koontz) of the major academic disciplines generally considered to be more or less relevant to the exercise of management, together with those theories of management to which they are especially related:

Field of Knowledge	Theory of Management
Decision Theory	Rational Choice
Economic Theory	Rational Choice
General Systems Theory	Applied Systems
Mathematics	Management Sciences
Political Science	Cooperative Social Systems
Sociology	Group Behavior
Social Psychology	Group Behavior
Cultural Anthropology	Group Behavior
Psychology	Interpersonal Behavior
Industrial Engineering	Socio-Technical Systems

In addition, there is, of course, that special field of knowledge concerned with actual situations and contingencies experienced by various enterprises, and with the study of the roles of individual managers, or groups of managers, under various conditions. This, together with applicable elements of all the fields listed above, relates to the so-called Operational approach to a theory of management—obviously a theory that purports to be virtually comprehensive.

It seems impracticable to project realistically what the future may bring in each of these fields of knowledge; to foresee how all such developments may impinge upon and interact with one another; and to anticipate adequately the resulting effects upon the practice of management. But, to the degree that such projections may be feasible, competent, and valid, they may be applied—at least hypothetically—to the managerial functions discussed above.

In this way, it should be possible to arrive at some degree of prevision of what may characterize at least some aspects of management and of what may be required of managers in the future.

Education for Managers of Accelerating Change

by

George Korey

We are now living in an era of very profound and fast changes, when the computer is a link between human expertise and the advanced world of mechanical and electronic technology. We are witnessing many changes that will transform our world during our lifetime in a dramatic way that cannot be compared to revolutions of the past. All of the previous revolutions of mankind have involved mainly changes in the distribution of power and property within a society. The approaching technological revolution will affect us in this way, too, but it will also affect the essence of our individual and social existence. It will have tremendous consequences for the way and the meaning of our life.

It is far easier to speak of the past than the future; we have no experience of the future. Nevertheless, we must speculate about it and try to visualize the changes it will bring, as we are educating a new generation that will live in a completely different world.

In North America, more than in any other part of the world, we live today in a society that is shaped—from the cultural, social, psychological, and economic points of view—by the far-reaching impact of science and technology. The computer has become a major force behind the acceleration of knowledge acquisition and the storage of this knowledge. There are clear indications that, during the next few decades, the human brain will become more and more powerful. Through the use of computers, people will also acquire additional powers that will expand the boundaries of human reasoning and potential. Man will have the capacity to determine the sex of his children. Through the use of new pharmaceutical products, he will have the capacity to influence and expand memory potential and the intelligence of his children. To meet the challenge of the approaching change, businessmen will have to forget about the ''trial and error'' approach. They will have to learn to use all possible and available management devices and scientific tools, thereby improving their process of decision-making and permitting a greater degree of precision.

Alvin Toffler, in his book *Future Shock*, said:

George Korey is president of the Canadian School of Management in Toronto, Ontario, Canada.

In the technological systems of tomorrow—fast, fluid and self-regulating—machines will deal with the flow of physical materials; men with the flow of information and insight. Machines will increasingly perform the routine tasks; men the intellectual and creative tasks.

The technology of tomorrow requires not millions of lightly lettered men, ready to work in unison at endlessly repetitive jobs; it requires not men who take orders in unblinking fashion, aware that the price of bread is mechanical submission to authority, but men who can make critical judgements, who can weave their way through novel environments, who are quick to spot new relationships in the rapidly changing reality.

In just a few years, we will be facing a world quite different from the one in which we live today. As a result of changes that will come, we must strive to make life better from the environmental, social, and economic point of view. There is no question that, as a result of technological progress, we can claim beneficial results, such as:

- improved health care
- the ability to harness and use energy
- a longer life-span (primarily in developed countries)
- replacement of manual labor by machines
- advances in mass audio-video and satellite communications
- progress in transportation and methods of travel on land, sea, and in the air
- improved production techniques and systems
- vastly improved access to knowledge and a generally better educated population
- the ability to manage complex physical and social systems
- increased per capita income.

But resulting from these achievements are certain accompanying problems, or "mixed blessings," that progress brings. These include:

- a certain loss of privacy
- erosion of traditional values
- dehumanization of ordinary work
- centralization of technological systems
- proliferation of weapons
- air, noise, land, and water pollution
- accelerated depletion of the earth's resources.

It seems that the abundance of material goods in technologically developed countries may have contributed to the growing scarcity of non-material goods—such as time, wisdom, stability, ethical values, and the influence that people exercise over certain areas:

We have a lot less **time** than people who lived before us.

While we are bombarded with a lot of irrelevant information, the **wisdom** to make right decisions is not increasing.

Stability is decreasing, with very quick changes in the character of whole communities.

Ethical values are often neglected by contemporary society.

Influence and impact that people could have on social systems is decreasing.

The challenge for educators and for managers of future change is to make technology more responsive to our needs—so that it will provide us with solutions to social problems as well. We have to balance our increased capacity to use knowledge for practical purposes with a sensitivity to human needs, an increase in human concern and ethical values to serve mankind.

An analysis of historical and current trends will help us master the future. Certain trends will probably continue (e.g., the overall growth of world population; the growth of human knowledge; the democratization of education; a trend toward further industrialization, specialization, and professionalization; the growth of leisure time; and cultural homogenization.

While technological progress may have some unpleasant side-effects, it is nevertheless essential for us to maintain the human side of this process, a high quality of life, by developing a matching change mechanism in the evaluation of concurrent human progress.

In order to accommodate business and industry to the needs of evolving society, we need people who will know what must be done and who will plan and think about how it should be done.

Obviously, managers in the future must assume a more active and creative role in attacking the ills afflicting the business world and the whole of society in general.

What this means, of course, is: (1) industrialists and businessmen must recognize the world outside their offices and respond to the challenges presented to them; (2) in order to master change, we have to understand the long-range goals of society and the mechanisms of control over the forces of change; (3) we have to educate managers of accelerating change. Linkage must be found between business and higher education through an acceptance of the industry's needs, an assessment approach, and the acknowledgement by universities of the lifelong learning concept and the idea of experiential learning.

The role of our generation will be to find an intellectual depth and a philosophical meaning in the technological age. The success of this search is vital—so that man and science may co-exist, so that man may still be happy, and so that society may adapt itself to the requirements of a changing age and to the social needs of the future world.

These changes of the new technological age—changes that will affect all of us personally—are already affecting, in a different way, the world of business and of industry.

There are already certain signs indicating that the role of executives in North American business is being altered by these revolutionary forces that have had an unprecedented impact on methods of business management.

The first of these trends has been the rapidly accelerating democratization of society that has opened opportunities of advancement for people of ability, people who increasingly insist on and enjoy the right of participation in basic decision-making. The result has been a demand, voiced loud and clear by middle management, for a meaningful role in company planning and a real opportunity to contribute importantly to that decision-making.

The second revolutionary force reshaping management practices is the information explosion, which forces the senior executive to rely more and more on his subordinates. Faced with today's new technology, every executive must learn to know what he does not know, and be prepared to curb his natural self-assertiveness.

A third force modifying the present-day style of executive leadership is the sheer bigness of business. Mass marketing has contributed to an enormous growth of business, not only in sales and income but also in the kinds of business activities, because of the diversification of companies. This diversification on top of growth will unavoidably broaden middle management's powers of decision-making. Similarly, it will further reduce the number of decisions the president of the company alone can reach in any one of the many businesses in which his corporation competes.

The fourth trend that has altered techniques of business management in recent years is the worldwide expansion of business opportunity, based in large measure on an insatiable demand for consumer goods among all income groups. The global approach to business forces executives to direct operations that may take place in several different industries or markets, each with its own unique requirements for success.

These new forces I have cited combine to limit the old-fashioned style of business leadership and to put stress not only on the senior executive's decision-making power, but on his ability to unleash the decision-making power of the company's middle management personnel.

In view öf the changes that have already occurred and the rapid acceleration of new changes and demands that management will face during this and the next decade, how are business schools responding to the challenge to educate future managers who will be able to manage the change?

The answer to this question requires a closer look at both traditional and alternative approaches to management education in our universities and colleges.

From the point of view of adult professional men and women, education is often seen as the acquisition of the art of the utilization of knowledge. As such, it constitutes a vital and necessary element in an individual's life. Educational programs recognizing prior learning and work experience provide an answer to the needs of mature students who already know what they wish to make of their lives and who are looking for the best, most direct way of equipping themselves for it.

As a proponent of *managerial andragogy*, I see that pioneering schools which think in terms of preparing managers for the future are starting now to play an essential role in this process by:

- Offering alternative educational programs based on the recognition that practical experience has a definite educational value that can be awarded credit in the pursuit of higher education, and that experiential learning in the form of past and current work experience can be assessed for academic credit toward a diploma or degree when documented.
- Preparing adults who already have considerable business and professional experience for managerial positions in their own field through

career-oriented degree, diploma, or certificate programs that combine specific educational objectives with academic excellence and integrity.

- Providing opportunities, through seminars and intensive continuing education, for the upgrading of professional qualifications and keeping up with the "state of the art" of management and to meet the accreditation needs of the growing professional credentialing movement.
- Undertaking and supporting research activities in the areas of business, industry, public, and health sector.

They see education as a lifelong process that must be related to the varied needs of people at different stages of their lives. They recognize that adults who know what they want to learn can learn what they need effectively and quickly.

Many adults, who have extensive practical work experience and had no opportunity to complete their university education, are now demanding that their managerial experience be validated and that they be allowed to complete their work toward a degree in a non-traditional way by combining a credit for prior learning, both formal and informal (management development, continuing education, professional association, industrial and government programs), and credits for practical managerial work experience.

Traditional post-secondary education has been based on certain key assumptions that do not appear to be universally applicable today, especially to many businessmen and other working professionals who wish to continue their education:

1. It was assumed that post-secondary education followed immediately on completion of secondary school program. Consequently, an overwhelming majority of students were young, with very little or no practical experience in any aspect of business or professional life.

2. It was thought that the main function of post-secondary education was to develop mainly general skills and approaches, to provide the student with a theoretical background that, it was presumed, he would then be able to utilize in business and the professions. In this way the school was believed to prepare the student for life and career.

3. Programs, curricula, and admission procedures all reflected this basic educational philosophy. They were based largely on clearly defined subject areas and curriculum units. Students proceeded in a definite order from one unit to another, and completed one educational level before being admitted to another.

These basic trends in educational theory and practice were so prevalent, so entrenched, that to most people they seemed based on age-old traditions, representing the only "natural" way of acquiring an education. But, in fact, as any student of the history of education knows, this is a mistaken view. Education over many centuries took many forms, most of them based on principles other than the ones that we have learned to accept as nearly "self-evident."

It might be argued that many of the "new" trends in post-secondary education represent in fact a revival of some very ancient insights and approaches. We might even say that we are experiencing a renaissance of the truly traditional, *practitioner-oriented approach* to education that was prevalent before comparatively modern times in most areas of the world.

Whatever the case may be, the merit of these new, or not so new, trends lies in the fact that they reflect the changing needs and patterns of our own time. They are characterized by breaking away from the high school-to-university-to-career model by the introduction of new approaches to assessment and evaluation of educational achievement, by the recognition of the value of experiential learning, by the tendency to combine theoretical, classroom learning with actual professional practice, and to look at the actual learning process less from the point of view of compartmentalized subject areas and more in terms of the total situation confronting the student in his professional work as well as in other areas of his life.

These new ways of looking at educational theory and practices received much of their initial impetus from the changes that have occurred in the last 25 years or so within the student population and especially the growing number of adult students attending centers of post-secondary education. In view of the complexity of today's business and approaching change, increasing numbers of adults find it not only helpful but even necessary to go back to school to provide an essential step to further professional development and success and to be able to manage the approaching change.

Education in business management still occurs, for the most part, within the framework of the traditional approach to education. This entails classroom instruction in which the instructor plays the leading role and scope for discussion is limited. The emphasis is on teaching theory. While such an approach might be sufficient for young students without significant work experience who are looking for entry-level positions, it is not good enough for people already in management positions. Little concerted effort is made to make the program more useful to these students with practical experience. Whatever the work experience, it is never counted towards credit. Instead, the mature professional must successfully complete a prescribed number of courses to obtain a degree in management.

When in 1964 the Union for Experimenting Colleges and Universities was established in the United States, it marked the beginning of an alternative approach to education in North America as these colleges and universities began offering what were termed "nontraditional" courses. Nontraditional or alternative educational programs are characterized by the belief that credit should be granted for documented, relevant work experience and learning acquired outside the college setting. Instruction is given in tutorials scheduled on Saturdays or evenings so that students in the work force do not have to sacrifice work and earnings to continue their education. The faculty, committed to the view that theory should be combined with practice, promotes the participation of students in the learning process by having them relate theoretical principles to their work experiences.

In Canada, an alternative approach to management education is offered by the Canadian School of Management. Founded in Toronto in 1976, and affiliated with Northland Open University, the school offers bachelor degree programs in business management and health administration and an Executive M.B.A. program. In all its programs, the emphasis is on meeting the needs of mature students by combining theoretical knowledge with practical experience, and in meeting the needs of the business, industry, public, and health sectors in preparing a cadre of experienced managers who will be able to manage accelerating change.

In Europe and the United States, considerable effort has been expended on the education of managers, and companies have developed in-house training programs for their managers. In the past, successful completion of such programs was not considered to be credit-worthy by universities and colleges. This situation has changed with the advent of the U.S. Program on Noncollegiate Sponsored Instruction. The program shows how colleges may grant credit towards a degree to persons who have successfully completed "educational programs and courses sponsored by noncollegiate organizations, including business and industry, government, and labor unions." Thus, this program makes post-secondary education more accessible to persons of all ages, and allows managers to validate their experience obtained outside of the traditional college classroom.

By making higher learning more accessible to working managers and by combining theory with practice in instruction, the nontraditional approach offers a means of increasing the flexibility of managers, individually and collectively. Thus, in the modern business environment, where the ability to adapt to changing conditions is crucial, the nontraditional approach harmonizes well with the needs of the business community for management education.

A growing percentage of the student population today is composed of working adults who wish and often have to continue their education, but who only rarely can afford to interrupt their careers to go back to school as full-time students.

In response to ever increasing knowledge specialization and organizational complexity, as well as the need to upgrade the competency of managers, it makes obvious sense to continue one's professional career while studying, not only for financial reasons, but also from the point of view of making one's education truly relevant to one's professional and other needs. But in order to accommodate and truly serve this type of student, some basic changes must be introduced into the traditional post-secondary educational system. New programs, new procedures, and new emphases are needed. They mean a departure from the concepts of *pedagogy*—or teaching of young people—and acceptance of the concept of *andragogy*—development of adults.

The following changes and new approaches seem most essential in this modern, alternative approach to management education, if we seriously think of preparing and educating managers for the accelerating change:

1. Traditional admission procedures and requirements must be modified. Evaluation of students' achievements should not be limited to formal courses taken at academic institutions and credits granted for largely classroom learning. Professional experience should also be given formal credit recognition. In other words, a student who has had an opportunity of developing skills and acquiring knowledge in any given field should be able to translate that achievement into credits if he applies to an educational institution for admission. This seems to be a minimum requirement.

Traditional educational institutions cannot be blamed for being suspicious of some of these new trends in credit-granting and pointing out possibilities of abuse. Nevertheless, some acceptance of experiential learning seems inevitable and necessary. It is incumbent on schools with nontraditional approaches to explore these new admission procedures, while at the same time making absolutely sure that high educational standards are maintained.

2. Changes are needed in the curriculum planning and educational requirements in academic institutions, especially those whose student populations contain a considerable percentage of adult professionals. Actual professional and other relevant experiences of every student should be given full weight and academic credit. Many skills assumed completely in young high school graduates should be recognized in more experienced adult students. The principle, therefore, must be to add to, to build upon, already existing skills and learning experiences, to organize and sort out the student's knowledge and to provide the means of developing it further.

Curriculum planning should be flexible enough to reflect the individual student's needs and background. Proven and obvious competence should be viewed as equivalent to some course work. For example, it would make little sense to require an experienced accountant to take a course in basic accounting just because a curriculum set up for mainly inexperienced students prescribes it, or for the same reason, to ask a personnel manager in charge of a large department to take an introductory course in personnel administration. This may seem obvious, and yet there are still very few academic institutions, at least in Canada, that are willing to grant academic recognition to experiential learning. In fact, this feature of the Canadian School of Management program and the keystone of its educational approach still raises quite a few academic eyebrows and causes much misunderstanding of its policies. The point is not to give credit away, but to give it where it is due.

3. Another very important feature of adult professional education should be to allow the student to set up his own goals and his own timetable whenever possible. As mentioned above, a program of studies can, and often should, be combined with a full-time professional career, and it should in fact take advantage of the learning possibilities offered by a day-to-day pursuit of a profession. Curricula should be structured around experiential learning wherever possible, rather than in competition or conflict with it.

4. Credentialing of professionals (or certifying an individual's level of competence, knowledge, skills, and professional experience) is a new and growing force of change. The credentialing process, often administered by professional societies, government agencies, and other organizations, presents a tremendous opportunity to progressively oriented post-secondary educational institutions as they face the approaching change. Licensing and regulation by governments concerning such professions as engineering, medicine, management consulting, nursing, or accounting have been instituted for public protection. The newly developing credentialing movement—a growing force for change—occurs not only for legal, health, liability, or safety reasons. As a result of competition and complexity in business, as well as the desire to better manage technological change, new professional groups and organized associations have emerged and will continue to grow (groups such as financial or economic analysts, computer programmers, strategic planners, insurance consultants, fellows in banking, real estate, profit planners, social economists, human resources managers, business presenters, health service executives, career planners, social work executives, organization development managers, manpower forecasters, environment engineers, etc.).

The scope of the credentialing movement currently exceeds 50 credentialing groups. As the awareness, knowledge, and commitment to the professional credentialing idea grows, continuing professional education will be the direction of many schools of management to assist such groups in upgrading qualifications, testing, and maintenance of established credentials—as many professional organizations will regard credentialing not only as a tool for the advancement of their membership, but also as a gauge of higher reputation of their organizations in the eyes of the public.

These are the basic changes of approach to post-secondary professional education that some of us are trying to explore and introduce. Some traditional educators view these trends with suspicion, fearing that they might lead to lowering of educational standards and goals. Yet it seems to us that these fears, however understandable, are not well founded. An experienced adult student, actively engaged in professional work, is surely less likely to accept poor teaching and lower standards than a young, inexperienced student, used to being a passive recipient of a product to which he is in many cases quite indifferent.

There are, of course, certain difficulties that many adult students face to a greater degree perhaps than young high school graduates. Some adults have been away from any kind of formal education for a considerable number of years and may lack certain skills and techniques of learning generally available to younger students.

They also have a tendency to underestimate their ability to cope with educational procedures and requirements. Some—very few—tend to overestimate it. But it seems to me that these difficulties are more than compensated for by the adult student's motivation, maturity of judgment, and ability for independent effort; furthermore, his professional and general life experience is an extremely important and largely untapped educational resource. It is the primary function of progressive educational institutions, fully aware of the demands that the accelerating change makes on us, the management educators, to give experiential education full weight and to utilize it in their educational policies and practice.

In the time of change that we are facing, a manager whose sole claim to his position is technical competence will become obsolete. He will be replaced by a new type of manager who combines excellent technical background with good business practices and a profit-oriented approach.

He must also understand the problems of ecology and the growing demands of the environment.

The new type of manager will understand computers and the benefits of scientific management, but he will also have to concentrate more on the problems of human-resource management. It is not enough nowadays to produce profits for the corporation and, at the same time, to disregard social problems, conservation, environmental pollution, the problems of inefficiency in government bureaucracy, or blatant incompetence all around us.

The manager of the future will be aware that his leadership qualities contribute to the community and country, and to his ability to produce profits. These criteria will, in turn, be used to measure his own overall performance.

The manager who develops the motivated team of people in the organization of tomorrow will reconcile the requirements of the company with the needs of its individual members.

The manager of the future will have an array of devices, techniques, and tools available to him to assist in the decision-making process and he will be proficient in their use.

Computers, which have scarcely begun to reveal their potential, will be developed to an extent that will permit future managers to couple human expertise in the most advanced mechanical and electronic technology with our rather limited knowledge of our highest capability—that of thinking. Only in this way can we learn the extent of the computer's flexibility and evaluative powers in order to make far better use of it.

To meet the challenge of the future, a new discipline or field of study has to be introduced. I am now working on introducing such a program at the Canadian School of Management. I call it *Managerial Futuristics*. I would like to share with you the proposed definition of this program, as it is pertinent to the topic we are discussing.

Managerial futuristics is a future-oriented discipline and activity based on the philosophy of futurism and the intellectual exploration of a future that seeks to identify, analyze, and evaluate possible changes and developments in human life and the world from the point of view of managerial leadership.

The basic assumption of the proposed course is that people can make meaningful forecasts about the future, if they take the trouble to understand fully the present conditions and trends in business, life, society, and the world in general. It is the objective of the proposed course to assist them in the process.

We are aware of the importance of the future. The past is gone; the present exists only as a short moment. Traditionally, scholars study the past and are not interested in the future. The crises of today have resulted from past failures to deal with emerging problems. We can do very little to improve the present world, because basic changes require time. We do have, however, the power to influence the future. By their very nature, managers are future-oriented, because management decisions of today affect the future. The important role of *managerial futuristics* is to provide a useful framework for decision-making and planning by developing reasonable assumptions about the future (expressed in terms of probability or possibility rather than certainty), based on an assessment of present conditions, the identification of future dangers and opportunities, suggesting alternative approaches to issues and evaluating alternative policies and actions—thus realizing that new future possibilities are open to us and increase the extent of our choice.

I see the need for the study and research of the possible impact of future technological, economic, and social developments and an assessment of their consequences for management people. Such a course would prepare management leaders to live in a changing technological, economic, and social world; it would develop their understanding of man's environment, the fundamentals of modern technology, genetics, evolution, and population dynamics; it would provide a better understanding of man and society, human progress, ecology, social psychology, changing occupational patterns, education, and employment; it would increase personal competence, develop access to information, and encourage independent learning styles. It would also assist in developing more effective communication for better management and an enhanced understanding of management strategic planning as a tool for dealing with the problematique of future change in all its dimensions (composite strategic planning, operational management planning, and tactical planning), seen through the prism of social responsibility of managerial leadership of the future.

I hope that a Managerial Futuristics program will play an important role in preparing managers of the accelerating change.

I would unhesitatingly list the following basic rules:
1. Understanding people.
2. Need for vision, courage, and creativity.
3. Ability to delegate properly.
4. Ability to make sound decisions.

An understanding of people is one of the most vital attributes to managerial success, and will not lose its importance in times of change. Instead, it will become more and more important in the management of future change.

Executives must understand why people act and react as they do; they must provide positive motivation for employees, derived from the higher needs and aspirations of human beings to develop. On the contrary, performance that arises from fear or insecurity is a result of negative motivation that should be eliminated completely from the sphere of industrial relations. Such performance, based on negative motivation, vanishes immediately anyway as soon as the threat disappears.

The manager of tomorrow will have to learn to identify drive as the highest priority for each of his employees, drive that can contribute most to the well-being of both the individual and the company. Thus, short-term and long-term positive motivation can be developed, and so lead to the identification of employees' personal ambitions with those of the organization.

A second vital attribute is the need for vision, courage, and creativity to make changes and to meet requirements imposed by changing times. Progress is the law of economic life. If a company ceases to progress in a changing world, it starts to fall back. We must be willing to make changes (not for the sake of change but when necessary and indicated), and to contribute new ideas and sell these ideas to our colleagues and superiors.

The third ingredient necessary for success is the ability to delegate properly. We have to learn that delegation of authority is an extension of our own achievement. At the same time, it improves the morale of the staff by giving them the feeling of sharing responsibility. This is what makes work interesting.

Finally, a few words about the ability to make sound decisions. As technological change and business grow more intricate and as constant requirements are being imposed on executives by changing conditions, a proper process of decision-making enables management to set its objectives in time and to determine its plans and strategies.

A good leader can face a crisis without panic, because he knows how to meet a problem; he knows that he has first to meet the problem, define it, put it in an organized shape, seek information that is necessary for its solution, analyze all the elements of the problem, and test in his mind all possible alternative solutions before reaching a final decision.

In conclusion, the future executive, in order to face and manage change, will have to be competent in a way that present managers are not. He will be aware of the most advanced technological and managerial tools that can help him in the complicated process of managing change. But above all, he will be able to apply his own knowledge to the analytical process required, and he will be able to motivate his staff in a positive sense through better understanding of the complexities of human personality.

Will the business leaders of tomorrow be able to meet the challenge of the changing times? It seems that the answer to this question rests with future managers, business leaders, and management educators. I think that the challenge to business leaders will be accepted, and that it will result in a major triumph for the manager of tomorrow. He will build on what exists; he will motivate people to improve; he will unite employees in constructive cooperation. He will do this because he is aware that the biggest challenge confronting the world today is to use the advances in research and technology to solve man's economic and social problems. We must solve these problems in order to narrow the gap between rich and poor nations. It is in this endeavor that managers of tomorrow will have a tremendous role to play.

While the industrial revolution of the nineteenth century can be said to have developed through a struggle for survival of the fittest, the technological age, in order to prosper, requires the effective mobilization of the most able and the most knowledgeable to manage the change.

Assessing Preferred Job Attributes for the New Manager of the 1980s

by

David Hopkins and Sandra LaMarre
with Jerry Thurber

I. Purpose and Importance of the Study

It is doubtful that any other "theory" has received as much attention in the literature regarding employee motivation as the "Hierarchy of Needs" proposed by Abraham Maslow (9). It is in many ways simplistic: it is **ethnocentric** in that it fails to account for cultural determinants that might alter the basic hierarchy; it is **static** in that it fails to account for changes in the hierarchy due to short-run situational changes; it is **rigid** in that it does not adequately account for the often observed non-sequential adherence to the categories of needs in the hierarchy; and it is perhaps **incomplete** in that it does not exhaust the kinds of needs that motivate human beings. Despite its shortcomings, it is nevertheless useful in describing the various needs that motivate human behavior. The purpose of this paper is to utilize the basic taxonomy presented by Maslow to describe the perceived job-related needs of the recent group of college graduates.

Why is it important to continually describe the "needs" of various occupational groups? As one author states, "If you want worker productivity, you must satisfy worker needs" (5:56). Concern for the continual decline in productivity in the United States relative to the Japanese and others is at the forefront of domestic concerns.

Secondly, understanding job-related needs is important due to the relatively high rates of absenteeism and turnover. Losing people who have been highly trained is very costly. Turnover at the managerial level multiplies this cost significantly and yet it has been increasingly characteristic for new college graduates to have several different employers in the first few years of their careers. Management turnover in 1960 among graduates out of college less than five years was 10%. Today the average corporation loses 50% of its college recruits within five years, according to the Sterling Institute, a Washington, D.C., management consulting firm (12). What appears to be happening in the American work force is a growing mismatch between company incentives and employee motivation. Today's employees simply are not responding to traditional rewards as they once did. Our own study indicates that over 70% of the new college graduates expect to work for at least two different employers in the first five years after graduation; nearly one in five expects to have three or more employers

David Hopkins is associate professor of management and public administration, School of Business and Public Management, University of Denver, Denver, Colorado. Sandra LaMarre is assistant professor of management, School of Business and Public Management, University of Denver, Denver, Colorado. Jerry Thurber is a graduate assistant at the School of Business and Public Management, University of Denver, Denver, Colorado.

103

in five years. As the chief psychologist for the Personnel Sciences Center in New York City commented in an interview for *U.S. News and World Report*, "younger workers feel they can pretty much call their own tune on a job; if they don't like what they see, they'll pick up their marbles and walk away" (15:63–4). For both productivity and turnover reasons, it is important to understand what people want from their jobs. As Karlins notes, "many contemporary managers can't satisfy worker needs because they don't know what they are" (5:56).

Finally, the purpose of this study is to provide descriptive base-line data from which to measure future changes in job-related needs. Our intent is to follow a significant sub-sample of our respondents during the first 10 years following graduation in order to document how and why their perceived job needs change. Armed with this knowledge, we believe management will be much better equipped to experiment with and design new types of incentive schemes. In the late 1960s almost half of all employed Americans viewed their work as a major source of personal fulfillment. Today that number has dropped to less than one out of four according to a recent survey by Yankelovich, Skelly and White (16).

II. Review of the Literature

There is a growing interest, among businesses and those involved in preparing individuals for the job market, in evaluating the value systems of current employees with hopes of developing more effective motivation techniques and job definitions. In reviewing the literature in this area, there is a consistent reference to a change in value systems. However, consensus does not exist in delineating the nature of the change. Yankelovich (16) suggests that:

> 1) fear is no longer a primary motivating factor—job security is very important but is considered a right rather than a goal; 2) money as an incentive remains crucial but is more difficult to use and is not in itself sufficient; and 3) the "work ethic" is no longer a predominant value brought to the job.

The U.S. Department of Labor (16) says in contradiction that "there appears to be an emerging work ethic which places a greater demand upon work. Work is viewed as an integral part of one's life." Further, they find American college seniors of 1972 in all academic areas to expect a resurgence of the importance of family life, and to be less concerned with money than their fathers and much more concerned about the nature and purpose of work. They appear to have a strong desire for career security and stability, put less emphasis on social status and teamwork, less emphasis also on the need to be original and creative, more emphasis on utilization of special skills and abilities.

Several empirically based studies have been conducted in this area. Again consensus appears to be lacking. Fretz (4) surveyed male college sophomores and juniors in five pre-professional curricula: law, medicine, engineering, education, and business. They were asked to rank order pay received, security, prestige, advancement, variety of duties, working conditions, independence, opportunity to use special talents, challenge, self-satisfaction, and fringe benefits. Although there was a small amount of inter-group differences, mean values indicated the top five areas of concern to be: 1) self-satisfaction, 2) pay received, 3) challenge, 4) security, and 5) independence. Business students ranked the occupational values in the following order: pay received, advancement, self-satisfaction, challenge, and security.

Mitchell et al. (10) attempted to predict occupational choice and to discover why certain students select business as an occupation. The method of this study was again a questionnaire administered to 141 randomly selected psychology and business majors in their junior year at the University of Washington. Significant differences between the two groups were noted. Business majors more highly valued autonomy and eliminating poverty.

Baker (1) studied differences in value systems between college students majoring in accounting and those majoring in other academic areas. The 565 students were selected at random from students majoring in sciences, the humanities, social sciences, and undergraduate and graduate accounting programs. They were asked to rank order terminal and instrumental values as delineated on the Rokeach Values Survey. The results indicated that accounting students gave statistically greater median rank to: 1) a comfortable life, 2) family security, 3) ambition, 4) cleanliness, and 5) responsibility, than all other students.

Zikmund, et al. (17) addressed themselves to the question, '' What are accounting students looking for when they consider their future careers?'' Fifty accounting majors at Oklahoma State currently interviewing for positions in anticipation of near-future graduation were surveyed. They were asked to choose from a series of job-offer pairs. The researchers paired salary-interesting work, salary-social responsibility, interesting work-social responsibility, and interesting work-opportunity for advancement. Results indicated that opportunity for advancement has the strongest impact on job choice. Interesting work was also highly significant, but was subject to salary negotiation (e.g., a high enough salary differential would cause the subject to select for money rather than job interest), and social responsibility had a positive impact also on selection but was more easily overcome by high salaries.

Cherrington, et al. (3) surveyed 3,053 workers in 53 companies to determine worker attitudes toward jobs, company, community, and work in general. It was found that the most desirable work-related outcome was a feeling of pride and craftsmanship in your work. The second most desirable work outcome was ''getting more money or a larger pay increase.'' The survey results indicated that getting more money was more important to younger workers, male and female, than to older workers. ''Unless they can obtain other valued rewards for their efforts, younger workers are likely to be less motivated than older workers'' (3).

Additional research has been done investigating the values of full-time MBA students and new employees. Ondrack (11) found that MBA students at the University of Toronto valued: 1) challenge in work, 2) good salary, 3) quality of peers, 4) opportunity for achievement, and 5) individual responsibility. Manhardt (7) considered value systems of recent college graduates employed in similar positions and found significant differences in orientations men and women bring to their jobs. Men tended to rate achievement/responsibility factors, which seemingly relate to long-range career success, significantly higher than women, while women gave higher ratings to factors that deal with the nature of the work environment (congenial atmosphere, etc.).

To summarize, while there is agreement that the new worker or near-future worker brings different values and expectations to the job than did his predecessor, and while there is a clearly demonstrated difference in value systems between individuals seeking careers in business and those seeking other types of careers, there is no clear determination as to what the most important values are. Money, job security, and job content seem to be consistently high-ranked, but much disagreement exists as to which is most important. It is clearly evident that security and high salary are no longer the primary set of values brought to the work situation. An increased emphasis is being put on job content, challenge, responsibility, participative decision-making, and availability of leisure time and/or the importance of family life.

Research that has been done in this area is somewhat limited and sample sizes have been small and parochial. Only Fretz (4) and the U.S. Department of Labor (13) have concentrated on delineating value systems of undergraduate students approaching graduation.

III. Methodology

Units of Analysis

The results reported here are part of a larger study that surveyed 1,930 graduating college seniors from 50 four-year institutions across the U.S. The institutions were selected by stratified random methods so as to be representative of the national population of such institutions on five different dimensions: size, competitiveness, affiliation (i.e. public, private, or church), environment (i.e. rural, urban, or suburban), and region of the country. The 50 schools selected were within 1% of the actual proportion of schools in each sub-category in the country. Once the schools were selected, a 20% sample of graduating seniors was systemically selected from lists of graduating seniors provided by the schools themselves. Of approximately 6,800 questionnaires distributed, 1,930 were returned for a return rate of approximately 28%.

Instrumentation

The results presented here were derived from the following question in our survey, which asked respondents to rank 20 different job attributes in terms of their preferences:

Please rank the following attributes in order of importance to you. (1 = highest priority, etc.) Each attribute completes the phrase, "I would prefer a job that has _____."

Due to concern that respondents would be unable to accurately rank a list of 20 items, we pre-tested the approach by having a group of approximately

60 students also answer this question on a "paired comparison" basis. That is, they were asked to choose only between two attributes at a time. This was done for all possible attribute pairs and the overall results of this approach were compared to the simple ranking of all 20 items by the same students. The two approaches yielded results that correlated at approximately .85. The similarity between the results of our national study and our pilot study also suggests that responses to this question yield reliable results.

The job attributes selected were culled from the literature to represent the five dimensions of Maslow's Hierarchy of Needs. A brief description of those dimensions and the related indicators is presented below:

Physiological Needs: The lowest rung on Maslow's hierarchy encompassses those needs involved with basic physiological requirements, i.e., air, food, water, shelter, clothing, sex, comfort, and convenience. While to some extent wages and salaries can be used to satisfy needs in all levels of the Maslow hierarchy, basic income is particularly relevant to the satisfaction of these basic needs. As Boone and Kurtz note, "Because minimum wage laws and union wage contracts have forced wage levels upward so that most families can afford to satisfy their basic needs, the higher-order needs are likely to play a greater role in worker motivation today" (2:163). We utilized the following four attributes to measure the dimension of "physiological needs":

- A Convenient Work Location
- An Adequate Wage and Salary
- Comfortable Working Conditions
- Free Organization-Provided Meals

Safety/Security Needs: The next category in the hierarchy is composed of safety/security needs. This involves the need to feel safe, secure, and protected. It includes "job security, protection from physical harm and avoidance of the unexpected" (2:163). In terms of the job, it might include protection against health and medical care expenses, safe working conditions, and security against inflation (e.g., cost-of-living increases). From these possibilities, we selected the following four attributes as being representative of this dimension:

- Good Insurance Benefits
- Substantial Job Security
- A Non-Competitive Atmosphere
- Clearly Defined Assignments

Social Needs: The next higher dimension is what Maslow describes as "social" needs. These take various forms. They describe a person's need to "belong" and be accepted by others. People desire social contacts and have a basic need to be affiliated with others. The work place provides several opportunities for people to satisfy these needs through work groups, clubs, committees, and meetings as well as formal and informal associations with peers, subordinates, and superiors. We selected the following four attributes to tap these needs:

107

- Co-Workers with Similar Beliefs
- Substantial Interaction Among Employees
- Friendly Co-Workers
- Organization-Sponsored Social Activities

Esteem Needs: Above social needs come "esteem" needs. These describe a person's desire to feel a sense of accomplishment and achievement. This has two parts: people need *external* validation of their worth and importance, but they also need an *internal* self-respect and sense of importance. There are several ways in which a person's job provides the opportunity to satisfy these "ego" needs: formal and informal feedback on performance, social recognition, and organizational titles and positions that indicate status and the ability to influence others. We have included the desire for a "high wage and salary" in this category. Like basic wages, high wages can be used to satisfy other needs as well (e.g., security). Nevertheless, we have equated basic wages/salaries with the satisfaction of basic needs, and the desire for high wages/salaries as a manifest indicator of one's worth in the eyes of others. Therefore, the four attributes used to measure esteem needs are:

- A High Wage and Salary
- Importance in the Eyes of Others
- Recognition for Good Performance
- Influence over Others

Self-Actualization Needs: Finally, at the top of Maslow's proposed hierarchy are what he has labeled "self-actualization" needs. Maslow himself had earlier described these needs, saying, "A healthy man is primarily motivated by his needs to develop and actualize his fullest potentialities and capacities . . . what man can be, he must be" (8:384, 392). On the job, these needs are expressed in the desire for self-development, autonomy, personal growth, responsibility and independence, self-fulfillment, and the ability to utilize one's creativity, special talents, and capabilities. We selected the following attributes as representative of this dimension:

- Freedom for Self-Expression and Creativity
- Opportunity to Use Your Skills and Abilities
- Interest and Self-Satisfaction
- Opportunity for Personal Development

The previously described job attributes were randomly selected as to their position on the questionnaire. The question and format were pretested in a pilot study of approximately 200 undergraduate seniors at eight four-year institutions in the Denver Metropolitan area.

IV. Results

Overall Results

In both our pilot study and our national study, some respondents indicated that it was fairly easy to pick their top five and their bottom five preferences. Distinguishing preferences for those job attributes in the middle was apparently more difficult. The top five preferred job attributes were:

1. Interest and Self-Satisfaction.
2. Opportunity to Use Skills and Abilities
3. Opportunity for Personal Development
4. Recognition for Good Performance
5. An Adequate Wage and/or Salary

In contrast, the least preferred job attributes were:

20. Free Organization-Provided Meals
19. Organization-Sponsored Social Activities
18. Influence over Others
17. Importance in the Eyes of Others
16. Co-Workers with Similar Beliefs

The fact that "an adequate wage and/or salary" is ranked as low as fifth is somewhat surprising and contradicts many current perceptions that *money* is the primary objective in job selection. The fact that "organization-provided meals" and "organization-sponsored social activities" are ranked last and next-to-last is not surprising. Nevertheless, one is struck by how different the ranking for such items might be in different cultures or for respondents entering the job market from different economic situations (e.g., non-college graduates).

Finally, the overall scores on the five Maslow need dimensions are shown in Exhibit 1. (These scores can range from 10, which represents a *high* preference for a need dimension, to 74, which represents a *low* preference). Given our categorization, the "self-actualization" dimension demonstrates an extremely high preference. Also surprising is the fact that the "social" and "esteem" dimensions are both lower than "physiological" or "security" in terms of respondents' preferences. However, the inclusion of "an adequate wage and/or salary" *only* in the "physiological" category undoubtedly gives greater weight to that dimension than it would have otherwise. Nevertheless, the overwhelming preference for jobs that provide opportunities to satisfy one's self-actualization needs is indeed striking.

Sub-Group Results

The preference orderings for various job attributes have also been calculated for various sub-groups of the overall population of respondents. Four broad sets of characteristics have been used to identify the subgroups: personal characteristics, academic characteristics, family characteristics, and institutional characteristics.

Results for Sub-Groups Defined by Personal Characteristics

The "self-actualization" dimension is the overwhelming preference among all these sub-groups; jobs that provide "interest and self-satisfaction" and "opportunity to use one's skills and abilities" are the first and second choices in all cases.

The responses of men and women are very similar. Compared to men, there is a slight tendency for women to prefer job attributes that provide

Exhibit 1
Overall Need-Dimension Graphs

	Low					High
Physiological:						
	74	61	48	36	23	10
	Low					High
Security:						
	74	61	48	36	23	10
	Low					High
Social:						
	74	61	48	36	23	10
	Low					High
Esteem:						
	74	61	48	36	23	10
	Low					High
Self-Actualization:						
	74	61	48	36	23	10

greater security (e.g., "a non-competitive atmosphere") while men have a slightly higher preference for job attributes satisfying esteem needs than do women.

Among age groups, the older respondents definitely appear to have stronger self-actualization needs, whereas younger respondents have a greater preference for satisfying social needs. Respondents over 35 years of age ranked "freedom of self expression and creativity" third whereas respondents under 22 ranked that item eighth. Similarly, younger respondents demonstrated slightly higher esteem needs while older respondents have slightly higher physiological and security needs.

Among broad racial categories, Negroes strongly prefer jobs that satisfy security needs, Orientals exhibit much higher esteem needs, and Caucasians appear to have a slight preference for satisfying social needs relative to the other two groups. Orientals ranked "an adequate wage or salary" significantly lower than Caucasians or Negroes, but ranked "a high wage or salary" substantially higher than the other two groups. On the dimension of social needs, Caucasians had a higher preference for "friendly co-workers" while Orientals had a higher preference for "substantial inter-action among employees." Negroes had significantly higher preferences for "clearly defined assignments" and "substantial job security" than other respondents. All racial sub-groups had equally strong preferences for satisfying self-actualization needs.

Foreign students expressed a stronger preference for jobs that satisfy physiological needs while American students had a stronger preference regarding security needs. Indicative of this was the foreign students' higher ranking for a "non-competitive atmosphere."

The amount of full-time work experience does not appear to translate to sufficiently different preferences among job attributes, though respondents with no full-time work experience showed a stronger preference for satisfying social needs. However, in terms of part-time work experience, there were significant differences among sub-groups and the reasons for this distinction are unclear. For example, those respondents with no part-time work experience have a preference for satisfying those needs further down on Maslow's hierarchy (i.e., physiological and particularly security). Those with more than three years of full-time work experience had a substantially stronger preference for satisfying esteem and self-actualization needs. Indicative of this pattern was the higher ranking for "an adequate wage or salary," "substantial job security," and "clearly defined assignments" among those with no part-time work experience. In contrast, those with more than three years of part-time experience had a stronger preference for "freedom of self-expression and creativity" as well as for a "high wage or salary." The amount of part-time work experience appeared to distinguish significant differences among sub-groups more than any other characteristic. Nevertheless, the Spearman's Rho (rank order correlation) between the ranks of those with no part-time experience and those with over three years of experience is still a very high .987. Spearman's Rho for the ranks of males and females is .999.

Results for Sub-Groups Defined by Academic Characteristics

There are some significant differences between academic majors. Business and public administration majors had lower preferences for job attributes that tend to satisfy physiological, social, and self-actualization needs than do other majors. However, they have higher esteem needs than do other majors. Relatively higher physiological needs were expressed by fine arts, humanities, and applied majors. A somewhat greater preference for satisfying social needs was demonstrated by social and behavioral science majors and pre-professional majors. Humanities and pre-professional majors had lower esteem needs. The highest possible preference for satisfying self-actualization needs was reflected by majors in the social and behavioral sciences, fine arts, and the humanities.

Students with grade point averages below 2.5 demonstrated greater preference for satisfying security needs and slightly higher preference for satisfying esteem needs than did students with GPA's of 2.5 and above. Students with better grades had slightly higher preferences in terms of physiological, social, and self-actualization needs. Nevertheless, the rank order correlation between the two groups is an extremely high .996.

We also looked at differences between student groups defined by who was paying for the majority of their academic expenses. The differences were negligible. However, students who had the majority of their expenses paid by sources other than themselves or their families (e.g., employers, government, etc.) did have slightly greater preference for satisfying "lower level" needs (physiological and security) and somewhat lower preference for satisfying self-actualization needs.

Finally, we looked at differences between students who intended to take jobs in the public, private, and non-profit sectors. Those aiming for the private-for-profit sector revealed weaker physiological and security needs, but substantially stronger esteem needs. Those students preparing to work in the non-profit sector had the highest self-actualization needs and the lowest esteem needs. Students who professed a desire to enter the public sector had the highest security needs. Indicative of these patterns was a significantly higher ranking assigned to "recognition for good performance" and a "high wage and salary" by those intending to enter the private-for-profit sector as compared to those aiming for the non-profit sector.

Results for Sub-Groups Defined by Family Characteristics

The results for various sub-groups defined by family and early childhood characteristics reveal that those from high-income families (i.e., gross income over $75,000/year) had higher preferences for satisfying Maslow's higher-level needs (i.e., social, esteem, and self-actualization) than did those students from lower-income families (below $25,000/year). Likewise, respondents from low-income families had a greater concern for physiological and security needs.

In terms of religious upbringing, there were few significant differences between broad religious groupings. Jews reflected stronger esteem needs than others. Similarly, Catholics had higher security needs than other groups. Finally, Protestants indicated a higher preference on the dimension of physiological needs, which was the result of a significantly higher rank given to "an adequate wage or salary" by Protestants than by Jews. Protestants ranked that attribute fifth whereas Jews ranked it twelfth.

We looked at differences between families with various work patterns. Those students who had two working parents when they were growing up had nearly identical preferences compared with respondents who had only one working parent. When both parents worked *some*, the results were also similar.

There was a noticeable difference between students who were raised in rural settings as opposed to other settings. Those from rural environments have significantly higher needs at the bottom of Maslow's hierarchy (i.e., physiological, security, and social) and lower esteem and self-actualization needs than those students raised in small towns, suburban, or urban environments. Differences between non-rural environments were negligible.

Finally, we examined differences between married and unmarried students. Again, the differences were insignificant. Married students had slightly stronger preferences for satisfying security and self-actualization needs and somewhat lower preferences for jobs that satisfy social needs. Nevertheless, in comparing sub-groups defined by all of these family characteristics, the overwhelming pattern is similarity, not diversity.

Results for Sub-Groups Defined by Institutional Characteristics

The results for students coming from various types of schools indicate that there do appear to be some regional differences. Students attending southern schools indicate higher security needs and lower self-actualization needs than those from other regions. For example, they ranked "substantial job security" fourth and "freedom for self-expression and creativity" eighth. Respondents from midwestern schools had the lowest security needs. Those from western institutions had the lowest esteem needs.

Respondents from less competitive schools had substantially higher security needs and somewhat lower self-actualization needs than those from more competitive schools. Indicative of this is the higher ranking they give to "substantial job security" and "good insurance benefits."

The affiliation of the school (i.e., private, public, or church) did *not* define dramatic differences between students. Students at private institutions had slightly higher self-actualization and social needs and slightly lower physiological and security needs than did others. Those from church supported schools had somewhat higher preferences for job attributes that satisfy Maslow's lower level needs and less preference for those satisfying higher level needs.

Students from small schools also expressed a stronger desire to satisfy lower-level needs (i.e., physiological and security) and lower preference for satisfying esteem and self-actualization needs. Students from rural schools demonstrated this same pattern of needs. However, institutional characteristics do not appear to create significant differences among job-attribute preferences. Similarity across sub-groups is again the rule rather than the exception.

V. Conclusions

First, the respondents in this study expressed an overwhelming preference for job attributes that satisfy what Maslow labeled self-actualization needs. The three top-ranked job attributes were in this category—"interest and self-satisfaction," "opportunity to use one's skills and abilities," and "opportunity for personal development."

Second, the preferences are extremely consistent across sub-groups. The rank order correlation for the preferences of the most diverse groups is above .95.

Third, there are some mild differences in preferences, which have been noted above. For example, a higher preference for satisfying *self-actualization* needs is indicated by older respondents (over 35), those with more work experience, those majoring in social or behavioral science, fine arts, or humanities, those having the majority of their academic expenses paid by their families or themselves, those aiming at jobs in the nonprofit sector, those raised in other than rural environments, and those who attended school in the East, Midwest, or West.

Those respondents who appear to have a higher preference for job attributes that satisfy *esteem* needs are Orientals, those with some part-time work experience, those majoring in business and/or public administration, those intending to enter the private sector, Jews, those raised in other than rural environments, and those who attended medium or large, urban or suburban schools.

A stronger desire to satisfy *social* needs through the job is reflected by Caucasians, those under 22, those with no full-time work experience, those from families with incomes under $25,000, those with no particular religious upbringing, and those raised in rural and small town environments.

Those indicating higher preferences for satisfying *security* needs were Negroes, American students, those with no part-time work experience, those with grade point averages below 2.5, those expecting to take jobs in the public sector, those from poorer families, Catholics, those raised in rural environments, and those attending small, church-supported schools in the South that are below average in competitiveness.

113

Finally, those respondents who put a relatively greater stress on job attributes that satisfy *physiological* needs were Caucasians, Negroes, foreign students, those majoring in fine arts, humanities, or applied subjects, those having more than half their academic expenses paid by sources other than themselves or their families, those intending to take jobs in the public or nonprofit sectors, those from poorer families, Protestants or those with no religious upbringing, those raised in rural environments, and those attending small schools.

Fourth, if groups of needs are satisfied in some sort of priority sequence as suggested by Maslow, then one would expect the scores on the various dimensions to reflect that ordering. They do not. On the other hand, Maslow suggests that needs which have been satisfied tend to lose their motivating power and are less sought after. If this is the case, it would appear that all but self-actualization needs have been relatively well satisfied for students just graduating from college. To take this a step further, social needs would appear to have been the most satisfied and physiological and security needs the least satisfied (aside from self-actualization). This makes some intuitive sense when one realizes that these respondents have just finished four (or more) years of college, probably with relatively low levels of discretionary income, and are just entering a stage in their lives when many will be attempting to get their first job. However, this scenario does not adequately explain why a person would be so dramatically concerned with self-actualization. As one looks at the various orderings of the five Maslow need-dimensions across various sub-groups, it is clear that there is not one dominant ordering. Nevertheless, this information does not necessarily fault Maslow's theory. One would have to know more about the individual situations of the respondents and which of their needs have already been satisfied.

Fifth, the job attributes that we have selected to represent each of Maslow's dimensions do not always hang together. For example, on the esteem dimension, the "recognition for good performance" is consistently ranked higher than other attributes on that dimension. Similarly, "friendly co-workers" is consistently ranked higher than other attributes on the social dimension. Not surprising is the fact that "an adequate wage or salary" ranks high among those attributes measuring physiological needs.

Bibliography

1. Baker, C. Richard, "An Investigation of Differences in Values: Accounting Major vs. Nonaccounting Major," *The Accounting Review*, Vol. 1, # 4, October 1976. pp. 886–893.

2. Boone, Louis E., and Kurtz, David L., *Contemporary Business*, Third Edition, New York: The Dryden Press, 1982.

3. Cherrington, David J., *The Work Ethic*, AMACOM, New York, 1980.

4. Fretz, Bruce R., "Occupational Values as Discriminants of Professional Student Groups," *Journal of Vocational Behavior*, Vol. 2, # 3. July 1972, pp. 233–237.

5. Karlins, Marvin, *The Human Use of Human Resources*, New York: McGraw Hill, 1981.

6. Lawler III, Edward E., "Compensating the New-Life-Style-Worker," *Personnel* May-June 1971, pp. 19–25.

7. Manhardt, Philip J., "Job Orientation of Male and Female College Graduates in Business," *Personnel Psychology*, Vol. 25, 1972, pp. 361–368.

8. Maslow, Abraham, "A Theory of Human Motivation," *Psychological Review*, July 1943.

9. Maslow, Abraham, *Motivation and Personality*, New York: Harper, 1954.

10. Mitchell, Terence R., and Knidsen, Barrett W., "Instrumentality Theory Predictions of Students' Attitudes Towards Business and Their Choice of Business as an Occupation," *Academy of Management Journal*, Vol. 16, # 1, March 1973, pp. 41–52.

11. Ondrack, D.A., "Emerging Occupational Values: A Review and Some Findings," *Academy of Management Journal*, Vol. 16, # 3. September 1973, pp. 423–432.

12. Rowan, Roy, "Rekindling Corporate Loyalty," *Fortune*, February 1981, pp. 54–58.

13. U.S. Department of Labor, *Job Satisfaction: Is There a Trend?*, Manpower Research Monograph No. 30, U.S. Government Printing Office, 1974.

14. U.S. Department of Labor, *Youth and the Meaning of Work*, Manpower Research Monograph No. 32, U.S. Government Printing Office, 1974.

15. Witkin, Arthur, "How Bosses Get People To Work Harder," *U.S. News and World Report*, January 29, 1979, Interview.

16. Yankelovich, Daniel, "New Approaches to Worker Productivity," a talk given at the National Conference on Human Resource Systems in Dallas, Texas, October 25, 1978.

17. Zikmund, William, Catalanello, Ralph, and Wegener, Steve, "The Accounting Student's Job-Rating Criteria: An Experiment," *The Accounting Review*, Vol. 52, # 3, July 1977, pp. 729–735.

Making Technology Work:
A Report from the Battlefield

by

James L. Horton

Friction is the only concept that more or less corresponds to the factors that distinguish real war from war on paper. The military machine . . . is basically very simple and therefore seems easy to manage. But we should bear in mind that none of its components is of one piece: each part is composed of individuals, every one of whom retains his potential of friction . . . . A battalion is made up of individuals, the least important of whom may chance to delay things or somehow make them go wrong. The dangers inseparable from war and the physical exertions war demands can aggravate the problem to such an extent that they must be ranked among its principal causes.

This tremendous friction, which cannot, as in mechanics, be reduced to a few points, is everywhere in contact with chance, and brings about effects that cannot be measured, just because they are largely due to chance.

—Carl Von Clausewitz, "On War," 1832 (taken from Princeton edition, 1976; edited and translated by Michael Howard and Peter Paret).

(*For "war," read "business"; for "military machine," read "company"; for "battalion," read "company unit."*)

Factory hands, dockworkers, mechanics, technicians, clerks, secretaries, salespersons, and middle managers are the ones who will make the future work because they do the business of any company.

But who is overcoming their fears that tomorrow's technology will cost them their jobs, humiliate them in front of lower-status employees, and force them to confront concepts they could not have learned in school? Work improvement and productivity are wonderful theories, but too often they bring lower-than-expected yields because the human factor is overlooked.

Item: The leader of one of America's largest corporations has threatened to replace workers with robots if wage demands are not moderated.

Item: By making managers type on computer keyboards, we ask them to abolish a fundamental distinction between themselves and secretaries.

Item: An employee wrestles with "user-friendly" software for 10 or more hours before giving up in frustration at making it work.

James L. Horton is associated with Robert Marston and Associates, Inc., New York, New York.

Item: Workers avoid a new high-production office machine because they have to get work out and they are not "comfortable enough" to use it. They already had several hours of training on the machine.

The author can document each of these examples and more.

The problem of change in organizations is well-known, but the introduction of computer, communications, and automated technology to every facet of the workplace is so vast that it is reminiscent of the industrial revolution and the rise of assembly lines. As anyone who has read Dickens and studied U.S. unionism can tell you, those shifts were botched. Workers rose in anger against appalling conditions and intolerable line speeds ordered by engineers palming stopwatches.

It is too early to predict disaster for the new technologies, but the warning signs are there and suspicion verges on paranoia in some parts of the workplace.

Unfortunately, there appears to be little organized effort to confront human problems and the unquantifiable risks they present. The drive is once again for the bottom line of the income statement. Cost-effective management should not impede respect for employees, but too often it does. Companies such as Emerson Electric, which attempts to meld aggressive, numbers-oriented performance with strong communications and worker concern, are rare.

As one who has been on the battle lines to get new technology into offices, it seems to me that some commonsense observations about people and management are pertinent to "Working Now and in the Future."

Technological Leaps Are Made Through Microsteps. The best introductions of new technology are tedious. They demand careful personnel planning, advance employee communications at all levels, "hard-sell" introduction, training, and new socio-cultural and organizational relationships.

Frequently, planning stops at calculations of return on assets, tax benefits, and production gains. And, unfortunately, this may be as much a result of education as anything else. For example, in the MBA program this author attended, nearly all planning was financial and revolved around discounted cash flows. Human aspects received glancing nods at best.

The importance of humanistic managerial communications has been much neglected or overburdened by studies on spans of control, optimum network configurations, and "pop" psychology. An old saying applied by many a general and "Bull of the Woods" is perhaps still the most pertinent when major changes occur: "The best management tool is a good pair of shoes."

One must go to the work site, look at the progress (or the lack of it), talk to employees at every level, demonstrate enthusiasm, show hands-on leadership, and exhibit real knowledge of the equipment to overcome problems and keep a project moving.

Credibility Is Hard Won and Easily Lost. Woe to managers who say new technology does not threaten jobs but then lay off workers. A breach of faith is not easily forgotten. It is better to be honest. But this error is made all the time.

Years ago, Chester Barnard noted that workers give labor voluntarily and can withhold it, too, when they no longer accept the authority of an executive. A manager is only credible if, when he or she leads, workers follow. Achieving this requires hard, long work to project one's ideas and goals to the bottom of the organization, to get employees to understand them, and, most difficult of all, to accept them and act.

When entire organizations are hostile to technology, it takes a dramatic, uncontested threat to gain credibility, such as the invasion of Japanese cars. If that does not work, the manager may replace the organization by moving the plant or forcing installation of machines. Neither are palatable. Dumping workers on society solves immediate problems, but it ignores taxes, government regulations, and other consequences arising from mounting unemployed who cannot be left to starve.

Stick to Fundamentals When Great Changes Occur. Side issues dilute efforts when new technology is introduced. Most of today's electronic equipment, for example, can do more than any previous machine. It is a trap to concentrate on gaining wonderful advantages before making sure that employees understand how a machine makes basic tasks easier, faster, and better.

No manager should presume that a manual, a seminar, and hands-on experience are enough to get employees used to new machines. It doesn't happen. Workers are overwhelmed by new concepts. Learning is slow, and volumes of information obfuscate. Two rules are of use:

- KISS: Keep It Simple, Stupid. (An old Army saying.)
- Tell 'em what you're going to tell 'em. Tell 'em. Tell 'em what you told 'em.

Identify the one key work-flow task and train employees to perform it well. Then, and only then, branch into new territory.

This has three advantages:

- Work-flow remains steady: there is less disruption.
- Performing key tasks gives workers time to become comfortable with equipment.
- Key tasks on new machines may be similar to tasks performed on older equipment. Employees may be able to adapt better and faster. For example, word processing depends on basic typing skills that nearly every secretary knows.

Conceptual Understanding Does Not Equal Applications Understanding. Before introducing new technology, the careful manager tests training, instructions, and other procedures on the least skillful employees. If they cannot grasp it, the manager reworks the program until they do. When roll-out occurs, chances of success are greater—but never insured. An engineer may know the principles of an auto but not be able to build one. A secretary might learn the concept of word processing but get hopelessly tangled in the buttons.

When Apple built its new "user-friendly" computer, *Lisa*, software was tested on unskilled employees during development and revised until nearly anyone could work the machine with 30 minutes of instruction. Although it is too early to determine whether *Lisa* will be commercially successful, it has been roundly cheered by nearly everyone who has worked with it.

Such testing means organizational changes occur slowly. During the fallow period between the start and finish of a roll-out, managers may suffer substantial abuse for "doing nothing" and may have to perform more than a few "symbolic" actions to keep top management and employees motivated.

Accept the Inevitable. For all the planning that occurs, some things just don't work. For all the training that is given, some employees cannot or will not adapt to new technology. Sloan, in writing of his years at General Motors, recalled vividly the lessons of the experimental copper-vaned engine on which the company nearly bet its existence.

Good managers prepare fallback positions during change to make sure that work gets out. And, if possible, they test new technology in a place where the guts of a business are not threatened. When it comes to recalcitrant employees, managers live with them, move them, or fire them. Humanistic leaders find this most unpleasant, but wise ones lay groundwork carefully—if they have time, and they usually do—so that both the employee and co-workers may see that a reasonable chance to adapt has been given and not reached.

Status Can Be a Trap. The prestige of having one's own microcomputer, robot, or terminal has reached the same proportions in some corporations as gold-plated golf clubs. Status, however, does not guarantee use.

Stories circulate of executives who have terminals but don't turn them on, or, worse, do not hook them up. New technology, in these cases, does not help the business and harms the individual. The executive does not take the machine seriously. When this happens, problems become self-fulfilling prophecies about why old ways are better.

However, if a manager tests a machine in one department, favorable usage reports and word of mouth on the grapevine will confer prestige quickly. Status then becomes a powerful management tool in rolling out the technology throughout the organization.

The Most Advanced System May Not Be Best. As high-speed engineering produces new machines, software, add-ons, advantages, and other enticements, the temptation is to get the most advanced system to guarantee greater productivity.

However, the manager must ask whether old dogs can learn new tricks and if so, how fast. It does little good to push people into the 1990s if they are still in the 1970s. Change should be gradual with easier-to-understand equipment. While it is best to upgrade by acknowledging the attitude of the organization, this does not mean that a company that is behind will remain behind. The smart manager pours resources of time and attention into highlighting the company's position and its goals.

Use a Time Rule and Make It Well Known. After working with a new technology, a rough pattern of acceptance emerges. In word processing, the author has seen a pattern of three and six months. During the first three months, there are problems with learning the equipment. By six months, there are manager clashes for available time on a machine.

Clashes are a sign of acceptance. It has been the author's policy when participating in new-technology introductions to make time rules well known to employees and top managers. It smooths crises that inevitably occur, and lets all know that their problem is part of a normal cycle rather than an imminent failure.

Failures Are Usually 90% Managerial and 10% Employee. It is easy to blame subordinates, the union, or anyone but oneself for poor progress in introducing new technology. If one accepts that most problems result from failing to present issues clearly to begin with, then searches can be simplified when things go wrong. Smart managers do not attempt to start a change before talking with several subordinates to learn how it is understood. This, too, is an old managerial rule: "If you want to see how you are communicating to subordinates, pull some of them aside two or three days after you announce a new policy and ask them to explain it to you."

Most managers are appalled to learn how their clear thought, strong leadership, and driving salesmanship have been distorted beyond recognition.

Blaming management, however, goes only so far. Credibility problems resulting in generations of unionism have institutionalized distrust and distort the best-intended messages. It takes cataclysm to break through the barrier—or years of hard labor and consistent strategy. It is not unlike the U.S. and the Soviet Union. While there may be cooperation, underlying assumptions and motives are at odds.

If one looks at the source of this distrust, he should find a failure to maintain employee and management focus on the true functions of the business. When (on the surface) workers see management aggrandizing, they will demand what they can get eventually. When technology threatens personal well-being, it becomes an intimate danger and not a business good. It is management's long-term task to maintain a clear picture of the business and the employee's part in it. This is rarely done.

Do It. Fix It. Try It. Some organizations plan in the nth detail, but never produce. Strategic exercises excuse decision-making. Solving new crops of risks becomes the prime task rather than facing them. At some point, good managers act or quit on new technology and do it decisively. They and their employees gain nothing by endless studies.

It is a fact of life that one can know as much as 90 or 95% of any given action, but the rest remains unknown. Managers who worry about the unknown too much fail themselves and subordinates. On the other hand, serendipity has led to great discoveries. Opportunistic managers use small, unforeseen insights to extraordinary advantage and the result may be far removed from the original plan for the technology.

Great Organizational Changes Require Great Leaders. Managing during great technological change is not scientific. It is art based on skill, psychology, stubbornness, timing, and luck. Thus far in U.S. industry, few companies have been survivors—gaining the full benefits of technology they sought to apply—without alienating workers.

Compare the travails of Chrysler Corporation with those of International Harvester. On the one hand, an executive has taken a moribund company and given it a chance to live. On the other, a leader hastened a corporation's ruin.

However, it is unfair to damn the executive of International Harvester while canonizing Lee Iacocca. Both men had successful records before assuming their posts. Both men faced similar tasks requiring reduction of bad managerial and employee practices and installation of technology that would regain productivity and restore company health.

For some reason, however, Chrysler held onto its employees' minds while International Harvester did not. Harvester's problem may well have been timing. The corporation took a strike at a time when real dangers were not yet apparent. The employees reacted bitterly, and help was not forthcoming when the company really began to plunge.

The corporate executive is a politician negotiating diverse organizational differences and trying to gain action. He is not a passive player. He must have a view of where the organization is going. Further, he must have time to take it there plus the skills to push his views through every level of the organization where the real work is done.

To do this, he must use all communications skills that a congressman considers essential. Unfortunately, too many executives have supplanted communications duties with planners, public relations departments, personnel administrators, information systems, etc. The result has been disintegration of the vision and aims of the organization. Departments eventually pursue their own goals to the exclusion of others. The executive must use every managerial skill he has to focus attention, and, of course, this must be done without creating irreparable hostility.

Carl Von Clausewitz said a leader needs "genius," an indefinable quality not susceptible to scientific management or textbook formulations. Another writer, Ralph Z. Sorenson, formerly a professor at Harvard, summarized his experiences as a manager in a series of observations that seem to be common sense. The good manager requires:

- Ability to express oneself.
- Leadership skills.
- Broad human understanding.
- Courage and a strong sense of integrity.
- The ability to make positive things happen.

This list is hardly complete or, for that matter, essential since effective leaders have failed in every one of the points. Moreover, it is disappointing. It would seem that, after thousands of years of discussing and writing about great leaders, we would reach a more scientific and technological definition to help companies face new technology and the future. Thus far, we haven't.

The problem may lie with the fundamental dichotomy between cumulative and moral knowledge. Cumulative knowledge can be written down to build a body of learning. Moral knowledge—ways of acting ethically and in relation to other humans—must be learned by each individual all over from birth through life-choice decisions and experience.

The Final Rule of Technological Change: There Are No Rules. There are numerous management and communications techniques, but no cookbook process that works in every case. For all the organizational behavior studies and case histories, each manager starts with the people at hand, the history peculiar to that organization, the cultural bias, and the change.

Applying a process rigidly or not at all should be less a matter of dogmatism and more a case of pragmatic judgment. What works 10 times in a row may not work the 11th. Thus each of the observations made above will have times of exception when they do not apply and should be discarded. For the orderly mind, it is frustrating. For the academic, it is a defeat of reason by illogic.

The author hopes that futurists who are highly optimistic about the impact of technology will take to heart this lesson. New technology works only if people make it work. And that's not easy.

The Segmented Work Force

by

Matthew J. Puleo

It was a simpler world back then. At the end of World War II, Americans had an insatiable appetite for consumer goods. For one brief decade, all we had to do to sell something was to manufacture it and put it on the shelf. Workers were also easier to manage. We subscribed to a common goal—to build the American business machine—and Theory X was seen as an appropriate management tool.

The rampant consumerism began to subside as the world moved into the 1960s. As competition increased, the marketing function moved to the forefront and became a critical business strategy. Marketers were under increased pressure to come up with the best recommendations for pricing, promotion, branding, etc. However, traditional market research, which produced demographic descriptions of the consumer marketplace, left a void. The information produced a vast array of techniques, facts, and figures, but there was no way to master this information in order to cut through the detail and focus sharply on new opportunities.

In the '60s, Daniel Yankelovich realized that buying decisions were based on factors other than demographic influences. He, therefore, began to collect qualitative, nondemographic forms of information. As a result, he developed what is now referred to as nondemographic *market segmentation*, revolutionizing how we define markets and brand products today.

For example, before market segmentation, the shampoo market targeted a demographic cut of the population, i.e., men, women, and children. In 1950, there were less than six major shampoos on the market. Nondemographic market segmentation allowed producers to expand their market share by focusing on incremental differences. This has resulted in considering the market as a number of segments in lieu of a nondifferentiated total "market." The result is that today there are over 100 shampoos catering to value preferences such as natural substances, conditioning of the hair, daily shampooing, etc. For the manufacturer, this method of segmentation has yielded a better return on investment.

Matthew J. Puleo is vice president, Human Resource Group, Yankelovich, Skelly and White, Inc., New York, New York.

The research we conducted as a firm to monitor the changing values and attitudes of the American public was expanded to look at the attitudes and values of the American work force. Several trends were beginning to emerge that would have an enormous impact on how we manage that work force. By the end of the 1950s, the idea that the U.S. was capable of nearly unlimited economic growth had become prevalent. With the rise of this unprecedented optimism came a new social phenomenon—a psychology of affluence. We as a society believed that affluence was no longer something for which to struggle. Instead, it was a logical by-product of America's endlessly expanding economy.

As we moved through the social revolution of the '60s and early '70s, the necessity for conformity and adherence to the Protestant work ethic was being questioned. Our classic American values, based on the Protestant ethic, with its flexible standards and requirement of self-denial and self-sacrifice, now seemed irrelevant. We asked ourselves, as a society, Why should we submerge our individuality in order to fit society's model of a desirable person? Why should we submerge our desires today for future rewards? And finally, Why should we submerge inclinations for pleasure in behalf of productivity?

The answer was an overwhelming "It's no longer necessary." The psychology of affluence was so prevalent that workers, particularly younger ones, became less willing to change masks when they crossed the corporate threshold. In addition, society pressured business to assume responsibility for its welfare and pressured government to step in and regulate business if it was unwilling to meet that responsibility.

The Need to Change

One of the ways corporate America responded to the changing work force was to focus on worker happiness rather than on worker productivity. The personnel function grew into the human resource function as a way to bring humanity into the workplace. Unfortunately, such approaches merely dealt with the symptoms and never developed a methodology for analyzing the causes.

Much like the dilemma facing marketers in the '50s, the work force became increasingly difficult to understand and manage. Perhaps it is because we adopted a monolithic strategy for a pluralistic problem.

The pervasive changes in society and the psychology of affluence legitimized the development of the segmented work force—a work force whose premise was a focus on self-needs—in opposition to an earlier one based on a submissive subservience to a common cause.

The focus-on-self perspective had allowed nondemographic influences such as attitudes, values, esthetic concepts, purpose, and individual needs to become factors to be reckoned with by management. These influences were identical to those marketers used in making branding decisions. In effect, the social agenda of the "fix it" era allowed consumers to play out their wants and needs in the workplace.

A New Definition

Work today is subject to the same pressures as products in the marketplace. It is as if it were a segmented product to be sold to workers, not a commodity we buy from them. Specifically, because the employer/ employee contract has changed, it is those factors which are negotiated in and determinants of the contract, such as compensation, training, career development, etc., that are subject to this market segmentation.

Before we continue, I would like to stress that traditional ways of making human-resource decisions should not be disregarded. Rather, they should be considered as only one of among many possible ways of analyzing the work force. In fact, the key requirement in taking a market segmentation approach is that the human-resource professional should never assume in advance that any one method of segmentation is best. The first task is to muster all probable segments and then choose the most meaningful one with which to work. This approach is analogous to that used in research in the physical sciences where the hypothesis that best seems to explain the phenomenon under investigation is the one chosen for working purposes.

The human-relations movement of the "fix-it" era focused on the segementation based on individual needs and satisfaction to the exclusion of all others and was primarily psychological in orientation. Human-resource systems, however, collected information on a predominantly demographic basis. Occasionally they converged and provided direction for recruitment, promotional policies, retirement planning, etc. But more often than not it just added to the confusion. For example, a recent finding from our ongoing study of the work force called "SIGNAL" shows a 50-point difference between top management and the total labor force on how well companies were perceived by the average employee in satisfying their needs as individuals. Even though we focused on individual needs, we fell far short of our mark.

The New Work Force

As we moved into the '80s, the work values became more entrenched and pervasive. Today we have five clearly defined groups in the work force, each one encompassing approximately one-fifth of the total. These groups have different priorities, different life-styles, and different stances vis-a-vis work and cut across traditional demographic segments.

It is easiest to think of these groups as old-values and new-values workers. The two new-values groups come from a focus on self-orientation. The first group we call "fulfillment seekers." A fulfillment seeker places more emphasis on a job and career than on interpersonal relationships. Commitment to fulfilling work is the key. There is a strong commitment potential to the organization if they find their work fulfilling. What clearly differentiates this group from the other new-values group is that money will not be taken as a substitute for psychic rewards. Demographically, they are highly educated, disproportionately professional, and have the highest concentration in high-tech industries.

The other new-values group is called "money or excitement seekers." They seek a full, rich life-style and the money necessary to achieve it. At work, money is the dominant consideration and they are willing to accept increased monetary rewards to compensate for lack of psychic

125

rewards from work. They are willing to commit to and do more for an organization, to a point. When they have sufficient money to pay for their level of satisfaction outside of work, they will not become involved in commitments that infringe on their life-style interests. Demographically, they tend to be of average education and disproportionately represented in white-collar clerical and sales positions. Interestingly enough, there are more women than men in this category.

Old-values workers, as the label implies, have their roots in the past. They adhere to the traditional work values that have guided American workers for decades—the Protestant work ethic. Old-values workers are categorized in one of three ways. First, there are the uncommitted. This is a segment of the population that is turned-off. They often have adopted an adversarial role or are disillusioned because they are unable to attain the rich, full life they thought they were entitled to. The second group is job-oriented. Specifically, they are interested in security and a job. The third are called the work-oriented. Work-oriented employees are comprised of a relatively well-educated group with a large proportion of professionals who are interested in strengthening their work skills and abilities. They are also strongly committed to their jobs and to working *per se*. However, there is little or no interest in maximizing earnings by making unattractive trade-offs.

It is clear to see from this brief description of the values groups how inadequate demographic information is in determining human-resource policies. Within both the new-values and old-values groups, workers and their needs differ dramatically. For example, although all new-values workers are relatively intolerant of a static ritualistic work environment, fulfillment seekers look for a different structure than do money seekers. Although both thrive on psychic challenges, they seek it differently. They look for career advancement but do not view money in the same way. Human-resources policies must, therefore, recognize that the work force is a segmented community.

New Rules

What are the implications of a segmented work force and the use of a marketing approach to deal with that work force? Several challenges and opportunities come to mind. For example, fringe benefits are a part of every corporate reward system. The pluralistic work force has created a need to move from a uniform benefits package to a "cafeteria" plan. With increasing emphasis on cost effectiveness, managers are looking for ways to "satisfy" employee demands while meeting bottom-line objectives.

A marketing approach provides a mechanism for determining what is really being asked for in a benefits package and how to get workers to buy into it. If we wanted to make health care more cost-effective, what would a marketing approach give us? The myth is that workers view health care as a non-negotiable item. The belief that workers are entitled to the best care money can buy, with someone else footing the bill, provides a major obstacle to cost-containment efforts.

"SIGNAL," however, indicates that values have shifted considerably and that workers are ready to address problems such as the increasing cost of health care. Specifically, we have found the following shifts:

- Workers are developing a new cost-effectiveness orientation. Benefits are now measured more against costs and less against abstract ideals.
- Workers are becoming "smart shoppers"; they are willing to plan, to depend on new information, and to trade off convenience for quality and value.
- Workers have decreased their reliance on traditional providers of goods and services. They are more apt to stress self-reliance and entrepreneurship and are bypassing traditional distributors, including professionals.
- Workers are demanding information about company plans and programs that affect their well-being and they are eager to participate in identifying solutions to problems.

In summary, workers have become more critical and inquisitive than in prior years. They are ready to examine the quality and cost of services such as health care rather than accept the services *carte blanche*. Above all else, they are eager to join forces with their company to solve joint problems.

Conclusion

What has occurred in the last two decades? A business creates systems to meet its own business goals. However, workers' values and attitudes follow the trends and norms in our society. As society and business move in their own particular directions, gaps occur. Marketing segmentation analysis provides a mechanism to define those gaps. Marketing work puts a manager in a position to bridge them.

Human-resources departments and professionals have been asked to fill those gaps by finding new ways to manage employees. Is not the marketing of work to a segmented work force the answer?

Computer Technology and Employee Resistance in Future Work Environments

by

Alan W. Ewert and Alison E. Voight

Computer technology is rapidly becoming an integral part of many administrative and management systems. In 1982 alone, over 1,440,000 computers were shipped throughout the world (Blundell, 1983), with one million of these units being used within the United States. Analysts expect this number to rise to 9.8 million units shipped annually throughout the world by 1990.

Indeed, a new revolutionary, technological wave has begun, bringing with it the promise of dramatic changes in the way people live and work, perhaps even the way they think (Friedrich, 1983). A wide variety of organizations are being touched by the wave of computer technologies. Many agencies are turning to computers as a more efficient and effective means of delivering human services (Sharpless, 1981). One of the first studies to produce data on computer use in human service delivery systems came out of the Public Policy Institute at the University of California, Irvine. Of the over 1,000 municipal governments that responded to the survey, 59 reported at least one computer application in use or under development for one type of human service delivery system: recreation (Sharpless, 1981).

As is true with any major revolutionary change, problems and conflicts may arise as a result. Computers have created a great deal of apprehension and resistance regarding their implementation and uses. This article will attempt to depict the prevalence of computer use in the workplace; staff resistance and deterrents to computer usage; the overall effect of computer usage regarding department functions and their employees; and suggestions for the alleviation of staff resistance.

Prevalence of Computers

Increased work loads, reduced resources, and tighter demands for accountability have forced recreation administrators to explore new and more efficient ways of doing their business. Computers are swiftly infiltrating

Alan W. Ewert is assistant professor, Department of Recreation and Park Management, University of Oregon, Eugene, Oregon. Alison E. Voight is assistant professor, Department of Recreation and Leisure Studies, Lyndon State College, Lyndonville, Vermont.

the management of human services as a more expedient method of delivering services and establishing accountability. Although many professionals feel that the computer is too impersonal for use in a human services field, it should be regarded as a tool, and used as such (Cheng, 1982, p. 14). The many areas in which it has already successfully been implemented include: financial accounting, attendance records, registration, scheduling, reservations, inventory control, and facility management (Cheng, 1982; Howe, 1982; Cheek, 1982).

Regardless of the prevalence of computers, their effectiveness among organizations will ultimately depend on the attitude of managers, administrators, and staff. The role of computers in agency operations and the information they are programmed to produce is placed on a foundation—the management system. If the management system is not functional, then the application from a computer will lead to either redundant information or the non-use of computer services (Siderelis, 1981, p. 121). Basically, the administrator/manager should strive for a usable end-product: a functional computer system, with workable programs, and a staff that *chooses* to work *with* rather than *against*, the computer, resulting in a comprehensive system that creates more positive benefits than negative results.

Generally, the reception of computers by management and administration agencies has been favorable. In a nationwide survey conducted by the Leisure Research Institute at Indiana University in May and June of 1981, 92% of the administrators who responded wanted to see greater use of computers in their departments (Sharpless, 1981). Seventy-five percent felt that computers would greatly improve the way departments do their work, and 76% agreed that computers could solve a great deal of the problems facing their organizations (Sharpless, 1981; Watts, 1980, 1981). But while administrators may be eager to implement computer programs in their departments, their employees, who must work directly with the computer, may be less enthusiastic. Despite the imminence of the computer and the many benefits associated with computer use, many professionals seem to resist the change (Cheng, 1982, p. 14; Malinconico, 1983a).

Staff Resistance and Deterrents to Computer Usage

It is natural for people to resist changes that deviate from a traditional method of operating (Siderelis, 1981). A simple reallocation of a worker's responsibility to accommodate the introduction of the computer may have unfavorable consequences on his/her organizational values and working relationships (Siderelis, 1981, p. 118). Ultimately, the success of the operation that implements a computer into its system will be dependent upon the acceptance of the new technologies by the staff. What is of paramount importance to many employees when faced with computerization and automation is their concern over losing their jobs and/or obtaining the necessary level of skills to be able to effectively use the technology (Strauss and Sayles, 1965; Elizur, 1970; Shepard, 1971; Dorf, 1974; Brod, 1982; Covert and Goldstein, 1980). Siderelis (1981) suggests that there are several reactions to the augmentation of computers, including **aggressive behavior** (attacking or sabotaging the information fed into the computer); **protective behavior** (blaming the computer for operational difficulties or projecting their own failures onto the computer); and **avoidance behavior** (ignoring computer printout information and only using existing information). While it is possible to mandate employee use of computers, negative behaviors might arise as a result of this authoritarian approach.

Because of their unique ability to perform tedious, rote types of tasks, computers are particularly threatening to people who have jobs involving tedious, rote types of work. Paradoxically, personnel involved in human services may find themselves in the uncomfortable position of replacing people with machines that are more efficient. Additional research has further substantiated the staff member's concern over lack of skills or obsolescent skills (Dalton and Thompson, 1970; Shaiken, 1981). The changeover of skills required by the implementation of a computer system can often precipitate an escalating error or anxiety cycle, with debilitating results for the organization as well as for the employee (see Figure 1).

Besides concern over loss of jobs or acquiring the necessary skills to work in a computer-facilitated operation, Shepard (1971) reports that computers can create three aspects of work alienation: powerlessness, meaninglessness, and normlessness. More specifically, introducing computers can cause staff to perceive a lack of control over the work process, an inability to identify one's role in the workplace (a provider of human services or a machine attendant), and a lack of confidence in proper rewards (i.e., the machine gets most of the credit).

Another deterrent to computer use is the wide spectrum of ethical, technical, social, and philosophical problems it may create. Because of their complexity and associated esoteric jargon, computers have the ability to give the appearance of change or increased efficiency while everything actually remains the same (Foster, 1970). Professionals must not fall prey to this ''aura'' of infalibility surrounding the computer. They should avoid the trap of assuming what comes out of the computer printout is completely factual and error-free. Information that is flawed to begin with will be transformed into erroneous data.

Although the high cost of computers is also considered a deterrent to their implementation, the major deterrent is the lack of computer knowledge by department personnel (Sharpless, 1981). So while modern technologies may elicit certain conditions, imagined or actual, the computer becomes a *symbol* of change within the workplace creating uncertain outcomes. This uncertainty produces a stressful condition (Brod, 1982) that may ultimately result in employee resistance to computer technology.

Alleviating Staff Resistance

Resistance to computer technology can be costly both in fiscal as well as human terms. Delayed schedules, staff polarization, and lowered performance all serve to decrease the viability of the organization. Anticipating and alleviating staff resistance to the computer system and the ''change'' it represents is a skill managers and administrators will need to deal with in future situations (Maynard, 1982). Strauss and Sayles (1965, p. 263) address this concern in their statement: ''An organization must anticipate changes by altering its own policies and structure in time to meet these new conditions.''

130

Figure 1

Computer/Employee Anxiety Cycle

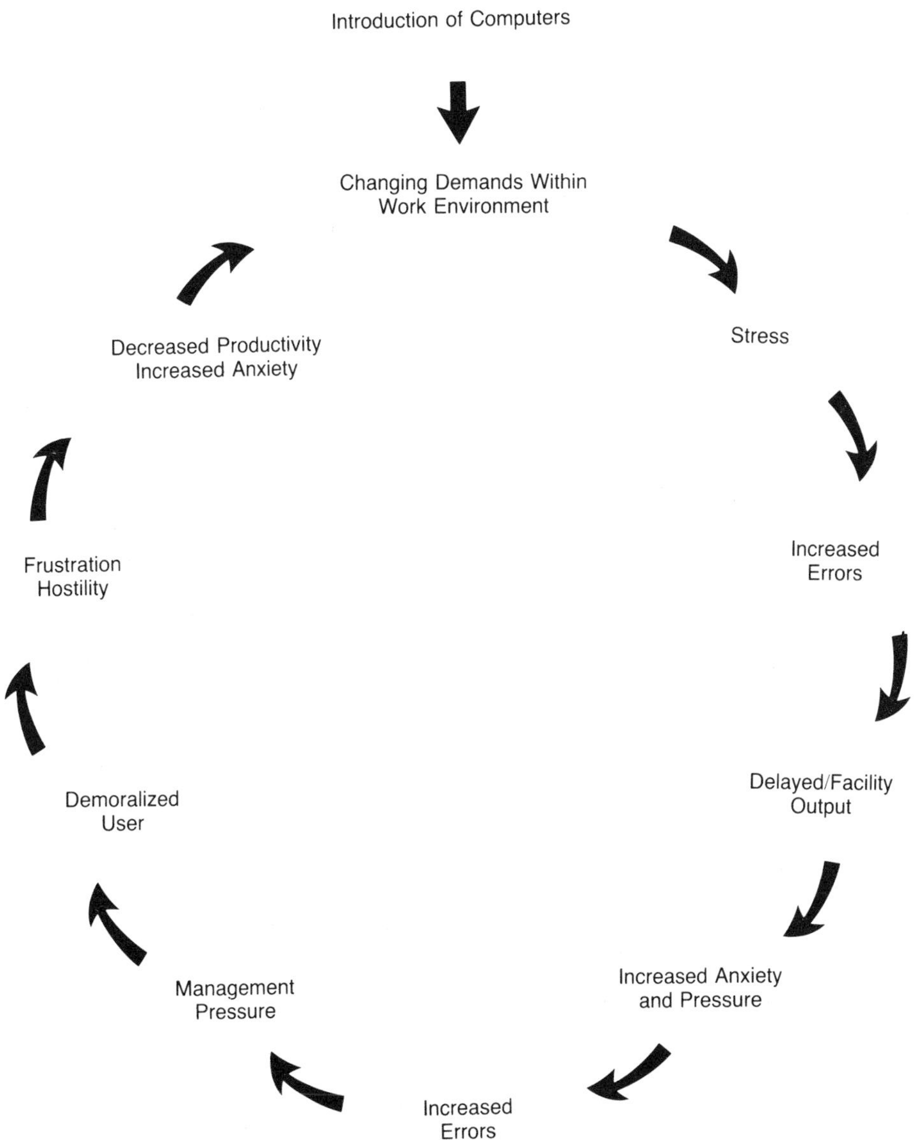

Introduction of Computers

Changing Demands Within
Work Environment

Stress

Decreased Productivity
Increased Anxiety

Increased
Errors

Frustration
Hostility

Delayed/Facility
Output

Demoralized
User

Increased Anxiety
and Pressure

Management
Pressure

Increased
Errors

It should be noted that the computer can, and usually does, bring about very positive results, such as greater efficiency in payrolls, employee records, and report filing. A problem often arises when only a limited number of staff realize these benefits. For example, the computer operator and the superintendent's staff may be the only people in the entire organization who can "see" the beneficial effects of computerization. Other employees only recognize the changing and often greater work requirements. While the benefits are real, the remaining staff may view them as nonexistent because of a lack of awareness. More often, they view the computer as generating more, not less, work for them.

Elizur (1970) reports that after initial resistance to computerization, staff members generally began to like the presence of computers. They found the work more varied but also more demanding, and were more satisfied with job security although upward mobility decreased due to the need for more education or training. Most of the workers studied disliked how the change-over was accomplished, as agencies provided little training and preparatory information. Shutz and Weber (1966) found that work performance did not suffer appreciably when employees were given enough time to adjust to changes brought on by computerization. Wilensky (1972) has suggested three approaches for dealing with any alienation and boredom associated with introducing automation through computers: compensating leisure activities, increased benefits, and job variability.

Along similar lines, Herzberg, Mausner, and Snyderman (1964) and Meyers (1964) investigated motivations to work and found the main motivators of workers to be: achievement, recognition, responsibility, growth, and advancement. If the research of Herzberg, Mausner, and Snyderman is correct, the computer can be a useful tool in providing pathways for greater staff achievement through recognition of growing computer skills, new levels of responsibility, and personal growth. Earlier research (Benne, 1956; Schein, 1960; Zander, 1950; Lewin, 1947) has substantiated the view of facilitating the growth of both the group and the individual through the change process. Zander (1950, p. 10) establishes this point by stating that:

> Resistance will be prevented to the degree that the changer helps the changees to develop their own understanding of the need for the change, and an explicit awareness of how they feel about it, and what can be done about those feelings.

Employers may find the introduction and utilization of the computer to be a useful process for both the development of their staff's specific skills and affective relationships. Short computer training seminars may be valuable in allowing the staff to deal with a subject in which everyone starts with basically the same skill level.

A Planning Strategy

The following strategy has been developed to aid the administrator/manager in planning and implementing a successful computer system for both the organization and the staff:

Time: Allow enough time to adequately plan and think through the system. Important concerns should include: actual needs for computerization; functions of a new system; cost of the system such as consultation,

132

maintenance, acquisition, extra equipment (peripherals), space requirements, supplies, and necessary personnel (Ceriello, 1982).

Personnel: Whatever staff may be "touched" by the computer system should be encouraged to express their concerns and make recommendations. Previous research already cited has confirmed the problem of lack of communication between the higher staff echelon and the line staff members. If appropriate, allow for group decision-making in areas such as: location, users, and training (Malinconico, 1983b). In using computers to aid in the decision-making process, the administrator/manager must be concerned with the following questions: Are decisions made as promptly with computers? Are the decisions as fair with computers as without? And finally, does the computer process offer adequate opportunity and time for reflection and decision-making?

Training: Staff should be made aware of what they can expect from the computer system in terms of changing work requirements and the operating procedures of the organization. Training, for those persons directly involved in the system, should identify the specific communication patterns, i.e., getting the machine to work for the individual, types of work, changing time patterns such as scheduling deadlines, task-related thinking functions, increased hand-eye coordination, and changes in the work environment. The primary goal is to give the employee a sense of control over the machine, rather than feelings of helplessness. Frustrations can be removed by reinforcing coping mechanisms that can lead to greater employee productivity and involvement with the computer. Finally, administrators/managers should strive to create productivity cycles to replace the anxiety cycles previously mentioned. Figure 2 illustrates a computer/employee productivity cycle.

Adequate time for training procedures should be allocated within the organization to allow staff members ample practice sessions with the computer system to upgrade their skills. A four-step procedure can be incorporated in the training phase of the organization: 1) preparing for new demands, 2) handling new demands, 3) evaluating that handling, and 4) improving upon that response.

Identifying Organizational and Individual Needs: While initially considered in the planning stage, organizational needs should be further defined using two criteria: prioritizing and flexibility. Prioritizing needs to occur in the areas of: projects in which the computer is critical, projects in which the computer can be useful, and projects in which other devices such as people can be as equally effective as a computer. Prioritizing can also answer the questions of who is in charge, who gets the information, and how the information can best be used (Rothman and Mosmann, 1976).

From an individual staff member's point of view, computers are often perceived dichotomously, that is, either as a useful tool or problem-causing entity (Lee, 1970; Cancro and Slotnick, 1970). Miller (1971) suggested that a person's attitude is the most important aspect of a successful human-computer relationship. Enabling an individual to see how the computer can improve their operations within the organization will be a powerful tool for the administrator/manager to use in facilitating the staff's transition to computer technologies.

Figure 2

Computer/Employee Productivity Path

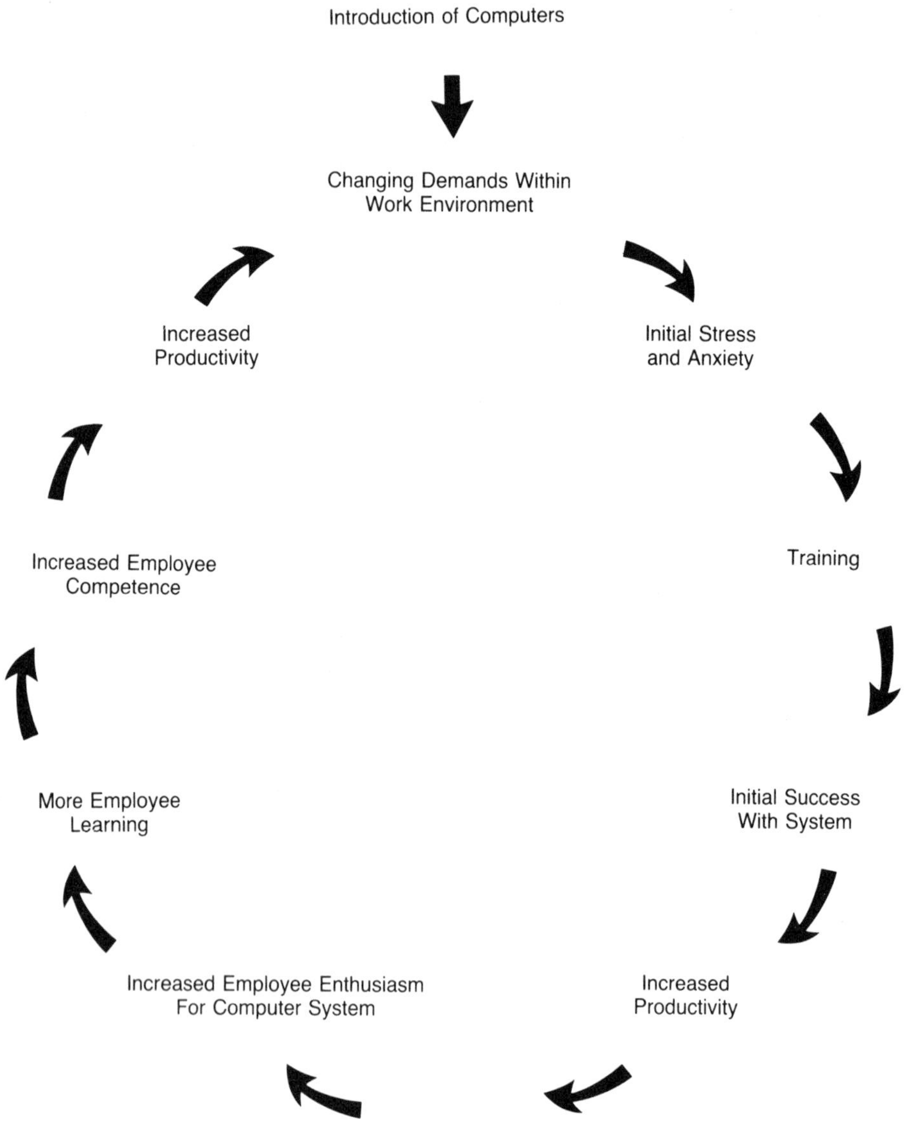

Introduction of Computers

Changing Demands Within
Work Environment

Increased
Productivity

Initial Stress
and Anxiety

Increased Employee
Competence

Training

More Employee
Learning

Initial Success
With System

Increased Employee Enthusiasm
For Computer System

Increased
Productivity

Evaluation of Computer Usage and Department Functions

Any strategy is prone to error through the two factors of conceptualization and implementation. While increasingly sophisticated computer systems will negate the manager/administrator's need for a high level of technical computer competence (Philipson, 1962), evaluation of the computer system in terms of technology and its effects upon the staff will also be important to the overall performance of the organization. In specific terms, the evaluation of the computer operation should include the following questions:

Does the system do what it is supposed to?

Is the system enhancing or deteriorating the morale of the staff?

Are appropriate staff being adequately trained?

Is polarization taking place in the staff—those who are aided by the computer versus those who remain wary of it?

In designing the evaluation format, Thompson and Dalton (1970) have warned against creating one grand performance appraisal to serve all of the administrative and management needs of an organization. Appraisal of the system and the staff's ability to deal with the system should be open and future-oriented.

If the administrator/manager is to implement and operationize computer technologies, care must be exercised in acquiring the proper equipment and integrating the staff with the technology. Computer-generated stress can reduce staff productivity and create alienation. If computers are to be successfully implemented into human-oriented organizations, it will become necessary to be more than mere technicians.

Future work environments will certainly involve a greater use of computerization (Naisbitt, 1982). In a similar fashion, the concern for employee productivity will manifest itself, in part, by a greater emphasis on the psychological and affective health of the worker. If these two "waves" are to work synergistically rather than in opposition, the organization must combine the high-speed efficiency of machines with the sensitivity and feelings of people in an effective but humanistic manner.

References

Benne, K. Deliberate Changing As the Facilitation of Growth. In W. Bennis, K. Benne, & R. Chin (Eds.), *The Planning of Change*. New York: Holt, Rinehart and Winston, Inc., 1964.

Blundell, G. Personal Computers in the Eighties. *Byte*, 1983, *8*(1), 166–182.

Brod, C. Managing Technostress: Optimizing the Use of Computer Technology. *Personnel Journal*, 1982, *61*(10), 753–757.

Cancro, R. & Slotnick, D. Computer Graphics and Resistance to Technology. *American Journal of Psychotherapy*, 1970, *24*, 461–469.

Ceriello, V. The Human Resources Management System: Part 1. *Personnel Journal*, 1982, *61*(10), 764–767.

Cheek, D. Visitor Surveys: A Snap with a Computer. *Parks and Recreation*, 1982, *17*(4), 55–56.

Cheng, V. Computers in Leisure Services. *Recreation Canada*, September 1982, 12–16.

Covert, M.D. and Goldstein, M. Locus of Control as a Predictor of Users' Attitude toward Computers. *Psychological Reports*, 1980, *47*, 1167–1173.

Dalton, G. and Thompson, P. Accelerating Obsolescence of Older Engineers. *Harvard Business Review*, November 1970.

Dorf, R. *Computers and Man*. San Francisco: Boyd and Fraser, 1974.

Elizur, D. *Adapting to Innovation*. Jerusalem: Jerusalem Academic Press, 1970.

Foster, D. Computers and Social Change: Uses and Misuses. *Computers and Automation*, August 1970, 31–33.

Friedrich, O. The Computer Moves In. Time, January 3, 1983, 14–24.

Herzburg, F., Mausner, B., & Snyderman, B. *The Motivation to Work*. New York: John Wiley and Sons, Inc., 1959.

Howe, C. Let Your Computer Do the Calculating. *Parks and Recreation, 17*(1), 70–72.

Lee, R. Social Attitudes and the Computer Revolution. *Public Opinion Quarterly*, 1970, *34*, 53–59.

Lewin, K. Group Decision and Social Change. In T. Newcomb and E. Hartley (Eds.), *Readings in Social Psychology*. New York: Holt, Rinehart and Winston, Inc., 1947.

Maynard, W. Skills Managers Need to Survive. *Administrative Management*, 1982, *43*(12), 33–71.

Malinconico, S. Hearing the Resistance. *Library Journal*, January 15, 1983, 111–113. (a)

Malinconico, S. Listening to the Resistance. *Library Journal*, February 15, 1983, 353–355. (b)

Meyers, M.S. Who Are Your Motivated Workers. *Harvard Business Review*, Jan/Feb 1964, 73–88.

Miller, R. Human Ease of Use Criteria and Their Tradeoffs. IBM Poughkeepsie Technical Report, 1971, TTRoo.2185.

Naisbitt, J. *Megatrends*. New York: Warner Books, 1982.

Philipson, M. (Ed.). *Automation: Implications for the Future*. New York: Vintage, 1962.

Rothman, S. and Mosmann, C. *Computers and Society*. Chicago: Science Research Associates, Inc., 1976.

Schein, E. Interpersonal Communication, Group Solidarity, and Social Influence. *Sociometry*, 1960, *23*(2), 148–161.

Shaiken, H. Microprocessors and Labor: Whose Bargaining Chips? *Technology Review*, 1981, *83*(3), 37.

Sharpless, D. Trends in Computer Use in Parks and Recreation. *Proceedings: National Workshop on Computers in Recreation and Parks*, 1981, 111–116.

Shepard, J.M. *Automation and Alienation: A Study of Office and Factory Workers*. Cambridge, Mass.: MIT Press, 1971.

Shultz, G. & Weber, A. *Strategies for the Displaced Worker*. New York: Harper and Rowe, 1966.

Siderelis, Chrystos. Setting Up for Computerization: An Informational Analysis Approach. *Proceedings: National Workshop on Computers in Recreation and Parks*, 1981, 117–141.

Strauss, G. & Sayles, L. *Personnel: The Human Problems of Management*. Englewood Cliffs, New Jersey: Prentice-Hall, Inc. 1965.

Thompson, P. & Dalton, G. Performance Appraisal: Managers Beware. *Harvard Business Review*, 48(1), 149–157.

Watts, R. Computers in Parks and Recreation Preparation for the Future. *Proceedings: National Workshop on Computers in Recreation and Parks*. 1980, 37–48.

Watts, R. Parks and Recreation Computer Education Survey. *Proceedings: National Workshop on Computers in Recreation and Parks*, 1981, 143–154.

Wilensky, H.L. *Work, Careers, and Leisure Styles*. Cambridge, Massachusetts: Harvard Information Office, 1972.

Zander, A. Resistance to Change: Its Analysis and Prevention. *Advanced Management*, 1950, *15–16*, 9–11.

Tomorrow's Work Dilemma:
Security vs. Access

by

Sanford B. Weinberg

The moving power behind the acceptance of computers is and has been the continuing spread of access to the machines. In the not-very-dim past, a priesthood of data-processing professionals stood guard against all newcomers, making certain that only the jargon-initiated few could ever really touch, operate, or control the holy equipment. But severe shortages of trained personnel, growing pressures for performance, and technological revolutions brought about a generation of machines that, after a number of substages, can be easily and comfortably used by the unwashed multitudes. Microcomputers using menu-driven programs can be operated effectively by any noncyberphobic literate person. Expected advances, to be introduced in the very near future, will replace modified keyboards and typewriter entry systems with voice-activated units, making it possible to verbally command a computer, word processor, or analogous machine, further increasing access and eliminating "literacy" as a condition for successful operation.[1]

There is, however, a more far-reaching matter in the area of increasing access. Accepting the apparently inevitable impact of computers on the workplace, a secondary and more potentially limiting dilemma can be anticipated. As one manager explained, "The only thing worse than me not knowing our inventory would be to have our competitors know as much as we do about it." The centralization of data inevitable in computerization raises a series of questions about the security of that data. The concern about that security may well prove to be the limiting force in the trend toward increased access, reliance upon, and use of computers in tomorrow's workplace.

Security

The FBI currently estimates corporate losses due to violations of computer security to be in excess of three billion dollars per year. The average detected computer theft nets $450,000. Even if discovered, the odds of the thief suffering a prison term are less than one in ten. Clearly, security problems are monumental, and deterrent forces are ineffective.[2]

Sanford B. Weinberg is department chairperson of administrative sciences, Saint Joseph's University, Philadelphia, Pennsylvania.

138

At present, little can be done to prevent computer-related criminal acts. Contrary to popular belief, most security violations do not require a high level of intelligence or esoteric knowledge of a system. Most password keys are poorly protected or easily guessed, and many computer systems will provide suggestions for bypassing internal controls if properly asked. The simple and frightening fact is that almost any trained employee with access to a computer terminal can abuse that access with little fear of serious consequences. Our major operating protections today are post hoc audits that have had only ineffectual success in doing more than halting discovered abusive practices; the basic morality of our working populace; and a series of fast-exploding myths about how complex computer security systems really are.[3]

As access increases, the potentials for violations of security progress geometrically. It becomes more difficult to pinpoint the source of a breach. It becomes more difficult to build in limiting controls. And opportunities for unauthorized tampering grow as remote units are scattered around a company or around the country.

Many units, for example, are connected to computer mainframes via phonelines. The potential to tap those lines, and hence monitor sensitive material or access restricted systems, has always been real. The recent and projected shifts to microwave and satellite-bounced phone transmissions make tapping even simpler, and even more difficult to detect. Incidentally, in light of recent court rulings there is some question about whether or not any post hoc legal remedies exist to deal with intercepted microwave transmissions. It may well be quite legal to use a dish antenna to listen in on your competitor's computer, gaining confidential information about pricing, finances, or personnel.[4]

The move toward increased access, unless coupled with a parallel and as yet unrealized move toward more sophisticated security systems, creates a serious dilemma. More users means an increase in remote stations, and thus greater opportunity for violation. The greater number of users weakens responsibility and forestalls apprehension possibilities. An increase in access encourages greater depth as well as breadth of exposure, providing increased opportunity to accidentally or purposely discover methods of bypassing existing security restrictions. In short, the pressures to increase access are running head on into the growing problems of computer security.

Scenarios

Some authors of science fiction have envisioned a world in which the dilemma is solved a la 1984. The society so predicted is filled with computers in every home, but police officers (sometimes in the same persona) looking over every shoulder. A few optimistic technologists have argued instead that new breakthroughs in security will allow us to slip between the horns of the dilemma, having universal access with tight privacy restrictions. Recently, for example, Honeywell introduced a system with a security protection guarantee, claiming it could not be violated in less than three years of intensive work. A Defense Department "tiger team" testing the system successfully breached it in less than 12 hours.[5]

The far more likely scenario, though, suggests a significant modification in the workplace, varying not only from the status quo of computer use but from the apparent trends of today as well. The conflicting pressures for increased access and more strict security are likely to produce a shift over the next five to ten years (until blueprint-stage technologies providing greater security are perfected) to a computerized workplace unlike that imaged by most theorists, dreamers, or industrial engineers.

Currently, networked intelligent terminals linked to a central data base predominate the market. Satellite stations used primarily for word processing, MIS applications, production control, MRP, and similar functions connect to common disk storage, printing, and processing facilities. Many managers, fearful of spiraling maintenance costs and trends toward departmental "empire building," have resisted requests for freestanding units, opting instead for the network systems. Diverse physical locations, too, argue strongly for the interactive and interconnecting units.

The effect is generally a company in which various departments interact with near simultaneous spontaneity with a central computer, using very limited local memory capacity to compensate for queuing delays and for handling brief word-processing functions. Departments can instantaneously interact with the main computer, greatly increasing the speed with which data can be accessed and transmitted.

The vulnerability such a situation creates, with the potential for abusive breach of internal restrictions, is not likely to continue to be tolerated. Compromises, including some loss of flexibility and speed, are likely to provide a necessary alternative in the name of stronger security protections.

Prediction

To balance the counteracting pressures of the need for security and a growing demand for free access to data and processing within a subsystem, we are likely to see a scenario relying with increasing commonality upon a network of microcomputers. Each free-standing micro could be used for different and secure computing functions, with a central switchboard linking them with specific authorization to shared or common data bases and programs.

The use of a telephone-type network is particularly appropriate, for it allows constant monitoring of shared access, it allows rapid and accurate networking, and it provides the security of a two-step linkage process. That is, completing a phone call today requires (a) dialing the proper access code and (b) speaking or interacting over the phone line. The connection and communication steps are electronically and physically separate.

Hypothesizing a continued need for rapid access and a growing security concern, what changes in the workplace can we reasonably imagine? The most reasonable expectation would be a continuing growth of telecommunication, using phonelines and equivalents to share restricted-access data while using high-memory (256K) disk drive connected microcomputers for most tasks. This combination requires a worker population with high user training but little expertise in technical and programming skills, and requires a general managerial acceptance of the presence and use of

140

the microcomputer units. Evidence of such acceptance will probably be realized when executives accept the substitution of magnetic (microcomputer) records for paper (printed) equivalents.

It is reasonable to expect, then, that the office of five to ten years from now will be equipped with one or more free-standing microcomputers, and with a security-controlled networking access device allowing linkage to other data bases. Managers will find themselves with responsibility for controlling the networking system to prevent the kinds of abuses that can result in a system reversal (and unauthorized access to internal systems). Workers will find increasing demands for computer literacy. On the other hand, the security pressures explained above will probably prevent a more widespread use of linked mainframe computer terminals, or of electronic systems with the potential to replace more carefully monitored human workers.

Conclusion

There is little or no doubt that computers will have a profound effect upon the future workplace. Most predictions, however, have failed to examine the impact of increased concern for security as a mitigating factor restricting the spread of general-access computer systems. The use of microcomputers, externally linked to shared data bases, will help to compensate for the counteracting access-security pressures.

Notes

1. Shorr, Melinda, "Voice Recognition," *Yankee Group*, September 1981.

2. Becker, Jay J., *The Investigation of Computer Crimes*, Dept. of Justice, Law Enforcement Administration, 1980.

3. Parker, Donn B., *Ethical Conflicts in Computer Science and Technology*, Arlington, VA, AFIPS Press, 1979.

4. Wurglitz, Alfred M., J. D., private interview, February 1983.

5. Kolata, Gina, "When Criminals Turn to Computers, Is Anything Safe?" *Smithsonian*, August 1982.

Innovation and
Economic Strategy

Innovation and New Institutional Structures

by

John Diebold

I've always been fascinated by the Industrial Revolution and I think one of the questions one immediately poses, as I did when I was doing my student work, is, Why was the Industrial Revolution a revolution? Was it the machines? The conclusion I came to was that it wasn't the machines: The steam engine, the cotton gin, the railway, the power loom— all were extraordinary inventions. But the reason they were revolutionary was because they were agents for great social change. They were revolutionary because they took people out of the fields and brought them into factories. They gave us mass production and, through mass production, the first society in which wealth was not confined to the few. The Industrial Revolution produced a sense of hurry, a sense of time, a sense of goal that simply didn't exist previously. It changed human society and that's what was revolutionary, not the machines themselves. And I think that today, looking ahead at what is happening, the same thing is true. I think that if you had asked Richard Arkwright or James Watt if they thought they were changing society, they certainly would not have thought so. They were simply concentrating on what they were doing. One of the problems is that we are changing society with many of today's computer technologies, and it's very important to be conscious of that fact, and to think much more widely, as many of our leading scientists are doing, of what the social consequences and what the human meaning might be.

Computers Will Revolutionize Other Businesses

The really interesting developments have either already started and will be increasingly important in the years ahead, or are not quite recognized yet but will be very important in the years ahead. The computer industry has developed and grown in the last 30 years to what is today a big industry, but it has already started to shift. It is no longer only a capital industry producing capital goods. It has also become a consumer product industry, and that is going to be a very important part of the years ahead—

John Diebold is president of The John Diebold Group, Inc., New York, New York. This article is based on a speech given at the World Future Society's Fourth General Assembly, "Communications and the Future," Washington, D.C., July 1982.

not only products, but services, and not only the direct products, but the indirect products, the incorporation of chips in automobiles and consumer products of all kinds, and in capital products of all kinds. There are a lot of consequences from this because it means that the main determinant of economic competitiveness internationally is increasingly going to be success in this field because this industry is going to determine success in almost all other services and in almost all other kinds of product areas. And the fact that it's not only becoming a consumer field but it's also going to materially change virtually all other businesses is of the utmost importance in terms of our own nation's well-being.

Humans Will Interact More Easily with Machines

The second observation I would like to make concerning the years ahead is the fact that the changes that are going on in the technology involve fundamentally extraordinary technical steps that will lead to material decreases in costs, which means that machines can begin to do more and more complex things that will make things easier for human beings. Basically, the human/machine interface is getting much easier, and that is what I think is the real meaning of the technological changes: for example, the voice machines that respond in any voice you want; machines that handle graphics and that you can communicate with in graphics; and the great portability of these machines. All of these technological changes mean that we can begin to build systems that are able to handle the flow of information, which is the principal determinant of our society, and that are friendly and easy to use and that can adapt themselves to the human need in this area. That's a very important kind of change and it's composed of hundreds of innovations.

The intertwining of this change with the other great developments of our times—the biological developments—is inevitable and obvious. The interesting part of the biological developments has to do with the fact that there are enormous volumes of information encoded within cells, which immediately shows you that we haven't gone as far as people think we've gone with regard to density of storage and the limits that we have in the current machine system. Obviously it's possible to go very, very much further than most of the people thinking about it from the outside realize.

The intertwining of these two developments is going to be formidable.

Several years ago, Vannevar Bush said we would end up with computers implanted in each of us, and we already have chips implanted in heart devices and we will have a multiplicity of increasing human involvements in this, but it also shows us the way toward doing a lot of things in terms of circuitry.

Computers Will Change What We Do

The third observation that I have is the fact that, so far, most of the use of automation has been to mechanize what we have done, what we do, to mechanize work that we've been doing. To a certain extent the second phase has started, and it will be an enormously important phase, and that is to change what we do. Already you can begin to find examples of the parameters of competition in business being totally changed as a result of the imaginative use of this new technology.

Computer games, for instance, constitute an industry that is already twice the size of the movie industry in the United States. The computer-game industry, which didn't exist a couple of years ago, is totally dependent upon interactive TV and computers.

We now are totally changing the structure of some industries—not by mechanizing what we did yesterday but by providing services that weren't provided at all previously. This will be the dominant characteristic of the years ahead: the fact that we will provide services and products that simply weren't provided in the past. It is no longer a question of mechanizing what we've done in the past, but of doing quite new things. And one of the things that I've always used as my own construction on the future is that first, you mechanize what you did yesterday; second, you find that what you do changes; and third, you find that the society in which you're doing it brings about the greatest change of all.

A few years ago, the stereotype was that developments in automation and computers meant rigid systems, highly centralized, monolithic types of structures that were de-humanizing. Today it's exactly the reverse. They are highly decentralized, very flexible, very human, increasingly friendly, and very easy to adapt in any way that people who are using them want. And what that means is, you make it easy to unleash human imagination and what that leads us to is something that we can hardly begin to guess. But it unleashes the most important force we have and that's really what is happening in this field.

New Policy Issues

My first observation concerning the future is that, to date, the developments in automation and computers have raised relatively few discernible public-policy problems. Some of us feel that a lot of problems have been raised, but very few people perceive them at this point. But the period immediately ahead of us will witness the appearance of an increasing array of public-policy problems relating to this technology, and it's a very wide array indeed. What's a branch of a bank? Is a terminal a branch? What kind of communications policy should our country have? What about the rest of the world?

We have a growing array of problems that increasingly encompass all areas of our public-policy process, but we have a very fragmented institutional structure to deal with them. One example is antitrust. I cannot help but feel that it would be a fascinating irony if what the two Japanese companies have been indicted for in terms of theft of information from IBM is precisely the information that the European Economic Community (EEC) is trying to achieve through their antitrust actions. The Europeans' proposed remedy in their antitrust action would give precisely the information that the Japanese, according to the indictments, have been responsible for stealing!

Another irony of that situation is that if the EEC prevails, the beneficiary will be the Japanese because the one thing the European organizations have demonstrated in the last 30 years is an inability to bring to market competitive products in precisely these areas, and the one thing that the Japanese have demonstrated is the ability to do so. But what I'm trying to point out is that we now face a lot of real public-policy problems, and

I believe we're going to find many more of them. The most pressing of these is how to maintain the dynamism of U.S. society in terms of innovation.

Our Real Problems

My second observation is that our problems tend to be debated at what I believe is an entirely incorrect level. The crisis issues of the moment—energy, or inflation, or interest rates, or whatever the current crisis may be—are not our real problems. Our real problems are a series of fundamental institutional problems. I've identified four. You can pick a much wider list, but four might give you an idea of what I mean.

Maintaining Our Ability to Innovate

The first problem is, How can we in the United States maintain the ability to innovate, which is what has put us in the leadership position that we enjoy in the technology of automation? We've led because we can innovate; that is the thing we are best at. The great strength of America is its ability to innovate. This ability comes from the mobility of the highly educated population, the American belief in backing small enterprises and in getting things started. There is a whole mix of things that have made us very dynamic in this regard.

But how do we ensure that the marvelous engine of cornucopia will continue to spew off the things that our society rests on, and that the marvelous stream of innovations from the Silicon Valley, Route 128, the Hudson Valley, and other parts of the country will continue. Our strength is innovation. What do we do to maintain it?

We now have a society in which more and more factors work against taking risk. How do we maintain one in which there is a value system that encourages risk? I think this is worth a lot of attention and is a major determinant of what happens next.

Lengthening Our Time Horizons

A second problem is our time horizons. We have a very short time-scale in our decision-making, and that is true both at the private as well as public level. We tend to use a variety of very sophisticated tools such as discounted cash flow, which lead to decisions favoring short- rather than long-term investments. This is particularly true in periods of high interest rates. We have a time-scale in the political system that is extraordinarily short when one considers it is an area where decisions should be made not just for the lifetime of our children, but also for their children's lifetime. This ought to be the scale of thinking, and it isn't at all. Once, in our society, it was. I think we have a serious problem, and a very complex one.

I've done some writing about it. It's not something we can quickly solve, because there are many factors involved. But I think that this is a problem that ought to receive a good deal of attention. At the very least, we ought to make decisions that are relevant to the lifetime of our children—which is not a particularly long period ahead to be thinking about, yet totally beyond the time horizon used in most decision-making today.

Trade-off Systems

The third problem is really a series of problems—problems of government and of the social structure that we operate within. For example, we have gradually built up a system in which there are thousands of places in which you can veto doing something, but we have no system of trade-offs—no organized method or way of going about setting priorities. We can block things all over the place—and every year we invent new ways, either legislatively or with the help of the massive numbers of lawyers we're turning out. We have gradually developed all kinds of veto points in society, but we have failed to develop trade-off systems. At some point, society has to be able to say, "We want to do all of these things but we can't," "This is more important than that," or "We can go so far on this and so far on that." We have very crude ways of making such decisions, but we really need a much better approach to setting priorities and providing trade-off mechanisms. We really don't have a workable system, and it's a very serious shortcoming in our society. It's very easy to find an authoritarian solution, but it's very tough to find a democratic solution, and that's what we need.

Another facet of this issue is our lack of an adequate coordinating mechanism. How do we bring about trade-offs and coordinate our actions when arriving at public decisions? For example, how do we, as a society, stay ahead in the field of computers and automation? We now are ahead in it but we have a lot of very complex issues affecting what happens next, and we don't have a very good coordinating mechanism for handling what the implications are. The current debate over communications is another very good example. We don't have a good mechanism for arriving at public policy in this area and for taking account of the many variables that need consideration from the standpoint of our society's future well-being.

We don't know how to arrive at such policy decisions and still keep flexibility and freedom, but it certainly ought to be possible to do so. I think that it may be easier to do that than to convert short-term to longer-term time horizons, but we certainly need to find a way to do it. The Germans and the Japanese both are able to do a better job than we do. The French go at it in their way. I don't think we should copy any of those, but devising our own approach is a task worth spending time on.

Understanding the implications of discernible future change is an area that we ought to be innovating in. Some years ago, I suggested that we create autonomous institutes of the future—publicly funded but not tied to current budgets and insulated by public boards not related to the administrations. The institutes could take contradictory positions on particular issues relating to the current impact of discernible future change, and to the future impact of current decisions. I continue to think that such institutes would be very useful. We clearly need some institutional invention in that area.

A Guiding Vision

The fourth and last problem is that of creating what I've characterized as a guiding vision for society. French president Francois Mitterrand has stated that France's future society and economy will be determined by computers and automation; Japan's Ministry of International Trade and Industry (MITI) has said that the main determinant of international competitiveness in the future in all fields is going to be the computer; and Singapore premier Lee Kuan Yew has made similar statements. These people have some kind of guiding vision and some view of how you draw things together. We need to invent a way to do that without decreasing our ingenuity or our individual initiatives, and without getting us into a structure that is not democratic or that goes against our history. We are going through an extraordinary social revolution and the changes in computers and in automation are one of the principal motive forces of that change. Our task is to try to ensure that this change ends up being to the benefit of mankind and not to its detriment. And the institutional change, the institutional inventing, and the political questions in this area are absolutely key determinants to our success. Regrettably, I see very little going on that is encouraging in that area. I see a lot that isn't.

Some people are trying very hard to come to grips with this, and I think many more people should be concerned. I think we need to rethink the institutional relationships within our society because the technology has outpaced them, and we have outmoded structures in many areas that keep us from unleashing the human forces in the U.S. and other countries so that we can make good use of the technology that we've created.

We must come to grips with the task of really making sure that we, as a society, use technology and science in an imaginative way. And it is that aspect that I think we should focus on in looking ahead at automation.

An Economic Strategy for the 1980s

by

Gary Hart

I'd like to offer some perspective on how the high-technology revolution can be helped or hindered by a conservative institution—our government.

When I use the term "conservative" to describe the federal government, I'm not referring to current political philosophies. I'm talking, from a more institutional viewpoint, about an enterprise responsible for balancing the needs and concerns of some 230 million people, an institution that historically has functioned best through incremental change, balancing of competing interests, and hard-fought compromise.

Furthermore, history shows that there's a considerable gap between the development of a new technology and an ability to comprehend and adjust to all its ramifications. Many of our elected officials, all our regulators, are products of an older generation that is basically computer-illiterate, and that is, at a minimum, a bit wary about where all this change is headed.

It could very well be that the only people who have an intuitive sense of how this technological revolution will affect our democracy are the twelve year-olds playing "Donkey Kong" over at the local convenience store. But until it's their turn to assume the political leadership of this country, we'll be dealing, to a certain extent, with a "lost generation" of political figures. We've got an incredible task ahead of us if we are to educate the federal government to work as an ally, rather than as an impediment, to our future progress.

There is also the awesome challenge of re-educating the American worker to accept this new infusion of information technologies in the workplace. The fact is the drive toward the highly automated factory will affect American jobs and jobholders on an unprecedented scale. We will see a radical restructuring of work; current work skills will be devalued and new ones will be created at an ever-increasing rate. As many as 45 million existing jobs could be affected by factory and office automation, and much of that impact will occur in the next 20 years.

One doesn't have to be an expert in political science to guess that the frustrations caused by this rapid change will be expressed in the political arena.

Gary Hart is a Democratic U.S. senator from Colorado.

I say this not in a spirit of pessimism, but merely to present an honest picture of the tasks we face. In fact, I'm very confident that the American system, more than any of our competitors, is well-structured to use the opportunities provided by "high tech" developments to strengthen our entire industrial base.

As a nation, we face a basic choice. We can engage in a battle between competing regions and competing industries for a share in piecemeal federal programs. Or we can try to get beyond the unnecessary and divisive sunrise/sunset and frost-belt/sun-belt debates and develop a strategy for encouraging the economic health of the nation as a whole.

That's what I believe we should do—but we're not doing it today. Today, the federal government is practicing an ad hoc industrial policy, made up of subsidies and benefits for individual industries. Just a few examples of current industrial assistance programs make this point:

- Total expenditures for research for commercial fisheries are five times higher than R&D on new steel technologies.
- $5 billion was spent on R&D for the nuclear power industry, but only $943 million for coal.
- Tax breaks to the timber industry in 1980 totalled $455 million, while the semiconductor industry received no direct assistance.

Look also at the "safe harbor" leasing provisions of the 1981 tax law. They were intended, in part, to encourage new investment by our older industries. Instead, they were used to shelter income by some of our biggest and most profitable oil companies. And tax law encourages hostile take-overs and mergers—with no new productive benefit to the economy—by making money borrowed for such purposes tax-deductible.

We need a more rational set of policies that takes into account the needs of our economy today and for the next decade. We need policies that will help growing industries succeed and older industries become and remain competitive. Let me outline seven elements of such a strategy.

First, we need a process, initiated at the highest level of government— by the president—to bring about industry-by-industry agreements on modernization and growth. Representatives of management, labor, and the major sources of capital would sit down together to design ways to help our major industries become more competitive in this changing economy.

Most importantly, this proposal of presidentially negotiated industrial modernization agreements is designed to make basic American manufacturing industries the most modern and the most competitive in the world. The notion that we can rely on foreign autos, steel, chemicals, textiles, and other manufactured goods is unacceptable to me and to most Americans. We can and must compete, but it will not happen by protecting worn-out industries—or by accident.

Second, our approach to trade must be revised to provide greater competitiveness and greater access for American products abroad. I introduced a bill to address the restrictive trade practices toward high-technology products by some of our competitor nations. The idea behind the bill, which has been incorporated largely into the trade bill reported by the Senate Finance Committee, is to promote trade liberalization, rather than have our government duplicate the protectionist policies embraced by our

152

competitors.

Third, we need to review and revise our regulatory policies to ensure that they are supportive of our efforts to strengthen American opportunities.

Fourth, we need to increase government support for research and development. The percentage of spending for R&D in this country has fallen behind that of some of our international competitors, especially in the area of "pure" as opposed to "applied" research.

The government should dedicate more attention to R&D and make more funding available for it. But we should also encourage cooperative research programs among private companies. Indeed, I feel that this is one of the key domestic initiatives needed to spur the development of our high-tech companies.

Fifth, we must invest heavily in education.

The first step is to establish excellence in education. Twenty-five years ago, the launching of Sputnik transformed our educational system and brought new emphasis to critical scientific and math teaching. Today, the challenge is no less serious, and we must once again bring our educational system into line with today's realities. To this end, I introduced the American Defense Education Act, which focuses on improving our deficient science, math, and language studies throughout our nation's schools.

At the university level, we are not graduating an adequate supply of scientists, engineers, and technicians. Plenty of students are eager to enroll, but our engineering and science schools do not have enough laboratories, equipment, or professional faculty to meet the demand. Moreover, more than a third of the doctoral degrees awarded by American universities in engineering last year went to non-U.S. citizens on temporary visas.

To break this bottleneck, federal support, through National Science Foundation grants, should be directed to universities for expanding and improving science and engineering facilities and for supporting faculty research and graduate students seeking advanced degrees.

More generally, we need to enact a "High Technology Morrill Act" that would concentrate our resources and energies and do for high technology what the first Morrill Act, the Land-Grant College Act of 1862, did for American agriculture.

Finally, training and retraining literally millions of American workers will be a, if not *the*, major employment challenge of the 1980s. We need a broad-scale, flexible program to meet the immense, changing, and diverse needs of American workers. One such system that looks quite promising is the Individual Training Account in which joint employer-employee contributions would establish for each worker an account that may be used, when the worker is displaced, for retraining and for relocation.

Sixth, we have to solve the most serious problems facing new enterprises—the need for capital. We can enlarge the pool of available capital by identifying and employing underutilized capital resources, such as pension funds. They constitute an enormous potential source of capital: $800 billion this year, $4 trillion by the year 1995. Pension funds have remained largely untapped because of regulations that are too restrictive and do not recognize the current capital-formation needs of our nation.

We should also consider altering bank regulations to encourage equity investment in small firms. And by easing regulatory and application requirements on small business loans, we can reduce the relatively high cost of obtaining them.

And at the state level, state development finance corporations should provide small businesses not only financial assistance but physical resources—such as computers, laboratories, and office space—and managerial resources—such as management counseling and assistance in labor negotiations—as well.

Finally, we should encourage entrepreneurial activity in all areas of industry. We should maximize the unique assets of the American industrial culture—and that means creating the necessary preconditions for entrepreneurial activity to expand and flourish. One reason I reject the Japanese model for industrial growth is that its emphasis on centralization and consensus works to inhibit the risk-takers, the entrepreneurs.

Entrepreneurial activity is opportunistic by its very nature, so no static federal model is going to work. But by working to eliminate many of the impediments to entrepreneurial success, we can allow the risk-takers in our society to reach the gold ring and succeed.

These are some examples of the kinds of creative approaches we could take if we had a well-thought-out national industrial strategy. The potential clearly exists for developing policies that will enable our high-tech industry and related businesses to compete aggressively in the future.

Americans, after all, are not afraid of change—we love it. No nation has been more willing to experiment, to take risks, than ours.

Technological Innovation and Economic Development

by

Fred Best

These remarks have been prepared to facilitate discussion of the role of technological innovation in the overall scheme of economic development. The following sections will discuss: (1) the growth and importance of high-technology industries to economic revitalization, (2) the activities and findings of the California Commission on Industrial Innovation, and (3) an exploratory framework for isolating and assessing economic problems and potential solutions.

The Growth and Importance of Technological Innovation

During the last few years, the United States has been confronted with waves of technological innovation that have provided hope for rekindling the dynamics of the American economy. Since the 1960s there has been discussion of the impacts of technology and automation on the American economy.[1] Although technological advances occurred at a crisp rate, nothing resembling the predicted tidal wave of change emerged until the last few years.

After years of forecasts, we are not confronted by wave after wave of innovations that are having profound effects on our personal and occupational lives. The advent and growth of the video recorder is just beginning to revolutionize communication and entertainment. Over three million Americans purchased home and personal computers during 1982, and some six million more are expected to make similar purchases in 1983.[2] If the cost of purchased or rented computer time continues to decline at its historic rate of 50% every 2½ years, and the complexity of utilization is reduced by "user-friendly" software,[3] the assimilation of computers into every aspect of our lives can be expected to explode at geometric rates.

The number of industrial robots used within the United States has grown from 200 in 1970 to 3,500 in 1980, and is expected to pass 35,000 by 1990.[4] Perhaps more important is the 'cybernetic' promise of integrating

Fred Best is president of Pacific Management and Research Associates, Sacramento, California.

computers and automated machinery. The growing use of CAD/CAM systems (Computer-Assisted Design/Computer-Assisted Manufacturing) now allows industrial planners to design products on computer screens and then reformat machinery on the shop floor by pushing a few buttons.[5] The implications for increasing productivity and product diversity are spellbinding.[6]

Other innovations in the areas of energy production and utilization, biotechnology, new materials, and medical services offer equally revolutionary implications.[7]

The direct and indirect importance of expanding "high-tech" industries to the U.S. economy promises to be phenomenal. Computers, robots, communication technologies, and other innovative products are overshadowing and sometimes displacing traditional markets. For example, the value of the home and personal computer market has grown from $1.8 billion in 1980 to approximately $4.9 billion in 1982.[8] If the number of "personal computers" sold worldwide grows from about 1.5 million in 1982 to the 11 million projected for 1990,[9] the market implications are startling.

The direct and indirect impacts on the job market are equally earthshaking. Nationally, the growth of employment in high-technology industries alone will account for some 7% of all new jobs between 1980 and 1990. In California, these industries will directly provide about 9% of all new jobs (see Tables 1 and 2).[10] Indirectly, these industries are expected to stimulate about twice this amount again in support and service jobs.[11]

Beyond job creation, the technologies produced by these industries will fundamentally alter the nature of work and skills required from employees in every sector of the economy. Word-processing and communication technology is just beginning to affect office work,[12] and CAD/CAM and robotics will drastically change the face of America's manufacturing and commerce sectors. These changes not only offer new hope for increased productivity, economic growth, and new job opportunities but also confront us with the challenge of negotiating institutional and human adjustments that have not been faced since the first "Industrial Revolution."

The challenges and opportunities presented by technological innovation are particularly pronounced in California. Since the early days of aerospace and atomic research, California has been an acknowledged leader in technological innovation. This lead has been maintained with computers, biotechnology, energy research, medical breakthroughs, and robot design. Clearly, encouragement of these industries and responses to the adjustments they foster is a primary policy concern of the state government.

The California Commission on Industrial Innovation

In an effort to assess the direction of technological innovation and encourage its growth within the California economy, Governor Edmund G. Brown, Jr., established the California Commission on Industrial Innovation by Executive Order during November 1981. This commission, for which I had the privilege of serving as deputy director, was chaired by Governor Brown. The commission and an interlocking set of advisory

156

Table 1

Sources of California Jobs, 1970–1990

	1970	1980	1990	Growth 1980–1990
Total Jobs	8,023.9	11,146.5	13,917.0	24.9%
High Technology	273.0	492.2	726.7	47.6
Computer Services	11.4	43.3	128.3	196.3
Computers	52.8	97.1	163.0	67.9
Instruments	50.3	123.1	147.5	26.4
Communication Equipment	102.9	130.1	163.3	25.5
Electronic Components	55.6	98.6	124.6	19.8
Service	1234.8	2082.9	2856.6	37.1
Trade	1530.8	2267.5	2917.2	28.7
Finance, Insurance, Real Estate	374.5	620.9	794.5	28.0
Other Manufacturing	1078.7	1338.9	1642.0	22.6
Mining	31.4	42.9	51.9	21.0
Aircraft/Space	217.7	213.3	237.7	11.4
Self-Employed, Household Workers, Other	1858.3	2321.1	2736.5	17.5
Government	1424.7	1766.9	1953.9	10.6

Table 2
Employment in California's High-Technology Industries

Industry	1980 Employment	1990 Employment	1980–1990 Growth Rate
Biotechnology	2,000	9,000	300.5%
Photovoltaics	1,000	4,000–10,000	900.0%
Robotics/Computer-Aided Manufacturing	1,000	5,000–10,000	900.0%
Computer Software and Data Processing Services	43,300	128,300	196.3%
Computers and Peripherals	97,100	163,000	67.9%
Electronics Components	98,600	124,600	19.8%
Aircraft and Space	213,300	237,700	11.4%
Instruments	123,100	147,500	26.4%
Communication Equipment	130,100	163,300	25.5%
TOTAL High Technology	709,500	993,400	40.0%
TOTAL California	11,146,500	13,917,000	24.9%

committees worked throughout 1982 to conduct analysis and develop recommendations. Attention was focused upon the three areas of:

1. Financing research and investment in technological innovation.
2. Adjusting education to better meet the needs of emerging jobs.
3. Encouraging more productive relations between management and labor.

The commission met six times during 1982. During this time, an emphasis was placed on open dialogue in an effort to avoid needless polarization of representatives from different interests and to foster productive "problem-solving" activities.

Over the year, the commission produced a series of technical reports assessing current trends and emerging developments in key "high-tech" industries,[13] and a final report titled *Winning Technologies*, which summarizes analysis and recommends policies to encourage technological innovation and facilitate their assimilation into the U.S. economy and society.[14] Highlights of this final report follow:

Introduction and History of Commission (Chapter 1): This chapter summarizes the formation of the commission and highlights some of the leading concerns of individual members.

Toward a National Industrial Strategy (Chapter 2): Issues are concerning whether or not state and federal governments should engage in a more explicit effort to work with business, labor and other groups to develop a "strategic plan" to encourage our most promising industrial sectors. California and United States policies are compared to those of European countries and Japan.

Encouraging Investment and Research in Technological Innovation (Chapter 3): This chapter reviews current data concerning investment and research and suggest a variety of approaches for accelerating these activities. Some of the recommendations include expansion of government grants and tax credits to encourage research and development, removal of unnecessary anti-trust barriers to cooperative research, elimination of long-term capital gains taxes, use of pension funds to encourage innovation and more reciprocal trade agreements.

General Educational and Job Training Needs for the Future (Chapter 4): A review of the best available state and national data concerning the nature of employment in the future suggests a need to improve and expand the caliber of math, science, and technical education, develop effective approaches for retraining mid-career workers, and provide general skills for living in a more technically complex society.

Elementary and Secondary (Chapter 4): This chapter, developed primarily by Michael Kirst, notes a critical shortage of math and science teachers at the K-12 level and suggests possible solutions, emphasizes the importance and potentials of computer training and computer-assisted instruction along with recommendations, suggests a variety of incentives that might be used to increase the study of math and science, and outlines potential revenue sources.

Vocational Education and Job Training (Chapter 5): This chapter recommends a "Master Plan" for vocational and job training that would emphasize performance assessment and integrated planning to insure optional use of resources; suggests improved linkages between education and work through job-based training, increased involvement of business and labor in educational planning, and selected use of private sector resources; proposes increased emphasis on updating teachers, curriculum, and educational facilities; and supports a variety of steps to provide effective retraining opportunities for established workers.

Higher Education and Graduate Training (Chapter 6): This chapter examines today's existing shortage of scientists and engineers and suggests expanding training capacities by selectively increasing faculty salaries, providing assistance and incentives to encourage graduate study in selected fields, and improving campus-based teaching and research facilities. Initiatives are suggested to improve the "technical literacy" of college graduates, including a "liberal science" program; and resumed emphasis is urged for campus-based research activities. Revenue sources and resource realignments are suggested.

Partnerships for Productivity (Chapter 8): This chapter discussed how undue polarization between management and labor can undercut the motivation to work and foster resistance to technological innovations that are essential to economic revitalization. Recommendations to give employees a "stake in productivity" include tripartite boards to encourage labor-management cooperation, technical and economic assistance to encourage productive application of new technologies in ways that benefit employees, and profit-sharing options.

The analysis and recommendations are not only supported empirically, but have also passed the first test of political viability in that they have been generally reviewed and supported by the commission.

Need for Comprehensive Thinking

The development and application of new technologies will clearly play a critical role in regalvanizing both the California and the U.S. economy. At the same time, it must be emphasized that technological innovation is only one component in the total formula for economic recovery. As such, efforts must be made to integrate the promise of these innovations into an overall economic strategy.

While there is widespread agreement that the California and American economies are faltering, there is considerable debate over the causes of this suboptimal performance and prospective solutions. Disagreement over the basis of today's economic problems ranges from belief that the economy is fundamentally sound and experiencing a short-term cyclic downturn to concern that we confront long-term structural problems dealing with technology, labor supply, investment levels, and other conditions requiring major institutional changes. Further, there is widespread disagreement over the relative importance of varied factors believed to be causing both short- and long-term problems. Needless to say, such varied viewpoints concerning the causes of U.S. economic problems have complicated the task of developing a working consensus concerning both the choice and interrelation of solutions.

Realistically, there is no one set of solutions that can be expected to solve all our economic problems. Indeed, the development and selection of solutions is likely to require trade-offs between objectives and the relative importance of objectives. As such, it is critical to develop an overview of the factors alleged to foster economic problems, empirically assess the existence and nature of alleged problems, and develop some consensus concerning the relative importance of documented problems as a prerequisite to policy development.

It is also likely that there is more than one set of solutions that might effectively combat any specified group of economic problems. At the same time, there is a danger that a chosen set of solutions may not be the best combination for combating problems or, even worse, entail contradictions that may undermine desired results. Hence, it is increasingly important that public and private sector policy makers strive to develop a working consensus concerning the overall nature and relative importance of today's economic problems.

Factors Contributing to Economic Problems

The final report of the California Commission on Industrial Innovation provided a provisional outline of factors that may be contributing to the economy's suboptimal performance. For purposes of discussion, this list has been grouped into seven major categories:

Poor Economic Climate and Attitudes. It has been suggested that the overall economic environment has undermined the confidence and economic performance of individuals and firms. Inflation and price instability are viewed as undercutting effective planning, savings and investment, and consumer confidence. Similarly, erratic and sluggish market demand is seen as leading to underutilization of capital and labor, as well as discouragement of business confidence to expand and modernize. It is generally agreed that the economic instability and pessimism discourage optional use of existing productive resources.

Obsolete and Inappropriate Technology. Some claim that the development and application of new technologies has become inadequate. It is suggested that declining expenditures on basic and applied research are causing the American economy to be noncompetitive with other industrial nations. Others suggest that the American industrial system has been too slow to assimilate critical technological innovations.

Inadequate Investment. It has also been claimed that high interest rates resulting from public deficits, high debt loads, and the instability of international loans have curtailed investment in industrial modernization, postponed replacement of obsolete and worn-out machinery, and allowed the basic economic infrastructure (roads, utilities, etc.) to degenerate. Others suggest that existing capital investments have not been directed to the most productive areas.

Indequate Organization and Utilization of Human Resources. There have been varied claims that human resources at both the managerial and line-employee levels have not been effectively utilized. Some focus on the supply and skill levels of workers, suggesting that workers are ill-trained for existing jobs, that work habits and motivation are poor, and that labor costs price workers out of jobs. Others argue that employees have been ineffectively utilized by management and that managerial decisions have been suboptimal. Specifically, there are claims that employees are ineffectively placed in jobs and given ineffective incentives, that human resources are wasted through needless unemployment, that little opportunity is provided for retraining and updating skills, that little attention is given to basic industrial operations, and that too much attention has been given to short-range profits. In sum, many opine that the human contribution to economic productivity could be improved.

International Competition. It has been increasingly noted that international competition has been capturing large portions of foreign and domestic markets that the United States had previously dominated. Among the reasons for these observations are global industrialization and economic development of previously noncompetitive nations, government subsidization of foreign competitors, noncompetitiveness of American industry, and unfair trade relations.

Inaccessibility of Raw Materials. It has been claimed that constraints in the supply of essential raw materials (most particularly energy) caused by natural depletion, institutional barriers, and international trade have caused the economy to function less productively than in the past.

Obstruction to Economic Revitalization. A number of factors have been identified that may inhibit the application of more productive economic activities. Foremost among such obstacles is the tendency of labor, management, and communities to resist the de-emphasis or realignment of established economic sectors. It has been suggested that labor's fear of job and economic loss impedes modernization and the disinvestment needed to shift resources to more promising uses. Additionally, it has been claimed that government regulation, costs of social welfare programs for those without jobs, and general political instability have curtailed the optimal use of economic resources.

As suggested above, the empirical existence of many of these alleged problems, as well as their relative importance, must be fully documented and elaborated by detailed discussion and rigorous empirical assessment.

Approaching an Economic Development Program

The above and other efforts to isolate and define the problems confronting the economy suggest important considerations for those seeking to develop economic development policies. Regardless of one's views concerning specific problems areas, there can be little doubt that today's economic difficulties have their roots in multifaceted causes. While specialized efforts must be made to attack specific problem areas, it is critical that those concerned with economic policy develop and maintain an awareness of the interrelated nature of the task they are undertaking. Given the severity of today's economic downturn, extraordinary efforts must be made to facilitate communication among those working on specialized areas and to create forums that foster broad problem-solving dialogue to build common understanding of problems and encourage integrated solutions.

The task of moving from a reasonably common agreement about economic problems to programs and policies is no simple matter. While there is a clear and critical need for new ideas, the problem does not lie solely with a lack of proposals. It also stems from the complexity of existing proposals, lack of effective elaboration of proposals, misunderstanding of proposals and their likely impacts, and failure to effectively negotiate resolutions to conflicting interests.

Notes

1. Howard Bowen and Garth Mangum (editors), *Automation and Economic Progress*, Prentice-Hall, Englewood Cliffs, New Jersey, 1966; Norbert Wiener, *The Human Use of Human Beings*, Avon Books, New York, 1950; and Walter Buckingham, *Automation: Its Impact on Business and People*, Mentor Books, New York, 1961.

2. "The Computer Moves In," *Time*, January 3, 1983, page 14.

3. "The Speedup in Automation," *Business Week*, August 3, 1981, page 60.

4. *The Impacts of Robotics on the Workplace and Workforce*, Department of Engineering and Public Policy, Carnegie-Mellon University, Pittsburgh, June 14, 1981.

5. Thomas Gunn, "The Mechanization of Design and Manufacturing," *Scientific American*, September 1982, pages 114–131.

6. One source reports that the use of CAD/CAM by Westinghouse resulted in a 25% reduction in manufacturing lead-time and a 400% increase in productivity ("The Speedup in Automation," *op. cit.*, page 60).

7. "High Technology and the California Workforce in the 1980's," *California Technological Future: Emerging Economic Opportunities in the 1980's*, California Department of Economic and Business Development, Sacramento, March 1982.

8. "The Computer Moves In," *op. cit.*, page 14.

9. Greggory Blundell, "Personal Computers in the Eighties," *Byte*, January 1983, page 168.

10. "Project Summary," *California's Technological Future: Emerging Economic Opportunities in the 1980's*, California Department of Economic and Business Development, Sacramento, March 1982.

11. Michael Kieschnick, "The Incipient California Industrial Policy," Office of Economic and Business Research, Department of Economic and Business Development, San Francisco, California, January 6, 1982.

12. Colin Norman, *Microelectronics at Work: Productivity and Jobs in the World Economy*, Worldwatch Institute, Washington, D.C., October 1980, pages 22–29.

13. Four studies of specific high-technology industries were contracted: Richard Osborn, Barbara Wachsman, Anne Markusen, and Peter Hall, *Computer Services: The People Behind the Machines*, August 1982; Elisabeth O'Malley and Marshall Feldman, *Biotechnology: The Next Green Revolution*, August 1982; Richard Dorf, *Robotics and Computer-Aided Manufacturing/Design*, August 1982; and Eugene Coyle and James Hawley, *Photovoltaics: Technology for Energy Independence*, August 1982.

14. *Winning Technology: A New Industrial Strategy for California and the Nation*, Final Report, California Commission on Industrial Innovation, Office of the Governor, Sacramento, California (Executive Summary Released September 1982 and Detailed Report Released October 1982).

Incentives
and
Motivation

Autonomy, Control, and the Office
of the Future:
Personal and Social Implications

by

Don Mankin

The key to understanding the potential impact of the office of the future is recognition of the essential duality of the technology itself. That is, the inherent nature of the technology makes possible a wide range of alternatives and designs. On the one hand, it is possible to use the technology to monitor job performance; increase managerial control over workers; subdivide and standardize jobs; regulate work schedules, location, and pace; and remove the most challenging and interesting aspects from many jobs by substituting computer routines for employee decisions and judgments. By now, most of us are familiar with such applications of computer technology in the work of secretaries in word-processing pools and order entry clerks in large commercial enterprises. In effect, these applications are information-age manifestations of industrial-age ideas about the most effective ways to organize work; they are F.W. Taylor's principles of Scientific Management and Henry Ford's assembly line dressed up in the new technology but exhibiting essentially the same ideas, values, elements, and substances—with the same dehumanizing consequences.

Other applications, designs, and forms are possible, however. The nature of industrial-age organizations reflected in part the need to "bring people together around a central energy source that fueled the means of production," Shoshana Zuboff of the Harvard Business School points out. They had to interact with various linked and frequently large and cumbersome production machineries, and to coordinate their activities in real time with the energy source, machinery, and each other. Since electronic information technology does not require work to be collective and synchronous, organizations employing this technology are less dependent on the location, scheduling, and pacing of inflexible machinery and nondistributable energy sources. Furthermore, since the substance of "computer-mediated work" (to use Zuboff's words) is symbolic and abstract (information) rather than physical (raw materials and products), this substance can be easily manipulated and transformed as long as the software nec-

Don Mankin is a research consultant with the Rand Corporation, Santa Monica, California. He is also the director of a U.S. Department of Education grant to develop undergraduate and graduate programs in information resources management for Antioch University campuses nationwide.

essary for these operations is readily available. As a result, more flexibility and employee control is possible in the execution of the job tasks than is possible in the rigidly structured and machine-defined tasks found in most manufacturing industries. Furthermore, the implementation of this technology and the design of the organizational context can support and extend this flexibility and control considerably. Involving users in the implementation planning process, developing training programs that show employees how to use the systems to aid them in their work, designing systems that are user-programmable and modifiable, and relaxing organizational policy concerning work hours and location are just a few of the ways in which implementation decisions and organizational policy can contribute to the flexibility and discretion of computer-mediated work.

To conclude, it is clear that automated office technology need not shape jobs and organizations in predetermined ways. How the technology is used, implemented, and supported, and therefore its impact on workers and society, depends as much on management ideology as on the technology itself. The same technology that can be employed to control, monitor, and deskill work can also be used to facilitate creativity, initiative, flexibility, variety, and employee self-management. In effect, the technology—and the work processes in which the technology is employed—*can* be used to increase the degree of control, discretion, and autonomy that workers exercise and experience in their jobs. The principal hypothesis of this paper, then, is that this autonomy and control, in turn, could have personal and social implications that go well beyond their already well-documented impact on work performance and job satisfaction.

Computer-Mediated Work and Stress

Mental and physical health is one of these implications. Control has long been implicated as a moderating factor in the relationship between aversive conditions and health. While stress research has often focused on the sense of or locus of control as a property of the individual, a growing body of research on work-related stress has begun to examine control as a characteristic of the job. For example, in a series of studies using a representative sample of the male Swedish labor force, workers whose jobs were characterized by heavy work loads and low control over their work situations were most inclined to exhibit symptoms of depression, excessive fatigue, cardiovascular disease, and mortality. The workers with the lowest probability of illness and death were those with moderate work loads combined with high levels of control over the work situations. In another series of experiments, also conducted in Sweden, catecholamine excretion—a neuroendocrine stress response—was highest for workers whose jobs were highly repetitive and machine-paced.

A study conducted in the United States by a research team at the University of Michigan also suggests an ameliorating impact of autonomy on stress. On the basis of this and related studies, Robert Kahn, an organizational psychologist at the University of Michigan, recommends an organizational change strategy for alleviating job-related stress that increases the extent to which employees "participate in the decisions that affect them . . . and the extent to which they are autonomous or controlling in their own work." If it is truly the case that work autonomy can moderate job-related stress, as this research strongly suggests, then automated office systems designed to increase the degree of control that employees have over the scheduling, location, pacing, and nature of their work should lower the psychological stresses they experience in their jobs and the physical problems typically associated with long-term exposure to such stresses.

Implications for Social and Political Participation

The office of the future also has implications for social and political participation. These potential consequences emerge from a tradition of research that focuses on work as an instrument of social learning. Much of the early research on this topic tried to account for the apparent lack of interest exhibited by many workers—particularly urban blue-collar workers—in work that was challenging and discretionary. The explanation typically offered was that these attitudes were at least partly a function of job experiences that had created the expectation that such opportunities were generally not available to them. Even when challenging and autonomous work was available, many workers would view these jobs with suspicion, treating them as a ruse by management for increasing their job responsibilities without commensurate increases in job level and pay. Or they would assume that they lacked the job and decision-making skills necessary for effective performance. These attitudes, the argument continues, were further reinforced by workers' perceptions of the job experiences of their parents, peers, and others with similar socio-economic and educational backgrounds. This learned passivity would spill over into such areas of their nonwork lives as leisure, family life, and community and political activities.

This argument leads in turn to the corollary that a way to decrease passivity and apathy is to gradually introduce acceptable and manageable increments of control and discretion into the jobs of those for whom little opportunity for control has previously existed. Not only would they learn step-by-step to exercise responsibility, discretion, and control in their jobs but they would seek out additional opportunities to exercise these newly developed skills in their jobs and in their nonwork lives as well—just as fit, coordinated, and well-toned athletes seek out activities that exercise and test their physical capabilities.

Probably the most thorough and explicit presentation of this thesis can be found in the writings of political scientist Carole Pateman, particularly in her book *Participation and Democratic Theory* (1970). Pateman argues that hierarchical, nondemocratic organizational structures socialize workers into passivity and political apathy, which is reflected in their poor turnout for elections, low levels of community service, and reluctance to participate in voluntary organizations and union, community, and political activities. If workplace authority structures were redesigned along democratic lines, workers would develop a heightened sense of political efficacy and, therefore, take a more active and participatory role in the political processes in the larger society. In Pateman's words: "We learn to participate by participating and . . . feelings of political efficacy are more likely to be developed in a participating environment."

Modest support for Pateman's thesis can be found in a recently published article by Maxwell Elden of the Norwegian Technical University (1981). In the research reported in this article, Elden collected data from a newly-built, highly automated manufacturing plant. The plant differed from older, more traditionally structured plants owned by the same company in its use of semi-autonomous, self-managed work groups. Using a questionnaire distributed to all the employees, Elden found a small but statistically significant correlation between self-management opportunities and a sense of political efficacy.

Additional support for Pateman's theory comes from one of the Swedish studies mentioned in the earlier discussion of job stress. In this study, conducted by Robert Karasek of Columbia University, a nationally representative sample of employed males between the ages of 18 and 60 were interviewed in 1968 and later in 1974. Those workers whose jobs had become more "passive" also became more passive in their political and leisure activity while those with more active jobs became more active outside of their work. In discussing his own research, Karasek's study, and several other similar investigations, Elden concludes that "empirical evidence which has become available since [Pateman's book] validates her contention that a democratically designed work environment induces the development of the type of political resources necessary for participation in and beyond the workplace."

What is the relevance of this conclusion to the subject of office automation? First, as argued earlier, office automation systems can be designed to provide employees with substantially increased control over the scheduling, location, pacing, and nature of their job tasks. While workplace democracy is frequently interpreted in terms of employee participation in organizational decision-making, either directly or indirectly through elected representatives, it can and often does include "democracy" at the level of the workplace or the individual job. Indeed, most of the research indicates that, of the two approaches—higher and lower level participation—the most effective strategy is to enhance worker control over their immediate job tasks and work environment. (These are generally compatible strategies in any case and should ideally be implemented at the same time so as to reinforce each other). Therefore, by giving workers control over the job conditions and context they actually experience throughout the day, office automation systems could have an immediate and profound impact on the development of participatory skills and attitudes.

Second, following Pateman's theory on the socializing influence of democratic job structures, workers exposed to autonomy-enhancing office automation designs would have the skills and be more inclined to participate actively in such nonwork activities as community affairs, public service, political lobbying, and voting.

Finally, since an increasing amount of research and organizational experience points to the important role of employee participation in organizational effectiveness, autonomy-enhancing approaches to office automation should gain increased favor. As these approaches proliferate, office automation could become a major factor in the development of a society where a majority of the citizenry regularly and actively participates in the processes by which organizations, communities, and nations are governed—that is, if Pateman is indeed correct about the relationship between workplace democracy and political efficacy and participation. Fulfilling the democratic ideal requires not only the opportunity for participation but a populace with the motivation and skills necessary for the effective use of this opportunity. As Elden notes; "Work democracy seems to be one way of creating an enduring propensity to participate in political affairs." And one way to create work democracy—a way that would be acceptable to managers as well as workers because of its impact on productivity and efficiency—is to implement designs for office information technology that support and liberate human function rather than constrain and control it.

Before concluding, I would like to inject a brief note of caution into the rosy picture of this technological utopia. We need to consider what, if any, negative consequences might arise from a society of active, autonomous citizens willing and able to participate in the political process for the purpose of influencing policy decisions and issues. Specifically, there is no guarantee that these citizens, with their recently developed skills and sense of efficacy organized into groups with competing interests, will agree on important decisions or even agree to compromise with other groups equally skillful and confident of their political potency but holding differing values and opinions. The result, as Daniel Bell notes in *The Coming of Post-Industrial Society* (1976), may lead to a seriously constraining paradox:

> The greater the number of groups, each seeking diverse or competing ends, the more likelihood that these groups will veto one another's interests, with the consequent sense of frustration and powerlessness as such stalemates incur . . . .
> Thus the problem of how to achieve consensus on political questions will become more difficult. Without consensus there is only conflict, and persistent conflict simply tears a society apart, leaving the way open to repression by one sizeable force or another.

The "zero-sum society," to use Lester Thurow's expression, could aggravate the problem as competing groups make increasingly contentious demands for a larger slice of a pie that may no longer grow as rapidly as it has in the past.

This need not be a reason for resisting the implementation of autonomy-enhancing office automation systems. Compensating policies and mechanisms can be developed: in particular, better means for resolving conflict among competing public interests and policies for expanding the "pie" so that everyone's slices can grow larger. Perhaps, the very existence of more challenging and autonomous work itself would lessen demand for certain forms of satisfaction outside of work.

169

But within the contents of this paper we can do little more than just raise the issues. These issues, along with further study of the ones discussed here and several that have not been addressed, comprise a research and policy agenda that needs to be examined before the revolution in office automation renders these issues faits accomplis in a manner little to our liking.

Tomorrow's Technical/ Communications Labor Force

by

Arthur B. Shostak

Dramatic and rapid advances in modern work practices promise to vastly increase the number and significance of a new type of nonsupervisory employee—the "hands-on" operators of large centralized computer workstations. Typified by panel watchers in chemical plants, oil refineries, nuclear power plants, TV and recording studios, and stock brokerage operations, among others, this new kind of American worker may hold the most responsible, the most stressful, and the best paid jobs in the non-college-educated labor force of the next 25 years.

Special insight into the problems and prospects of these distinctive data processors has been offered by the demands and fate of the U.S. air traffic controllers' union, the Professional Air Traffic Controller's Organization (PATCO). Conventional wisdom had it that the highly sophisticated work of the controllers, performed in modern settings and reliant on elaborate computer technologies, should have presented few, if any, labor problems. A bitter strike, and the ensuing dismissal of 11,400 controllers, however, revealed otherwise, and work experts have since concluded that "the demands being made by the controllers are the kind of demands that can be expected from workers in other sectors of the economy that depend on advanced technologies."[1]

If we are to maximize the gains in work that advances in communications make increasingly possible, it is imperative that we improve the management of our workplace human resources—and begin by learning from present-day mistakes. The controllers' strike, for example, marked perhaps the first time in history that American workers, in effect, "gave up their jobs because they had been mismanaged."[2] Another specialist warns that the controllers' demand for relief from excessive workplace stress will be raised over and over again by similar occupational types ("Stress is the black lung of the technical classes.").[3] And a third commentator insists that the controllers' demand for better equipment to ensure safer air travel foreshadows many similar pleas from other conscientious employees: The

Arthur B. Shostak is a professor of sociology at Drexel University, Philadelphia, Pennsylvania. A founding member of both the World Future Society and its Philadelphia chapter, he is the author of 12 books and nearly 100 articles on social issues.

rapid automation of industry is thought likely to generate new controller-like jobs responsible for the safety of whole factories or offices and their contents—material *and* human.[4]

Supervisory malpractices, the prevalence of debilitating job stress, and doubts concerning equipment with which to ensure the safety of "souls" (or passengers in the aircraft being "handled" by the controllers) are harbingers of labor discontent likely wherever this new breed of controller and controller-like worker is brought into being.[5] PATCO's strike, accordingly, can be understood as a historic milestone—the first major rebellion of nonprofessional workers against hardships in the technological shift from producing things to controlling information. If we intend to reduce the pressure for many more such upheavals, we *must* attend to the reform lessons contained in PATCO's noble, if ill-fated, stand.

PATCO Strike "Lessons"

Drawing on my two years of involvement as a survey researcher for the union, and on lengthy discussions of work issues I have held with controllers at the O'Hare Tower (the world's busiest), on the Philadelphia airport PATCO picket line, and at union headquarters in Washington, I want to highlight seven guidelines I draw from controller discontents that might help improve the work *and* worklives of controller-like employees.

First, technical workers with jobs like those of air traffic controllers are likely to desire and prosper from collegial rather than authoritarian approaches to supervision. This type of worker seems to have a keen need for sensitive support from supervisors when inevitable human errors occur. They appreciate supervisory praise when inevitable crises at work earn an extraordinary response. And they expect an honest and constructive effort from supervisors in the performance-appraisal process. Controllers, and other data communicators like them, apparently do their best when the workstation feels chummy and collaborative: little wonder that an outside expert insists that "on the face of it, the [tower] should be the ideal location for quality of worklife experiments."[6]

Second, technical workers with jobs like those of the air traffic controllers may need to create a workplace culture that deliberately alleviates inordinate stress. For example:

• During their eight-hour shift, a controller rotates through several positions (clearance delivery, ground control, flight plans data, helicopter control, second approach control, etc.).

• When a controller is having a bad day, others will discreetly "carry" him, as by extending their time in the hot spot to reduce the time he must spend in it.

• Every controller is given leeway, and even covert support, to create maintain, and enhance a distinctive style of "working traffic" (as with using one's hands like a traffic cop, even though pilots cannot see this; or, mimicking the accent of different pilots; or, occasionally substituting CB jargon for more common air-control language).

Confronting a work flow largely outside of their command, and challenged by rapid changes in the character of work (as with weather reversals or emergency landing demands), air traffic controllers, and other data

172

communicators like them, apparently require considerable latitude to alter the culture at work.

Third, technical workers with jobs like those of the controllers are likely to spotlight mental health, rather than yesteryear's physical health concerns. In contrast to grimy and sooty factories, the computer communicators work in soaring, antiseptic, climate-controlled "cabs," and their discontent focuses away from traditional rage over the absence of a clean place to sit down in the average mill, warehouse, or assembly plant. Instead, the controllers are preoccupied with the strain the job puts on their minds, moods, marriages, and general mental well-being. Many think the chronic anxiety, ulcers, high blood pressure, sleeplessness, nightmares, and impotence to be more of a toll than the job ever need entail—and they especially resent management's reluctance to admit or to deal with this situation. Accordingly, to extrapolate cautiously from the situation of the controllers, their counterparts in the work force of tomorrow can be expected to push the dialogue on a relatively new issue about which labor and management must reach an accord—the entitlement an employee has to the reduction of negative (and counter-productive) stress at (and from) work.

Fourth, technical workers may desire a larger say than other non-professionals in items commonly and erroneously thought to concern only well-educated professional types. Controllers, for example, are eager to help guide management in making crucial decisions about updating safety rules, the better to reduce fraud and hypocrisy in the matter (". . . regulations are violated every day, day in and day out, in order to handle the volume of planes we have to handle.").[7] As well, controllers are understandably concerned about the quality of the basic equipment ("The computer-radar combination is subject to far too frequent failure . . . . Working the system is like, as a surgeon, having to perform delicate operation after delicate operation knowing the operating room lights could, and probably will, go out any time. Under conditions like that, a few seconds in the dark can be a lifetime.").[8]

Accordingly, many controllers have technical notions about how to improve the hardware and software of their trade, though most have long since come to despair of gaining a fair and encouraging hearing from management. Be that as it may, air traffic controllers, and other data communicators like them, may be looked to as an eager source of productivity-aiding insights—a source, however, that can go sour if denied.

Fifth, technical workers may challenge many prevailing notions about the significance of time at work. Controllers insist that the sustained nature of mental stress in their computer-driven jobs makes a shorter workweek (32 hours) a necessary prop for productivity and client safety. As well, they point to their 80% "burnout" rate, or the fact that four out of five go out on disability before reaching the retirement minimum, as evidence of the need to reduce the length of time required to qualify one for retirement (15 instead of 20 years). Above all, however, they rail against the casual insistence by management on an "insane" rotating shift schedule (". . . one of the greatest hazards to the flying public is the schedule we have to work.").[9] Accordingly, data communicators with controller-like jobs can be expected to pressure employers for shorter hours, shorter retirement-qualifying terms, and far more leeway to say "no" to rotating shift schedules that wreak havoc with family life and personal fitness.

Sixth, controllers and similar others insist they are worth much more than they are presently being paid, and they fully intend to win more! Confusion and controversy abound in the matter, since these employees reject comparison of their earnings with others who also lack a college education or are also as young (most controllers are not college graduates, and 80% are under 36). Instead, they contend that their distinctive job requirements (mental alertness, stamina, quickness, decisiveness) and their demanding job responsibilities (close teamwork, solo order-giving, extraordinary life-and-death decision-making) set them quite apart from other classes of workers.

Consistent with this, PATCO respondents in each of four attitude surveys conducted over 18 months before the strike ranked "salary increase" their foremost demand (with "shorter hours" and "earlier retirement" a close second and distant third). The rank-and-file also used the surveys to register strong resentment over having their compensation levels determined by an impersonal and removed Civil Service system. Computer-aided controller-like workers, in short, can be expected to press increasingly for substantial salary and fringe benefit gains consistent with their self-image as a fairly unique cadre of hard-working, larger-than-life "communicators."

Seventh, controller-like workers are likely to appreciate the indispensability of collective bargaining protection, the 1982 demise of PATCO to the contrary and notwithstanding. "Computer technology creates the false illusion that problems with the workplace are over," a student of technological change explains, adding that, "the controllers were exhibiting old attitudes, the attitudes of coal miners."[10]

Prime among such proud and self-assertive attitudes was strong resentment against unwarranted irritants (PATCO's 1976 contract finally compelled management to relax its IBM-like dress code for controllers). The union had fought to humanize work rules (PATCO forced management to agree not to change a controller's day off only hours before it was to begin). The union had also moved to protect controllers who feared management retribution in the event of a human error (". . . a major source of stress is the fear that in the event of a crash the FAA will do whatever it feels it can get away with to 'hang' the controller with responsibility for the accident.")[11] Above all, the union compelled management to reckon with a formal grievance procedure, one that provided the 85% of all controllers who voluntarily joined PATCO with trained representation at every level of the process, high-powered legal counsel, and an invaluable sense of countervailing power.

Little wonder, then, that when I surveyed PATCO members shortly before their strike, they expressed ringing confidence in Organized Labor, outdoing every demographic category in the most recent (1979) Gallup national poll in this matter.

As some 42% had made use of the PATCO grievance process, it was not surprising to find that 80% felt the union's problems were also his or her own problems, and that 93% believed most PATCO members preferred to be represented by a union.

Where labor militancy was concerned, these white-collar technical workers were not shy: although only 20% had had any previous experience as a unionist, and only 15% had ever walked a picket line before, the vast majority approved of allowing public employees like themselves to strike (84% voted "yes" where teachers were concerned; 81% approved in the case of postmen; 68%, firemen; 68%, policemen). Above all, 84% affirmed their intention of supporting a properly sanctioned PATCO strike, a vote of co-worker solidarity that the White House was mistakenly led to believe did not exist.

Air traffic controllers, and other data communicators like them, should be regarded as employees skeptical of management's good intentions, and inclined instead to meet power with power. Given the intransigence of abusive managerial ways—as revealed in the insistence of nonstriking controllers six months after PATCO's decertification that management attitudes remain "centralized, rigid, and insensitive"[12]— reason exists to suspect more, rather than less, union organizing and labor militancy from tomorrow's growing numbers of technical workers.

Summary

Critics have branded the 11,500 controllers dismissed by President Reagan as "irreverent malcontents,"[13] while admirers insist that PATCO's strike forced management to significantly improve work practices (as in increasing the staffing of the towers and requiring more spacing between flights). Critics second-guess whether non-strike tactics like a "rulebook" slowdown might have sufficed, while PATCO supporters remind all that federal employees have struck the government in 20 earlier labor disputes, even as they take quiet pride in judging theirs the "most monumental job action ever directed at the Federal Government."[14]

Controversy here will persist, of course, for as long as the supervision of human beings remains a critical art form in increasingly automated workplaces. It already seems clear, however, that controller-like employees stand apart in the challenge they pose to any post-industrial scenario of preference: These technical employees are likely to insist on sharing the managerial decision-making process. They want to directly profit from experience-gained insights into how to do the job better. They mean to reduce negative stressors and protect their quality of life on and off the job. They intend to earn more for their labor, and, as a form of insurance that all these objectives will be met, they prefer to stand together as trade unionists and not rely instead only or especially on enlightened personnel relations.

While middle-class in level of earnings and middle-of-the-road politics, and while white-collar-like in job content and work setting, this new kind of worker is potentially more assertive and militant than commonly understood by outsiders. Operating large centralized computer workstations, they are steadily coming to realize the exceptional power they command— and its very real limitations (as in the ability of FAA supervisors to step down and help operate a scaled-back system after PATCO had struck). As well, technical employees of this sort live with nagging insecurity about technological displacement (as with the FAA's new 20-year plan to modernize the aging air traffic control system and have one controller soon do what three or four do at present).[15]

Not surprisingly, therefore, these workers remain a volatile and problematic element of the changing labor force—strong in their six-point agenda of workplace reforms, yet weak in their recognized vulnerability to "technological scabbing" and technological displacement. Especially well-satisfied when their jobs are going strong, the commitment of these workers to the work ethic could not be greater. Accordingly, as the potential vanguard of exactly the high-quality, high-contribution labor force that the U.S. requires, controller-like technical workers merit a much fairer, calmer, and far more constructive hearing than PATCO ever received—if we intend to salvage vital lessons of value from the nation's first workplace rebellion of tomorrow's communication "controllers."

Notes

1. Serrin, William, "Controller Called Typical of New Breed of Worker." *New York Times*, August 16, 1981, p. 38.

2. Shrank, Robert, formerly of the Ford Foundation, as quoted in *ibid*.

3. Aronowitz, Stanley, a labor activist, writer, and teacher (Columbia University), as quoted in *ibid*.

4. Helpful in making this point clear is Raben, Joseph, "Toward a Nation of Controllers." *New York Times*, September 27, 1981, p. 18-E.

5. Weil, Henry, "Those Ultracool, Death-Defying Air Traffic Controllers." *Cosmopolitan*, May 1976, p. 259.

6. Lawler, Edward J., professor of organizational behavior at the University of Southern California, as quoted in Serrin, *New York Times*, *op. cit.*

7. Rose, Sam, controller, as quoted in Biggs, Don, *Pressure Cooker*. New York: W.W. Norton, 1979, p. 136.

8. Biggs, *ibid.*, p. 189.

9. McCloskey, Will, controller, as quoted in *ibid.*, p. 152.

10. Shaiken, Harley, an MIT research associate specializing in advanced technologies, as quoted in Serrin, *New York Times*, *op. cit.*

11. Biggs, *Pressure Cooker*, *op. cit.*, p. 226.

12. Jones, L. M., *et al.*, *Management and Employee Relationships Within the Federal Aviation Administration*, Washington, D.C.: FAA, March, 1982, pp. 41, 67–69.

13. "One of the saddest parts of this tragedy is that a group of people whom I know to be decent and generous will forever be branded as irreverent malcontents." Poli, Robert E., "Why the Controllers' Strike Failed," *New York Times*, January 17, 1982, p. E-1. Poli was the PATCO president who led the strike, and resigned in January 1982.

14. "A judgment advanced in a forthcoming book by two PATCO members, Gary Greene and Tom Holliday, entitled *Strike: The PATCO Nightmare*; as reported on in *Flightline Times*, June 30, 1982, p. 1.

15. Witkin, Richard, "Revamping of Air Control System in Next 20 Years Proposed by U.S.," *New York Times*, January 29, 1982, p. 1.

Industrial Democracy

by

Edward Cohen-Rosenthal

Workplaces can become more democratic. In fact, the growth of industrial democracy in all Western industrialized countries is practically inevitable. The term industrial democracy has a wide variety of meanings and applications. On a limited scale, it can mean a somewhat restricted socio-technical tinkering with existing industrial-relations structures. In Europe, this approach is represented by a new coterie of worker-directors who sit on corporate boards. In the U.S., it is found in expanding programs geared toward greater sensitivity to the opinions of workers and job enlargement.

However, industrial democracy can mean a new way of structuring production and power in a post-industrial world, which transfers much greater influence and responsibility to workers and their unions. This is far more than the nominal power of boards or sophisticated suggestion boxes, but rather the infinite power of pooled human purpose. In another vein, industrial democracy can lead to greater economic democracy for citizens to be able to voice their concerns on the direction of corporate activity. Workplace democracy can establish a new relationship between sources and production that attends greater thought to both the consequences and means of production.

The future surely bears increasing numbers of companies and unions experimenting with shop-floor workers' and union leaders' participation in issues previously reserved as exclusively management prerogatives. These include such areas as work pace, hiring and firing, training design, occupational safety and health, equipment engineering, and purchasing. In some countries, there is worker involvement in considering long-range investment policy, marketing, plant closures, product selection, plant expansion, and social accounting.

These new patterns of work are presently manifesting themselves in many Western European countries and Japan. Both in board representation and shop-floor experiments, serious discussions of proposals are presently under way in the United Kingdom, New Zealand, and Australia. In the United States, there has been a marked increase in experimentation with participatory management. Flavored by their own cultural and political backgrounds, there are variations on the theme under way in Yugoslavia and Israel and in many developing countries, including Tanzania and India.

In Sweden, the old notion of man as "human capital" or man as solely the merchant of his labor has been replaced by the idea of man as a social being whose rights extend into the workplace. To many Swedes, industrial

Edward Cohen-Rosenthal is president of ECR Associates, Laytonsville, Maryland. This paper is drawn from a longer unpublished manuscript.

democracy represents a way to generate justice in the workplace. They perceive it as an evolution improved from expansive and expensive social welfare approaches. Industrial democracy places responsibility squarely where it belongs: on the shoulders of all of the people concerned, not just an elite managerial corps. One's humanity does not stop at the factory gate. One's brain is not disengaged as the office door is closed. There has to be a better way to work. Endless laws can only attempt to prevent gross abuses. But creativity and commitment do not come by laws—even good laws. The nature of relationships at work does not conform neatly to legal formulations. This new way of working is much less encumbering, therefore more responsive and effective.

Worldwide, the demand for improved occupational health and safety has assumed an unprecedented position of importance. In a study released by the U.S. Department of Labor, the topic of greatest interest to workers for participation in decisions was safety and health. Seventy-six percent of workers think they should have all or some say. (See chart *Decisions in the Workplace*.)

Decisions in the Workplace

Workers sometimes have a say in decisions at their workplace, even though they are not supervisors or managers. How much say do you think workers *should* have about . . .

Type of Decision	Base N	Complete say	A lot of say	Some say	No say at all
			Percentage		
Safety of equipment and practices	2256	13.3%	62.5%	22.8%	1.3%
How the work is done	2254	4.8	36.0	55.1	4.1
The wages and salaries paid	2235	3.6	26.8	58.9	10.7
The particular days and hours people work	2245	2.7	16.7	50.2	22.4
Hiring or layoffs	2224	2.6	13.0	45.1	39.4

Source: Robert P. Quinn and Graham L. Staines, *The 1977 Quality of Employment Survey*, Survey Research Center, Institute for Social Research, University of Michigan, Ann Arbor, Michigan, 1979, p. 178.

The present critical importance of industrial health is but a forerunner of other demands on the workplace to put people first.

The next decade will probably plot an interesting future for the growth of industrial democracy. Efforts utilizing worker participation will slowly gain ground in the next five years. There is a rising accumulation of experience in this field. Projects have been under way at such corporate giants as General Motors, U.S. Steel, Exxon, Weyerhaeuser, and General Foods. Unions such as the United Auto Workers, the International Wood-workers, the United Steelworkers, the Oil, Chemical, and Atomic Workers Union, the International Association of Machinists, and the Communications Workers of America have jointly engaged in projects. In over eight cities such as San Diego, California, and Columbus, Ohio, and in several hospitals, experiments have been conducted in the public sector. That every state in the nation and over 130 different national unions are involved in some way is documented by reports of the National Center for Productivity and Quality of Work Life.[1] They are not all successful, but they provide a base for learning even if they don't last. There is a growing documentation that these new ways to work are not only more in tune with the people in them but are more successful economic units.

However, in the 1985-1990 period, the number of companies and unions moving in the direction of industrial democracy should expand dramatically. A number of factors should coalesce by this period. Emerging worker values fueled by rising levels of education should precipitate new demands from workers. A need for renewed purpose on the part of unions and a drive to organize white-collar and younger employees should thrust expanded participation in workplace decisions to a higher priority. A need for productivity improvement and more than a decade of experimentation should convince many companies to try greater worker participation. When toted up, it yields a prospective boon in the United States for new styles of decision-making. In a modest way, the current phenomenal growth of quality circles is evidence of this. The joining of new values, demographic trends, and economic necessity is fortuitous for steps in the direction of industrial democracy.

The likelihood of greater participation by workers in the future has been noted and written about by numerous commentators. One of the best glimpses at this future is provided by James G. Affleck, chairman of the board of the American Cyanamid Company, who writes:

> The future of management is "non-management." It will be the development and utilization of people organized to employ all their individual and creative talents to the maximum, within an environment of continuous and dynamic change. The rigid and highly structured organizational framework of the past will be replaced by a cohesive interdependence of thought and action, perhaps without conscious direction or apparent leadership as we have understood it. Management's main job will be to exercise sensitivity and an educated intuition to draw the maximum from a highly skilled and intellectually sophisticated force of managers and workers. . . .
>
> Up to now organizational structures have served to treat people as surrogate machines, or to replace them with machines wherever possible in the name of efficiency. In the future, we as managers will have to develop new attitudes and practices if we are to lead the men and women of the last quarter of the twentieth century and give them the kind of rewarding and fulfilling work experience they are being conditioned to expect. We are going to have to employ people as people, taking into account all of the interests, habits, attitudes, and learned skills which when properly exercised lead the human being to new heights of individual and collective achievement. We are going to have to employ 100 percent of the individual, not the 20 or 50 percent which may fit the current job description.[2]

The critical role of trade unions in industrial democracy should be discussed. In most European countries, it is the unions who are the most active proponents of further efforts for industrial democracy. In the United States, some unions look warily at work reorganization efforts; in them, they often see management gimmicks, more responsibility with no increase in compensation, and weakening of the contract. With real justification, some unions see workers' participation as undermining efforts for wider unionization. After all, collective bargaining is in itself a basic model for democratic participation in the workplace. The union is not an abstract institution but a reality where workers elect their representatives and ratify their contracts. A union is an instrument for workers' expression and protection. Encouragingly, an increasing number of labor leaders are viewing quality-of-work-life efforts as a way to extend previously won benefits while maintaining the security of the contract. More and more are involved in various labor-management committees and in worker-participation projects. Their motivation is caused not only by an ideological attachment to human dignity and democracy but also by many of the same pressures that are forcing companies to explore new styles of participation. These pressures are exerted in the form of the broadened concerns of primarily the younger membership for good wages and benefits *and* an improved quality of working life. They want both. Unions are squeezed by international and regional competition, by lower wage markets or higher productivity growth thereby threatening jobs and the hard-fought gains in their standard of living. Declining or stagnant union membership as a percentage of the labor force calls for bold action in organizing the service sector and other workers eager for more meaningful participation in the processes of work. Worker participation could be the demand of the eighties and nineties.

Irving Bluestone, retired vice president of the United Auto Workers, has written about emerging trends in worker participation:

> Participation by workers in decisions involving management of the job is fundamental to the fulfillment of the ultimate goal of achieving industrial democracy. It seems inevitable that workers will demand increasingly to be part of the decision-making process, particularly with regard to those aspects of work-life which are of most immediate importance to them in the performance of their job. In a real sense the trend toward worker participation in decision-making is an extension of the democratic values into the workplace which the worker enjoys as a citizen in society.[3]

Non-union employers are increasingly using these kinds of participative programs. For some, it is a genuine concern for inclusion. However, some employers are trying to develop these programs to demonstrate that unions are unnecessary. Their programs are often sophisticated versions of company unions. All European experience and much of what has transpired in America shows to the contrary that strong union organization is not only important for the workers on the job to provide collective strength in community, national, and international affairs, but also at the enterprise level in the successful operation of worker participation and productivity improvement. Rather than wither away, unions remain necessary to combat management smugness and provide a positive vision of workers' needs.

Industrial Democracy and Education

In my talks with workers, union officers, and managers in many parts of the world, increased learning is one clear outcome stretching across

180

the industrial democracy spectrum. An enormous new demand for further learning is released. It stands to reason that this will occur. In representative models of industrial democracy, worker directors and members of work councils dealing with complex issues find that there is much they need to learn to function effectively. Shop-floor participants are brought into contact with areas of knowledge and operation where they previously have had little exposure. Participants not only learn facts and theories but a lot about the people and human dynamics involved.

There have been a number of examples of this learning connection. In Europe, both companies and unions have designed education programs for representatives. The classic example in the United States is the in-plant school established by members of the United Auto Workers employed at Harmon International. In this automobile mirror plant in Bolivar, Tennessee, workers were, on their own initiative, learning a wide variety of subjects from welding to anthropology. In Norway, the educational redesign of seafarer's schooling based on the outcomes of participative decision-making is another sterling example of new demands on education rising out of new demands on the workplace.

For most people, real participation is not easy. In order to participate effectively with other people in reaching workable and informed answers to real-life problems within reasonable time limits, workers need to focus on how to do it well. There is a definite need for training in a variety of process skills that assist workers in understanding the techniques of problem-solving, group dynamics, information-gathering, and a range of other process aides that clarify ways to make decisions better. There is also a wide band of content skills, which differs according to the nature of the industry and the idiosyncrasies of the work organization. However, some content skills such as an understanding of the history of industrial democracy, the range of alternative work patterns available, and a general understanding of economics would be important for most if not all participants.

The style of worker participation will put new process demands on schools and colleges. Since horizontal work teams cut across occupational titles, workers will expect and want interdisciplinary and problem-centered curricula. Since workers will have more of a say in the operation of their workplaces, they will expect more of a say in the operation of their schools and participation in setting the goals and objectives of their learning experiences. The use of new behavorial-science techniques to facilitate participation in the workplace will make standard lectures as arcane as company pep talks. Though functional on occasion, didactic, one-way communication needs to give way to more interactive approaches to learning.

Industrial democracy is an answer to the paradox of advancement through education. Up until recently, more education has been an effective entree to positions of authority and challenge. While expectations of education's payoff remain high, the ability of the existing system to absorb people at either their level of aspiration or their level of talent is dim. A society based on frustration of talent or drive is in a serious predicament. The only real solution is to broaden participation and expand the number of "good" jobs. Any attempt to brainwash people into lower expectations or to ignore the problem will fall flat on its face. Industrial democracy is a way to buy out of the mentality of laboriously climbing the hierarchical ladder. Though new types of work will uncover talents that have been previously submerged and better match individuals and jobs, this concept of democracy does not offer a way for individuals to reach "the top" by stepping on the backs of co-workers. Industrial democracy implies a shared growth where success has new definitions.

The three issues identified earlier in this essay—cybernetics, democracy, and ecology—help to understand the particular direction that new forms of industrial democracy should take. In the workplace, we need to know how to sort out the mountains of data to select important information without ignoring evidence helpful for full understanding. At work, like elsewhere, the more people who participate in decisions, the more information they in turn create. They then have to wrestle with the frustrating task of coping with even more intimidating mounds of data. In addition, the useful life of data is open to serious question. Things became irrelevant or passé so quickly. So common that they fail to shock anymore are stories of the obsolescence of knowledge as in the case of engineering students who are out of date by the time they graduate. What is unclear is how the emerging workplace will learn—if at all—to sift and order its wealth of know-how. How will it improve its cybernetic capacity?

A true industrial democratic system is a much more intricate animal than formal organizational charts with lines between departments. The difficulty of communication grows with increased complexity. Unfortunately, we don't know enough about how to involve large groups of people in effective decision-making. When it does work well, democracy is a powerful social tool. Cooperative decision-making needs to be taught from the earliest years to the end of life. Unless we learn and relearn this skill, increased participation will represent a two-edged sword. On one hand, even good decisions will be rejected unless arrived at in a democratic fashion. On the other, by their very lack of focus, amoebic and anarchistic "democracy" could stifle or divert any effective resolution of problems.

Concerning the ecological dimension, we need to encourage holistic decisions at the workplace that give due consideration to the social and environmental ramifications of proposed actions. Workers and managers need to learn better how to broadly frame issues to assess their impacts on social and environmental well-being. Enterprises in France and Scandinavia are required by law to prepare a report on corporate impact on the community and their workers. This impact statement is a new field called "social accounting." Another example is found in the United Kingdom, where workers at the Lucas Aerospace Company are thinking of more humane ways to employ technology. A Center for Alternative Technology has been established by the Lucas Aerospace Combined Shop Stewards Committee in conjunction with researchers and academics in order to find viable alternatives to the production of military hardware. One of their successful ideas was to bid on a new type of light rail transportation system suitable to Tanzania. In the United States, workers are beginning to realize that, contrary to scare tactics, not only has environmental action failed to cause the promised massive layoffs but in fact more jobs were created. In an age of limited resources and a more intimate "global village," workers need to be able to understand and act on the environmental consequences of their actions. In India, environmental protection is one of the locally mandated functions of worker participation councils. Given the opportunity, new ways can be found to save energy and redesign products to suit a new ecological consciousness with the cooperation and imagination of workers—instead of being viewed with distrust as a threat to job security.

Welded together, these three concepts help inform a version of industrial democracy that is deeply participatory, keenly informed, and broadly concerned. It is a kind of work experience that can help stimulate more justice inside the workplace, produce better goods and services, and fuse better with expanded notions of leisure and education. Industrial democracy is a workstyle for the future.

Notes

1. National Center for Productivity and Quality of Working Life, *Directory of Labor-Management Committees*, Washington, D.C., Spring 1978
2. James G. Affleck, "Constructive Orchestration of Chaos," in Lewis Benton, ed., *Management for the Future*, McGraw Hill Book Company, New York, 1978, p. 3.
3. Irving Bluestone, "Human Dignity Is What It's All About," Industrial Union Department, AFL-CIO, *Viewpoint*, Vol. 8, No. 3, Third Quarter 1978, pp. 21–25.

Careers and
Work Trends

Jobs with a Future

by

Marvin J. Cetron

Forecasters, as opposed to other futurists, must use very specific yardsticks to measure the likelihood of a prediction actually taking place. These yardsticks include technical feasibility, economic feasibility (cost effectiveness), social acceptability, and political acceptability. If any of these are not applicable to a projected change, it will not rate a positive forecast.

For example, a futurist might look at solar energy and determine that it is the way of the future since it is clean, nonpolluting, and there is an inexhaustible supply. However, in making a forecast about the use of solar energy, even though it is technically feasible and acceptable socially and politically, it will not become economically feasible until the price of oil goes up to $54 per barrel. Therefore, solar energy will not be the way of the future.

When applying these tests and measures to occupations, one thing is sure about tomorrow's job markets: major shifts will occur in employment patterns. These changes are going to affect the work force of the future, and are going to precipitate changes in the education and training of both potential and existing workers.

Major shifts in the job market do not necessarily mean major changes in the numbers of people employed anywhere inside the job market. What it does mean is that many of the old jobs will disappear—and not just because of robots and computers. Manufacturing of products will consume only 11% of the jobs in the year 2000, down from 28% in 1980. Jobs related to agriculture will drop from 4% to 3%. The turn of the century will find the remaining 86% in the service sector, up from 68% in 1980. Of the service-sector jobs, half will relate to information collection, management, and dissemination.

Unemployment will continue to be a problem. If the current recession were to end tomorrow, probably 1.2 million of the more than 11 million unemployed today would never be able to return to their old jobs in the automobile, steel, textile, rubber, or railroad industries.

Marvin J. Cetron, a pioneer and expert in the areas of technological forecasting and technological assessment, is president of Forecasting International, Ltd., Arlington, Virginia. This article is adapted from his forthcoming book Jobs with a Future, *to be published by McGraw-Hill in January 1984.*

About one-sixth of the 1.2 million jobs will be eliminated by foreign competition in low-wage countries; another one-sixth will disappear because of the nationalization of many major industries in other countries, which results in "dumping" of products on our market, undercutting our prices. "Computamation" (robotics, numerically-controlled equipment, CAD/CAM [computer aided design and computer aided manufacturing], and flexible manufacturing) will assist in the demise of the remaining two-thirds of the jobs eliminated.

As this technological transition takes place, productivity will increase. For example, the use of robotics or CAD/CAM in the automotive industry can replace up to six workers if operating around the clock. Quality control increases four-fold, and scrap is reduced from 15% to less than 1%.

Japan is already using some of these new jobs and technology. It had no choice. Presently, 96% of its energy is imported. By the year 2000, it will rise to 98%. Eighty-seven percent of all of its resources come from outside the country. These statistics form a base for the decision to go robotic, but the essence of Japan's problem is that, between 1985 and 1990, 20% of the entire work force will retire at 80% of their base pay for the rest of their lives. They were forced to go robotic to remain productive. The United States, too, will be filling many of today's blue-collar jobs with robots. The displaced workers will have to learn the new skills necessary to build and maintain the robots.

White-collar workers in the offices of the future will see some dramatic changes in their jobs, also. Currently, about 6,000 word lexicons are in use. After a person dictates into the machine, it will type up to 97% of what was said. In addition, it can translate the material into 9 languages (including Hebrew, which it types backwards, and Konji symbols, which it types sideways and the user reads down the columns). Machines such as this will lead to the demise of 50% of all clerical and stenographic jobs. But instead of going to an unemployment line, these workers will find jobs controlling the robots in factories with word-processing equipment.

Not only will types of jobs change, but so will the definition of full employment. Currently, a 4.5% unemployment rate is considered full employment. By the year 1990, 8.5% unemployment will be considered full employment. This is not as disturbing as it first appears, for at any given time 3.5% of the work force will be in training and education programs preparing for new jobs. This will be made possible, in part, because of the job shift patterns. In 1980, 45% of the households had 2 people working. In 1990, this will increase to 65%, and in 2000, 75% of family units will have 2 incomes. This shift will allow easier entry and exit from the work force to the training programs and back to the work force. Forecasts estimate that, every 4 or 5 years, one or the other of the spouses or partners will leave the ranks of the employed to receive the additional knowledge and skills demanded by changes in technology and the workplace.

With these changes already taking place, Americans must acquire the knowledge and skills they will need for today's new jobs and for the future jobs that will soon need to be filled with qualified workers. Vocational educators and trainers must gear up to provide this vital education and training to the work force of the next two decades. The future will include jobs related to robots, lasers, computers, energy and battery technology, geriatric social work, hazardous waste management, and biomedical electronics. (See table for some of the jobs that are disappearing and others that are growing in the shifting job market).

The Shifting Job Market

Some jobs that will be disappearing by 1990:

Occupation	% Decline in Employment
Linotype operator	−40.0
Elevator operator	30.0
Shoemaking machine operators	19.2
Farm laborers	19.0
Railroad car repairers	17.9
Farm managers	17.1
Graduate assistants	16.7
Housekeepers, private household	14.9
Childcare workers, private household	14.8
Maids and servants, private household	14.7
Farm supervisors	14.3
Farm owners and tenants	13.7
Timber cutting and logging workers	13.6
Secondary school teachers	13.1

Some jobs that will be growing until 1990:

Occupation	% Growth in Employment
Data processing machine mechanics	+157.1
Paralegal personnel	143.0
Computer systems analysts	112.4
Midwives	110.0
Computer operators	91.7
Office machine service technicians	86.7
Tax preparers	77.9
Computer programmers	77.2
Aero-astronautic engineers	74.8
Employment interviewers	72.0
Fast food restaurant workers	69.4
Childcare attendants	66.5
Veterinarians	66.1
Chefs	55.0

New Occupations for the 1990s

The following occupations are among those that we can expect to become increasingly important. Included with each is a short description, starting salary, average salary, and training requirements. The descriptions have been prepared by Clyde Helms and Marvin Cetron, president and vice president of Occupational Forecasting, respectively.

Energy Technician—650,000 jobs starting at $13,000, averaging $26,000. Jobs will dramatically increase as new sources of energy become marketable. Demand will greatly exceed available supply of labor in nuclear power plants; coal, shale, and tar sands extraction, processing, and distribution; solar systems manufacturing, installation, and maintenance; synfuels production; biomass facilities operations; and possibly geothermal and ocean thermal energy conversion operations.

Technicians, inspectors, and supervisory positions will require a high-school education and the equivalent of two years of technical college.

Housing Rehabilitation Technician—500,000 jobs starting at $14,000, averaging $24,000. In the next 35 years the world population will double, intensifying housing demand. This will lead to mass production of modular housing, using radically new construction techniques and materials. Modular housing will be fabricated with all heating, electric, waste disposal and recycling, and communications systems pre-installed.

Technicians, inspectors, and supervisors will require a high-school education and the equivalent of two years of technical education plus appropriate experience such as formal apprenticeship.

Hazardous Waste Management Technician—300,000 jobs starting at $15,000, averaging $28,000. Many years and billions of dollars may be required to clean up cities, industries, air, land, and water. Additionally, tens of thousands of jobs will be added to each area as breeder reactors and coal, shale, and tar sands mining and processing reach commercial stages. When the requirements for collection, transportation, and disposal of radiological, biological, and chemical wastes are included, the total workers needed could well exceed 1.5 million.

Highly specialized technical training will be required for workers, supervisors, and managers in this very hazardous occupation.

Industrial Laser Process Technician—600,000 jobs starting at $15,000, averaging $25,000. Laser manufacturing equipment and processes, including robotic factories, will replace many of the machine and foundry tools and equipment. The new equipment, processes, and materials will permit attainment of higher production quality at lower production costs.

High school, technical training, and retraining requirements will vary with levels of skill required under a severe system of job evolution.

Industrial Robot Production Technician—800,000 jobs starting at $15,000, averaging $24,000. The microprocessor industry will become the third largest industry in the U.S., facilitating extensive use of robots to perform computer-directed "physical" and "mental" functions. Millions of human workers will be displaced. New workers will be needed to ensure fail-proof operation of row after row of production robots.

Knowledge and skills requirements will compare with present-day computer programmers and electronics technicians.

Materials Utilization Technician—400,000 jobs starting at $15,000, averaging $24,000. Future materials are being engineered and created to replace metals, synthetics, and other production materials not suited for advanced manufacturing technologies. Materials utilization technicians must be trained in working with amorphous and polymer materials and others that may be produced at the molecular level through the process of molecular beam epitaxy, involving atomic crystal growth. In addition, there will be genetically engineered organic materials. These and other "man-made" materials will substitute for natural-element metals and materials now being depleted.

An education level equivalent to that of an electronics technician, tool and die maker, nondestructive materials testing specialist, or industrial inspector will be required. Two years of technical college will be the minimum requirement.

Genetic Engineering Technician—250,000 jobs starting at $20,000, averaging $30,000. Genetically engineered materials will greatly improve upon and supersede present organic materials and will also produce beneficial effects upon some inorganic materials processes. These engineered "man-made" materials will find extensive usage in three general fields: industrial products, pharmaceuticals, and agricultural products. Completely new and modified materials and substances will be produced under laboratory-like conditions and in capacities comparable to industrial mass-production quantities. Technicians must be educated and trained to work under laboratory-type controls without inhibiting production of some of the materials in tonnage lots.

A bachelor's degree in chemistry, biology, or medicine will be helpful in the initial industrial production work, but production operations will be accomplished by "process technicians" with high-school and two-year postsecondary technical education and training.

Holographic Inspection Specialist—200,000 jobs starting at $20,000, averaging $28,000. Completely automated factories will use optical fibers for sensing light, temperature, pressures, and dimensions and transmitting this information to optical computers that will compare this data with holographic, three-dimensional images stored in the computer. Substantial numbers of inspectors and quality-control staffs will be replaced.

Specialists working in this new technology will require a minimum of two years of postsecondary technical education and training, with emphases on optical fibers characteristics and transmission, photography, optical physics, and computer programming.

Bionic-Medical Technician—200,000 jobs starting at $21,000, averaging $32,000. Mechanics will be needed to manufacture the actual bionic appendage (arm, leg, hand, foot) while other specialists work on the highly sophisticated extensions of neuro-sensing mental functions (seeing, hearing, feeling, speaking) and brain-wave control.

These technicians will require appropriate technical knowledge of microprocessors and specialized accredited education in the respective anatomical, physiological, and psychiatric disciplines equivalent to a minimum of four years of college work. Medical professionals who establish a reputation will move into the higher six-figure levels of earning.

Automotive Fuel Cell (Battery) Technician—250,000 jobs starting at $12,000, averaging $18,000. These technicians will schedule and perform tests and services for new fuel cells and batteries used in vehicles and stationary operation, including residences. Such fuel cells may be charged and discharged by direct electric inputs from conventional electric distribution systems, by solar cells, and by exotic chemicals generating electricity within the cells.

These processes include potential hazards but can be safely serviced by technicians with a vocational high school education.

On-Line Emergency Medical Technician—400,000 jobs starting at $16,000, averaging $29,000. The need for paramedics will increase directly with the growth of the population and its aging. In forthcoming megalopolises and high-density residences, emergency medical treatment will be rendered on the spot with televised diagnoses and instruction from remote emergency medical centers. Despite reports of a forthcoming glut of doctors, they and other professional and paramedical specialists will become part of emergency medical teams, traveling in elaborately equipped mobile treatment centers.

To meet the needs for more complete treatment on site, education and training must be upgraded to an extent comparable to that required for registered nurses.

Geriatric Social Worker—7000,000 jobs starting at $15,000, averaging $22,000. These workers will be essential for the mental and social care of the nation's aging population. By the year 2000, the birthrate of native-born Americans will merely equal the "replacement rate"—zero population growth. Improvements in food, medicine, and life-extending medical processes will create the need for hundreds of thousands of workers to serve the aged.

Education and experience requirements comparable to those for licensed practical nurses, recreational specialists, mental hygienists, and dieticians will enable GSWs to find financially and physically rewarding employment.

Energy Auditor—180,000 jobs starting at $11,500, averaging $15,600. Using the latest infrared devices and computer-based energy consumption and controlled networking, energy auditors will work with product engineers and marketing staffs in the production, sales, operation, and management of energy conservation and control systems for housing, industrial plants, and machinery. They will help architects and cost accountants achieve significant cost reductions through use of sophisticated heat sensing and measurement devices and systems, appropriate construction and insulation materials, and energy enhancement and recovery systems.

Technicians, inspectors, and supervisors will require a high-school education and the equivalent of two years of technical college education plus appropriate apprenticing or on-the-job experience.

Nuclear Medicine Technologist—75,000 jobs starting at $18,000, averaging $29,000. With the advanced understanding of medicines and serums using radioisotopes, a substantial increase in demand for this technologist will be needed. As the isotopes are absorbed in tissues and muscles, diagnosticians can observe functions of normal and/or damaged tissues and organs and can determine treatment needs and responses to medication in the central nervous, cardiovascular, pulmonary, digestive, and metabolic systems. Flow of medicines and effects can be traced and viewed directly on computer-enhanced video displays, thus reducing the incidence of surgery.

Technologists must be trained to work in laboratory conditions, become familiar with sophisticated equipment, and be prepared to assist doctors and nurses in handling equipment and patients.

Dialysis Technologist—30,000 jobs starting at $16,000, averaging $25,000. With the use of new portable dialysis machines and a greater number of hospital dialysis machines available, the demand for more dialysis technologists will grow.

These technologists must be educated and trained to work under laboratory conditions in a two-year postsecondary technical education program including a four-week computer-assisted training program and instruction from other dialysis technologists.

Computer Axial Tomography (CAT) Technologist/Technician— 45,000 jobs starting at $13,000, averaging $20,400. Though more than a decade has passed since development of this technique for using X rays with computer technology to give sectional views of internal body structures, the supply of qualified technicians has not kept pace with the growth of this non-invasive diagnostic science and equipment. Jobs for technicians to install, maintain, and operate CAT scanning systems and assist in the analysis of these scans will offer attractive employment situations for thousands of qualified people.

Minimum requirements for technicians include two years of postsecondary education and on-the-job training on the actual equipment in a participating hospital or equipment manufacturer. Minimum requirements for technologists include two years of instruction in anatomy, biology, and medicine. Fully qualified professionals will need further education leading to a baccalaureate degree.

Positron Emission Tomography (PET) Technician/Technologist— 165,000 jobs starting at $14,500, averaging $17,500. PET scanners are used for diagnoses of disorders of the human brain. Requirements for qualified workers in this field will increase with the growing use of this science, advances in human and computer technology, and research in human intelligence. Due to specialization in several technological and medical disciplines, technicians will be specialized.

Minimum requirements for technicians will include two years at the postsecondary level. They will specialize in equipment, chemistry, physics, or computer programming. Technologists must be qualified at the professional level, including a baccalaureate degree. Both occupations will require on-the-job experience.

Computer-Assisted Design (CAD) Technicians—300,000 jobs starting at $18,000, averaging $30,000. New uses for applications for this new design, engineering, and production technology will create hundreds

193

of new occupations for CAD specialists, both professional and nonprofessional. Millions of workers—including blueprint file clerks, draftspeople, designers, engineers, researchers, inspectors, secretaries, and artists—will find the computer can do more, better, and faster than traditional methods. Whether designing modes of transportation, dwellings, or other products, CAD will affect the education, employment, and ways of work more than any other single technology.

Education and training requirements will include high-school diplomas and at least two years of postsecondary technical school

Computer-Assisted Graphics Technician (CAG)—150,000 jobs starting at $20,000, averaging $35,000. Rapid growth of computer-assisted graphics will affect the education, training, and employment of all graphics technicians as no other event in graphics pictorial history. Demands for artists and technicians will increase tenfold with an increase in demand for new forms and dimensions of graphics to portray objects, schemes, and scenarios before they are actually produced.

Basic education and training will still include the physics of color, layout, dimensions, etc., along with instruction on specialized effects attainable through computers, computer programming, and business potentials and effects.

Computer-Assisted Manufacturing (CAM) Specialist—300,000 jobs starting at $20,000, averaging $31,000. CAM systems will permit all the design, development, specification, and logistics data to be pulled out of CAD and CAG data bases and be reprogrammed into computer-assisted manufacturing programs, which will then operate most of the production facility. This permits the attainment of Flexible Manufacturing Cells (FMC) in which every step of producing a product is determined and programmed sequentially for accomplishment without or with minimal human intervention. Education and training requirements must be changed in almost all occupations, especially in industrial and business management and personnel administration.

Education and training will include a high-school education and at least two years of training in postsecondary or technical institutions.

Computerized Vocational Training (CVT) Technicians—300,000 jobs starting at $14,000, averaging $22,500. Hundreds of thousands of these technicians will be employed in education and training materials development firms as this art becomes a new science to use in programs at all levels and in all disciplines in public and private educational institutions. Utilizing the demonstration capabilities and versatilities inherent in CAD software, in conjunction with the art and color expression of computer graphics, educators and trainers will be able to depict any object and any action with a vividness and dynamism that will produce higher learning benefits than any mode ever employed. Students will be able to assemble or disassemble the most complex mechanisms, construct the most artistic forms, and design dwellings and structures without ever leaving their computer terminals. While "hands-on-training" will remain an essential part of vocational training, terminology and work sequencing will be learned at the CRT. Textbooks and lesson plans, lengthy lectures and dissertations will become passé in the coming decades of learning by doing at the computer terminal interface. Up to 75% of all instruction will be acquired at the computer console, allowing teachers to spend much more time helping students learn actual on-the-job work skills with actual products and processes.

Technicians working in this new area will specialize in graphic arts, computer programming, educational and learning theory and practice, and technical competence in respective vocational technologies. At least two years of technical education after high school will be required.

Strategies to Provide Training for New Jobs

To upgrade and update the capacity of vocational education to provide the education and training needed by the labor force of the future will require addressing three areas of concern: acquiring competent teachers; changing prevailing attitudes toward education, training, and new technologies; and updating teaching methodology and instructional materials.

Attracting Competent Teachers

Currently, competent teachers are not attracted to the profession due to low salaries and low status. Competent teachers in vocational education, math, and science can earn 50–60% more in positions in the private sector. The decline in the profession can and must be stopped. Over the years, teacher-education programs have encountered declining enrollments—due, in part, to low salaries, to oversupplies during baby-boom years, and to the high status of working in the private sector. To counteract the declining enrollments, teacher training programs lowered their standards for entry, which resulted in not only attracting a lower caliber of student into the program, but also making teacher training a curriculum of last resort for those students who could not make it in other curriculums.

To reverse this trend, long- and short-term strategies must be instituted nationwide. Teaching can be made more attractive through the support of administrators and by raising the salaries of teachers, especially in areas of high demand such as vocational education, math, and science. Raising the salaries by 20% across the board, and by an additional 20% in those areas of high demand, will attract teachers back from the private sector and encourage a higher caliber of student to enter undergraduate teacher-preparation programs. The law of supply and demand will work if other constraints, such as inflexible pay scales and tenure laws, are lifted; but standards must not be lowered.

For long-term solutions to assuring a supply of competent teachers, a series of three hurdles must be instituted by teacher-preparation programs and departments of education on a national basis:

1. Before acceptance into a teacher education program, students must have scored at least 850 combined total on their SATs and have passed a proficiency test in reading, writing, and computational skills.

2. Before continuing in a teacher education program, students must maintain above average grades (3.0 GPA or the equivalent) for the first two years of undergraduate work (or the equivalent).

3. Before receiving permanent certification, a teacher must pass a competency examination and receive positive evaluations from supervisors, administrators, and/or peers.

These are not new suggestions; each has been implemented successfully in several states already. The implementation of these standards will not happen without controversy. Witness the furor caused by Penn State's Joe Paterno and the NCAA when they decided to require a total of 700 on the SATs before accepting college athletes. But for assured positive impact on the teaching profession as a whole, each of the three (entry standards, maintenance standards, and certification standards) must be initiated and maintained on a national basis.

Requiring each prospective teacher to overcome these hurdles will tighten the profession's standards and limit the numbers entering to the best. The resulting shortage of teachers will raise salaries and attract more from other places. The downward spiral will be reversed and the status of the teacher will rise, along with the salaries and the level of competence. If we do not reverse the trend, we may be forced to use teachers from foreign countries, similar to the medical professions' solution to maintain medical services in rural America.

To relieve the short-term lack of math, science, and vocational teachers, rather than tolerate less than the best, the best retired teachers or business people in these fields could take a 1–2 month refresher course and return to the classroom for a year or two. To further alleviate the shortage, corporations could be encouraged to make available some of their skilled technical people to provide some teaching.

Along with limiting entrants into the profession to the best, schools must continually retrain their good teachers. For example, computer literacy for every high-school student and every teacher must be required. In-service programs provided by school districts or departments of education should be available, and every teacher should be able to pass a computer literacy test within four years. If teachers do not fill the gap in their skills, they should be phased out on the basis of failing to keep current with the requirements of the profession. To win the salaries and esteem that the profession deserves, schools cannot keep deadwood on their faculties.

Changing Prevailing Attitudes Toward Education, Training, and New Technologies

Across the board, the gap is closing between the highest and lowest students. Special programs help the lower students come up to their capacities; however, few programs help the truly brilliant students perform at their capacities. In general, teachers who are brighter and capable of making more money are going into other occupations and are being replaced by less adequate teachers, so the students with the greatest potential are not getting the necessary support.

The latest report by the National Commission on Excellence in Education states the problems with the U.S. educational system very bluntly: "If an unfriendly foreign power had attempted to impose on America the mediocre educational performance that exists today, we might well have viewed it as an act of war." The commission found that some 23 million American adults are functionally illiterate, nearly 40% of the 17-year olds cannot draw inferences from written material, and two-thirds of the 17-

year-olds cannot solve a math problem. College entrance tests show a steady decline in scores in such subjects as physics and mathematics.

The commission strongly recommends increasing the length of the school day from six hours to seven or eight hours and the length of the school year from 180 to 210 days. (Additionally, I recommend one and a half hours a *day* of homework instead of the current one and a half hours a week.) But the report doesn't say who will pay for the extra hours of teaching, how the economy will absorb the additional 10–12% of women who will join the work force because their children are at school longer, or what will happen if large numbers of the children now in private schools return to public schools as a result of the longer school day.

There are, however, other steps that can be taken to improve education in the United States:

- Increase the number and competence of math and science teachers.
- Adopt more rigorous measurable standards of academic achievement.
- Adopt a curriculum that requires four years of English, three years of math, three years of physical and biological sciences, three years of social sciences, and one-half year of computer science. If a person is planning to go to college, there should be an additional two years of languages required.

America must encourage its youth to be proud of their skills in science, math, and vocational subjects. Students in any of these areas of study should not be made to feel inferior to anyone. Traditional funding sources, as well as parent/teacher groups, boosters clubs, etc. should be encouraged to make money and give funds to "mathletes" and "chemletes" as well as athletes. Students should be given letters in math, physics, chemistry, and vocationally-related extracurricular activities, similar to athletic letters. Finally, schools should be pouring dollars into computers rather than stadiums.

Education must equip people to change. As important as math, science, and vocational skills are, they are not enough. As society changes, so will the skills and knowledge needed to be productive and satisfied. The higher levels of cognitive skills must be learned as early as possible. People must be taught skills in decision-making, problem solving, creativity, communications, critical thinking, evaluation, analysis, synthesis, and the structuring of problems to understand what the results ought to be. We must make people think.

Updating Teaching Methods

Keeping vocational education programs up to date always has been a problem. The rapid pace of technological change accentuates and widens the gap between programs and the cutting edge of knowledge. Budget cutbacks make the problem even greater. The same problem has hit industry. Consequently, businesses are turning to computerized training to lessen the cost and, at the same time, maintain or improve the quality of their programs. At the forefront of this nationwide trend is the PLATO computer-assisted instruction system developed by Control Data Corporation.

The applications for PLATO are as limitless as the range of business and industry itself. Such diverse industries as manufacturing, petroleum, banking, real estate, finance, aviation, and emergency medicine find PLATO indispensable. Individual companies and associations training with PLATO include American Airlines, General Motors, General Mills, Shell, DuPont, Federal Express, National Association of Securities Dealers, Bank Administration Institute, Con Edison, and Merck Sharp and Dohme.

Computer-assisted instruction (CAI) is easily adaptable for short-term training. Many of the unemployed need two or three months of training for a job that will exist. CAI is practical and effective. Currently, over 12,000 hours of training make up the body of PLATO, with more added constantly. The information is absolutely up-to-date. If this or similar programs were implemented in vocational-technical schools, every teacher and every student would have immediate access to the most recent information available. Students could learn theory and related content on the computer. Teachers could then work individually with students for the hands-on training that is so vital in vocational education. This method requires a different kind of thinking by teachers. Insecure teachers will feel threatened by the computer if they have not yet become computer literate. But the computer is a tool to make teaching more efficient and more effective—not a replacement for the teacher.

Maintaining a skilled work force will take an enormous expenditure of resources. Operating training programs in vocational, technical, and industrial facilities 24 hours a day will eliminate much of the need for duplicating expensive equipment.

Even more importantly, we must use our training dollars only for jobs that exist or will exist in the near future. In the past, the training programs sponsored by the Comprehensive Education and Training Act (CETA) did not give Americans what was promised. Sixty percent of the money was used for administration; the remaining 40% went into training. Only 3% of the trainees actually obtained jobs. The people were trained for jobs that did not exist and will not exist. For example, up until 1979 people were still being trained to be linotype and elevator operators, even though a need for these skills had not been identified for the preceding 10 years. In fact, the equipment these people were trained to operate had not been manufactured for 15 years preceding 1979.

The new Job Partnership Training Act has tried to correct this by requiring that 70% of the funds go to actual training programs and limiting administration to 15%. The remaining 15% is designated for basic literacy education and for childcare services for trainees.

Conclusion

The jobs of the future are changing in nature. America needs to make short- and long-term changes to avoid disastrous consequences.

The first step is to begin to encourage the unemployed to upgrade their skills and take lower-paying jobs as temporary solutions. The next step is to get the education system back on track to produce educated minds that accept the challenges of the future and want to learn more. Strong emphasis on education is necessary; however, it is not sufficient. Training for the occupations of tomorrow is also needed. Finally, Americans must admit past mistakes and do what it takes to make the country strong and stable in the future.

References

Cetron, Marvin, and O'Toole, Thomas. *Encounters with the Future: A Forecast of Life in the 21st Century.* McGraw Hill: 1982.

National Assessment of Education for the Last 13 Years. Educational Commission of the States, Denver, Colorado, January, 1983.

A Nation at Risk: The Imperative for Educational Reform. National Commission on Excellence in Education. April, 1983.

Knowledge, Technology, and Professional Motives for the Future

by

M. Kent Mayfield

Paradigms for social change are rapidly shifting. D.N. Chorafas, for example, argues that the industrial revolution is over, superseded by a knowledge revolution that will result in upheavals as great as any spawned by the industrial revolution.[1] Peter Drucker outlines the emergence of a knowledge society where the systematic collection, organization, and application of information is the basic foundation for work and productivity.[2] Alvin Toffler tells us that society is now riding a wave of revolutionary change that will provide civilization with more, and more precisely organized, information than could have been imagined even a quarter-century ago.[3]

The concept of a "post-industrial society," particularly as outlined by Daniel Bell, is probably the most widely known analysis of the coming social order.[4] Bell describes his society along five dimensions. First, the economic sector of society is experiencing a shift whereby a greater proportion of the labor force is engaged in providing services rather than working in agriculture and manufacturing. Second, the number of individuals engaged in professional and technical employment is increasing. Third, theoretical knowledge gains rising importance in contrast with the primary use of empirical knowledge that characterized industrial society. The central role of technology requires, according to Bell, the continuous opening of new technological frontiers. Therefore, a fourth dimension of post-industrial society is a future orientation that involves the deliberate planning and assessment of technological growth. Finally, post-industrial society experiences the rise of a new intellectual technology to handle multi-variable problems.

A common theme in the literature is that the emerging society is a technologically-based service economy with a work force dominated by highly professionalized groups whose elite status is based on their possession, manipulation, and application of specialized knowledge.

The emphasis that social forecasters give to the role of knowledge, the emergence of technological elites, and the service orientation of the economy are all themes that have great appeal to the professions. The danger

M. Kent Mayfield is director of education for the Medical Library Association, Chicago, Illinois.

is that, in their enthusiasm to serve and join the elites of the post-industrial society, social forecasters may adopt the uncritical attitudes that seem to have characterized earlier efforts to respond to social change and the tacit acceptance of social goals formulated by elite segments in American society whose main objective was and is to preserve the status quo.[5]

Eager as professionals may seem for increasingly important roles in the knowledge-based society of the future, change of long-established practice does not equal the velocity of technology itself. Technology adoption follows a regular pattern: In the first stage, technology replaces manual or traditional methods, and activities are performed faster and more effectively; in the second stage, technology fosters new applications and things are done that were never done before; in the third stage, technology transforms or changes lifestyles. And, Kochen warns, "The flow of technology is so rapid it can acquire a momentum of its own and sweep us into lifestyles we may not like . . . We have barely enough lead time to prepare for an effective control."[6]

Yet, in a day when the world of corporate business is promoting the use of new communicative technologies to close the gap between an exponentially expanding information base and its effective management, the professional community lags far behind in its response to the immediate question of organizational information resource management and the far-reaching, and certainly more serious, issue of managing the intellectual resources on which society is based. The Conference Board raised the issue in its 1971 information management policy analysis study;[7] educational groups and medical associations have more recently voiced similar concern.[8] The intellectual professional community is familiar with the question. The assumptions of scholarly professional activity are not far removed from notions of information as a resource or a commodity to be managed nor from the considerations of the access to and transmission of knowledge or information as essential elements of professionalism. Why, then, so cautionary a posture on the part of the professions?

Nina Matheson, in her report on "Roles for the Library in Information Management," suggests that "the major barrier to change is often not the love of the status quo but the lack of a clear picture of where technology leads . . . . Without a vision . . . a concrete demonstration of feasibility, change is difficult to initiate."[9] Therefore, she sets forth three scenarios describing how the evolution of the present environment into more advanced stages might proceed.

Matheson describes the outlook for one profession, that of medical librarianship, but it resonates with significance for the professions more generally. But, intriguingly sketched as her canvases are, they lack the very dimension by which Matheson commends them to our consideration. Concerned with the organized surveillance of information, possessing special skill in manipulating knowledge, and therefore justifiably eager to foresee what impact technology will have on their world of work in the future, for what purpose, toward what goal, with what *intent* does the profession now define itself? No engaging, commanding, humane social or professional motive is evident. Nor, then, is there that motive that can enliven a profession's practice. Lacking that, although technologically sophisticated and organizationally complex, the work of the professional in the future she describes may be routine, mind-deadening, clerical, inconspicuous—a downward rather than an upward linear projection of the status quo.

The critical characteristic of any occupation recognized as a profession has been its grounding in a coherent body of theory, and in the technical "lore" grounded in its theory. The profession protects itself both by monitoring and controlling growth through research and by managing the distribution of private knowledge through venerable institutions or agencies. Only those persons surviving a prescribed protocol of training, indoctrination, and scrutiny are allowed to apply knowledge in practice. The exclusive right vested in a profession by society for the use of such knowledge has been the basis for the profession's autonomy and the practitioner's authority over the client.

The monopolization of specialized knowledge is now seen as fundamental to the emergence of the technological elites in the post-industrial society. However, the monopoly of knowledge and the status of traditional professions are threatened by the increase in the level of education of the general public. The gap narrows between the professional and the client, even in areas of professional expertise, through books, articles, television programs, and other media. Consumer health groups sponsor workshops on self-help health care. "The law belongs to the people. Pass it on," reads a recent advertisement from a law book publisher.

The intrusion of technology, especially the computer, also breaks down the monopoly of knowledge. Computers are becoming an important tool for all professions, forcing the practitioner to rely on specialists for access to and analysis of information in the professional field. Furthermore, information can be made widely accessible. "No longer," according to Haug, "need knowledge be packed only in the professional's head or in a specialized library, where it is relatively inaccessible. It can be available not just to those who know, but also to those who know how to get it."[10] As clients become more knowledgeable and have greater access to specialized bodies of knowledge, we move closer to the self-service society. It will be those occupations that create the techniques and service that increase the direct access to information and who pursue that intent with vigor that will experience the greatest increase in status.

The expansion of knowledge, seen as a harbinger of the post-industrial society, could in itself have a contra-professional effect. True, the growth of knowledge increases the number of specialists and experts vying for professional status, but it also leads to greater specialization and segmentation within professions. The proliferation of experts and the fragmentation within occupational groups diminishes the distinctive role of a specific profession and again reduces its ability to monopolize a body of knowledge and a system of technical lore. It is, then, increasingly difficult for the lay person to distinguish who is and who is not a professional.

On the other hand, the client is in the advantageous position of having a wider range of expertise to draw upon. Information on a particular financial problem, for example, might be supplied by a lawyer, accountant, real estate broker, financial advisor, social worker. or librarian. As clients become more knowledgeable and have a wider range of experts at their disposal, they become more self-reliant and demanding, require greater accountability for professional decisions, and assume a greater role in the governance of individual professions through lay representation in professional bodies.

Social change will undoubtedly have an impact on the established and emerging professions, but this change is not necessarily leading to a highly professionalized knowledge-based service society, at least not in the form often predicted by prominent futurists. Instead, it may be a time when clients are more self-reliant, depending less on professionals whose occupational structure is based on the monopolization of a specific social service and the knowledge upon which it is based. What we could see is the emergence of a self-service society requiring a new kind of professional, a professional who helps the client become more self-sufficient. Indeed, this is now occurring; occupations that are often cited as the emerging or semi-professions with little chance of attaining the full professional status of the recognized professions can now be shown to be, in fact, a new distinct type of profession, the goals of which are consonant with those of a changing society.

William Bennett and Merle Hokenstad, expanding on the work of Paul Halmos, have made the challenging case that there is a group of "people-working" or "personal professions" significantly distinct from the traditional professions. In contrast to such accepted professions as medicine, law, architecture, and engineering, which prescribe solutions to the client's problems, the newer professions, such as education, social work, and the mental health sciences, "function as catalysts who, through the communication of information and sharing of insights, attempt to help the client help himself."[11]

The elite professional uses his or her knowledge to help the client but does not share the knowledge, while the personal professional shares the profession's knowledge so that the client is better able to cope with his or her problem. The client's problems are often social or economic and may have a political or spiritual aspect to them in that the professional may serve as an allocator of a beneficial resource—information, welfare, salvation. Because of the nature of the problems, then, the knowledge-base of the personal professions also differs from that of the impersonal (older or elite) professions. It is less substantive, more technique-oriented, especially with regard to interpersonal skills and strategies for transferring knowledge. It is the ideal of the personal professional that the client grows or changes through the meetings with the professional and in the future can handle the problem without the professional.

In short, the professional and the client become more like each other. This is in sharp contrast to the elite professional, whose clients are expected to return for any recurring problems and are not expected to become self-sufficient at any point.

While it may be difficult to ascertain what course of action is specifically appropriate for the professions, it is clear that attempts to protect the ideologies and structures of the elite tradition alone would be a retrogressive step if the professions are to meet the challenge of social change.

A few propositions may be important in identifying professional motives for the future:

1. The professions must clarify who they are, what and whom they care about, what they have a talent to do, what kind of world it is into which they have been thrust, and where and how that being and caring and doing can change the world in the direction of their highest aspiration for it.

2. The professions must adhere to the practice of encouraging the growth of persons—competent, integrated, sufficient—and of demonstrable human outcomes.

3. The professions must be committed to insuring the greatest access to knowledge, opposing censorship and the monopolization of information by the private sector and promoting freedom of information and increased access for all clients.

4. The professions must not be limited to outmoded models of professional identity that would limit their contribution to social change. Instead, they should reflect on Haug's observation that "perhaps the term 'professional' with all its upper class implications will become obsolete or even a pejorative term, symbol of an earlier, pre-modern era. Some new word to signify the human service expert will emerge in the 21st Century."

5. The professions must not feel threatened by the emergence of other occupational groups concerned with the organization and dissemination of knowledge nor see in them the occasion for compromise or accommodation, but instead approach them as allies.

Perhaps these are little more than a reiteration of long-standing principles of exemplary professional practice, not always adequately applied but still valid. It is the critical and forceful application of these concepts that will be the challenge to established professional groups as they cope with knowledge, technology, and the selection of motives for the future.

Notes

1. Chorafas, D.N., *The Knowledge Revolution*, London: George Allen and Unvin, 1968.

2. Drucker, Peter E., *The Age of Discontinuity*, Harper, 1968, pp. 263–380.

3. Toffler, Alvin, *The Third Wave*. Morrow, 1980, p. 193.

4. Bell, Daniel, *The Coming of Post-Industrial Society*. Basic Books, 1973.

5. Harris, Michael H., "Portrait in Paradox: Commitment and American Librarianship, 1876–1976," *Libri*, December 1976, pp. 281–301.

6. Kochen, Manfred, "Technology and Communication in the Future," *Journal of the American Society for Information Science*, March 1981, pp. 148–156.

7. Kozmetsky, George, Ruefli, T.W., "Information Technology: Initiatives for Today—decisions that cannot wait." New York: The Conference Board, 1971.

8. Sawhill, T.C., "Curriculum Priorities for the '80s: Beyond Retrenchment," *Current Issues in Higher Education*, 1980. Vol. 4, pp. 13–33; Tosteson, D.C., "Science, Medicine, and Education," *Journal of Medical Education*, January 1981, pp. 8–15.

9. Matheson, Nina. *Academic Information in the Academic Health Sciences Center*. Association of American Medical Colleges, 1982, pp. 27–29.

10. Haug, Marie R., "The Deprofessionalization of Everyone?" *Sociological Focus*, August 1975, pp. 197–213; Helena Z. Lopata, "Expertization of Everyone and

the Revolt of the Client,'' *Sociological Quarterly*, Autumn 1976, pp. 435–47; Adam Yarmolinsky, ''What Future for the Professional in American Society?'' *Daedalus*, Winter 1978, pp. 159–74; Rue Bucher and Anselm Strauss, ''Professions in Process,'' *American Journal of Sociology*, January 1961, pp. 325–34.

11. Bennett, William J., Jr., and Merle C. Hokenstad, Jr. ''Full-time People Workers and Conceptions of the 'Professional''' in Paul Halmos, ed., *The Sociological Review Monograph*, University of Keele, 1973, pp. 21–45; Paul Halmos, *The Personal Service Society*, Cardiff: University of Wales Press, 1966.

Education:
What Do We Do?

The Reindustrialization of Vocational Education

by

Amitai Etzioni

"Vocational education is not a priority," lamented Richard Arnold, division manager of the Community Educational Relations Department of AT&T. "The Business Round Table decided not to take it on," confided one of my colleagues. When I ran into David Goslin, the top social science staffer of the National Academy of Sciences on the way to a "VocEd" meeting, he wanted to know, "What are *you* doing here?" When Congressman Carl D. Perkins launched hearings on possible renewal of the massive five-year program of federal aid to vocational education (which was due to run out September 30, 1982), the opposing views did not make the network news, indeed were barely reported at all.

Vocational education may not be a prestigious or "in" subject, but it requires attention in this era of national turnabout. Call it renewal, revitalization, or—I naturally prefer my own term—reindustrialization, the quality and preparation of human capital is a vital part of the renewed attention to economic growth. Few if any would contest the elementary truth that even if government intervention in the marketplace is slashed, its guzzling of resources is effectively curbed, and R&D and the formation of capital are encouraged, labor will still remain an essential factor in any equation defining the elements of productivity and economic growth. Indeed, a pivotal element of the first industrialization of America, roughly between the 1820s and the 1920s, was the mass preparation of immigrants and farmers for work in factories, including acculturation, general education—and vocational education.

The Condition of Human Capital

Many corporate executives find vocational education—and, more widely, preparation for jobs—a subject best delegated to someone in personnel, a topic not nearly as worthy as return on capital, new technologies, or even labor relations. The same executives are nevertheless keenly aware of the bottom line of the condition of human capital, the frequent absence of "employable skills." There is an acute shortage of persons with some specific skills (computer programmers, toolmakers, engineers, secretar-

Amitai Etzioni is university professor at The George Washington University, Washington, D.C., and is also director of the Center for Policy Research, New York City and Washington, D.C. This article is based on his book An Immodest Agenda: Rebuilding America Before the Twenty-First Century *(McGraw-Hill, 1982).*

ies). Moreover, in the groups of workers, blue collar and white collar, who are available in abundance, many are reported to be unable to read a blueprint, query a work processor or computer, compose a coherent report, or do simple calculations with assurance. "When I told her to use the yellow pages," a Washington-based executive says about his new secretary, "she said she couldn't." It turned out that she did not have a firm grasp of the alphabet, nor was she trained in the use of a simple index, two "skills" without which the yellow pages become quite unwieldy. The U.S. Army, one of the greatest users of raw human capital, found out in a recent tank-battle simulation that the messengers and radio operators were unable to "decipher" rather simple, but urgent messages.

Indeed, complaints about the lack of skills of the youth who graduate (or drop out) from American high schools, whether regular or vocational programs, have reached the level of a common cliché. It is less widely recognized that in fact the poor skills level of many of America's youth is an important reason for "youth dispreference" in hiring. In a study conducted by a White House task force in preparation for the administration's 1980 youth employment initiatives, employers said they could not find enough young people who have the basic skills of reading, writing, and arithmetic to perform white-collar jobs; they sometimes have to interview 12 to 15 young people to find one who can qualify for even an entry-level job. The literacy gap among applicants was a serious problem; major employers reported that over 60% of young applicants fail entry-level job exams. It is estimated that almost 23% of those who begin school will never receive a high-school diploma; even among those who do, many lack elementary preparation for work. Complaints about the decline of work-ethic are similarly common.

Social scientists, whose job it is to be skeptical about all widely-held assumptions, are less sure. Economist Edward F. Denison, a leading authority on productivity, is "skeptical that a sudden drop in willingness to work is responsible for the recent retardation of productivity." His skepticism, he explains, is

> largely attributable to having heard similar generalizations all my life and having read them in the works of observers who wrote long before my birth. It was well before 1967 that I wrote, "Like the supposed decline in the spirit of enterprise, there seems always to be a popular belief that people are less willing to put in a hard day's work than they used to be, but this is scarcely evidence."

Another leading authority in the field, the National Institute of Education's Henry David, in *A Policy for Skilled Manpower*, published 27 years ago, wrote "It was contended that workers are no longer governed by internal standards of work; that they display less of the old-time willingness to please the boss. . . ." Among the factors cited at the time were schools that no longer stress discipline, and decline of supervision at home because many mothers are employed.

The truth may well lie somewhere between employers' complaints and social scientists' doubts. Assuredly, matrons in ancient Rome complained that "you can't get good help anymore," but there is some evidence that the quality of America's human capital has indeed deteriorated over the last decades. A recent study by the National Assessment of Educational Progress found that the average quality of the writing of 17-year-olds is somewhat lower than it was in 1969, while the descriptive writing of 13-year-olds showed a "significant decline." The study concluded, "It appears that a considerable proportion of young people—from 10 percent to 25 percent—do not understand the nature and conventions of written language." Similar data have previously been published on declines in ability to compute and most other things.

And, despite his doubt about the decline in willingness to work, Denison found that great increases in the proportions of inexperienced workers—young people and adult women—among the employed caused a reduction of productivity, albeit not a major one. While the entry of so many young people and women into the labor force did increase total labor input and output, it added "less than an employment expansion of similar size would have done if it had been distributed like existing employment."

The data indicating decline of the work ethic are much weaker and less clear, but still point toward less motivation to work hard, and more demand for using work for self-development rather than a day's pay. A recent survey conducted by Louis Harris for Sentry Insurance found that among labor leaders, business leaders, and the public, two-thirds to three-fourths endorse the views that people take less pride in their work than a few years ago; that their work motivation is not as strong as it used to be; and that people are not working as hard as they used to. Daniel Yankelovich reports in his recent book *New Rules* that the quest for self-fulfillment has drastically reduced the proportion of Americans who believe in "hard" work.

In short, it seems that employers may be bitching as usual, but also may have more to bitch about.

"Wait a moment," I can practically hear the reader exclaiming. "Willingness to work and employable skills are not the product of vocational education alone." Quite right. They are a kind of an educational bottom line that reflects all that preceded employment, from the condition of the home on. Was learning—and work—appreciated in the family? Was the primary school adequate? And so on. Vocational education builds on all this, and if the pillars are shaky the roof cannot be stable. Vocational education cannot make up for years of underpreparation for the world of work, of jobs. The more general term "job education" seems preferable when one wishes to include all work-relevant educational "inputs," leaving "vocational education" to refer to educational preparation for a specific vocation or for skills applicable to several categories of jobs. In these terms, job education may be more at fault than vocational education, at least the place where matters first go awry. But call it any name, preparation for work seems to be deteriorating.

Minorities, Women, and the Business Community

Preparation for work is gaining renewed attention as the United States undergoes a major turnabout in its national priorities. After three decades of pumping up public and private consumption, social priorities, and concern with "inner" growth and the environment, the national focus is shifting to rebuilding economic vitality and growth.

As part of this turnabout, emphasis on minimum competence is replacing social (or automatic) promotion in schools, and emphasis on standards and structure is returning to colleges. While this shift in emphasis grows out of a general concern about falling skills, both its advocates and its detractors often use "minimum competence" and "standards" as code words for positions specifically concerning minorities. Social promotion in schools (and open admission in colleges) came to be favored, after compensatory education largely failed, to help minorities catch up with educational requirements. Many kids, especially in minority groups, were three to four years behind in math and English; instead of being held back to repeat classes endlessly, and suffer stigma on top of deficient skills, these young people were promoted—and graduated—automatically. Now, the call that schools demand at least some demonstrated competence is often perceived as aimed first and foremost at minorities.

Moreover, for long, too long, the media have tended to depict unemployment as first of all a problem of inner city, minority, especially black youth. Major federal programs have been evolved to try to increase the employability of these young people. Indeed, preparing minorities for work is one of the two top priorities of the federal vocational education program. The program's other social justice target is women. States receive funds to hire "sex equity coordinators," whose tasks include reviewing all vocational programs in a state for sex bias and helping local education officials to improve vocational education opportunities for women.

Indeed, the whole federal vocational education program smacks of the sixties. It began in 1963 with the passage of the Vocational Education Act, which significantly expanded federal aid to vocational education and established such funding as "permanent." In 1968 and again in 1976, Congress amended this act to inject social considerations into vocational education. The amendments provided that portions of the money appropriated to vocational education programs were to be earmarked for special "target" groups, especially women, minorities, and the handicapped.

Through these amendments, the federal government has been trying to spur the states to direct vocational education toward federal priorities rather than their own. It provides the states with only a fraction of the money that is spent on classroom vocational education, about 9% of roughly $6 billion spent annually on such training; the rest is provided by the states and local boards of education. (Of course, training on the job is provided mainly by the industry as well as a sizable growing number of schools run by corporations, especially big ones such as AT&T and GM.) Nevertheless, the federal government has been trying to be the tail that wags the dog. Francis Tuttle, state director of vocational and technical education in Oklahoma, sums it up: "Under existing federal laws and guidelines, the federal government furnishes less than 10 percent of the money but is attempting to drive 100 percent of the programs. I don't think any of the states think this is appropriate." Most states, in turn, have tried their best to take the federal dollars and follow their own views as to what is

212

to be done. Tuttle notes, "What we have had to do sometimes is work around the federal rules in order to accomplish what we see as our priorities."

The focus of vocational education on "special targets," the hardcore unemployed, equity, and *social* change, has led to a wholesale disregard of industrial and business needs. Young people have often been trained for jobs that did not exist and have ended up, in droves, working for local governments, not in the private sector. In its 1978 report on employment and inflation, the Joint Economic Committee concluded:

> The problem of teenage unemployment is not the inability to hold a job, but to get one in the first place . . . . The central focus of eliminating [this problem] must be to provide better mechanisms to match job seekers with jobs. Schools, businesses, and unions should expand the scope of the activities that link classroom activity to work.

The Committee also noted, "Poor or nonexistent counseling often results in coursework choices which are irrelevant to future jobs."

Employers and their representatives second this complaint. Robert L. Craig, communications director of the American Society for Training and Development, an organization of private-sector job trainers, comments:

> Vocational education wastes a lot of money because the education people don't get together with the people from the world of work. There's a big gap between education and work, and the employer has to fill it. . . .

Craig Musick, training director of the Graniteville Company in South Carolina, notes the discrepancy between education and industry in his own state:

> The technical colleges in South Carolina are trying to develop technicians (2 years) and skilled craftsmen (1 year) for business and industry. . . . However, corporations have been slow to accept the technician concept because they do not have such a slot in their salary administration plan and corporate structure. . . . Both units (college and industry) are training people but not working together.

In addition, labor representatives have protested the lack of contact between educators and unions. Rod DuChemin, assistant director of human resources development for the AFL-CIO, notes that

> the split between the thought processes of the vocational education people and the business community is very wide. The vocational education people never really spend any time trying to learn what [union] apprenticeship programs are all about.

Widening the gap between vocational education and the business world is provision of vocational education mainly through public schools, the majority of which are comprehensive high schools and community colleges that offer both vocational and academic programs of study. There are nearly 5,600 such institutions, compared to 700 vocational high schools, technical institutes, and other specialized schools that offer instruction primarily in technical education, and 1,900 area vocational schools and centers offering technical education on a part-time basis. Most comprehensive high schools tend to treat vocational education as a third cousin at best, while they favor liberal arts. Moreover, subjects that are not specifically vocational are increasingly taught in a way that makes them more academic—relevant to college but not jobs—as witnessed by recent changes in mathematics, economics, and natural sciences courses.

A push in the same direction comes from the structure of the advisory vocational education boards states must set up if they are to receive federal funds. The federal government spelled out in fine detail 20 categories of people that must be represented on these boards. The advisory boards must include members concerned with the education of women, the handicapped, ex-cons, and people whose knowledge of English is limited; a VocEd student; and so on; but few are required to represent or understand the needs of the client of vocational education, the business community.

Beyond this general, almost incomprehensible inattention to the client, the preoccupation with social priorities and liberal arts distracts attention from two other obstacles to rebuilding human capital for reindustrialization: inappropriate psychic preparation and the mismatch between jobs and the labor force.

Skills or Self-Discipline?

Inadequate preparation of the labor (typical, by the way, of underdeveloped countries, which the United States is slowly coming to resemble) is *not* limited to some minorities, women, or inner cities. Large numbers of white males are also graduating from high school (or dropping out) unable to do elementary computation, and functionally illiterate, unable to follow a training manual, even one simplified to comic-book level. Moreover, to the extent that the widely-used term "lack of employable skills" focuses attention on cognitive deficiencies (inability to read, write, and compute), it is, I believe, deeply misdirected.

As I see it, the quality in which large segments of the labor force are particularly deficient is self-discipline, the basis of the ability to work with authority figures, with co-workers, with rules, and to do routine tasks. Indeed, this deficient psychic preparation seems to me to be a main cause of both deficient cognitive preparation and unemployability. Intelligence is rarely the issue; even a person of relatively low IQ can memorize the alphabet *if* he or she is able to mobilize self for this elementary level of concentration and effort—in other words, has self-discipline.

The intellectual demands of using an index system, reading a blueprint, or querying a computer are quite low, but these tasks do require an attention span, a level of concentration, and a systematic approach that exceeds that of impulse-ridden, unfettered minds. Behind most complaints about lack of skills (quite valid in themselves in that the person does not command the skills) is the lack of adequate psychic preparation. Thus, the inability to compose a simple memo, indeed a paragraph, is not so much intellectual as psychic—the inability to adhere to simple rules—a sentence must have a subject and a verb and end with a period, and so on. (I refer here not to effective essay writing, but to straight composition.) Similarly, simple math requires first and foremost a level of self-discipline to mem-

214

orize some basics (e.g., multiplication tables) and to adhere to a few rules. As I see it, the shortage of secretaries reflects a shortage of people willing to deal with routines (such as filing), to memorize (as in stenography), and to submit to authority. The key attribute of a good toolmaker is precision; precision is not a matter of high IQ, but of considerable self-discipline.

Indeed, give me a self-disciplined person, motivated to work, able to deal with others, with authority, and with rules, and having reasonable intelligence, and I will teach that person all the "employable skills" in short order. And give me a person lacking in these essential psychic traits, and I will find that person very difficult to teach—and to employ.

Why the deficient psychic preparation? In an America in which most, if not all, institutions have eroded, each institution tends to load part of what it should do in a well-functioning societal division of labor onto the next one, creating multi-institutional overload. The result is an institutional domino theory: as one institution underperforms, it leans on the next and strains it.

Laying the psychic foundation of self-discipline is first the task of the family; the formative years are crucial, and parents (and siblings) provide the first and most important "role models." True, even in good old America, not all families did their basic educational thing. But recently, with both parents often working outside the home, with "parents" often rotating (through divorces, a sequence of boyfriends or girlfriends, re-marriages, stepparents, grandparents temporarily playing parental roles, etc.), and with a widespread notion that normless permissiveness is the childrearing practice to follow, many kids reach the educational institutions woefully underprepared, from a psychological viewpoint.

Schools are supposed to be the bridge from the family to the world of work—the first experience of dealing with rules, authority, time-specific "work" units, structured achievements and rewards—but in many of the nation's educational institutions the experience is quite different. These schools are overloaded with excessive and conflicting demands; suffer from a breakdown of inner discipline and structure; and are equipped with a boundless permissive psychological philosophy and burned-out staff. Particularly among schools in the inner cities, the breakdown of discipline has turned many institutions from educational establishments to inefficient warehouses, where the entrance of young people into the labor force is delayed while they indulge themselves, act out, and otherwise hinder those who wish to teach or learn. In these schools, protecting teachers from rape and assault, and the building from vandalism, is often itself a consuming and inadequately performed task. Teaching does occur, but the sum of the educational experiences generated in these schools is a better preparation for a world of street gangs, drug-pushing, numbers-running, or sporadic work laced with drugs and alcohol than for "a day's work for a day's pay."

Even where there are but few disadvantaged students, as in the many suburban public schools, the quality of psychic preparation varies a great deal. In many, the psychic message is based on a version of developmental psychology according to which the teacher focuses on the person, not on his or her ability to function within a team or community. The result is well depicted in *The Class of '65*, a book about the graduates of an upper-middle-class school in Pacific Palisades, California. The students, typically the products of parental neglect or boundless permissiveness, had been faced by a school that set no clear standards, promoted no positive values, and "understood" the need to act out. Ten years later, only two of the graduates seem able to function in an adult work world. Others have committed suicide or had nervous breakdowns, are religious freaks or in a Turkish jail for drug smuggling, and so on. Some will eventually straighten out, but no thanks to their families or schools.

Not all American schools are like that certainly; but maybe half of the nation's kids pass through such schools. Not all of those who appear at work's gate are underprepared psychically; about half of the youth is a reasonable estimate.

When many families and schools are not doing their psychic preparation, their job-education, the task falls on the high school's vocational education programs, junior or community colleges (often openly perceived as remedial institutions for what the high schools neglected), or special programs, such as vocational schools. Many of these focus on cognitive elements (teaching remedial English or applied math). Other vocational programs do succeed in making up, to some extent, for previous deficiencies because they select youth in a way that screens out the psychically underprepared; or because they keep the kids day and night (the various "academies") and so can penetrate deeper into their pupils; or because training is closely tied to available, sought-after jobs at the end of the schooling—a powerful incentive.

Often, though, the load is passed to the next institution in sequence, the workplace. Large corporations end up spending hundreds of millions of dollars not on vocational training, or fine-honing skills to their needs, but on elementary job education and on attempts to cope with the consequences of deficient psychic preparation. Smaller corporations face even greater difficulties; unable to set aside the resources for schooling, they commonly have to make do with what they can hire: raw or underprocessed human capital.

Mismatch

Not all the difficulties arise from deficient psychic and cognitive preparation of workers; the world for which workers are being prepared has also changed. Henry David, who has led a major study of vocational education for the last five years, gives a telling example: twenty-five years ago a cabbie could be illiterate; today he must be able to write, because he is required to keep a log. Generally speaking, while the distribution of innate talent within the labor force may well not have changed, job requirements have escalated, with a decline in blue-collar and an increase in professional and semi-professional jobs. The computer revolution, the so-called onset of the post-industrial society, is but part of all this. No wonder less-skilled workers are in surplus and skilled ones in great demand.

Reindustrialization of Human Capital: What Is to Be Done?

All this suggests that there has been a wide decline of "employable skills," not one limited to minorities; that it is due first of all to institutional erosion and lack of self-discipline, not cognitive deficiencies; and that the federally imposed priorities of the sixties helped separate Vocational Education from the world of work; and that changes in job specifications have added to the difficulties.

If the preceding analysis is roughly correct, not too much is to be expected from attempts to straighten out the last domino of a teetering series. To ask vocational education in public institutions to provide "employable" workers is to ask its often unappreciated staff, thrust aside by general educators and often ignored by business, to correct for underpreparation by the family and the schools in both personality and cognitive areas, as well as to make up for what God and nature have not provided, an *expanding* pool of innate talent to suit raising job demands. Sure, some benefits can be squeezed out by using up-to-date instead of obsolete equipment (e.g., electric instead of manual typewriters). And a remedial course in English will somewhat improve the reading and memo writing of some. And if it is possible to forecast with reasonable accuracy where the jobs will be, and train people for them rather than for jobs that are vanishing, motivation to study will be improved. But these measures won't do the whole job.

Greater benefits might be generated by basic organizational changes. First, remove federal direction and let states and localities run vocational education. Second, increase the representation of business in the vocational education state advisory board and reduce the role of general education, which tends to foster an anti-vocational educational orientation. Third, increase the contact between vocational education representatives and the business community by forming local business *visiting committees.* Harvard has committees of outsiders who come to visit regularly with its departments, review achievements, and advise on directions to be followed. Vocational education programs would gain in relevance, reality, clout, and status if local employers would be invited to form committees to regularly advise these programs. Employers, increasingly concerned, might volunteer—especially if they felt their advice would be heeded.

To get at the two core issues, however, the growing labor-job mismatch and psychic underpreparation, quite different approaches are necessary. For the mismatch, one must recognize that as a rule it is easier to restructure the job than change the person. Thus, in the new anti-tank Cobra helicopter, the U.S. Army found that if the guiding mechanism breaks down, it is more efficient to unplug the "black box" and plug in a spare one than to call for, or train, repair personnel. Auto repair shops will benefit once computers start doing much of the diagnostic work, since fewer and fewer mechanics have the needed "insights." New typewriters, linked to processors, are equipped with a memory of the spelling of 50,000 words; if one is misspelled, the screen flashes. Using these may turn out to be more efficient than teaching anyone to spell all these words. Even more than before, we need to look at the job-worker match as a two-sided dynamic, without limiting our efforts to suit one to the other, not to make room for self-actualization but to be more cost-effective.

As to psychic preparation, "remedial" work is best achieved through surrounding the person with a constructive total environment—not in specialized classes, in which what is gained in class is lost in other environments. Hence, for those who come to work underprepared, the best hope lies in on-the-job training, not in additional schooling, though in many instances some additional schooling is needed before on-the-job training is practical, or must accompany it.

In the long run, the pass-the-overload system will need to be reversed. Rather than stacking more and more remedial institutions on top of one another, families and schools will have to do more of their elementary duty: to prepare persons able to function in an adult work world. This is not something that employers can command, but in the renewing America—in which the public has come to favor a tax cut for business over one for itself—the concern with our national and economic future may be carried over to a greater attention to the human capital, especially in the psychic formation of the next generation of Americans. It is as necessary as fighting inflation and securing investment in capital if economic growth and social stability are to be provided for the future.

New Work and Education:
Socio-Technical Work Theory
and
School Learning

by

Arthur G. Wirth

In the past several decades, an extensive literature has emerged that has identified a variety of ways in which schools correspond to the needs of the work world.

In this paper, I shall argue that the kind of systems efficiency influence from the corporate world that bore down on schools in the 1970s is being challenged by a counter set of factors in the 1980s. The challenges derive from two interrelated changes taking place in work: the emergence of democratic social-technical work theory, which, in turn, is being supported by some forms of high technology.

I shall make a brief reference to influences on schools of the systems efficiency rationale. Then I shall examine implications for education of emerging socio-technical work design by turning to theory/practice examples that have emerged from Norwegian Work Research Institutes where socio-technical theory has received its most serious attention. The Scandinavian experience may be seen as a model from which Americans might learn if the socio-technical trend already under way in the United States becomes a serious force in the economy.

Systems Efficiency and Schools in the 1970s

In the past decade, schools have been influenced heavily by the cost-benefit model of systems efficiency theory from industry. Pressures have mounted to treat education as a production function. As C.A. Bowers has pointed out, this has infiltrated the ways that teachers are led to think about their work; they begin to use the restrictive language of technocratic ideology—inputs, outputs, behavioral objectives, competency-based criteria, etc. Life in school gets narrowed down to "mastering" measurable components of instruction engineered by outside experts. In Bowers's words:

Arthur G. Wirth is a professor of education at the Graduate Institute of Education, Washington University, St. Louis, Missouri. This article is based on research for his forthcoming book, Productive Work—In Industry and Schools: Becoming Persons Again, *and also appears in modified form in the Fall 1983 issue of* The Teachers College Record.

. . . (The) application of systems theory to the teaching process . . . is likely to transform teaching and learning into a mechanical, positivistically oriented process . . . In effect, it creates an encapsulated technological universe where only technological and management problems are real.[1]

A turn in this direction became the strategy of educational policy makers in the '70s. It was their response to concerns about decreases in productivity that were plaguing both industry and education.

While the tendency of educators to seek answers through technocratic efficiency techniques might be understandable, there was also an irony in the move. At the very time when schools were turning toward refined versions of Taylorist control, that model was being declared dysfunctional by growing numbers of thoughtful leaders in industry.

They began to entertain the idea that the malaise of people at work might be an outcome of the very technocratic expertise introduced to correct it. They concluded that the old remedy of stepping up supervisory controls over a reluctant work force producing shabby work was no longer viable. They could continue to apply the failed treatment—or try something else. One surprising alternative was to turn to the concept of socio-technical or industrial democracy work design theory. It was based on the peculiar notion that the revitalization of human productivity might depend on a return to the neglected values of democracy under conditions of modern technology.

Before delineating features of socio-technical work theory and how it might affect education, I want to comment on several factors in the larger society that have supported this development: (1) the success of American education in producing an "over-educated" work force, and (2) certain trends in high-technology work.

American ideology holds that democratization of opportunity is provided by access to public schooling, which opens possibilities of upward mobility and personal satisfaction. The twentieth century, in fact, witnessed an impressive expansion of the school system aimed at accommodating all aspirants seeking better work. Success, however, became a source of trouble. Educational expansion has produced a larger number of educated persons than the economy provides jobs for. There is much evidence that a highly educated work force tends to be more resistant to the authoritarian social relations of the scientific management tradition. The discontents of "over-educated" workers could result in disruption of productivity and capital expansion. Concern about this potential has led to awareness of the need to address disaffection at work. One response has been to increase worker participation by various forms of workplace democracy. In the view of Henry Levin, who wrote the article "Education and Work" for *The International Encyclopedia of Education* (1983), moves toward greater worker participation and collective decision-making could have profound implications for schools. If the emerging system of production requires more collaborative, problem-solving human interactions it, in turn, could require school experiments with more liberalizing forms of learning for students *and* teachers. The conditions begin to arise for a new stage of work/school "correspondence."

One test of whether there is evidence for the possibility sketched by Levin is to see if it gets any support from developments on the frontier of new work—high-technology production.

High Technology and Learning at Work

We get a vivid sense of this in Larry Hirschhorn's analysis of the situation in the high-technology nuclear power industry, with events at Three Mile Island as an illustration.[2] There is a growing awareness, Hirschhorn says, that cybernetic technology does not replace human work, but leads to workers, technicians, and supervisors actually taking on more complex roles. A basic reason is that inevitable failures of cybernetic processes built into production require a higher order of coping responses.

In his analysis of events at the Three Mile Island accident, Hirschhorn identifies lessons we are beginning to learn: "The more complex the machinery, the more complex are the possible varieties of machine failure. There are moments when only human intelligence can diagnose and correct unforeseen breakdowns. To prevent catastrophes, machinery must be designed to permit human intervention, and workers must be trained as problem solvers, not merely machine tenders."

At Three Mile Island, there was a lack of flexible response to the complicated set of events that unfolded. Multiple failures included poor maintenance, bad design of the console and the control room, error of judgment, and inappropriate training. These "errors," says Hirschhorn, did not derive from failures to operate a machine correctly, but reflected a failure by the engineers and managers to design a system that integrated effectively worker intelligence and technical processes. Analysis of the situation reveals basic contradictions resulting from a conflict between old industrial mind-sets and the actual demands of the new post-industrial production systems.

On the one hand, the philosophy and training of engineers leads them to create designs based on the ideal of the regularity and lawfulness of the solar clock. In technical systems, "feedback" controls are designed to cope with *predictable* errors and failures. Workers are treated as extensions of the mechanical system. The aspiration is to control their actions through training programs and system design so that their responses will be specific and predictable. On the other hand, cybernation is a product of fallible humans. It cannot eliminate errors and, in fact, raises failures to new levels of complexity. Hirschhorn's analysis of the failures at Three Mile Island leads him to conclude that "workers in cybernated systems cannot function as passive machine tenders, looking to instruction manuals for the appropriate response. This suggests an entirely new definition of work in a post-industrial setting. Skills can no longer be defined in terms of a particular set of actions, but as general ability to understand how a system functions and to think flexibly in solving problems."

In spite of this, Hirschhorn finds that the traditional mind-set of engineers and managers makes them reluctant to help workers gain insight into system designs, or to train them to think conceptually beyond lists of responses to a series of anticipated problems. He found that training by utilities at nuclear plants is typically conducted by utility officials or vendors who sell training packages to companies. They are technically competent, but their courses are usually geared to the Nuclear Regulatory Commission's qualification examinations. The aim is to test competence on routine tasks and familiarity with specific emergency procedures. The aim is not to deepen workers' understanding of the physical, chemical, and system features of the reactor process. The result is a kind of training that ignores requirements for the kind of expanded learning that would equip workers to cope with the unexpected.

Even while these mismatches between concepts of training and the new technology continue to happen, there is growing experimentation with alternatives. The general trend in cybernated industries is to locate workers in control rooms where they manage from a distance the manufacturing process. In the chemical industry, for example, continuous "batch processes" are controlled by microprocessor operations. While not subject to nuclear catastrophe possibilities, failures in the system can become a major cost of production. Workers must not only be prepared to respond to emergencies but also to adapt appropriately to the introduction of new machinery or new products. Some manufacturers are recognizing the need to create designs that permit fruitful interactions between technology and human intelligence. Thus, a Canadian plant that manufactures alcohol which has to be "customized" for use in a variety of things such as soaps, carpets, containers, etc., designed a computer process not simply to automate production but also to supply workers with technical and economic data so that they could solve problems of customizing and could test their own production decisions. Workers who develop a facility for experimental decision-making become more knowledgeable and contribute to a constant upgrading of the manufacturing process.

Moves in these directions involve a fundamentally different conception of the interactions of workers and machines. Hirschhorn points out that the emerging logic of post-industrial workplaces tends to leave both management and unions in a paradoxical position.

Management, to operate and protect the new machinery, needs highly trained workers, trained to think independently; but its traditional interest in control mandates a work force with limited skills and aspirations. There is an uneasiness among some utility owners that moves toward autonomous work teams with highly trained problem-solving skills could become threats to the basic prerogatives of management.

Other problems are posed for trade unionists. Traditionally, union solidarity has been secured by emphasizing a class division between management and workers. But this tradition is in conflict with the professional character of work transformed by cybernated processes. In fact, unions, to protect workers, need to seek upgrading of competencies and broader worker involvement in plant operation. They need to assure workers' rights to understand the technology that they use. Such moves, which recognize the paraprofessional status of better-educated workers, may further blur the increasingly unclear line between workers and managers. There is fear among union officials that this could lead to erosion of union security. It could also lead, however, to new and different opportunities. There is growing dissatisfaction among engineers, middle managers, and other professionals who chafe at being underutilized or being victimized by bureaucratic size and politics. Imaginative unions might become a counterpoint to represent all employees, workers and managers, who are seeking new perspectives and goals for work life. They might assume leadership of an "oppositional culture" aiming at a new integration of company goals with protection of professional competence and needs for professional growth.

Hirschhorn concludes:

> The logic of the post-industrial workplace may force a radically different conception of production work upon both managers and trade unions. Managers may be forced to share real power with their workforce, not for the conventional purpose of improving morale or smoothing industrial relations, but because technological exigencies and market pressures simply demand more knowledgeable, autonomous workers. The old-fashioned class politics of industrial society is giving way to a new post-industrial politics, in which representation of worker interests by trade unions will turn on a very different set of issues, such as education and access to information.

The implication is clear that, for effective performance in work like that described by Hirschhorn, new modes of learning are needed that move beyond "training" concepts' of the classical scientific management model. The implication also seems clear that school learning based on narrow technocratic influences from industry will likewise be dysfunctional.

As we indicated in the introductory remarks, an alternative concept of work—democratic socio-technical work theory—has been emerging as a vigorous challenger. It is a growing force in the United States, but there is a longer history behind it in Scandinavia. Since we are concerned with linkages between the new work concepts and education, we can benefit by looking at projects developed at the Norwegian Work Research Institutes. They represent the most serious efforts to explore education/"new work" linkages.

Socio-Technical Work Theory and Education

The contemporary origins of democratic socio-technical work theory may be found in the interrelated work of a variety of thinkers such as Philip G. Herbst, Einar Thorsrud, Fred Emery, and Eric Trist, who, though scattered from Norway to Australia, have been associated with the English Tavistock Institute of Human Relations and the Norwegian Work Research Institutes. American theorists like Louis Davis and Michael Maccoby (influenced by Erich Fromm) have moved in similar directions.

A basic insight of socio-technical theory is indicated by the term itself. It holds that the fundamental flaw of the technical efficiency model is the "technical fix error," i.e., the insistence on seeking purely technical solutions in systems that are, in fact, *socio*-technical. "Socio" refers to the human part—the personal, intentional, creative aspects of human reality.

This is not the place to explicate in detail this alternative philosophy of work, which seeks to tap worker involvement as a corrective to the technical-fix error.[3] My purpose is different. I work from the assumption that educators must accept the reality that their work will be influenced significantly by the master economic institution and the world of work. When technocratic ideology and systems efficiency are unchallenged in industry, schools cannot escape their influence. But what kinds of educational implications might arise if significant sectors of American labor and management bring under question the Taylorist system of work design? What if there is a significant turn to democratic, workplace theory as a means of economic survival? Are there implications for the philosophy and practice of education when the work of teachers and students in schools is viewed from this perspective?

Formal writing on the subject is meager. Philip G. Herbst, one of the most creative thinkers of the Norwegian Work Research Institutes, has been the most direct in addressing the question of the relation of socio-technical work philosophy and education. I shall refer to his writing in exploring the question.[4]

He and his colleagues in the Norwegian Industrial Democracy Project took the position that growing concern about the quality of life at work and the need for democratic alternatives to hierarchical bureaucracies is not merely an aberrant wish of impractical humanitarians. It is rooted in fundamental changes in man's relationship to his environment. The bureaucratic model worked when man's fundamental relation to his world was the physical environment and the technology he developed to act on it. The environment could be conceptualized as an aggregate or cluster of elements that could be manipulated for human gain. Classical economic and management theory incorporated humans as constituent elements of the aggregate.

The socio-technical theorists maintain that we are entering a new stage marked by the emergence of a turbulent environment. The source of the turbulence lies in the shift from a situation where the physical environment and technology functioned as the medium for the relation of man to man. This derives from man's own conceptualizing, which confronts humans with rapid, profound, often unpredictable change. "The turbulent environment is man himself and efforts to solve turbulent type problems with procedures based on principles of the mechanistic, aggregate model increasingly break down."

Norwegian work redesign in areas like the new high-technology merchant marine is based on the assumption that the rate of change in technological design increases so that it has now become necessary to build learning capacities into the organization of industrial work teams. Herbst and colleagues decided that this can be achieved only by creating relatively autonomous matrix organizations in which neither task roles nor work relationships are fixed. Within this framework, work teams of persons engaged in on-going learning become capable of doing reseach both to find ways to improve production and to develop strategies for coping with changes in tasks. Linkages are established with university and other research units.

In the new Norwegian Merchant Marine, there was a growing recognition that the sophisticated computerized technology of new ships was not amenable to old-style organization of ship personnel. There is a steady flow of newness in equipment and operations, which requires crews capable of ongoing learning and collaborative trouble-shooting. It cannot be met by organizational systems in which relations are impersonal, inflexible, and unstable due to rapid turnover.

To try to retain the old organizational forms seemed irrational, and Norwegian leaders also were increasingly dissatisfied with the disjunctions between the democratic values and relations in community life and the authoritarian traditions aboard ships. The basic decision was to experiment with alternatives to hierarchy so that Norwegian ships would become more democratic places in which to live and work. These developments, in Herbst's view, point toward the possibility of a new emerging post-industrial work model for some significant portion of the population:

> A society in which there will be relatively little difference in the educational level and status of those who work in industrial, educational, research, and service organizations. Persons will differ more as regards their focus of orientation than as regards the nature of their work. The leading elements in the transitional stage of development are the rapid increase and diffusion of complex technologies which can be operated by a small number of persons, and the rapid increase and diffusion of higher education . . . As development continues, the traditional hierarchical type of organization based on the separation of doing, planning and deciding will be replaced by primary work groups in which these functions are integrated. The members of these groups will to an increasing degree be able to participate in policy decisions and be capable of using specialists as consultants.

In *Socio-Technical Design: Strategies in Multidisciplinary Research*, Herbst devotes attention to the implications of "new work" philosophy for educational organizations. The assumption is that constant technological and social innovation is the dominant reality with which institutions must cope. The need grows to create educational organizations that can equip persons to adapt to *indeterminate* change. Educational institutions themselves experience turbulent change due to rapid growth in knowledge and shifts in expectations of their clienteles.

Herbst's premise is that the possibility for creating educational organizations appropriate for any era depends on the model used for structuring educational tasks. He makes a socio-didactic analysis of the basic assumptions that have been built into twentieth-century schools and finds that educational tasks have been structured on a simple "production-process model" paralleling the organizational features of the traditional factories. They have not yet responded to the learning characteristics of the new work world, which is still very much in the minority.

To clarify his thesis, Herbst differentiates two fundamentally different types of work tasks: determinate tasks and indeterminate tasks. *Determinate* tasks are those where every element is specifiable and the outcome is predictable. (The manufacture of Model T Fords would be an example.)

Regarding *indeterminate* tasks, Herbst identifies three varieties, which progressively become more indeterminate:

1. There may be a *given initial* situation and a *required* outcome and the *indeterminate* factor is the means to use to get from the initial state to the outcome. For example, the engine room of a ship (now full of sophisticated technology) may need to be cleaned. The means may be left

undetermined if the crew is permitted to create its own task force, which will take initiative in reaching the goal. In this case, it becomes a *research-type task*. On the other hand, if the methods are prescribed in detail and executed under bureaucratic scrutiny, the work has remained as a production-type determinate task.

2. We may have a task where *new material* is given, and the two indeterminate tasks become ''what can we do with it?'' (end product) and ''how can we use it?'' (means). For example, if a school gets a microcomputer, the staff might be brought into the thinking about what ends to use it for and how to use it.

3. Finally there is the fully *indeterminate task* where no element can be fully specified at the outset: This is the type of task that increasingly emerges with advanced technology. For example, in the case of the Norwegian merchant marine, as changing computer-oriented technology transformed the nature of the ships, the old production-type model increasingly became dysfunctional. New training programs could not be implemented before technological changes upset the planned design. The new type of ship emerging required flexible, multiple-skill trained personnel who could identify the problems and form themselves into flexible autonomous matrix groups to help the ship perform its mission. All workers who participate in this kind of indeterminate work task are actively engaged in a learning process.

We can understand why the socio-technical work theorists repeatedly refer to Jean Piaget's *To Understand Is to Invent*. Those who are at work in indeterminate-type tasks cannot be people who know only the discrete steps of a manual or workbook. They have to understand the whole system in terms of the interrelation of the parts.

A basic point in Herbst's socio-didactic analysis is that the way school tasks are structured affects all aspects of the dynamics of school life. The basic distinction is between production-type tasks and research project-type tasks. He quotes the findings of Dutch researchers (1969) who showed that students spot with high consistency the difference between production-type ''schoolish'' teachers and ''non-schoolish'' research-project oriented teachers. Herbst says that the production-type teacher

> . . . splits his subject into small isolated bits, which have to be worked on and learnt one at a time. Students are required to follow rigid instructions. The performance of students, both in terms of following instructions and in terms of the results obtained, is judged simply as right or wrong. The teacher claims complete autonomy for himself as an expert, while allowing little or no autonomy to his pupils. Subjects that especially lend themselves to being taught in this manner are mathematics and foreign languages. A machine teaching programme is an extreme example of this type of teaching technique.

Research-project type teachers

> . . . give their students autonomy to investigate, discuss, and find out for themselves. The teacher defines his role as a resource person for the activities of his students. . . . Where drill is needed, the purpose and meaning are explained. Judgment of performance is not simply in terms of right or wrong, but in terms of the development of increased ability, competence, and independence.

The "production-type" teacher aims to have his students follow instructions and to perform precisely a predetermined program. Original ideas of students are seen as non-compliant behavior, so curious students are often forced to choose between being passive or being seen as rebellious. This type of school organization fulfilled its function to produce human beings who were attached to traditional production processes and who were to subordinate themselves to the control of managerial authority. It also produced alienation from school tasks.

On the basis of his analysis, Herbst sees growing discrepancies between the task definitions in schools and the task definitions in industries under turbulent change. Secondary schools typically are organized around separate subjects. The research problem-oriented tasks of higher-technology industry do not split up the field of knowledge in the same way as the school subjects, and they require a type of organization based on cooperation rather than on competition. "Many types of problem encountered on the shop floor, in a hospital, or in a family require an understanding of social-psychological, economic, technological and political aspects and their inter-relationships."

A major project of the Norwegian Work Research Institute was a 10-year study of progressive changes in the design of work on the ship *Balao*.[5] As Norwegians on the *Balao* began to work more and more in the "indeterminate research learning" style rather than the traditional "production task" mode, they discovered they had to turn attention to the schools that were training personnel for the merchant marine. They found that the schools and teachers who were not in touch with the new developments were becoming isolated from maritime reality. The younger personnel were losing respect for out-of-date teachers and programs. A decision was made to bring teachers aboard the ships. Teachers were integrated into the work process itself, which gave them a sense of being on the frontiers of learning and enabled them to communicate as equals with ship's personnel who were working in the autonomous, matrix task force mode. Teachers, however, also taught classes in their specialized skill areas, which were valued as components of an integrated training program. When teachers returned to their schools on shore, they began to introduce problem-oriented projects consistent with the emerging learning style they had seen on ships.

Later I was able to visit a secondary school in Stavanger that was pointed out to me by the merchant marine researchers as a place exemplifying moves in the new direction. It has established working relations with the Jonas Øegland plant, which produces bicycles and industrial robots. This plant has moved in the direction of shop-floor democracy, with autonomous work group teams. Major changes were introduced in the modes of production and quality control, with workers taking over functions of managers and supervisors.

At the school, I observed classes in electronics where students were working on project problems that had been identified in consultation with factory work groups. For example, several students were working on a problem from the industrial robot division. Teachers, students, and factory representatives jointly planned strategies and evaluation procedures. A school steering group was created, composed of elected pupils and teachers and representatives of work groups from industry. The steering committee will allocate study projects into several courses of study: electronics, calibration, physics, etc.

Beyond this, the director explained that Norwegian education officials and representatives of collaborating industries are developing a plan for a postgraduate thesis program that can be completed by people who have entered industry. A practical or theoretical industrial problem will be identified by a candidate. His plan for thesis research will be placed under the supervision of the head of the appropriate department (for example, a department of professional engineers), and there will be consultation with appropriate personnel in the university. If the thesis is well executed, the candidate will be assisted in entering advanced training in a university. The director saw these developments as giving continued encouragement to students who like research-type learning. He said that places like the Øegland Plant industry begin to be a learning place for both workers and management—and move in the direction of the label described by Herbst where "everyone ought to be a researcher."

Industries of this type have to become capable of "learning" to meet change. In order for students to be adequately prepared for entrance to such places, the young should learn in schools that also are capable of "learning as institutions." Ironically, many schools whose programs are rigidly prescribed by centralized authority have less capacity for "learning" than some of the newer workplaces. Teachers and administrators are worn out by keeping the system running, by being made subordinate to prescriptions of external authorities, and by having to keep tabs on reluctant charges.

Herbst calls for more autonomy for individual schools, with meaningful roles for some representative committees like the Steering Committee of the Viderengaende Skole in Stavanger. Centralized boards of education would still have system-wide responsibilities but their consultative, facilitative roles would rise sharply in importance and their prescriptive, control functions would diminish. Pride would be taken in fostering schools skilled in getting students and teachers involved in personal learnings that relate to the changing social reality.

In Herbst's view, this does not mean that all "schoolish" type teaching is bad. There are needs for systematic specialized learning experiences. One of the avenues to be explored seriously in the 1980s will be to see how many of these can be programmed into computer-assisted instruction. That dimension is a necessary complement to the "research-project, non-schoolish methods" that now need to be expanded.

The Norway example illustrates the following: When people start down the socio-technical road, questions about the nature of learning and schooling tend to be raised.

If "new work" requires the empowering of people to learn reflectively and to act based on that learning (features of the liberalizing ideal), then continuities are needed between "new work" and schooling. The notion arises that the kind of learning that needs to be supported in both institutions is the liberal "freeing of intelligence" type learning.

If we seek ideas about how to make schools centers of liberalizing learning, we might turn to these new workplaces for useful clues. The question of what conditions support the freeing of intelligence (or what thwarts it) can be pursued productively both within schools as workplaces and within workplaces themselves.

Herbst himself defends the idea that this work theory has significant implications for societal transformation at the broadest level. He sees the possibility of a transition between a late-industrial stage and a potentially less destructive post-industrial era. Socio-technical work design is seen as a "leading edge" toward the forming of a social order based on the principle that productive development depends on human conservation or "well-faring" of all. Herbst uses the concept "world model" to compare present social features with a possibly emerging alternative.[6]

In the late industrial (or "modernist") model, the significant challenges seen as problematic for survival are located in the properties of the environment. The fundamental characteristic of the environment is that it is a cluster or aggregate of elements. This is the model in terms of which classical science built its theories of universal determinist laws. Armed with the tools of science, man stands apart from the environment and against it. This results in a basic contradiction in his condition.

In the active mode, standing godlike outside the world, man controls, masters, and subjugates the environment. In the passive mode, it is the environment that shapes, governs, and determines his behavior.

The orientation of a science that is atomistic, mechanistic, and deterministic, which permitted mastery of the environment, also provided the conceptual base for the creation of bureaucratic organizations based on the principle of uniform replaceable parts. When "fixing" is needed, one turns to the engineering expert who provides the thinking required "to restore efficiency." Others follow orders.

The pathologies of this model emerge, Herbst wryly observes, "when man begins to treat man as part of the physical environment. In the active mode he perceives and masters others as objects. In the passive mode he experiences himself as object, as a cog in the machinery." In this engineer's view of the world, "the function of insight and understanding is no longer a liberating one but the pragmatic one of meeting the challenge of the environment."

But the organizational patterns designed to increase control are themselves increasingly marked by unruly complexity, size, and dysfunctional change that becomes increasingly repugnant and unacceptable to humans. The principles of hierarchical bureaucratic control no longer provide the conceptual base for understanding the problems of the present turbulent environment. "This is because the behavior of man, the relationship of man to man, and the social ecologies that have come into being do not conform to the universal and immutable principles of classical science." The capacity to deal successfully with this order of change depends now on building a human choice-making capacity into the system itself.

The Taylorist tradition based on the separation of doing and thinking becomes increasingly inappropriate and is replaced by work groups in which these functions are integrated. "The members of these groups will to an increasing degree be able to participate in policy decisions and be capable of using specialists as consultants." The shift, then, is from a feeling of alienation to a feeling of autonomy.

The "well-faring world model" requires a kind of science of man that is not ethically neutral but has a responsibility to determine the choice of technologies that support the learning and growth of all persons in the system. According to Herbst, the shift to the new world model requires the capacity and opportunity to participate in "research style" inquiry type learning. This requires the values that John Dewey said are essential to engage in scientific inquiry—values of individuality and community. A forerunner of work of this type may be seen in some high-technology work processes where a relatively small number of well-educated workers need to respond to random unpredictable events.

Herbst himself, however, argues that high technology itself is not a guarantee of humanistic reform. Computer technology, for example, may be designed to bring closer the goal of complete, rational machine control that requires no human participation or intervention. "It is possible that god-like mysterious power will be projected upon computer programs, to which effective decision-making authority will be transferred and which may for a time permit the survival of centralized hierarchical organizations."

Herbst and colleagues simply point to the waste that results when human capacities are unutilized; and that technical and social health can be restored when people are "brought in" as whole human beings—as demonstrated with low-skilled workers in assembly plants as well as people in high-technology industries. These may be seen as "leading edge" examples of a well-faring world model where ethical choices about uses of technology and social relations are made for sane social and personal development. No one knows if they are aberrants or forerunners. They are beginning to appear, however, in the master institution. They might function as laboratories where growing numbers of people begin to raise questions about the quality of life under technology.

My personal conviction is that democratic/ecological third ways beyond main-line capitalist and state socialist systems need to be created. Producer cooperatives of the type developed in Mondragon Basque communities in Spain provide one promising example. We should seize the chance, however, to find out if working through corporate structures with the values of socio-technical, democratic work theory can become one serious source for effecting liberating social change.

Footnotes

1. C.A. Bowers, "Emergent Ideological Characteristics of Educational Policy," *Teachers College Record*, Vol. 79, No. 1, September 1977, p. 50.

2. Larry Hirschhorn, "The Soul of a New Worker," *Working Papers Magazine*, Vol. 9, No. 1, January/February, 1982, pp. 42–47.

3. Arthur G. Wirth, *Productive Work—In Industry and Schools: Becoming Persons Again* (Washington, D.C.: University Press of America, 1983).

4. Philip G. Herbst, *Socio Technical Design* (London: Tavistock Publications, 1974), and *Alternatives to Hierarchy* (Leiden: Martinus Nyhoff, 1976).

5. Ragnar Johansen, "Democratizing Work and Social Life on Board M. S. *Balao*," Report of Ship Research Group, Work Research Institute, Oslo, Norway, 1979. Supplemented by interviews with Mr. Johansen, Oslo, May 14, 1980.

6. For an elaboration, see Fred E. Emery and Eric L. Trist, *Towards a Social Ecology* (New York: Plenum/Rosetta, 1973).

Getting Ready for the Next Industrial Revolution

by

James O'Toole

The Japanese have finally gone and done it. They've built a factory in which, untouched by human hands, robots make robots. From the initial delivery of parts and materials, through the stages of cutting, grinding, molding, casting, welding, assembling, painting, and packaging, to the final warehousing of the finished product, machines do all the work. The "offspring" of this process are now being installed in American factories where they soon will be making cars, tractors, jet planes, and nearly every other manufactured product currently made by the hands of men and women. In the near future, automation will start even prior to the manufacturing stage of production: miraculous computers are now capable of actually designing products and then "sending orders" to robots on the shop floor telling them what to make and how to make it.

Revolutionary changes of this magnitude always entail a mixture of blessings and curses. For example, the nineteenth century industrial revolution ultimately led to the great advances in living standards, social equality, and democracy enjoyed today in Europe and North America. But along the way a heavy price was paid as workers were exploited, traditional community values were destroyed, and Dickensian slums were created. From what we can tell, America is on the verge of a second industrial revolution made possible—indeed, compelled—by the computer in its many manifestations. Like its predecessor, the next revolution will have both benefits and costs.

The benefits to the nation promise to be impressive. The advances in productivity provided by the new technologies are likely to increase America's standard of living, make the economy less inflation-prone, and, perhaps, make our industry once again competitive in world markets. On the personal level, machines will relieve humans of almost all dirty, dangerous, strenuous, menial, and repetitive tasks. In factories of the future, the only human workers will be engaged in installing, programming, monitoring, and repairing the robots that will do all the direct labor.

James O'Toole is a professor of management at the University of Southern California's Graduate School of Business Administration, Los Angeles, California. This article is reprinted by permission from National Forum: The Phi Kappa Phi Journal, *Vol. LXIII, No. 1, pp. 16–18.*

In offices of the future, word processors, intelligent copiers, and automated information systems will eliminate such drudge work as filing and stenography—and probably do away with the rote work of the typing pool. Already, such diverse workers as farmers, lawyers, accountants, nurses, journalists, managers, technicians, teachers, postal employees, auto mechanics, retail clerks, real estate agents, and military and police officers are finding subtle alterations in their jobs thanks to the new computer-based technologies. In the future, such changes will be profound and, in most cases, beneficial.

The office worker who once used only lower-level skills to sort, copy, and file will soon have access to information that formerly was the purview of managers only. The secretary of the future will hence be able to use her higher-level analytical and reasoning skills to make challenging decisions. Similarly, the industrial worker, who now uses her lower-level abilities to drag parts around and feed them into a machine, will soon have access to managerial information—and, hence, the ability to engage in tough and interesting problem solving along with her supervisor. In effect, the new technologies blur the invidious distinctions between the secretary and the boss and between the blue- and white-collar worker. This presents tremendous opportunities to those office and factory workers who are prepared by experience and education to accept increased responsibilities.

Unfortunately, this general upgrading of jobs comes with a negative side: the new technologies are beginning to erode the already poor employment prospects of the disadvantaged. While the coming wave of automation probably will not reduce the *total* number of jobs, it will decrease dramatically the number of lower-level jobs that typically go to the least-educated workers. Unskilled and semi-skilled industrial workers, clerks and typists in offices, and even service workers who do routine tasks will all see their jobs eliminated as sure as humans make little green Apple computers. Everywhere one looks there are signs of oncoming job losses: In an aircraft factory, labor that once required the efforts of 12 men is now done by a robot and one man monitoring its performance; in an auto corporation, work that once took a draftsman three weeks is now done in a day by an engineer with the aid of a computer; in an insurance office, letters that were once typed by a secretary are now entered directly into a computer by the boss himself, and sent electronically to other managers. Even in relatively high-technology industries, the impact of the miraculous new machines is being felt: the introduction of the computer to the telephone and telecommunications industries has eliminated some 100,000 jobs. In workplaces around the country, hundreds of thousands of people are being made redundant by automation. If current trends continue, the already-high levels of unemployment among the unskilled, the disadvantaged, and factory workers will rise to depression levels in the years ahead.

This forthcoming revolution is not a matter of if, it is quite simply a question of when. While the current prolonged recession has slowed the introduction of the new technologies, it has not altered industry's long-range automation plans. For example, before the recession, General Motors had planned to be as fully automated as its Japanese competitors by the end of the 1980s. That date has been set back because of GM's inability to raise the capital needed for expensive robots. But as soon as the economy turns around and capital starts flowing again into corporate coffers, GM and every other industrial giant is planning to convert its cash into new machines—*not* into hiring new workers.

These are not idle plans. Nor are the changes that are soon to occur the mere fantasies of dreamy futurists: they are real. Moreover, the coming industrial transformation promises not only quantitative but qualitative change. Indeed, the very nature of the economy is already being altered. As the power of computer technologies has increased exponentially by over 25% *annually* since the mid-1960s, and the cost of computer capability has fallen while the cost of labor has risen, the curtain has been lowering on the industrial age. For example, half of the U.S. work force is currently engaged in information work: the processing and manipulation of words, data, and ideas. The future promises more such changes. In vanguard post-industrial cities like Los Angeles, something like three-quarters of all advertised job openings are for information workers. In factories, we find the obverse of these white-collar trends. General Electric, for instance, has built a factory in which one enormous locomotive engine frame is produced daily in a process that involves *no* production workers at all. The plant replaces one that employed 68 workers who produced only one such frame every 16 days. The difference in the rate of productivity between the old and new plants is staggering; the resulting loss of employment alarming. Over the next decade, automation will reduce the total number of manufacturing jobs in the economy by 25–50% (the rate will depend on the speed of economic recovery).

In order to save the remaining jobs of the least-educated industrial workers, union and minority leaders will be tempted to call for limitations on the introduction of new technologies and on the closing of outmoded plants. Already, the International Association of Machinists is proposing a "Technology Bill of Rights" to protect displaced workers. But Luddite movements never succeed. Automation brings too many benefits to too many people to be denied. On this score, history is always cruel to the few for the good of the many.

But there is no reason why we need stand by helplessly and watch our most vulnerable citizens victimized by the onrush of technological progress. The only policy that can protect them in the long run is to begin educating them so that they will be prepared to enjoy the fruits of the second industrial revolution. The years to come will see tremendous demand for knowledge and information workers: analysts, engineers, scientists, technicians, managers, and the like. Unfortunately, America is failing to educate an entire class of citizens to realize these occupational opportunities. In the current system, general, basic, liberal educations are provided to the children of the privileged, who then are able to pursue advanced, specialized education in preparation for good jobs. In contrast, narrow vocational education is given to the children of the disadvantaged, who then enter the kinds of jobs that technology is eliminating. This system has always been undemocratic and unjust—now it is becoming economically untenable as well.

The only hope for the disadvantaged is for them to learn to read, write, and compute so that they can then acquire the skills needed for the jobs of the future. Soon there will only be work for those who have the skills of speaking, listening, observing, and measuring, and the confidence to use their minds to analyze and solve problems. Those who will succeed in the work force will be those who have learned how to learn—the unthinking jobs all will be done by machines. The French have anticipated this phenomenon. They have remade their once class-segregated educational system into a single-track in which all children now receive the same basic liberal education that was, until recently, preserved for only a privileged few. This new system complements a national effort to be in the forefront of the computer revolution.

The Japanese, too, have anticipated the age of automation. Recently, they have outpaced us in providing high levels of basic education to all their children and youth. Consequently, Japanese workers and unions welcome the introduction of labor-saving technology. Unlike Americans, the well-educated Japanese workers are able to be rapidly retrained for better jobs when their current jobs are automated. Domestically, we seem to be moving in the opposite direction, compounding the undesirable side effects of automation. For example, there are now misguided calls for increased high school vocational training of industrial workers. (We never seem to learn: after the Watts riots, the federal government trained young, black Angelenos to be elevator operators—oblivious, as late as 1967, to the inevitable dominance of the automatic elevator.)

Vocationalists go wrong, in part, because they cling to an outmoded assumption that the typical worker is, and will continue to be, a lathe operator (or some other factory or manual laborer). While the assembly-line worker *was* the representative employee of the industrial revolution, Drexel University's Arthur Shostak suggests that the air controller is the prototypical worker of the future. Unlike factory workers of the past who worked mainly with their hands, air controllers (and similar nonprofessional controllers of machines in factories and power plants), work with their minds. Their computer-based jobs are highly sophisticated, critical to the safety of their enterprises and the public, directly affect productivity, and are indispensable (one can't get machines to make human judgments about other machines). Thus, the worker of the future is not the manual laborer of the vocationalist's imagination, but a "data communicator" with heavy responsibilities—both technical and moral—that require the judgment and analytical skills that are characteristic of the broadly educated person.

Perversely, calls for outdated, vocational training often come from liberals and leaders of minority communities. There seems to be an unspoken conviction among many in these groups that black and brown children can't handle the same educational challenges as whites, and that many nonwhites are uneducable for good jobs. These assumptions overlook evidence coming from the few inner-city schools lucky enough to have teachers and principals who refuse to let students cop out of learning with the excuse that they are disadvantaged. Where teachers demonstrate high expectations of their students, poor nonwhites respond to educational challenge as well as do their suburban, white counterparts. Once they have the confidence that they can learn—and are provided with a sound, basic educational curriculum—minority students quickly form appropriate habits of study and work and develop the language and numerical skills needed in all jobs in the second industrial revolution. Fortunately, such a curriculum has come along at exactly the moment it was needed: *The Paideia Proposal* by Mortimer Adler and his colleagues outlines exactly the form of education that can prepare disadvantaged and advantaged students alike for life and work in a technologically advanced society.

What educators must avoid is overreaction. For example, in California, Governor Edmund Brown, Jr., has called for the remaking of all education into high-tech education. In schools across the state, administrators and principals are directing every spare nickel into computers and software. In a trendy rush to be on the cutting edge of the latest social movement, California's politicians and school administrators are overlooking the fact that computers are tools—albeit powerful tools—but merely tools nonetheless. While students must be trained at an early age to make full use of these tools, it must be remembered that computers are means, not ends. Computers are no substitute for sound, basic educational preparation for life's many activities and roles: work, leisure, family, citizenship, and lifelong learning. Certainly, there should be a place for a computer in every classroom, as there will be a computer in every aspect of life in the future. Still, the computer must be kept in its proper place. In California, unfortunately, some schools have let the computer drive the educational process. For example, the vocational preparation of computer programmers has been pushed at the expense of liberal learning. Ironically, this has occurred just as self-programming computers are being developed. This is no better than training elevator operators.

Caveat: I have not addressed a related and potentially tragic issue. America has not come to grips with the shorter-term problem of finding work for the many 40- and 50-year-olds whose jobs are being decimated by automation. Hundreds of thousands of factory workers in the auto, steel, and rubber industries of the Northeast and Midwest may never again know gainful employment—most certainly not employment at the high pay they once received. These semiliterate men and women—people who never learned the skills of lifelong learning when they were young—cannot readily be retrained to work in the new semiconductor industries or in jobs in computer maintenance, monitoring, or programming. Unless government and industry can find imaginative ways to retrain, even to educate, these people, they will face bleak life prospects. And society will face the terrible burden of an angry and dispossessed working class.

More and better education for all is the only policy that can prevent terrible social consequences from accompanying the introduction of the new technologies. Either America must begin now to educate the disadvantaged in the manner it educates the privileged, or expect a nightmare future. For the social consequences of millions of unemployed workers could make the side effects of the first industrial revolution appear benign in comparison. Fortunately, such consequences for our youth, at least, are not predetermined. They can be avoided if America acts now to make the reform of elementary and secondary education a high social priority.

Current Models for the Future Education of Workers

by

Sharon Rubin and Amy Thomas

As we consider work in the future, it's necessary for us to think about the education of future workers as well. The challenge is substantial. There will be huge numbers of new workers, including more women and minorities than ever before. They'll be doing new work, serving an information society. Both large corporations and small businesses will have new needs as they manage technological change, prepare new employees, keep workers from becoming obsolescent, and retrain them frequently. Workers will change careers more often and enter and leave the work force and educational institutions more frequently. How will higher education respond to these challenges?

As we look at present higher education, we see patterns surprisingly like those of 20 and 30 years ago. Although adults are returning to school for training or personal development in record numbers, most colleges still don't accommodate adults with ease. For every college that gives credit for life and work experience, another treats old transfer credits as if they were carriers of contagious diseases. For every course a major university offers in a distant part of the state on weekends, a dozen colleges continue to offer courses in three one-hour segments per week during the middle of the day. Corporations, frustrated by the inability of colleges to respond to their needs, develop more and more specialized training courses, but for every company that creates new in-house training, another cuts the training budget immediately when the bottom line is unhealthy. For every company that encourages employees to develop their abilities by taking college courses, another reimburses by the grade, discouraging employees from taking the truly rigorous or challenging courses.

If the general outlook for future-oriented worker education is gloomy, that gloom is not unrelieved. There are presently a number of programs that bring colleges and businesses together in ways that anticipate future trends, that use resources wisely, and that fill the needs of businesses and employees while supporting the mission of higher education, as well. These programs provide models that can be used as they are or readily revised for new circumstances.

The workers whose numbers will be increasing in the future—females, Hispanics, blacks, older workers—are those who have traditionally not

Sharon Rubin is director, Experiential Learning Programs, University of Maryland, College Park, Maryland. Amy Thomas is a research associate at Experiential Learning Programs.

237

been trained to enable them to pursue careers in technical fields. Three programs have found innovative ways to prepare such workers.

Evergreen Valley College, in San Jose, California, began its *Transition into Electronics* program to give displaced homemakers, the disadvantaged, and reentry students both exposure to technical industries and the confidence that they can be workers in such fields.

The 10-week program, initially funded through the Displaced Homemakers Act, combines classroom instruction with experiential learning, a curriculum geared to help each student make "realistic and knowledgeable career decisions."[1] The hands-on training includes constructing a transistor radio. Students report that this experience helps them "overcome their anxiety and fear of working with machines, tools, and other things technically-related." Other experiential learning includes a number of plant tours, so students can see different actual work environments. Classroom instruction is provided by "role model" instructors, many of them women employed in area industries. Students report that such instructors have had a major impact on them in creating an awareness of different occupations where they can "fit in."

Most of the students who enter the *Transition into Electronics* program are not already students at the college, but many decide, after completing the course, to become regular full-time or part-time students, continuing studies in electronics, data processing, electronics drafting, and engineering technology.

Women are rapidly becoming the largest population of new workers. Chase Econometrics estimates that, by 1990, 70% of working-age women will be in the work force.[2] Although women are entering the work force in record numbers, they are still concentrated in low-paying, low-skill jobs. Full-time employment responsibilities, in addition to family responsibilities, often prevent women from pursuing the extra education and training they need for job advancement.

The banking industry can serve as a model to study the difficulties of advancement for women in the business world. The National Association of Bank Women, an organization of women banking executives, conducted a study of its membership in 1972 and found that only 12% of the members had college degrees. This lack of educational credentials affected both the women's immediate positions as bank professionals and their prospects for future promotion. For instance, because of lack of education, women bank workers were primarily in the personnel, operations, and retail side of banking, but the line to senior management tends to be in the more technical commercial and lending areas.

NABW decided to develop an undergraduate management degree program to provide its members with the financial, analytic, and problem-solving skills they needed for promotion. NABW's original proposal, developed with Simmons College, Boston, was funded by the Carnegie Corporation in 1974. The NABW/Simmons program has been so successful that NABW decided to expand the program, and it is now offered at Louisiana State University in Baton Rouge and Mundelein College in Chicago as well.

The program is geared to the full-time banking worker, who can earn a bachelor's degree in management in three to five years without quitting work. Students attend six Management Institutes, two two-week sessions for each three years. The Institutes are designed to provide the student with in-depth instruction in the structural and behavioral aspects of finance, accounting and control, operations management, and marketing.[3] By completing the Institutes, the student earns between 36 and 42 credits; the remaining credit hours are earned in liberal arts and business-related courses, which vary by institution, and by credit for prior work and life experience.

Both bankers and banking institutions have acknowledged the program's immediate benefits. Women who complete the NABW program comment that the knowledge and experience gained are useful immediately to their current jobs. Over 85% of the program's participants have received promotions since first enrolling in the program. Sponsoring banks have witnessed increases in participants' productivity, professionalism, job satisfaction, and commitment to their banks.

Although employment opportunities have improved for minorities in fields traditionally closed to them, many obstacles remain. The number of minority executives has shrunk since the mid-1970s, despite efforts from major corporations to recruit minorities into management. This problem extends from the executive suite to the university classroom, where there continues to be low minority enrollment in undergraduate and graduate business programs.[4]

The Leadership Education and Development program (LEAD), established in 1980, is a national effort to increase the number of minority students in business schools and the business world. The program exposes high school minority student leaders to educational and career opportunities and to role models available to them through special summer programs.

Talented minority high school juniors and seniors participate in four-week intensive business and management curricula at LEAD-cooperating universities. The students are then monitored throughout their undergraduate careers and are encouraged to pursue liberal arts degrees, followed by professional business programs.

The students' role-model exposure extends beyond the classroom into the business world itself. All students participate in three-year part-time internships with the companies of their choice. At the end of each student's third year of undergraduate study, LEAD will assess the student's progress and plan a program of "upward mobility."[5]

LEAD, which started in 1980 at the University of Pennsylvania's Wharton School of Finance, has spread to Northwestern University, the University of Michigan, Columbia University, and the University of Maryland, which has a joint program with Howard University. By 1985, the program will operate in 10 major business schools.

These three models are different in intent and scope, yet they each have major implications for the successful integration of new populations of workers into the labor force.

As a result of the speed with which the United States is turning into a service economy, many companies have developed programs to upgrade their employees' abilities as effective service workers. Their definitions of "effective," however, have varied by both industry and philosophy.

INA, one of the nation's largest financial services organizations, with worldwide operations in property-casualty insurance, life insurance, employee benefits, health care, and investment management, has identified the liberal arts as the basis for giving employees organizing, planning, decision-making, and creative skills, along with leadership, oral communication, and interpersonal abilities.[6] As Ralph S. Saul, INA chairman has noted,

> Education in the liberal arts plays an important role in developing managers. It provides a vital perspective on the interrelationship and growing complexity of business and society. As a multinational company doing business in 145 countries around the globe, INA recognizes the need to understand not only our own business, but also the diverse and complex social, political, economic and cultural environments we work in. It is no longer enough for managers to be well trained; they must be well educated. The demands of business and society require them to explore and act on dynamic and wholly new concepts that accept no traditional solutions. For that they will need to know the best that has been thought and said by generations before them, and that is the benefit of a liberal arts education for business decision makers and leaders.

Other companies having philosophies similar to INA's often introduce top executives to the liberal arts through special summer programs, such as those at Amherst or Williams. INA, however, has imagined liberal arts eduction in a much broader context. With the University of Pennsylvania, INA has developed a liberal arts degree program that makes attending school as attractive and convenient as possible for INA employees. For instance, all courses are held at INA headquarters from 4:30 to 7:10 in the evening. A complete selection of liberal arts courses leading to a degree with a major in the social sciences is offered with regular University of Pennsylvania faculty. Courses are tuition-free to qualified students, and INA pays all tuition bills in advance of each semester. A full-time coordinator is available to help employees discuss their educational plans, to facilitate application to the University of Pennsylvania, and to provide information and counseling to students.

Although the program was originally intended for employees of any level seeking to enhance their liberal arts backgrounds, the program has been most attractive to clerical personnel who do not already have college degrees and who see the program as a route to long-term mobility within INA, as well as a chance for personal enhancement. INA is now considering graduate courses to give professional staff and middle managers motivation to develop their liberal arts competences, too.

Companies wanting to improve their employees' service abilities often sponsor short-term training or even offer college courses specifically linked to job performance. INA feels it has taken a truly future-oriented step by investing instead in an on-site baccalaureate program in the liberal arts.

Although shifts in the economy are gradual in some fields, in others they are more drastic. A typical case of major change occurred at Western Electric's Columbus Works, due to the restructuring of the Bell System. Plant operations were being switched from production of electro-mechanical systems to computer-based systems, and heavy layoffs occurred. A work force of 6,500 was reduced to 3,000. Even remaining employees were not immediately transferable to newly-designed positions, and most were told that they had to become computer-literate if they were to keep their jobs.

Franklin University had been working with Western Electric since 1978, when the Western Electric employee development club had approached Franklin to ask them to offer business administration courses. It was therefore natural that Western Electric should again come to Franklin for help.

The first orientation meeting that Franklin arranged for Western Electric employees drew 125 people. Although Western Electric had planned the program for some of its technical and engineering employees, the majority of employees at the orientation were regular production line employees who did not have the mathematics skills to take the college-level mathematics prerequisites for computer science courses.[7]

Although Franklin and Western Electric could have restricted the program to those few employees who had the background necessary to begin programming courses, Western Electric made the decision to open the program to all its employees and Franklin quickly restructured the program to offer re-entry mathematics to interested employees.

In the summer of 1982, the program began with over 30 employees enrolled in on-site remedial mathematics and over 30 employees enrolled in on-site introduction-to-algebra courses. In addition, technical employees who did have good mathematics skills were enrolled in a computer programming course on the Franklin campus.

Although there is nothing particularly unusual about universities offering courses at company sites, both Western Electric's willingness to retrain rather than replace, and Franklin's willingness to provide a more basic program than anticipated speak well for the effectiveness of the collaboration.

Shifts in the economy lead to a scarcity of potential employees in fields where they were overabundant just a few years before. In the early 1970s, electrical engineers were having a hard time finding jobs; now those with graduate degrees are becoming more and more difficult to find. According to a recent survey by the U.S. Bureau of Labor Statistics, there will be 10,500 openings for electrical engineers per year through 1990, but colleges will produce only 35% of the electrical engineers needed in the next half-decade.[8] The University of Maryland at College Park and Fairchild Industries have therefore developed a cooperative master's degree program in electical engineering, emphasizing communications, systems, and software engineering.

Cooperative education programs have a long and honorable history since they began at the University of Cincinnati in 1906. Today, 210,000 students at over 1,100 colleges participate in full-time or part-time, concurrent or alternating semester programs. The Fairchild Scholars program, however, is unique in several regards. As in the original Cincinnati model, students work three days a week at Fairchild's Germantown facility and take two days of courses each week at College Park. They receive full salary and full employee benefits as well as a full-tuition fellowship. Half of the 15 students who enter the program each year are selected by Fairchild and half are selected by the University of Maryland.

The students find the daily switch from courses to the work world is a valuable one. One student noted, "Here, at Maryland, I'm in an academic environment with well-known faculty whose intent is to promote knowledge. In the work environment at Fairchild, I am concerned with getting a product out. It's a good combination." Another student noted, "If the nation's industries, especially the auto industry, could have benefitted from such cooperative ventures in the past, they wouldn't be in such bad shape now."

Whether economic shifts are gradual or drastic, every industry needs to think about how to ensure that the effective worker of today is not the obsolete worker in 10 years, and how to guard against the problem of technical employees who become managers and who are then unable to re-enter specialities when they wish to, or when the company needs them to.

Monsanto Company developed a program in 1977 with Washington University that can be characterized as preventive retraining. Each year, about 20 individuals are selected to participate in an intensive one-year program at Washington University. Monsanto pays tuition, continues salaries, and even arranges several family options so that participants can move their families to St. Louis or visit them every third weekend. Students, many of whom have been out of school for up to 20 years, are immersed in a five- to six-day-a-week program that emphasizes problem-solving, analytic computer techniques, and fundamental concepts in engineering and their application.[9]

The success rate of students who are retrained is extremely high. Of 73 people who participated in the first four years of the program, 68 completed it successfully and have gone on to challenging positions within the company. The program has been operating so successfully, in fact, that it has been expanded to include a career-broadening option for top performers in the company who wish to gain expertise in the specialty of process control.[10]

The program solves several problems for Monsanto besides the obvious one of obsolescence. Employee morale is strengthened by the knowledge that the closing of a plant does not necessarily mean termination for a good employee. In addition, it is an effective alternative to recruiting scarce and expensive chemical engineers. As for Washington University, the engineering faculty had had the opportunity to rethink midcareer engineering education. In addition, some of the cooperating professors in the program "perhaps relearned the value of practical applications and problem-solving in the classroom.[11]

242

It's easy, when thinking about the education of future workers, to assume that the teachers of those workers will magically develop the new skills and knowledge they need to prepare their students for employment. Conferences, journals, continuing education courses, and visits to places of employment can all give faculty new ideas and information for curriculum revision, but all these means are one step away from the realities of technological change. At the community or technical college level, in particular, the changing needs of national and local industries must be kept in mind by faculty members as they design courses and programs. Spartanburg Technical College has been sending faculty out into the field since 1978 to see and try new ways of doing things.

To help instructors gain current technical knowledge and an effective awareness of the world of work, faculty members who volunteer or who are chosen by their respective deans are placed in local industries for a minimum of two weeks and a maximum of a full academic quarter. This "Return to Industry" program has managed to alleviate one of the major problems faculty members have of staying current with new practices: maintaining a regular full teaching schedule. Because faculty are paid by the college but are replaced in the classroom, they can devote full time to gaining new expertise.

Over 30 faculty members have done internships in over 50 industries. The results have included over 70 curricular revisions and 8 custom-designed courses that now take the newest trends in technology into consideration. Faculty report that their activities are stimulating, and local companies know their needs will be met by future workers. As one local automobile dealer noted, "The average mechanic today will see more diesel engines in the next several years. Modifications will be needed and faculty will need to be taught new basics. We must retrain faculty as often as we retrain mechanics."[12]

As economic and technological change occur, the self-employed and owners of small businesses often have a particular problem of access to new information. Most business-higher education collaborative efforts are funded by businesses, but small businesses can often not afford to pay for the management and technical assistance they most need. The Center for Industrial Research and Service, connected with the cooperative extension service of Iowa State University, is funded partially by a grant from the Small Business Administration and partially by the state of Iowa, to serve Iowa's small businesses. The Center has subcontracted with colleges and schools of business at Drake, the University of Iowa, and the University of Northern Iowa to use their faculty and graduate students to provide counseling to firms throughout the state. Services of the program are publicized through newsletters to bankers, county extension directors, and Chambers of Commerce, and through press releases, TV public service announcements, and word of mouth.[13]

Generally, assistance with problems concerning production and manufacturing, management, marketing and sales, and research is provided free of charge. Special programs, such as computerized cash flow analysis, management clinics, and technical and marketing analysis for inventions, are provided for a fee. Innovative services include special programs for inventors, a regional waste exchange, trade area analysis, and international trade information for small businesses.[14]

Owners of small businesses not only get the benefits of services of the Center for Industrial Research and Service. By using those services, they become familiar with students and faculty at cooperating universities and find out how to use such college resources as library information and publication data base searches, advisory services, and workshops. The access that major businesses often have to university research and facilities is thus made accessible to small businesses as well.

Although the model of the university consulting center, such as Iowa State's, is hardly unknown, Henry Ford Community College in Dearborn, Michigan, has taken the idea much further by seeing the needs of small-business people and taking solutions to them instead of offering already-available courses or waiting to be asked.

The college happens to be across the road from Fairlane Town Center, a regional shopping center managed by the Taubman Company. As the director of Henry Ford's Center for New Directions was discussing problems of small-business people with the Mall's managers, certain typical problems emerged. Salespeople were often promoted to store management to fill a sudden vacancy without having any management skills or training. Problems of cost reduction, employee motivation, and management-tenant relations were frequent for these new managers.

In order to serve the mall tenants, the Center for New Directions developed a program geared to these typical store-management problems. To help make it as convenient as possible, the program, which came to be known as Sunrise Seminars, was held in a mall restaurant for two hours before the stores opened for the morning. Store managers were formally invited to attend by the center's management staff, but both groups were given equal status in the course and were encouraged to work as teams by the college faculty, who acted as neutral presenters. Participants completed "problems questionnaires" and all tenant problems were addressed during the series.

The seminars have been even more successful than either the college or the mall management could have anticipated. Participants have commented that the program is "precise, to the point, up-to-date, very informative," that "the interaction between the managers was of tremendous value," that "I use the principles of the course with my employees to help them perform better."[15] In fact, the program has resulted in "better tenant-center management relationships, increased profits and a reduction of costs, increased interaction of store managers with each other, and community involvement through the local community college."[16] The model is now being used in 21 malls throughout the United States in conjunction with 18 colleges; over 3,200 retail establishments have participated.

Each of the preceding programs offers the solution to one or more problems of employee preparation or retraining in a changing economy. However, they have generally depended on one business or organization, or a small number of businesses, working with one college or a small number of colleges. The idea of a systems approach, which makes it possible for many colleges to work with many employers and individual employees in a coordinated, effective way, is still very unusual, but it does exist.

Because colleges typically guard their territories vigorously as they compete for students, for 38 colleges to develop a cooperative relationship to serve the needs of an entire region's adult population is as likely as Pepsi and Coca Cola joining hands. Yet the Compact for Lifelong Educational Opportunities (CLEO) is a consortium of 38 colleges in the Delaware Valley "working together to improve and extend the support of the adult development process in the region."[17]

CLEO's services for adults are both individual and company-based. For instance, one telephone call from an inquiring adult will result in information on the courses, programs, and educational services at all the participating colleges and universities. Career and academic counseling or assessment of learning acquired through life and work experience can be obtained through CLEO, as well. However, CLEO also serves as a broker for education and training courses for industry, offers customized seminars for companies wishing to provide placement services for displaced employees, provides career-development planning seminars for groups of employees, and even offers testing services.

CLEO's activity as a liaison between higher education and business is successful because it keeps decision-making about training and education off its doorstep. CLEO will complete a request for proposal based on a company's training needs, circulate it to all member institutions, collect responses, and provide the company with full information, but the company contracts directly with the college it selects.

CLEO's brokerage has been useful to colleges not only for establishment of training collaborations but also economically. Advertising about all 38 colleges is included in CLEO brochures, advertisements, and newsletters. In addition, with CLEO's coordination, 17 colleges are now part of a national project offering telecourses to adults via local Public Broadcasting System affiliates. Because of CLEO's coordination, the group was able to license the courses at lower rates than they could have individually. In addition, CLEO offered a series of teleconferences to help individual schools market the telecourses, as well as teaching faculty how to "develop an instructional system based on telecourses and how to integrate them into college curricula."[18]

CLEO is now forging connections with area churches, public school districts, radio and television stations, and social service agencies, as well as continuing services to individuals and businesses, in order to support the education of adults in, or seeking to be in, the work force in as effective a way as possible.

For employers, the programs we have described provide models for training and retraining employees but also models for improving the quality of work life as well. For instance, a number of participating employers mentioned the increase in productivity of workers who had gone through special training, and their increased longevity of tenure in their positions.

Employees being trained mentioned being stimulated by their experiences and being encouraged by their company's interest in their welfare. Other workers mentioned more positive morale, as they saw others being retrained instead of fired, and promoted as a result of the new training.

For colleges, these programs provide models for excellent collaboration with a world not always familiar or open to advice from the educational sector. In addition, these programs give indication that systematic, future-oriented educational activity rather than crisis intervention can be a function of higher education.

For both colleges and businesses, these programs show that even with current resources and current knowledge, workers can be served both humanely and effectively to prepare them for their futures.

Notes

1. Andrew McFalrin, letter to authors, February 14, 1983, p. 2.

2. *TAP 17: The Changing Nature of Work*, American Council of Life Insurance, 1977, p. 3.

3. *NABW's Bachelor's Degree in Management Program*, pamphlet, p. 5.

4. Audrey Bishop, "UM Tries to Attract Blacks to Business," *The News American*, September 29, 1982.

5. Stephany D. Graham, "LEAD Program Merges with Howard U.," *The Black Explosion*, October 14, 1982.

6. *The Productive Partnership: The University of Pennsylvania Program at INA*, pamphlet, pp. 7–8.

7. Peg Thomas, interview with authors, February 17, 1983.

8. Anne Moultrie, "Maryland and Fairchild Plug into Tomorrow," *Maryland Today*, January-February, 1982, p. 6.

9. Trudi Spigel, "Retrofitting," *Washington University Magazine*, August 1982, p. 22.

10. Nancy J. Perry, "Recycled" Engineers Provide Talent and Technical Expertise at Monsanto," *World of Work Reports*, Vol. 7, No. 6., June 1982, p. 1.

11. M.P. Dudokovic, G.T. Kennedy, J. Maguire, "Industry-University Program for Long-Term Retraining of Engineers," *Chemical Engineering Progress*, June 1982, p. 21.

12. Howard Gombert, handout on Spartanburg Program.

13. Lloyd E. Anderson, letter to authors, January 31, 1983, p. 2.

14. *Management and Technical Assistance for Iowa Industry*, pamphlet, pp. 2–3.

15. Robert J. Kopecky, "An Overview of Sunrise Seminars," Henry Ford Community College.

16. Sunrise Seminars abstract.

17. "What is CLEO?" handout, p. 1.

18. *CLEO* Faculty/Staff News*, Fall 1981, p. 4.

The Future Impact of Technology on Work Skills

by

Henry M. Levin and Russell W. Rumberger

During the war . . . the Second Industrial Revolution . . . managers and engineers learned to get along without their men and women. . . . It was the miracle that won the war—production with almost no manpower . . . . Machines were doing America's work far better than Americans had ever done it. There were better goods for more people at less cost, and who could deny that that was magnificent and gratifying? . . . Now you people have engineered them out of their part in the economy, in the market place, and they're finding out—most of them—that what's left is just about zero . . . Maybe the actual jobs weren't being taken from the people, but the sense of participation, the sense of importance was.
                                    —Kurt Vonnegut, Jr., *Player Piano*, 1952

There is little doubt that technology will profoundly affect jobs in the future. Current technologies in biomedical engineering, computer design, and communications have already altered work in a variety of settings. The September 1982 issue of *Scientific American* documented how work in agriculture, transportation, offices, and even design has already been transformed significantly by technological advances. Future breakthroughs, especially in microelectronics, will bring even more changes and further spread the impact of high technology.

There is much more uncertainty about how technology will affect the number and composition of jobs in our future economy. Many business leaders, government officials, and citizens believe that an increasing number of jobs will be in high-technology occupations, such as the engineering and computer fields. Robots and similar devices will eliminate some of the more mundane and boring jobs in society, freeing workers for more rewarding and creative jobs. And since more and more jobs will involve the use of computers and other highly sophisticated technical products, the skill requirements of jobs will generally be higher than they are today.

Henry M. Levin is a professor in the School of Education and the Department of Economics and also director of the Institute for Research on Educational Finance and Governance, Stanford University, Stanford, California. Russell W. Rumberger is senior research associate and economist at the Institute for Research on Educational Finance and Governance, Stanford University.

247

As a result, future workers will need more education and training to acquire these skills.

Despite the popularity of these beliefs, available evidence does not support them (Levin and Rumberger, in press). Recent employment projections by the Bureau of Labor Statistics (BLS) of the U.S. Department of Labor show that many more jobs will be created in low-skilled service occupations than in high-skilled professional ones. Between 1978 and 1990, the BLS projects more than 600,000 new jobs for janitors and sextons, compared to 200,000 new jobs for computer systems analysts; and 800,000 jobs for fast-food workers and kitchen helpers, compared to 88,000 jobs for computer operators (Carey, 1981). While occupations in high-technology areas will grow by 45% between 1980 and 1990—almost three times as fast as employment growth overall—they will generate only 7% of the new jobs (Coleman, 1982). Just 20 occupations will generate 35% of new jobs during the 1980s and not one relates to high technology. In fact, only two of those jobs—elementary school teachers and accountants—require a four-year college education.

Of course, these figures are only estimates. But they are based on sophisticated, econometric techniques that are constantly revised by the BLS to reflect new advances and information (see Oliver, 1982). What they fail to show, however, is how technology will affect jobs in the future, particularly the skill levels of jobs. In the remainder of this paper, we will speculate on how technology is likely to impact on the number and composition of jobs in our future and why. We will then discuss the social implications of these changes.

Technology and Jobs

Technology will affect the number of jobs in our future economy as well as the skill composition of jobs. Both of these impacts are important. Some people fear that robots and other devices will eliminate an increasing number of jobs in our future economy. Others fear that the impact of technology on existing jobs will be equally disastrous by removing much of the discretion and creativity from jobs, leaving workers to simply monitor and respond to the demands of their machines. How likely are these fears to be realized?

The Number of Jobs. Technology will eliminate jobs, but it will also create jobs. The important issue is whether it will create more jobs or fewer jobs than it eliminates. One difficulty in addressing this issue is that the jobs created are frequently in different industries than the jobs eliminated.

Consider the case of robots. Robots have been used primarily to replace operative positions in manufacturing industries, such as automobiles and steelmaking (Ayres and Miller, 1983). One estimate suggests that robots could replace up to 3 million operative jobs during the next 20 years and eliminate all 8 million operatives by 2025 (Ayres and Miller, 1982). But the increasing use of robots will create jobs in those industries involved in their design, development, production, and maintenance. Another recent estimate suggests that robots will eliminate 100,000 to 200,000 jobs by the year 1990, while creating 32,000 to 64,000 new jobs (Hunt and

Hunt, 1983). Thus, it appears that one major technology has the potential to eliminate more jobs than it creates.

In order to assess the net impact of technological changes on the level of employment, one must account for the effect of economic growth. Economic growth creates jobs. So even if technology has the potential to eliminate more jobs than it creates, economic growth could produce enough new jobs to offset this tendency. Yet with the number of unemployed currently so high—12 million persons at the end of 1982–the economy would have to sustain a long period of high growth to both reduce the current level of unemployment and offset future displacement due to technology. Recent government forecasts suggest unemployment will remain high for the next five years even without further displacement (U.S. President, 1983; U.S. Congressional Budget Office, 1983). So while economic growth may help to offset the displacement effects of technology, there is no assurance that the requisite levels can be attained in the near future.

Another threat from technology is that it may facilitate the movement of production from the United States to other countries. Even high-technology firms themselves are not immune to this development, as the recent announcement of 1,700 layoffs by Atari demonstrates (*Washington Post*, February 27, 1983). Technological developments in production, even sophisticated electronics products, now permit these processes to be carried on by workers in other countries who receive much lower wages—$1 per hour versus $9 per hour—and have much less education—5 years versus 12 years—than American workers (*San Jose Mercury News*, February 28, 1983). Future technologies could accelerate this tendency.

The Types of Jobs. It is not only important to consider how technology will affect the level of employment in our future economy, but also the types of jobs in the economy. First, will the jobs created by technological advances be more skilled or less skilled than the jobs eliminated? Second, will the impact of technology on existing jobs tend to raise or lower requisite work skills?

It is unlikely that technology will ever eliminate the most skilled, creative, and demanding forms of work in our future economy. Yet technology is unlikely to eliminate the least skilled and most mundane jobs in our economy either, at least in the near future. It is much more profitable for companies to employ new technologies to eliminate jobs that pay $12 per hour than it is to replace jobs that pay the minimum wage of $3.35 per hour. Robots, for example, have been used primarily to replace operatives whose earnings are well above the minimum wage.

Other examples also suggest that technology is most likely to eliminate middle-level, skilled and semi-skilled jobs. A series of technological advances in the printing industry, from machine typesetting to computer-aided phototypesetting techniques, have eliminated large numbers of skilled craft jobs for composers and typesetters (Zimbalist, 1979a). Automatic teller machines are eliminating jobs for bank tellers. And computer-aided design (CAD) may soon eliminate the 300,000 current positions for drafters (Gunn, 1982).

It is much more difficult to predict the types of jobs that will be created as a result of these changes. Many of the new jobs will be in high-technology firms where these new products are designed, developed, and produced. While high-tech industries do employ a larger proportion of engineers, computer specialists, and other high-level, technical workers than other industries, the majority of jobs in these industries are at the semi-skilled level—operatives, clerical workers, and managers. Further, high-tech industries are only expected to generate about 5% of all new jobs between 1980 and 1990 (U.S. Bureau of Labor Statistics, 1982). Thus, it appears that the skill levels of jobs created through the increasing use of technology in the workplace will not differ significantly from the jobs eliminated. To the extent that jobs in high-tech industries themselves become less skilled because of technology, the net impact of technological change will be to lower skill levels.

The impact of technology on existing jobs will be much more important in determining the skill requirements of jobs in our future economy than the jobs created and lost through technology. Of course, technology alone does not change the skill requirements of jobs. It also depends on how the tasks associated with jobs are changed. As Adam Smith first recognized in *The Wealth of Nations* over 200 years ago and Charles Babbage more carefully documented 50 years later, if job tasks are fragmented into their respective parts, employers can hire less-skilled workers to perform the simpler tasks and pay them lower wages than workers who perform the more complex, skilled tasks (Braverman, 1974, p. 77–83). As a result of fragmentation, some jobs become "deskilled."

Technology can aid this process as machines take over some of the tasks formerly performed by workers. The assembly line developed by Henry Ford was based on the principle of job fragmentation—some workers assembled one portion of the car while other workers assembled other portions. The introduction of machinery automated some aspects of the process, such as the movement of the automobiles down the line (Gartman, 1979). Automation also allows employers to better control the production and work process (Braverman, 1974, p. 195).

One way to predict how technology will affect the skill levels of jobs in the future is to examine how technology affected the skill levels of jobs in the past. A number of studies have examined the implementation of past technological innovations on the skill requirements of jobs. One of the most thorough of these was conducted by James Bright, a professor at Harvard University. Bright examined the impact of automation in a variety of U.S. manufacturing firms during the 1950s. With increasing levels of automation, he observed that the skill requirements of jobs first increased and then decreased as many formerly skilled workers were simply required to tend machines (Bright, 1958). Other studies support the conclusion that past technological innovations have tended to reduce the skill requirements of jobs (e.g., Zimbalist, 1979b). Moreover, the skill requirements of jobs in the U.S. economy as a whole appear to have changed very little over the last 20 years despite the growth of professional and technical employment (Rumberger, 1981a).

Present and future technologies promise the same impact. Computers, for example, have become easier and easier to use. Early computers were initially programmed in machine languages that required extensive training. Since that time, computer software has become increasingly "user-friendly" so that people can use computers with little or no computer background. A recent sales ad for the new LISA computer claims that workers can use the system with only 20 minutes of training. Current systems available with a "mouse" cursor and future systems commanded by voice may soon eliminate the need for most keyboard functions.

While early technologies primarily displaced physical labor, computers and other electronic technologies threaten to displace mental labor and thereby reduce requisite work skills. Word processors now correct spelling mistakes and hyphenate words, thereby eliminating the need for those skills in secretaries. Computer-aided machines can now diagnose many of the problems that develop in these products, thereby reducing the requisite knowledge and skills of repair technicians. There appears to be virtually no area of work where computers cannot take over some of the mental tasks and make the judgments that were formerly the domain of individual workers. Computers also offer employers better ways of controlling the work process and monitoring the output of their employees (*Wall Street Journal*, May 6, 1983).

Social Implications

One implication of these changes is that our future economy may not be able to fully employ all those who wish to work. Similar fears were expressed during widespread automation of U.S. manufacturing firms during the 1950s. Those fears turned out to be unfounded as the United States experienced rapid and sustained economic growth during the 1960s. Yet the uneven economic growth of the last 10 years at least cautions against too much optimism over our country's ability to achieve the high growth rates of the past. Moreover, the future impact of technology on the workplace is likely to be much more widespread than past changes, increasing the potential for job displacement. If our economy is unable to generate sufficient jobs in the future, then our present system of distributing income based on work may have to be revised (Leontief, 1982).

Another implication of these changes is that work may become increasingly repetitive and boring in more and more jobs. Adam Smith (1937, p. 734) not only recognized the rationale for fragmenting jobs, but also the result:

> The man whose life is spent in performing a few simple operations, of which the effects too are, perhaps, always the same, or very nearly the same, has no occasion to exert his understanding, or to exercise his invention in finding out expedients for removing difficulties which never occur. He naturally loses, therefore, the habit of such exertion, and generally becomes as stupid and ignorant as it is possible for a human creature to become.

Similar concerns were expressed in the government-initiated *Work in America*, which appeared 10 years ago (U.S. Department of HEW, 1973).

Declining skill levels of jobs is particularly troublesome in the U.S. because education attainments, and hence skill levels, of the American work force are moving in the opposite direction. Currently, more than one out of every four young workers entering the labor market has completed four or more years of college (Rumberger, in press). As young workers with more schooling continue to replace older workers with less schooling, the average education level of American workers will continue to increase. Underemployment among college graduates is already widespread and will get worse even without further reductions in the skill levels of jobs (Rumberger, 1981b). Workers whose skills are underutilized display higher levels of job dissatisfaction and may be less productive as a result (Rumberger 1981b, Chapter 5). This not only poses a problem for individual employers, but for the country as a whole.

While the influence of technology on work is inevitable, its impact on the level and composition of jobs in our future economy is not. The influence of technology will depend on what technologies are developed, but its impact will depend on how it is employed. And that, in turn, depends on who controls the technology. Computer-generated medical diagnosis, for example, is unlikely to displace the need for physicians or their high status in the work world because they can control how this technology is employed. Most workers cannot. In most cases, employers determine how a particular technology will be employed and whom it will affect. Increasingly, unions have recognized the importance of bargaining with management over the use and impact of technology. The issue is likely to become more important in the future, especially as the threat of displacement becomes more apparent.

To the extent that the workers affected by technology can help determine how it is employed, some of the negative consequences may be mitigated. But even that may not be enough. The widespread influence of technology may require that all citizens become involved in setting policies over its use (Walton, 1982).

References

Ayres, Robert U., and Steven M. Miller. 1983. *Robotics: Applications and Social Implications*. Cambridge: Ballinger.

Ayres, Robert U., and Steven M. Miller. 1982. "Industrial Robots on the Line." *Technology Review*, 85 (May/June): 35–46.

Braverman, Harry. 1974. *Labor and Monopoly Capital*. New York: Monthly Review Press.

Bright, James R. 1958. "Does Automation Raise Skill Requirements?" *Harvard Business Review*, July/August: 85–99.

Carey, Max L. 1981. "Occupational Employment Growth Through 1990." *Monthly Labor Review*, 104 (August): 42–55.

Coleman, Garrett V. 1982. Memorandum compiled from revised BLS employment estimates, 1980–1990.

Gartman, David. 1979. "Origins of the Assembly Line and Capitalist Control of Work at Ford." In *Case Studies in the Labor Process*, edited by Andrew Zimbalist, pp. 193–205. New York: Monthly Review Press.

Gunn, Thomas G. 1982. "The Mechanization of Design and Manufacturing." *Scientific American*, 247 (September): 115–130.

Hunt, H. Allan, and Timothy L. Hunt. 1983. *Human Resource Implications of Robotics*. Kalamazoo: W.E. Upjohn Institute for Employment Research.

Leontief, Wassily. 1982. "The Distribution of Work and Income." *Scientific American*, 247 (September): 188–204.

Levin, Henry M., and Russell W. Rumberger. In press. "The Low-Skill Future of High Technology." *Technology Review.*

Oliver, Richard. 1982. *BLS Economic Growth Model System Used for Projections to 1990.* Bulletin 2112. Washington, D.C.: U.S. Government Printing Office.

Rumberger, Russell W. 1981a. "The Changing Skill Requirements of Jobs in the U.S. Economy." *Industrial and Labor Relations Review* , 34 (July): 578–590.

Rumberger, Russell W. 1981b. *Overeducation in the U.S. Labor Market.* New York: Praeger.

Rumberger, Russell W. In press. "The Job Market for College Graduates, 1960–1990." *The Journal of Higher Education.*

San Jose Mercury News, February 28, 1983, p. 1.

Scientific American (September 1982).

Smith, Adam. 1937. *The Wealth of Nations.* New York: The Modern Library.

U.S. Bureau of Labor Statistics. 1982. "Current Employment and Projected Growth in High Technology Occupations and Industries." Testimony submitted to the Joint Economic Committee, August.

U.S. Congressional Budget Office. 1983. *The Outlook for Economic Recovery.* Washington, D.C.: U.S. Government Printing Office.

U.S. President. 1983. *Economic Report of the President.* Washington, D.C.: U.S. Government Printing Office.

U.S. Department of HEW. 1973. *Work in America.* Special Task Force to the Secretary of HEW. Cambridge: MIT Press.

Wall Street Journal, May 6, 1983, p. 1.

Walton, Richard E. 1982. "Social Choice in the Development of Advanced Information Technology." *Technology in Society,* 4: 41–50.

Washington Post, February 27, 1983, p. F1.

Zimbalist, Andrew. 1979a. "Technology and the Labor Process in the Printing Industry." In *Case Studies in the Labor Process,* edited by Andrew Zimbalist, pp. 103–126. New York: Monthly Review Press.

Zimbalist, Andrew, ed. 1979b. *Case Studies in the Labor Process.* New York: Monthly Review Press.

Human Capital:
A High-Yield Corporate Investment

by

Anthony Patrick Carnevale

It is human nature to waste anything that seems abundantly supplied. At the moment, there seems to be an overabundance of American workers. Our economy apparently is overflowing with underemployed, unemployed, and expendable people. As unseemly rates of unemployment hover in double digits, we are told that labor-saving machinery will soon make us all redundant. The bogeyman of technology is loose again.

We Americans are predisposed to the view that there are too many people. Our recent history encourages us to accept the notion that people are superfluous while machinery, financial capital, and the tangible fruits of the earth are scarce. Since 1946, we have been forced persistently to reshape our economic and social structures in order to bear, feed, clothe, educate, employ, and house the 76 million members of the American baby boom. As a result, *while we have learned to value people for their purchasing power, we have not seen them as critical resources for production.*

Things are rarely as they first appear. Upon closer examination, the apparent oversupply of Americans proves illusory. Unfortunately, our misconceptions and the biases of our recent history are threatening our nation's economic future. There is some risk that we will be misled by the notion that people are oversupplied and beguiled by our recent past into a national investment strategy that favors machines and resources extracted from the earth over people. This would shortly prove a serious economic error.

As the following evidence will demonstrate, the economic and social yield from investing in human resources is high and increasing. Our economic growth and productivity are becoming ever more dependent on our human resources.

Increasing Yield from Human Capital

The nation's economic history tells us with deadening statistical regularity of the increasing yield from human capital investment. The evi-

Anthony Patrick Carnevale is presently a consulting economist and is also a research associate at both Harvard and Ohio State University. This article is an executive summary of a study prepared for the American Society for Training and Development (ASTD); information on the full study can be obtained from ASTD, 600 Maryland Avenue, S.W., Suite 305, Washington, D.C. 20024.

dence, as summarized in Figure 1, divides the increase in national income between 1929 and 1978 into its human resource, land, capital, and productivity components. Figure 1 also shows a middle-of-the-road projection of the growth in national income and its component parts through 1990. The evidence demonstrates clearly the overwhelming historical and projected contribution of human resource factors to the increase in national income. By way of comparison, human resource inputs are shown to be consistently more important than capital. Further, land continues to slip as a critical economic resource. *For every year measured since 1928, and projected through 1990, human resources have been the dominant factor accounting for growth in national income.*

Figure 2 provides additional detail on human contributions to growth in national income. It breaks the human contribution into its component factors: hours worked, age/sex composition, and education. "Hours worked" have a nearly persistent negative effect on the human contribution to national income. The reason: People are working fewer hours and enjoying more leisure time. Thus it becomes a happy problem when understood in the context of another set of trends—the simultaneous rise in wages and worker productivity. Between 1929 and the mid 1960s, American workers managed to increase their leisure time, their wages, and their productivity all at the same time. The negative impact of "hours worked" is, therefore, good news. It is testimony to the ultimate success of the American economy throughout most of this century. It demonstrates that *American workers have been working smarter, not harder.*

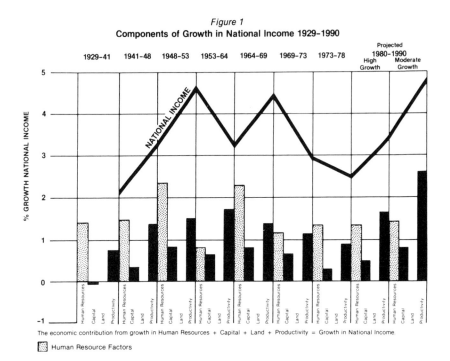

Figure 1
Components of Growth in National Income 1929-1990

The economic contribution from growth in Human Resources + Capital + Land + Productivity = Growth in National Income.

Human Resource Factors

255

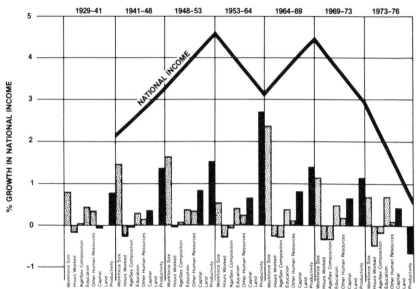

Figure 2
Components of Growth in National Income 1929-1976

Growth in economic contribution from Human Resources (workforce size, hours worked, age/sex composition, education, other human resources) + Capital + Land + Productivity = Growth in National Income.

▒ Human Resource Factors

The changing composition of the work force also has had a negative effect on growth in national income. This negative effect of labor-force composition is due mostly to the much publicized influx of youths and females into the work force. As the "baby boom" moved into the work force and as the number of females in the work force increased in the 1950s, a growing proportion of working Americans were relatively uneducated, untrained, and inexperienced. The concomitant lack of human capital investment and on-the-job experience in this group progressively reduced the contribution of human resources to income growth throughout the fifties, sixties, and seventies. However, as can be seen in Figure 2, with added training and experience on the job, the negative impact of young and female workers on national income growth will turn positive in the 1980s and should remain so throughout the twentieth century.

Perhaps the most remarkable finding is the sizable, positive influence of increased education on growth in national income. The nation's commitment to educational attainment has increased at an accelerating rate. Between 1940 and 1978, the median number of school years completed among American workers increased from 9.1 to 12.7. Over the same period, the proportion of all workers with a grade school education increased from 50% to 91%, those with a high school diploma from 19.7% to 41.4%, and those with four or more years of college from 5.7% to 17.7%.

256

The effect of education is all the more remarkable as it is probably understated. Its effect on national income measured in Figure 2 does not include the substantial investment by employers in formal employee training and development. Estimates of this investment run higher than $30 billion. Even more substantial is the amount of informal, on-the-job training excluded from the measured amount of education in Figure 2.

Productivity: Human Decisions and Work Attitudes

Productivity is the human art of getting more with the same or fewer resources. This can be accomplished by increasing the intensity with which we utilize resources (working harder) or by increasing the efficiency with which we mix and use available resources (working smarter). Both depend on the skill and work effort of labor and management. *In short, productivity at its roots turns on human decisions and work attitudes.* The quantitative snapshot provided in Figure 3 demonstrates the overwhelming importance of the human factor in productivity growth. It accounts for the greatest proportion of productivity increases between 1929 and 1973.

Growth in on-the-job know-how, the reallocation of labor, and the increase in the quality of labor through education, training, and health care have consistently accounted for more than three-quarters of productivity increases since 1929 and for most of our growth in national income. By comparison, the amount of machine capital per worker has contributed a consistent, and disappointing, 20% or less. Figures 3 and 4 verify that,

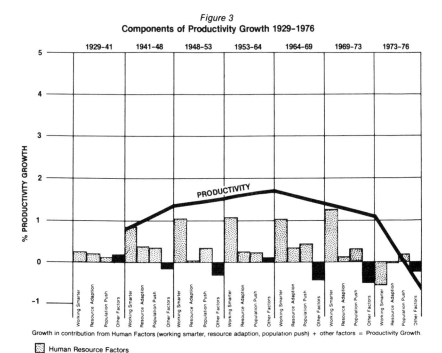

Figure 3
Components of Productivity Growth 1929-1976

Growth in contribution from Human Factors (working smarter, resource adaption, population push) + other factors = Productivity Growth.

Human Resource Factors

257

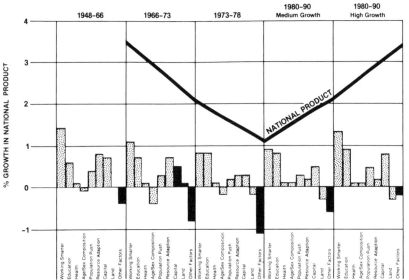

Figure 4
Components of Growth in Economic Output 1948-1978 and Projected Through 1990

Growth in contribution from Human Factors (working smarter, education, health, age/sex composition, population push, resource adaption) + Land + Other Factors = Growth in Economic Output.

Human Resource Factors

in the absence of the human contribution, productivity would have been virtually non-existent throughout most of this century.

The economic history of the modern world is a tale of the inexorable shift from natural and machine resources to acquired human skills as the basic building block of production. In 1890, resources from the earth, including minerals, energy, and food, accounted for 50% of the gross national product. Today, these same resources account for less than 10%. Over the same period, human resources grew to account for more than four-fifths of the nation's total economic output. The acquired skills and abilities of the human population have become the master resource because they are the agents that transform the environment into usable goods and services.

In the last century, for instance, economists routinely listed land, labor, and capital as the factors essential for economic production. In the shift from an economy based on agriculture and other resources extracted from the earth to the post-industrial economy, land has virtually been eliminated as a prime factor of production. Available data suggest that land had no impact on economic growth between 1948 and 1966 and a negative impact on national income between 1966 and 1978.

In the United States, real earnings per hour of work have increased fivefold since 1900. Fully 75% of national income now derives from earnings. Nobel laureate Simon Kuznets's classic studies of economic growth show a rapid growth in the value added by the human factor relative to other factors of production. Kuznets finds that over this century, the

258

share of national income attributed to property declined from 45% to 25% while the human contribution to national income increased from 55% to 75%.

In 1817, an American laborer earned the equivalent of two bushels of wheat per week. By 1890, weekly wages were equivalent to nine bushels of wheat. Wheat dropped in price by half between 1900 and 1970, which means that if human labor had remained in rough proportion to agricultural output, workers could have expected the equivalent of 18 bushels per week in 1970. Instead, the weekly compensation of manufacturing workers was equivalent to 96 bushels.

Not only has the economic system demanded an increased quantity of human capital, it has rewarded an ever-increasing quality. Manufacturing workers received only two cents per hour more than unskilled workers in 1900. By 1970, the absolute difference was 79 cents. Teachers, the nation's lowest salaried professionals, received only 24 cents per hour more than unskilled labor in 1900. Their margin has increased to $1.90 per hour in 1970.

A Service and Information Economy

In the latter portion of the twentieth century, the dominance of human resources in the American economy will continue and accelerate. *We are presently in the midst of a shift to a post-industrial service and information economy where productivity will increasingly be embodied in persons, not raw resources or machines.*

We already have come full circle since the early nineteenth century. In 1820, more than 70% of the labor force worked on the farm. In 1980, only 3% work on the farm, and 70% of the work force has moved through manufacturing and into services and information industries. What is more, the current shift from manufacturing to the service and knowledge industries will likely accelerate with new labor-saving technologies. Peter Drucker and others claim that the current 32% of our work force employed in manufacturing could shrink to 5% as early as 1995.

The coming of post-industrial society will not eclipse industrial production, nor the importance of the more highly skilled workers who will remain in industrial production. Agriculture did not disappear with the advance of industry. It became mechanized and more productive. In 1850, for instance, one farmer provided for four other people. In 1982, one farmer provides for 78 others. In much the same fashion, manufacturing and basic industries will rely more heavily on machinery and a smaller, more highly skilled work force for increased productivity.

An inevitable and accelerating economic trend underlies these data. That trend is what economists refer to as the ''rationalization'' of the world economy. Rationalization is the process by which high-skilled, high-technology intensive production concentrates in developed countries and, correspondingly, lesser skilled, technology-poor production concentrates in lesser developed nations. It is the sorting out of national competitive advantage in the world economy.

The competitive advantage of the lesser developed nations begins with their low-wage, low-skill labor pool. Our own competitive advantage relies on the application of technological advances and our ability to maintain and accelerate the skill level of our labor force. In the long term, we cannot protect the U.S. share of unskilled production. Ultimately, we cannot match sweat equity with 950 million Chinese. We cannot compete for low-wage, low-skill production markets.

Our real competitors are the other, "more-developed" countries. As the pace of technological change accelerates, competitive advantage depends on our ability to adapt, to apply new technologies to production, and to integrate human skills with new machine technology. Adaptation will be all the more difficult as product life and skill life become shorter and shorter. *Ultimately, it is the rate at which we apply new technologies and integrate them with ready labor that will determine our success.* As the international rationalization process accelerates, the constant and optimal shifting of human and machine resources will be required, as will the constant retraining of the work force.

The evidence of the economic impact of human motivation is compelling. Convincing data show that the key difference in productivity among firms and nations cannot be attributed to the quantity of resource inputs but to some unmeasurable qualitative human "factor x." Research shows that productivity differences between workers in the same plants with the same pay and equipment can vary by a factor of four, and differences between plants with identical equipment, labor, and pay can vary by 50%. According to available research, the variation in "x" efficiency is rooted in motivational and cultural differences. Recent advances in the measurement of motivational factors in the workplace suggest that a 10% improvement in motivational factors allows for a 1% reduction in product prices.

The world of standing room only will never come. Births are influenced heavily by economic and social conditions. Births rose with income during the early agricultural development of economic systems and declined with the coming of industry and urbanization. In fact, declining birthrates have characterized the United States and other industrial nations for more than 200 years. The single exception to that trend occurred in the United States between 1946 and 1964 when 76,441,000 babies were born. This was 20,000,000 more births than in the previous 20 years (1926–1945). By all reports, however, the "baby boom" is an exception. It passes into history while the dominant trend toward low birthrates reasserts itself.

The economic effects of population decline are already upon us. Overall shortages of workers are hidden, however, under the cloak of the current high rates of unemployment. Recovery will reveal this overall shortage quickly and dramatically. In the 1970s, for instance, even the slower rates of growth produced 19 million new jobs for new workers. As the effects of population decline begin to impact in the 1980s, there will be only 16 million new workers. If the eighties achieve even the middling rates of economic growth characteristic of the seventies, the economy will generate a minimum of 19 million new jobs, creating a gap of 3 million jobs for which there will be no workers.

The anxious notion that we draw our resources from increasingly inaccessible reservoirs is scientifically unfounded and statistically unproven.

Human economic and social institutions always will adjust to the available supply of economic resources. Increased prices for scarce resources create incentives to expand supply. When rising prices fail to generate new supplies, substitutes become cost effective and available resources can be remixed in the production process. In the rare cases where the cost of extracting more resources becomes prohibitive, human tastes will adjust to accept substitutes or other goods and services.

The Bottom Line

The long view of economic history teaches us that people are the master economic resource. They are the master resource because they use their acquired skills and abilities as the catalytic agents that combine tangible elements and intangible ideas to make machinery and usable goods and services. In spite of that fact, there is a great temptation for employers to ignore the long-term value of human investment. This is especially true in times such as these when investment capital is short and unemployment lines are long. Secondly, in the short term, individual employers are faced with the prospect of losing their investment in people. Employees are mobile and machinery is not. When one employer invests in training and development, another can invest in wages and pirate employees at the completion of their training. Lastly, when jobs are in short supply, there is an equally greater temptation to rely on a quantity of cheap labor rather than a quality few. With jobs available for only one in ten unemployed workers, it is indeed a buyer's market.

Although employers generally appreciate the long-term yield of current investment in human resources, the press of daily business and the realities of the labor market encourage them to win their share of the nation's skilled workers through wage bidding and not through human resource development. *We, as a nation of employers, have been going to the well for some time for skilled workers without replenishing the source of supply.* As a result, the long term finally is arriving, as evidenced in a spate of statistics that suggest mounting skill shortages, reduced overall quality in the American labor force, shoddy workmanship, unsatisfactory maintenance, and wages that are not balanced by worker productivity. Further, attempts to improve productivity by increasing machine capital are proving costly and are resulting in protectionist resistance among current workers who are concerned for their own job security. Individual firms that once found it profitable to buy skilled workers by bidding up demand now find the price high, the supply short, and the quality low. What was good for individual employers has proven costly for all.

As a society, we will have to discover new mechanisms for employers to realize the longer-term benefits of employee training and human resource development. Public incentives that place investment in human resources at least on a par with investment in machinery will help. Federally operated training programs for skill shortages which do not have the accountability of the workplace will only be marginally effective. In the final analysis, resolution of the problem depends on the willingness of employers to look beyond the short-term economic dynamics that discourage human resources investment. In the absence of employer-based strategies, however, public programs and regulations are inevitable.

Source for Figures 1–4

Anthony Carnevale, computed from Edward Denison, *Accounting for Slower Economic Growth: The United States in the 1970s*, Brookings Institution (Washington, D.C., 1979); 1973–78 data computed from John Kendrick, "Productivity Trends and the Recent Slowdown: Historical Perspective, Cause Factors, and Policy Options," American Enterprise Institute (Washington, D.C., 1979); 1980–1990 data computed from C. Jackson Grayson, "The U.S. Economy and Productivity: Where Do We Go from Here?" Joint Economic Committee (Washington, D.C., 1980), p. 44.

Needed: New Model Adult Universities

by

Gerard G. Gold and Nancy B. Blackman

Three years ago, two administrators of a university institute arrived in Washington on an annual grantsmanship pilgrimage. Their institute, located in the midst of a midwestern industrial-commerce-education-agricultural region, dealt with a variety of social issues, including work, families, and education. What, they asked one of this article's authors, were the hot topics and the up-and-coming hot topics to be? Where was the money?

Perhaps, it was gently suggested, they were looking in the wrong direction and asking the wrong questions. Was there not talk and serious likelihood that auto and steel and other manufacturing plants in their region were in trouble? Some major plants were already marked for closing. Perhaps it would serve their institutional and personal interests better to ask: Where are people hurting, where are patterns of chronic human needs emerging, and where are sets of salient, clearly definable problems that universities and the kinds of research and program development skills that universities tend to accumulate could help resolve? Perhaps, it was suggested, looking closer to home would lead to discoveries and leadership that would assure not only assistance to those in need of university skills but also continuity, survival, and perhaps even more prestige for the institute and its staff.

It would not be rewarding to pursue the history of this dialogue. Whether the problems of regional economy were so foreboding as to overwhelm academic initiative, or whether the complexities of collaborative efforts required too long a time line to satisfy short-range fundraising requirements, or whether local needs simply seemed uninteresting is not for us to know. What we do know is that across the nation the same colleges and universities that never shirk opportunities to advise governments on economic policies, or help engineering or pharmaceutical firms develop the latest computer tooling of high-technology plastics, or work assiduously to cure cancer, or do any of the thousands of practical applied

Gerard G. Gold is senior program officer at the National Institute for Work and Learning, Washington, D.C. Nancy B. Blackman is director of the Center for Work and the Family, University of Rhode Island at Kingston.

research or teaching tasks that help keep America ticking, have not been a presence felt by American workers, their families, and their communities.

Today, as the needs of America's industrial workers finally receive the glare of media and political attention, the kinds of understanding and imaginative suggestions that might have come from serious research and empathetic collaboration are not to be seen. What we see instead is a reactive, shortsighted, and sadly uninformed desire to offer to America's workers snap solutions that have not worked in the past. For the most part, these snap answers to systemic problems call for skill retraining as short and as quick as the adult worker can be "readjusted" into a new job, if one is available (and not to worry about what it pays).

We have stated the situation rather bleakly and baldly. We recognize that there are exceptions. More importantly, we recognize that the growth of the community colleges in the last two decades presents an assortment of educational strategies and responses that could not have been considered during the Great Depression 50 years ago. We also recognize that employers, unions, and educational institutions alike have access today to a far more sophisticated understanding of human development theories and programs than was the case 50 years ago. That the credit for these changes in institutions, theories, and program development concepts is owed to academia is the one thought that encourages us in our search for ways to make higher education more understanding and institutionally effective in serving not only displaced workers, but adult learners generally.

In fact, we are persuaded that the administrators, faculty, and students already located in America's colleges and universities are capable of meeting this challenge. But we doubt that the institutional structure of higher education as it now stands is capable of developing, organizing, motivating, or rewarding the hundreds of individual efforts needed to help workers, managers, and whole communities rebuild not only their jobs but their lives. What do we need to do to tap the riches of talent, training, energy, and commitment that can be found on almost any college campus?

A Minor Modification: New Model Adult Universities

Unfortunately, the pace of change in the workplace and in the needs of all adult learners can no longer tolerate the relatively lethargic pace of change in higher education. As much as colleges and universities are part of the solution to the present crisis in adult learning, they are also part of the problem. Higher education has moved much too slowly in absorbing and improving the processes of informal, self-directed learning that play such a major role in human affairs. While learners and other societal institutions actively seek more efficient, more sensitive modes of learning, higher education remains too tied to its rituals of passage. Higher education still places innovation and lifelong learning on the periphery of institutional affairs. Is it unfair to contrast this style of leadership with those manufacturers of computer hardware and software who have made the creation and marketing of "user-friendly" systems the very core of their institution-building strategies?

The concept of a New Model Adult University (NMAU) is our tentative solution to this conundrum. We propose that each state establish such a university with its own central campus, or as part of an existing campus, and with the broad mission to create and implement statewide imaginative, high-quality, and effective programs serving adults and institutions alike.

Functionally, the NMAU would perform instruction, research, program development, and evaluation activities as well as engage students and faculty in community service. It would be authorized to maintain credit banks, authorize credit, and award degrees and certificates. It would have its own facilities and its own administrators, faculty, regional coordinators and adjunct faculty, and students.

But how would the NMAU differ from the mass of existing postsecondary institutions? From what sources would it derive its energies? How would it work to improve either the lot of adult learners or the credibility and prestige of colleges and universities?

Perhaps the most important question to ask is this: How will New Model Adult Universities in each state be able to attract and retain the most creative, spirited, and dedicated staff—people who will grasp the opportunity to design and successfully construct a whole new set of relationships between educators and learners? There is no doubt in our minds that campuses have on them today many individuals who will jump at the chance to be involved in an undertaking of such importance. These individuals' current alienation from routine and pettiness is simply the flip side of their desire to contribute productively to the lives of others.

The first requirement is a combination of leadership and collegiality. This is not a case of dependence on charismatic solutions and *ad hominem* logic. Rather, the requirement points to the need for administrative freedom operating within a structure of few but crucial constraints. For this reason, we suggest that the staffing of the NMAUs should be conducted on an entirely voluntary basis, with all applicants chosen first from current state university system staff and with those selected for NMAU positions retaining the tenure and seniority rights they have established at their current positions. Tenure and seniority, however, would be held in reserve at their current campuses and not transferred to their NMAU positions, where they would work under renewable term contracts. Selection of NMAU staff would be the responsibility of the new university's president and the core administrative team selected by that president.

But how would the critical post of president be filled? It would be imperative that the leadership of the adult university be filled by someone of imagination and energy respected alike by leaders from business, labor, government, and community service sectors across the state. In most cases, we would hope that this person would be an educator, already highly respected within her or his own profession. But the current crop of educational leaders might not fit the bill in every state. Therefore, the selection of the president should be determined not exclusively by the state board of higher education, but rather by a multi-sector selection committee appointed jointly by the state board and the governor. The committee members would in most cases also be well-suited to serving as advisors to the NMAU president during the design and early implementation of NMAU policies and practices.

It should be clear by now that the New Model Adult University must be a serious venture backed by substantial political and resource commitments to the independence and broad scope of the undertaking. Nothing less will attract the risk-taking leadership required. In part, these commitments will involve special legislation and budgeting in each state, and formal agreements, enforced by the state board of higher education, establishing working relationships between the NMAU and other parts of the state's public and private postsecondary system.

The agreements with other postsecondary institutions will be critical because the NMAU will not be a campus-centered organization. Rather, the administrative core unit will serve as a nerve center for a network of satellite centers scattered across the state. Many of these centers will be best located on other college campuses, hence the need for clear and formal agreements of roles and functions.

It is probably inevitable that the NMAU will be perceived as threatening to current campuses although that need not be the case. There is no reason why any campus would have to discontinue its current continuing education programs. To the contrary, the role of the NMAU will be, in part, to develop new programs and enrollments benefitting the most convenient and suitable campuses. Statewide programs developed in negotiation with groups of unions or businesses might be implemented simultaneously on several campuses. Statewide voluntary organizations and professional associations might use the NMAU to develop degree programs subject to competitive proposals from strategically located campuses.

The NMAU, in other words, would fulfill some of the functions of an external degree program coupled with the program development and institutional brokering role of a group like the New Hampshire College and University Network. Furthermore, by being a dedicated source of expertise in the design of programs for adult learners, the research and institutional faculty of the NMAU would have a major technical assistance and training responsibility to assist colleges and universities statewide. While some conflict is probably inevitable, with proper leadership and support the NMAU is more likely to become a respected catalyst for creative competition among campuses. By strengthening the abilities of colleges and universities to use and compete with new sources of learning being created by corporations and telecommunications innovations, the NMAU will come in time to be accepted as a factor in shoring up all of higher education.

But organizational issues should not divert us from the order of priorities that first brought forth the need for a New Model Adult University: the historic changes being wrought upon the American working class. Glenn E. Watts, president of the Communications Workers of America, describes this development as "the crest of a wave of technological change like nothing the world has ever seen."

The impacts of new office, manufacturing, and information technologies are only beginning to be felt, much less understood. Industrial workers, far from being an exception, are at present merely the most visible group being negatively affected. Substantial turmoil with layoffs and retraining at mid-management and mid-career levels among white-collar workers proceed apace but with less publicity and less uniform human hurt. In

266

effect, we have entered a period of enormous uncertainty about the future of occupations, requisite skills, and commensurate opportunities for financial income, career advancement, and lateral career mobility. Put another way, basic assumptions about the quality of American life are being put to the test, starting at the workplace and rippling out to affect our leisure, our families, and our values.

In this context, it would be a profound error to stereotype the New Model Adult University as a proposal benefitting primarily or exclusively displaced industrial workers. Rather, we view the crisis in industrial occupations as an exciting opportunity, a moment when assumptions and established patterns of behavior are being unfrozen, a moment when creative people and meaningful resources can be applied to a set of serious problems. In the process, these pioneer efforts may be able to demonstrate the potential power now hidden in the diffused and discouraged minds of higher educators.

Staffing, organizing, and legislating on behalf of a New Model Adult University will only make sense if those entrusted with these responsibilities have a clear, communicable sense of the university's mission and priorities. Planning groups, presidential selection committees, and the faculty and core administrative team should all be working from a consensus regarding critical needs and intended outcomes guiding the first few years as the NMAU establishes its identity.

In most states, we think the first order of business should be a sophisticated, sensitive, and systematic campaign to eliminate adult illiteracy and fear of learning as causes of (and excuses for) unemployment and nontransferability of skills. Such a campaign, thoughtfully planned and conducted, will be no simple matter. Combining action research with the best of outreach, counseling, and instructional strategies, and depending on the active leadership of churches, community organizations, corporate training departments, and union education staff as well as colleges and universities, the New Model Adult University faculty will be working to solve a complicated societal problem through collaborative action. It would make sense to start first in a few communities in each state, apply the lessons of initial experience to program refinement, and then expand the literacy-network process to other communities.

A second, and parallel, order of business should be to collaborate with state government, employers, and unions in the design and testing of innovative "packages" of income support and re-education services for unemployed workers of all skill levels, including displaced managers. Federal and state government programs may be the financial and programmatic foundation, but these programs and funding mechanisms are greatly in need of reexamination and creative coordination. Additionally, private sector employers, unions, and nonprofit organizations should be more closely involved in the responsibilities of preparing individuals and communities for the discouragements and rarely used opportunities of unemployment. Governor Pierre DuPont of Delaware has already proposed one such package of information, training, and survival assistance. The New Model Adult University should be in the thick of this action, helping state agencies and others to think through the issues, design effective services, involve statewide educational resources, and assess progress. To the present, higher-education institutions have largely failed to participate in efforts to rationalize this nation's often self-defeating quasi-system of employment and training practices and policies. Repairing that fault should be high on the NMAU's agenda to better serve the needs of adult learners.

A third order of business should be to institutionalize across the country a network of researchers concerned with better understanding the motivations, cultural contexts, and institutional resources shaping learning and work and service opportunities for adults. This is a tall order, but one essential to the anticipation of future national traumas generated by economic, political, and demographic realignments. It is also essential that the longer time perspective built into theoretical and issue-centered analysis be tested in the real world of institutional and individual needs and conflicts. Therefore, research at the NMAU should be integrated with practical program design responsibilities, yet also serve as a point of synthesis for less-applied research on-going in other colleges and universities. The NMAU should be a convenor of research symposia where academic researchers can communicate with practitioners in more fruitful ways than is the case today.

A fourth order of business must be to establish the pattern of services to be offered to adult learners statewide. Many states already offer external degrees, and some have credit banks where adults can accumulate college and graduate credits from various institutions. But only one state (New York) has a nationally recognized service recommending credit for qualified instructional programs provided by employers, unions, and professional associations. The New Model Adult Universities would do all this (or could make cooperative agreements with other providers such as the American Council on Education or the New York Regents). Additionally, the satellite offices of the NMAU would be staffed by faculty prepared to design and coordinate portfolio assessments of experiential learning and to assist regional postsecondary education institutions in developing their assessment and experiential learning programs. Regional offices would also coordinate courses and services offered by adjunct faculty and would assist other institutions to develop their off-campus programs. The NMAU program development staff and regional coordinators also would work with area consortia of postsecondary education institutions to initiate collaborative councils and other forms of industry groups. One practical aim of such groups would be to facilitate proposal and contract relationships between employers and higher education. A more ambitious purpose would be to establish more effective patterns of communication at leadership and mid-organizational levels cutting across the major sectors of sub-state regions.

Finally, by starting from the problems and needs of individual adult learners, the faculty and supporters of the New Model Adult University would be aiming to build meaningful relationships between adults and their communities, using the resources and problems of communities as a curricular base. Self-knowledge and self-exploration, which are so much at the heart of the mission of all higher-education organizations, should be the starting and finishing point for the activities of the Adult University.

By removing barriers to learning, the NMAU will stimulate the desire to learn. By supporting learning with empathetic research, counseling, program design, and instruction, the NMAU will generate support from learners for higher education.

Learning Never Ends. That motto of the federal Department of Education is found on posters in education organizations across the land. But that motto, conceived in hope, is being perceived today as a progressively more imposing threat by the very adults that educators say they would like to serve. As formal learning becomes less voluntary and more involuntary, less a choice for some adults and more a necessary compulsion for almost all adults, tensions will grow between those adults and the traditional patterns of providing higher education. The New Model Adult University is proposed as one key part of the response that all colleges and universities serving adults will need to make in order to extend the power and hope of personal learning throughout the land.

Preparing California's Work Force for the Jobs of the Future

by

The California Commission on Industrial Innovation

California confronts a major challenge to provide workers with the training necessary for employment, and to insure that the development and application of important innovations is not constrained by a lack to skilled workers. A growing portion of tomorrow's workers will be directly and indirectly involved with increasingly technical jobs ranging from complex electrical assembly work to engineering research. New and more technical skills will not only be necessary in our exploding high-technology industries, but also in established sectors seeking to apply the multiple innovations created by these industries. Beyond basic training during youth, public and private educational institutions must work with employers and employees to facilitate the retraining and possible transition of workers to expanding economic sectors. Thus education and training will be a critical investment toward improving the productivity of California's economy.

This paper explores the role of education and training in fostering economic revitalization and the growth of high-tech sectors. First, the likely employment and social conditions of the future will be isolated to determine the types of education and training we are likely to need. Second, the capacity of our varied educational system will be briefly reviewed.

Skills for Tomorrow's Jobs

A variety of trends suggest that education and training must be adjusted to more effectively prepare individuals for life during the coming decades. Foremost among these adjustments concern the training and retraining of individuals for changing employment opportunities. Similarly, educational institutions must also prepare our citizenry for the daily tasks of living in a changing technological society.

This article was published as chapter four of Winning Technologies: A New Industrial Strategy for California and the Nation. *Final Report of the California Commission on Industrial Innovation, Office of the Governor, 1600 Ninth Street, Suite 100, Sacramento, California 95814. December 1982.*

270

Where Will the Jobs Be?

Job-related skills requirements are being altered by major changes in the nature and distribution of occupations and industries. However, these changes are not new. Indeed, changes in our industrial sectors, and the types of workers required by these sectors are part of an ongoing economic transformation that began with the Industrial Revolution. The basic nature of this transformation is a gradual shift of human work effort from physical labor to the use of machines to the processing of information and services.[1] This trend is aptly demonstrated by the gradual decline in the proportion of our work force employed in agriculture and manufacturing and the accompanying growth of service and information-oriented employment. Specifically, the proportion of American workers involved in agriculture and manufacturing declined from 83% to 30% between 1920 and 1980 while services expanded in a complementary fashion.

Recent trends and projections indicate that this historic transformation will continue, if not accelerate. In the medium-range future, this will not mean an absolute decline of jobs in agricultural and manufacturing sectors, but a relative decline as the size of the work force increases.[2] However, as advanced technology is applied to heavy industry during the last decade of the twentieth century, it is expected that the proportion of the work force employed in manufacturing will gradually decline to around 3% over the next 50 years.[3] This relative decline of employment does not, however, indicate that manufacturing and agriculture will become less important to our economy. Rather, it is expected that these sectors will become more productive with fewer workers. Just as the number of persons fed by the average American farmer increased from 9 to 25 between 1940 and 1962,[4] advances in technology and management will allow workers in manufacturing and other sectors to produce far more per hour of labor.

In general terms, the industrial distribution of California is shifting along much the same lines as national trends (see chart).[5] Indeed, the large proportion of high-tech industries in California is likely to accelerate projected rates of change.

Although unforeseen events may alter current projections,[6] an idea of the skills required for jobs in the 1980s can be gained from forecasts of job and occupational growth. Although the growth rate will be slower than the 1970s, the next decade will be likely to bring significant job growth at both the national and state level. Specifically, the number of jobs in the United States is projected to increase 15.9% from 103 million between 1981 and 1990, and the number of jobs in California some 24.9% from 11 million to 14 million during the same period.

Projections to 1985 from the California Employment Development Department indicate considerable variation of job growth among different occupations.[7] These forecasts, which roughly parallel those for the nation, indicate a greater than average growth rate for most technical occupations, as well as skilled craft and operative occupations. Many observers believe that these forecasts are unduly conservative concerning the growth of California's high-tech industries and the demand for highly trained labor.

It is important to recognize that the demand for different skills is not

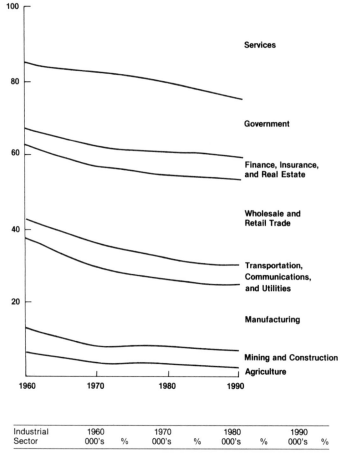

Actual and Projected Distribution of California Employees by Industry 1960-1990

Industrial Sector	1960 000's	%	1970 000's	%	1980 000's	%	1990 000's	%
Agriculture	372.1	7.0	277.6	3.9	383.1	3.8	355.0	2.8
Mining	30.6	.6	31.4	.4	42.9	.4	51.9	.4
Construction	294.8	5.6	303.0	4.2	431.3	4.2	596.8	4.7
Manufacturing	1,317.2	25.0	1,558.0	21.6	2,001.1	19.7	2,478.1	19.4
TCU	356.9	6.8	459.1	6.4	542.5	5.3	669.9	5.2
Trade	1,067.6	20.3	1,530.8	21.2	2,267.5	22.3	2,917.2	22.8
FIRE	243.2	4.6	374.5	5.2	620.9	6.1	794.5	6.2
Government	874.0	16.6	1,424.7	19.7	1,766.9	17.4	1,953.9	15.3
Services	711.7	13.5	1,266.2	17.5	2,126.2	20.9	2,984.9	23.3

Source: Data and projections for 1970, 1980, and 1990 cited from *California's Technological Future: Emerging Economic Opportunities in the 1980's,* Project Summary, Department of Economic and Business Development, State of California, 1982, page 47. Data for 1960 provided by the Employment Data and Research Division of the California Employment Development Department.

limited to the new jobs created in given occupations. Rather, the demand for workers with specific skills is the number of new jobs plus the number of existing positions vacated by persons leaving the labor force for retirement or other reasons. For example, California will create 1.4 million more jobs in 1985 than existed in 1980. At the same time, some 1.8 million jobs will be vacated by persons withdrawing from the labor force. As such, California employers will be hiring a net average of some 3.2 million workers to fill positions in a changing occupational structure.[8] While a significant portion of these new workers will come from interstate migrations, jobs changers and the re-entry of persons into the work force, many will be persons newly trained or retrained by our educational system.

High-Technology and Changing Job Skills

As in the past, shifts in the skills required for employment will be driven by technological change.[9] As such, the growth of the high-technology sectors of our economy will be critically important because they will increase the proportion of the new jobs created over coming decades, and change established industries and the types of workers employed throughout the economy.

While the nature of "high technology" industries is not universally defined,[10] it is generally agreed that these industries include sectors of the economy that develop and produce major technological innovation. High-technology sectors tend to be heavily composed of "basic industries," which produce goods and services that can be exported to other states and nations.[11] For analytical purposes, "high-tech" industries have frequently been defined as including the four basic industries of computers, communication equipment, instruments, and electronic components; as well as the non-basic computer service industry.[12] Aerospace, which also deals with advanced technology, is occasionally included in the "high-tech" category. Additionally, there are a variety of fledgling enterprises scattered throughout the economy that will ultimately be defined as high-technology industries as they mature. Some of these emerging industries include energy innovations, biotechnology, robotics, chemicals, new materials, selected medical products, and home entertainment equipment.[13]

Direct Employment Impacts of High Technology. Although high technology now employs a relatively small proportion of the total work force, job growth within these sectors has been phenomenal. Between 1970 and 1980, job growth for the five previously noted core "high-tech" industries within California was 80.3% as compared to 38.8% for the entire state work force.[14] During the 1980s job growth for these same high-tech industries is projected to be 47.6% as compared to 24.9% for the state. In absolute terms, moderate projections indicate that the number of jobs in these core high-tech industries is expected to increase from 591,795 to 726,700 between 1980 and 1990.

When available data on the growth of aerospace and fledgling high-tech industries are included, the importance of this sector becomes even more dramatic. The aerospace industry is expected to add at least 24,400 new jobs (possibly more due to recent defense contracts) to the California economy during the 1980s, and fledgling high-tech enterprises are likely to add another 10,000 jobs during the same period.[15] Consolidation of all high-tech related industrial growth suggests that these sectors will account for approximately 268,900 new jobs during the next decade. To put these figures in historical perspective, these high-tech industries and enterprises directly created 6.9% of overall California job growth during the 1970s and are expected to account for 9.7% during the 1980s. Some studies have forecast even faster growth. For example, one source suggests that the same combination of industries and enterprises may create as many as 327,900 new jobs, which would amount to 11.8% of California's expected job growth for the 1980–1990 period.[16]

It is also pertinent to note that a particularly large proportion of total U.S. "high tech" jobs have been located in California. Specifically, some 33.4% of the 655,500 non-aerospace high-tech jobs created nationally during the 1970s were in California. This trend is expected to continue, in somewhat muted fashion, with 23.3% of the nationwide gain of one million non-aerospace high-tech jobs for the 1980s occurring in California.[17] As a result of this growth, some 20.1% of all U.S. non-aerospace high-tech jobs were in California in 1980, and the comparable figure for 1990 is projected to be 21%.[18]

Most accounts suggest that the pronounced growth of these sectors within California has been and will continue to be encouraged by the ready availability of a diverse and skilled labor force, the strategic trade location of the state, industrial clusters allowing proximity to other high-tech firms and research institutions, and the general attractiveness of the state to managers.[19]

Preliminary projections based on available data[20] indicate that the skills required by California's growing high-tech industries will require more extensive and diverse training than that required by the workforce in general. This point is dramatized by the projection that 25.7% of the employees in California's five core high-tech industries will be engineers, scientists, technicians, or computer specialists in 1985. The proportion of the total California work force in these same occupations will be 5.7% in 1985. Further, between 1980 and 1990, the number of high-tech employees in these highly trained occupations is expected to grow some 58%. As a result, the proportion of high-tech employees in these occupations is projected to be 28.7% by 1990.

Recently, there has been considerable controversy over the demand for engineers.[21] While some claim that there is little or no problem with the supply of engineers,[22] others contend that shortages are rapidly approaching a crisis level that will cripple California's high-tech industries for years to come.[23] For example, the American Electronics Association estimates that the California demand for electrical and computer engineers alone will top 15,700 by 1985, a figure that they claim will be many times the supply.[24] While more moderate projections fail to portray such an extensive imbalance of supply and demand, it is clear that a shortage of engineers will exist in coming years. Available projections based on state data indicate that California will need some 58,000 new engineers between 1980 and 1985. Some 26,000 of these are estimated to be replacements for retirement and other forms of attrition, and another 32,000 will be the result for an overall increase in the demand for engineers.[25] High-technology industries will comprise about one-third of this demand. Specifically, by 1985, it is likely that the five core high-tech industries will need to replace approximately 6,500 engineers lost through attrition, as well as recruit another 10,500 engineers due to increased labor demand.

The growth technology industries will also foster an increasing demand for other technical, scientific, and skilled workers. Notably, trends indicate that there will be a demand for 31,800 additional computer specialists among the five core high-tech industries between 1980 and 1990, as demand increases 106%. Similarly, the demand for technicians will increase about 46%, and the demand for qualified assemblers and operatives by about 30% over the same period. As a result, high-technology industries can be expected to need 19,000 additional technicians, 21,000 additional skilled crafts persons, and 44,000 more qualified assemblers and operatives by 1990. Correspondingly, there will be a demand for managers, clerical workers, and other support personnel that are familiar with basic technical issues. As noted earlier, this growth in personnel needs will be intensified by the need to replace workers lost through attrition.

Indirect Employment Impacts of High Technology. While the growth of high-technology and its direct need for well-trained and technical employees is a major phenomenon in its own right, the primary significance of this emerging sector concerns its impacts on society and the economy as a whole. The assimilation of the knowledge and products generated by high-tech industries promise to fundamentally alter the nature of work, the processes and goals of education, and countless dimensions of personal lifestyles. The new technologies have the potential to galvanize economic growth and job creation, alter the skills required for employment, cause significant displacement and relocation of workers, and increase the technical demands of daily life and citizenship.

A major implication of the Information Revolution is that it will increase productivity and foster general economic expansion. High-tech products themselves are components of domestic and international trade. This "basic industry" characteristic will encourage the development of secondary enterprises and jobs to service the organizations and employees of high-tech sectors. It is commonly estimated that one basic job in high-tech industry will ultimately stimulate the growth of two additional secondary jobs.[26] Hence, it is assumed that the projected addition of 268,000 high-tech jobs during the 1980s would directly and indirectly create a total of 806,700 new jobs within the California economy.

Indeed, the implications for direct job creation through high-technology could be even more extensive. If the application of technological innovations leads to significant increases in productivity and product quality, domestic and international demand for lower-priced output could stimulate general economic growth, allowing even greater expansion of service and other secondary jobs.[27] In some cases, increased output per labor hour could foster a reversal of current trends to export selected production tasks to nations with lower labor costs.[28]

Perhaps the greatest indirect employment impact of high technology entails the potential for pervasive changes in the nature of work throughout all sectors of the economy.[29] The availability of innovations from high-tech industries, combined with intense international competition to produce more and better products more efficiently, is altering the nature of manufacturing and material processing industries. The historic trend toward mechanization is becoming increasingly sophisticated as robots and computer coordinated operations assume routine and dangerous tasks now performed by workers. For example, the installation of robots in the United States has been growing at a rate of 30% a year as the number of robots increased from 200 in 1970 to 3,500 in 1980. Moderate estimates indicate that there will be 35,000 functioning American robots by 1990, and that applications will skyrocket during the last decade of the twentieth century.[30] Correspondingly, the availability of small, decentralized computers, increasingly sophisticated sensors and servo-mechanisms, and design and control instruments that are progressively easier to understand and use is moving us rapidly toward highly integrated and flexible productive systems.

These changes will cause some employee displacements, which will be discussed later, and major adjustments of the types of work performed within manufacturing and material processing industries. Many existing employees will have to be retrained and reassigned to perform new tasks. While some of these tasks may not require greater skill,[31] many will necessitate an understanding of new and more complex technologies. For example, General Motors Corporation predicts that the percentage of skilled tradespersons will be 50% in the year 2000 as compared to 16% in 1980.[32] At the same time, it will be necessary to hire larger numbers of highly trained personnel such as engineers, technicians, computer specialists, and managers with basic technical skills.

High-technology products will also profoundly affect the nature of work in the office and service occupations. New capacities for information processing promise to revolutionize the ways in which information is created, stored, and processed. These changes will be made possible by dramatic reductions in the cost of computer time, the affordability of small offfice computers, the development of "user-friendly software" to simplify the use of computers, and the availability of high-speed printers and cable and satellite communication systems.[33] These developments will produce nothing less than a fundamental shift from paper to electronics as a medium of operation.[34] Typewriters, file cabinets and mail systems will be progressively replaced by word processors, computerized data storage-retrieval systems, and communication via video transmission.

These changes will not occur overnight. However, just as we have moved from carbon copies and manual typewriters to memory typewriters and copying machines over the last few decades, offices will progressively adopt technologies that will vastly increase the efficiency and output of information processing, as well as alter the majority of white collar and service jobs. As in the case of manufacturing and material processing, many jobs will become unnecessary. Mail deliverers, file clerks, stenographers, and other occupations will be progressively in less demand. Most particularly, from manager to secretary, familiarity and skill with computers, and the multitude of tasks they can perform, will become essential.[35] In overview, one reputable source has estimated that 20 to 30 million of today's existing white-collar jobs will be notably affected by office automation by the year 1990.[36]

In sum, the products of information technology can be expected to cause major changes in the nature of work and the skills required for employment throughout the economy. In many senses, the success of high-technology and other industrial sectors, and the supply of needed skills to both, will be closely interrelated. Evidence suggests that the capacity of established California industries to compete for domestic and international markets against foreign competition will depend heavily upon the swift application of new technologies. At the same time, established industries will not be able to apply these technologies, and high-tech industries will not be able to produce them, without an appropriately trained work force. While high-tech industries will probably always require a disproportionate share of highly trained technical workers, assimilation of new technologies by established industries will also increase their demand for such workers. For example, *Business Week* estimated that as much as 45% of existing jobs will be significantly altered by technological changes over the next 20 years, many through an upgrading of skills.[37] As such, our institutions of education must play a critical role in training and retraining our labor force to meet the potentials made possible by high technology.

Despite the widely acclaimed benefits of high-technology, there is considerable concern that productivity gains made possible by technological advances will lead to a significant reduction of jobs and displacement of workers. Concern over this possibility has long historic roots, stemming from the Luddite resistance to early industrial mechanization. However, to date, the prevailing opinion has been that, despite isolated cases of worker dislocation, technological advances have fostered economic and job growth.[38]

Current fears of worker displacement are based on the speed and pervasiveness of current technological changes. In the manufacturing sectors, the use of robots has been a cause for alarm. While the application of robots in this sector is expected to increase tenfold during the 1980s,[39] it is expected that this increase will only lead to a 4–7% reduction in current manufacturing jobs.[40] Given that roughly 15% of today's manufacturing work force will retire between 1980 and 1990,[41] this reduction should be easily absorbed by attrition without causing serious worker displacement.[42] By 1990, however, the comparative cost advantages of robots are expected to reach a "take-off" point,[43] leading to a reduction in the number of jobs in manufacturing to less than one-fourth of the 1980 figure by the year 2030.[44] While natural attrition would absorb large portions of this job loss, there would be some displacement. In the past, new labor force entrants and displaced workers have shifted to the growing white-collar and service sectors as jobs declined in agricultural and manufacturing sectors. However, current advances in information processing and other technologies suggest that white-collar and service sectors could undergo job losses due to automation that are equal or greater than those expected within the manufacturing sector.[45] Thus, some observers fear that we may be entering an era of "jobless growth," where, despite the limited emergence of some new jobs in high-tech and other sectors, increased economic output would occur while job growth remains at best stagnant.[46]

There is indeed some evidence that technology-induced productivity gains have caused low job growth and worker displacement. While there is little in the way of comprehensive data, a number of specific examples can be cited:

- National Cash Register reduced its U.S. work force from 37,000 to 18,000 between 1970 and 1975 because of productivity gains from using micro electronic as opposed to mechanical parts.[47]
- The General Motors plant in Lordstown, Ohio, reported reducing its work force by 10% after the introduction of welding robots increased productivity by 20%.[48]
- The Rhode Island *Journal Bulletin* decreased the number of its printing staff from 242 in 1970 to 98 in 1978 as a result of new typesetting technology.[49]

If nothing else, these examples underscore the fact that workers have indeed been displaced as a result of technology. A question, however, remains as to how extensive such displacment has been and will be in coming years.

The prevailing opinion seems to be that technological displacement of workers is an exception rather than the rule, and that the likelihood of major displacement in the future is remote. The key to this optimistic prediction is that technological advances allow an increase in the quality and quantity of products at lower costs. Because costs are lower, producers can afford to sell at lower prices, which in turn commonly cause consumers to increase market demand by purchasing more. As a result of increased demand, producers generally employ as many or more workers as before technological innovation to increase output. When this process occurs throughout the economy, the result is generally economic growth with higher real wages and an increase of employment due to the direct hiring of primary producers, and the growth of secondary jobs to service primary firms and workers.[50]

Two historical examples aptly illustrate this process. During the early stages of the Industrial Revolution, the introduction of Hargreaves's Jenny in 1770 ultimately allowed one worker to produce as much as 200 spinners without the jenny. Yet, employment in Britain's textile industry increased from less than 100,000 in 1770 to about 350,000 in 1800, because increased productivity allowed major reductions in price leading to even more dramatic increases in market demand for textiles.[51] Another more recent example comes from the introduction of the assembly line by Henry Ford. As a result of this combination of machinery and industrial organization, it took 56% fewer hours to produce the average car in 1920 than it did in 1910, leading to a 62% reduction in the real dollar price of an automobile. Consumers who previously could not afford a car began to buy; sales increased 10 times and employment by Ford rose from 37,000 to 206,000 in just 10 years.[52] In both these cases, workers may have been given new assignments and shifted to new parts of their plants, but displacement and aggregate loss of jobs does not seem evident.

If the past is an indication of the future, the innovations being introduced by today's high-technology industries present generally positive potentials, but also an unavoidable choice. In recent years, California has been plagued by another form of displacement. Plant closures resulting from a lack of technological and geographic competitiveness have accounted for over 80,000 displaced workers during 1980 and 1981.[53] Business failures and work force cutbacks, many of which are also the result of failing competitiveness, add greatly to this toll. While technological innovation is likely to cause some hardships in the form of worker displacement and reassignments, all indications suggest that failure to make these changes will cause the California economy to lose pace with national and international competition, and ultimately result in even greater loss of employment and economic growth.[54] There is growing concern that the incidence of such displacement is accelerating.

At the same time, it cannot be ignored that technological change frequently leads to undesired reassignment within organizations and occasionally displacement. Fundamental changes will be occurring in workplaces and the labor market. Old skills will lose their value and new skills will be required. This will require that business, labor, government, and the educational systems place high priority on working together to retrain workers so that they can be effectively reassigned within organizations and, if necessary, moved with a minimum of hardship to new jobs.[55] The success of such cooperation will not only determine how productively we utilize our human resources, but also whether workers view the applications of new technology and improvement of productivity as a threat or an opportunity.

In addition to the changing job-skill requirements created by technological innovation, a brief note should be made about the skills required for day-to-day living and citizenship. Technological change will not only affect us through our jobs, but also through countless adjustments of our personal lives. The growth of video entertainment appliances, home computers, programmed auto maintenance warning systems, automated bank tellers, biotechnology advances, energy conservation devices, and countless other innovations open exciting opportunities and the need to become aware of a bewildering array of new skills and responsibilities. Developing and maintaining "technical literacy" about our changing world will require a sound basic education and recurrent formal and informal learning that will place new demands on the educational systems of the future.

Implications for Education and Training

The growth of high-technology industries, and its impacts on the economy and society at-large, indicate a number of important implications for education and training:

Highly Trained Workers. The growth of high technology is predicted to increase the demand for highly trained workers. At the professional level, there will be a pressing need for more engineers, scientists, computer specialists, technically knowledgeable managers, and, as will be discussed later, educators. There will also be increasing demand for well-trained technicians, crafts persons, skilled assemblers, as well as clerical and service workers trained to utilize high-tech facilities. The demand for these workers will be particularly acute for high-tech industries, but will be manifest throughout the California economy. Specifically, the demand for the above noted professional and skilled workers within the core high-tech industries is expected to grow 22% by 1985. In the California economy as a whole, demand for these types of workers is expected to increase 17.1% over the same period as compared to 12.8% growth for all occupations.[56] Clearly, the growth of high-tech sectors and the economy as a whole will depend on the capacity of our educational system to prepare workers with these skills.[57]

Recurrent and Transition Training. Technological change will cause widespread redesign of jobs, reassignment, and some displacement of workers. For the most part, job reassignment resulting from technological innovation will take place gradually as employees are shifted to different tasks within organizations.[58] In cases where technological innovation, and perhaps other related factors, cause displacment, the problems of transition will be more severe and demanding for both individuals and society. In both cases, there will be a critical need for business, labor, and educational institutions to work cooperatively to encourage and facilitate ongoing training and skill-updating in order to facilitate internal realignments of workers, and to provide effective transition training and placement for workers dislocated by technological and economic change.[59] Significant policy initiatives in this area will be a key element of our ability to develop a popular consensus for necessary technological change. Further, such changes may have profound implications for future relationships between education and work over the life cycle of individuals.[60]

Basic "Technical Literacy". The capacity of workers and citizens to understand and utilize the potentials of high technology will depend upon the ability of our educational systems to provide quality general education and exposure to emerging technological developments. Without a general education in communications skills, math, science, and computer literacy, the foundations for learning and updating basic and advanced technical skills will be limited. Further, without a general educational foundation and some exposure, during both youth and adulthood, to emerging technological advances, workers and citizens frequently develop apprehension toward changes that they do not understand. The result can be individual and institutional resistance to necessary and beneficial innovation. As such, the successful application of high technology to our jobs and ways of living will depend upon the capability of educational institutions to insure that the California population has the basic foundations of knowledge necessary for continued learning throughout life and exposure to the technological tools of our time.

Education and Training for the Future

How will employers, workers, and citizens obtain the skills and knowledge necessary for the future? The task will require major realignment of existing educational institutions. First, basic educational foundations must be gained from primary and secondary schooling. Second, job-related skills required for the production and utilization of high technology must come from reservoirs of unused labor, various forms of on-the-job training within work places, and education and training programs. As such, the California educational system must play an increasingly active role in working with employers to effectively integrate curriculum with on-the-job training, develop and maintain a variety of basic training and retraining programs to produce skills that match emerging job opportunities, and identify and facilitate the use of reservoirs of workers that have unused or underutilized skills that might be effectively transferred to industrial sectors experiencing pressing labor shortages.

Notes

1. Daniel Bell, *The Coming of Post-Industrial Society*, Basic Books, New York, 1973, pages 47–120; and Peter F. Drucker, *The Age of Discontinuity*, Harper and Row, New York, 1968, pages 263–311.

2. Valerie A. Personick, "The Outlook for Industry Output and Employment Through 1990," *Monthly Labor Review*, August 1981, page 38; and *Projections of Employment by Industry and Occupation, 1980–85*, Employment Data and Research Division, California Employment Development Department, Sacramento, September 1979, pages 14–15.

3. *The Impacts of Robotics on the Workforce and Workplace*, Department of Engineering and Public Policy, Carnegie-Mellon University, Pittsburgh, June 14, 1981, page 1.

4. Leonard Broom and Philip Selznick, *Sociology*, Harper and Row, New York, 1963, page 662.

5. "Project Summary," *California's Technological Future: Emerging Economic Opportunities in the 1980's*, California Department of Economic and Business Development, Sacramento, March 1982, page 47.

6. It should be emphasized that the state and national projections cited in this report are moderate, best-estimate speculations based on existing trend data. Such forecasts can prove inaccurate by alteration of the assumptions upon which they are based. Thus, changes in consumer demand, technological innovations, fluctuations of the economy, access to raw materials, public policies, and a myriad of other factors can produce occupational and industrial trends that are significantly at variance with the most sophisticated of projections. (Paul M. Ryscarage, "BLS Labor Force Projections: A Review of Methods and Results", *Monthly Labor Review*, April 1979, pages 15–22).

7. *Projections of Employment*, California Employment Development Department, *op. cit.*., pages 27–30.

8. *Ibid*, pages 58–62.

9. Karl Polanyi, *The Great Transformation*, Beacon Press, 1967; and T.S. Ashton, *The Industrial Revolution, 1760–1830*, Oxford University Press, London, 1973.

10. *High Technology and High School: Preparing Students for California's Changing Economy*, Office of Appropriate Technology, State of California, Sacramento, April 1982, pages 19–22.

11. "The California Economy: 1970–1990," *California's Technological Future: Emerging Economic Opportunities in the 1980's*, California Department of Economic and Business Development, Sacramento, March 1982, page 2.

12. Ibid., pages 5–14.

13. *High Technology and High School, op. cit.*, pages 19–22; and "High Technology and the California Workforce in the 1980's," *California's Technological*

Future: Emerging Economic Opportunities in the 1980's, California Department of Economic and Business Development, Sacramento, March 1982.

14. "The California Economy: 1970–1990," *op. cit.*, page 10.

15. *Ibid.*, pages 40–42.

16. Michael F. Kieschnick, "The Incipient California Industrial Policy," Office of Economic and Business Development, San Francisco, January 6, 1982, page 10.

17. "The California Economy: 1970–1990," *op. cit.*, page 47.

18. *Ibid.*, pages 10, 12, 43 and 46.

19. *Ibid.*, pages 11, 38 and 39.

20. *Ibid.*, pages 10, 12, 43 and 46.

21. John S. DeMott, "Help Wanted: Engineers", *Time*, May 10, 1982, pages 88–89 and *High Technology and High School, op. cit.*, pages 31–42.

22. "The 'Shortage' Myth," *Recent Efforts Newsletter*, Committee of Concerned Electrical Engineers, Massapequa Park, New York, No. 106, January 1982; Fred Landis, "How Many Engineers will Graduate During the Eighties?" *Engineering Education*, May 1981, pages 784–788; Ronald Rosenberg, "Keeping Track on 'The Engineer Shortage'," *The Boston Globe*, December 15, 1981; and *Occupational Outlook Handbook*, Bureau of Labor Statistics, U.S. Department of Labor, Washington, D.C., 1980–81 Edition, page 283

23. Henry Petroski, "Who Will Teach the Engineers?" *Washington Post*, January 21, 1982; John S. DeMott, *op. cit.*, pages 88–89; and "Readers Comments." *Electronics*, July 14, 1982.

24. Patricia Hubbard, *Technical Employment Projections of Professionals and Paraprofessionals, 1981–1985*; American Electronics Association, Palo Alto, May 1981.

25. *Projections of Employment*, California Employment Development Department, *op. cit.*, page 58.

26. Michael Kieschnick, *op. cit.*, page 10.

27. Richard K. Vedder, *Robotics and the Economy*, Staff Study, Subcommittee on Monetary and Fiscal Policy, Joint Economic Committee, U.S. Congress, Washington, D.C., March 26, 1982, pages 25–27.

28. Colin Norman, *Microelectronics at Work: Productivity and Jobs in the World Economy*, Worldwatch Paper No. 39, Worldwatch Institute, Washington, D.C., 1980, pages 40–51.

29. *Ibid*, page 7–39; Daniel Bell, *op. cit.*, pages 263–311; and Alvin Toffler, *The Third Wave*, Bantam Books, New York, 1979, page 168–288.

30. *The Impacts of Robotics on the Workforce and Workplace, op. cit.*, pages 1–4 and 30; and "High Technology and the California Workforce in the 1980's," *California's Technological Future, op. cit.*, pages 16–23.

31. "The Speedup in Automation," *Business Week*, August 3, 1981, page 63; and Marcia Friedman, *Labor Markets: Segments and Shelters*, Allanheld, Osmun and Company, New York, 1976.

32. "The Speedup in Automation," *op. cit.*, page 63.

33. *Ibid.*, page 60; and Colin Norman, *op. cit.*, pages 22–39.

34. *Ibid.*, pages 22–24.

35. *Ibid*, pages 22–39; and *High Technology and High School, op. cit.*, pages 16–19.

36. "The Speedup in Automation," *op. cit.*, page 62.

37. *Ibid.*, pages 62–67; Richard K. Veddar, *op. cit.*, pages 12–30; *Technology and the American Economy. Report of the National Commission on Technological Economy, Report of the National Commission on Technology, Automation and Economic Progress, Washington, D.C., Vol 1, February 1966, pages 9–32; and Howard R. Brown and Garth L. Mangum (Editors), Automation and Econmic Progress.* Prentice-Hall, Englewood Cliffs, New Jersey, 1966, pages 10–22.

39. *The Impacts of Robotics on the Workforce and Workplace, op. cit.,* page 3.

40. *Ibid,* page 17; and Richard K. Veddar, *op. cit.,* page 1. A more alarming forecast is that 100,000 of the one million automobile assembly jobs will be eliminated by robots between 1980 and 1990 (Marley Shaiken, "A Robot is After Your Job," *New York Times.* September 3, 1980, page A19).

41. *Projections of Employment,* California Employment Development Department, *op. cit.,* pages 48–62.

42. Richard K. Veddar, *op. cit.,* page 1.

43. *Ibid,* pages 12-15; and *Impacts of Robotics on the Workforce and Workplace, op. cit.,* pages 48-58.

44. *Ibid.* pages 1 and 17.

45. Colin Norman, *op. cit.,* pages 22–29; and "The Speedup in Automation," *op. cit.,* page 63.

46. Roy Rothwell and Walter Zegveld, *Technological Change and Employment,* St. Martin's Press, New York, 1979.

47. European Trade Union Institute, *The Impact of Microelectronics on Employment in Western Europe in the 1980's,* Brussels, 1979.

48. Colin Norman, *op. cit.,* page 34.

49. J. Stark, "Hold the Front Frame," *New Socialist,* November 30, 1978.

50. Richard K. Veddar, *op. cit.,* pages 15–30.

51. *Ibid,* pages 25–26 (cited from Phyllis Deane, *The First Industrial Revolution,* Cambridge University Press, Cambridge, Great Britain, 1979, pages 90–91).

52. Richard K. Veddar, *op. cit.,* page 26 (Derived from *Historical Statistics of the United States, Colonial Times to 1970,* U.S. Department of Commerce, Washington, D.C., 1975).

53. Figures provided courtesy of David Jones, Employment Data and Research Division, California Employment Development Department, Sacramento, June 1982.

54. "The Speedup in Automation," *op. cit.,* page 63.

55. *Ibid.* pages 62 and 67; Richard K. Veddar, *op. cit.,* pages 19–20; Colin Norman, *op. cit.,* pages 54–55; and *The Impacts of Robotics on the Workforce and Workplace, op. cit.,* pages 8 and 22–23.

56. These percent growth figures were computed for engineers, scientists, science and engineering technicians, miscellaneous technicians, computer specialists, mechanics, repairers, installers, and assembly occupations.

57. "The Speedup in Automation," *op. cit.,* pages 62 and 67; and *High Technology and High School, op. cit.,* pages 29–44.

58. James J. Byrne, "Occupational Mobility of Workers," *Monthly Labor Review,* February 1975, pages 53–59; and Dixie Sommers and Alan Eck, "Occupational Mobility in the American Labor Force," *Monthly Labor Review,* January 1977, pages 3–19.

59. *The Impacts of Robotics on the Workforce and Workplace, op. cit.,* pages 22–23; "The Speedup in Automation," *op. cit.,* pages 62 and 67; Colin Norman, *op. cit.,* pages 54–55; Richard K. Veddar, *op. cit., pages 19–20; Howard Bowan and Garth Mangum, op.cit.,* pages 22–38; and *Technical Change and Economic Policy,* Organization for Economic Co-operation and Development, Paris, France, 1980, pages 79–108.

60. Fred Best, *Flexible Life Scheduling: Breaking the Education-Work-Retirement Lockstep,* Praeger Publishers, 1980, pages 3–11 and 20–48.

Work, Life-style,
and Leisure

Telecommuting:
Its Impact on the Home

by

Jane Kingston

This paper presents a brief look at the phenomenon of telecommuting, a new way to work. After a general overview of the issues involved in telecommuting, I'll examine a particular issue—the impact of telecommuting on the home life of the worker—and make some suggestions to optimize the usefulness of telecommuting, and to minimize its drawbacks.

Telecommuting is a term coined by Jack M. Nilles, director of the Center for Futures Research Information Technology Program at the University of Southern California's Business School. It is defined as working at home (or some similar site remote from the employer), using personal computers or computer terminals that are connected to one's employer's central computer by electronic means (usually telephone lines).

Background

The nature of work in the United States is changing drastically. We often are referred to as the *post-industrial society*, a phrase coined by Daniel Bell in 1957. According to the author of the famous book *Future Shock*, the term implies an "economy . . . largely based on service, the professional and technical classes dominate, theoretical knowledge is central, intellectual technology—systems analysis, model building, and the like—is highly developed and technology is, at least potentially, capable of self-sustaining growth" (Toffler: 1970, p. 490). Thus, we are no longer concerned so much with the manufacture of goods as with the provision of services, which is based upon the collection, analysis, and distribution of information. Examples of the service or information industries now spreading in our country are communications of all sorts (TV, radio, telephone, satellite), health and life insurance companies, banking, education, publishing, retailing, marketing, etc.

Paul Strassman, vice president of the Xerox information products group, said in 1980:

> Gradually and almost imperceptibly, the U.S. economy since 1940 has been engaged in a transformation that is unique in the history of mankind. By the mid-1950's our working population was predominantly engaged in information

Jane Kingston is a program officer of the Publications, Instruction, and Evaluation Project at the Center for Information Technology, Stanford University, Stanford, California.

handling; more people were involved in the manipulation of information than were employed in mining, growing crops, raising cattle, manufacturing goods, or providing personal services. The "information society" became in fact a proper expression of predominant societal characteristics. (Strassman: 1980, p. 55)

Later, he goes on to say:

> While the total U.S. labor force is expected to increase by 20% in the course of the '80s, technical and professional jobs will grow by 30%. Actually most of this growth is projected for jobs that might best be described as "quasi-professional" (though that's not a term often used by labor statistics). These jobs will require a measure of specialized skill, but a skill primarily acquired on the job rather than through extensive formal training.

> Whatever their level of formal education, all members of that greatly expanded technical and professional category foreseen by the automation enthusiasts will use advanced information processing machinery in their work, partly for such nuisance tasks as digging information out of the files but mostly for intensive direct interaction with co-workers as well as with customers and other contacts outside the organization. (in Kirchner, p. 255)

Some Estimates

The preponderance of jobs requiring the ability to manipulate, process, and store data; to turn that data into information; and to use that information to generate knowledge is increasing at a notable rate. People who do these jobs are often called "knowledge workers," and most people, whether in low-level, mid-level, or top-level jobs, are knowledge workers. According to one analyst, "something like 10 million office employees in the U.S. already work with video terminals, and this number is bound to keep rising sharply, considering the 40% growth rate that the office automation industry is expected to sustain into the mid-'80s" (Kirchner, p. 252). Knowledge workers use computer terminals, often called visual display terminals (or VDT's), to do word processing, report preparation (including report formatting and typesetting), transaction recording, financial modeling and analysis, filing of information, statistical calculation, and communication, to mention a few of the many possibilities.

The interesting fact, in terms of the scope of this paper, is that one can work at a computer terminal 50 feet away from the computer, or 50 miles, or even 5,000 miles as long as there is some form of electronic/telephonic linkage available. The computer doesn't care where the terminal is as long as the signal is clear, and there is no significant loss in communication time between the user and the computer if there is any distance involved. So telecommuting has naturally evolved as a new way to work.

The current estimate of the number of people who are telecommuting in the United States is about 10,000, according to International Resource Development (Tangorra, p. 52), Nilles estimates that no more than 1,000 of these telecommute full time (Tangorra, p. 52). Elisabeth Allison of Data Resources estimates that there is a potential for 15 million knowledge workers to work at home via telecommuting, doing work such as computer programming, financial analysis, and writing (*Business Week*, p. 66).

Experts agree that there are about 35 company-initiated "home work" programs developing in the United States, and some of them extend back to 1978. Some companies are therefore training managers how to supervise from a distance, and also realize the need to develop new systems of compensation (*Business Week*, p. 66). The ability to work for one's employer at home has far-reaching implications, and many organizations are coming to terms with these implications, which are both positive and negative. Let us look quickly at some of these implications:

Positive Implications

- Telecommuting allows workers to have more control of their time. It is possible to work a full eight-hour day over a longer period, leaving time available for other obligations.
- Workers, especially women, can continue to work while caring for children.
- New job opportunities are opened for the handicapped and the elderly.
- Expenses connected with working can be cut if one doesn't need a "career" wardrobe, a car or other transportation, or child care. Employers can save on office space allocations. Employees can sometimes get a tax deduction for the space used in their residences for working and/or for the computer equipment, if they need to buy it (Tangorra, p. 54).
- Workers do not have to be tied to a geographical area. It is possible to live in California and work for a company in Massachusetts, for instance. It is also possible to travel and work.
- Working at home can avoid the interruptions and noise of the typical office, thus increasing one's ability to concentrate and be more effective.

Negative Implications:

- Telecommuting can tend to isolate the worker, socially and psychologically.
- There is danger of a breakdown of the supervisor/worker relationship.
- Companies concerned with maximum efficiency will worry about their ability to monitor workers and lose control over their performance.
- Patterns of living, already established in the home, may be disrupted.
- "Home workers" are often not covered by the same protective legislation regarding safety and non-exploitation that office workers are, and are not guaranteed benefits such as sick leave and vacation leave.

These positives and negatives often go together, as Charles McClintock points out:

> Telecommuting from home may reduce transportation costs but require expensive changes in the size or design of the home to accommodate the new equipment and work patterns. It may reduce role conflicts with co-workers in the office, but create role conflicts at home among family members. It may give one greater control over geographic and schedule constraints related to filling a particular job, but impose control by restricting the employee to the home. It may increase physical privacy, but decrease privacy regarding the pace and quality of work if centralized monitoring is in effect. (McClintock, p. A8.2.2).

Likewise, in a summary document recently published by the Canadian government, the negative implications of telecommuting seem to be a particular worry for certain groups, especially women, to whom telecommuting poses potential setbacks in the struggle for equal job opportunities:

> Another theme that surfaced repeatedly in the briefs we received was apprehension about working from home ("cottage industry"). We were cautioned that while working out of the home could be an ideal setup for some workers including specialized professionals, disabled workers, people living in rural areas, and women with young children, the potential problems are significant. Women pointed out that there is a serious danger of exploitation in a system of home work. They further emphasized that home work can lead to the re-isolation of women in the home, and in the case of women with young children, burdening them with two jobs instead of one. Isolation might mean little or no opportunity for advancement. The absence of effective labor standards for home workers, such as proper wages, good working conditions, sickness, accident, and pension benefits were cited often.

> No one is sure how many women are now working at home, and are connected to main computers located at an employer's headquarters. But isolated stories in the newspapers and sporadic comments by employers about future possibilities of decentralization of work make this issue a matter of serious concern . . .

> Research has proved that workers cannot contribute their best efforts if the working environment is intimidating and lacking in human sensitivity. Clearly, the new technology, intended to eliminate 'dirty' routine work and drudgery, does not have to mean a more fragmented and boring work environment. The concerns about the introduction of microelectronics technology, more particularly deskilling, the monotony of work, the social isolation of the worker, invasion of privacy, greater centralization of decision making and a more rigid and less human organization of work do not augur well for creating an environment that would lend itself to higher productivity. (Labour Canada, p. 57)

Clearly, the marvels of the "electronic cottage" (Toffler: 1980, pp. 194–207), so well described to us in the media, are becoming clouded with drawbacks, exceptions, unanticipated events, and hesitations; this is often the case when something that looks so bright in the future gets a little closer, and a little more within the realm of possibility. The question becomes one of whether the negative implications will outweigh the positive implications, and whether there is room for making adjustments toward an acceptable compromise, if necessary.

This paper seeks to examine some of these positive and negative implications, particularly with respect to the impact of telecommuting on the home and the life of the people in the home, and to begin to seek directions to minimize the negative aspects. This is a preliminary study, by no means definitive, and seeks only to gather information for more definitive studies.

Survey of the Literature

A more thorough approach to this topic would include a survey of the literature on the history of work, its place in the home, its exit therefrom, and the social, political, and economic implications of the transitions. This study, being preliminary, will limit itself to a survey of some of the

290

more recent literature on work in the home, especially when it involves telecommuting. One problem with the literature in this field is that it is so new that it appears to a large extent in the more popular press than in the scholarly journals, so some of the articles were not found. No doubt there will be more quantitative, experimental findings in the future.

Two interesting articles came from McClintock's list of references: Near, Rice, and Hunt, and Lopez and Gray. (McClintock, p. A8.2.4). The first, "The Relationship between Work and Nonwork Domains: A Review of Empirical Research," is a significant work. They review major sociological viewpoints regarding work. According to them, Durkheim "suggested that basic work-related divisions of labor produced interdependence among institutions," which could lead to either social integration or fragmentation. (Such fragmentation, according to Durkheim, would produce "feelings of estrangement and normlessness," which "would then produce both feelings of anomie and anomie behavior" (Near, p. 415). Another sociological point of view is represented by Weber, who sees work strongly affected by the nonwork part of our lives. These views lead to two hypotheses: the compensatory hypothesis ("If work lets you down, you can find happiness in other parts of your life."), and the spillover hypothesis ("Trouble at work will make trouble at home, and vice versa."). The authors find plenty of theories and hypotheses, but few attempts at a systematic overview. They attempt to assess the actual social structures of work affecting life away from work, and the social structures of "beyond-work" affecting work. They find that "the research reviewed supports the finding that moderate correlations exist between both pairs of variables," and urge that further research be pursued. The usefulness of this paper is its overview of current sociological thought on the relationship between work life and nonwork life, and the directions it points to for further research.

The paper by Lopez and Gray is called "The Substitution of Communication for Transportation—A Case Study." Although it is not a study of telecommuting as we are defining it, i.e., working from the home, it does look at the concern of an insurance company over the problem of moving large numbers of people into a central area to do work, and the innovative solution of moving the work to the people by decentralization of office location, and the use of telecommunications. The paper is distinctly quantitative, dwelling upon the development of an optimization model whereby the company can make the best decisions regarding its pending decentralization.

Charles McClintock is a social psychologist at Cornell University who has been studying the phenomenon of telecommuting over the past few years. His paper "Working Alone Together: Managing Telecommuting" is preliminary work toward addressing a major question facing the future of telecommuting: its effect upon worker productivity. His paper introduces "variables and their causal directions that intervene in the relationship between telecommuting from home and productivity" (McClintock, p. A8.2.2). His work is toward the development of a model that will allow more rigorous testing.

The Canadian government report *In the Chips* is an 89-page report prepared and compiled by a six-member task force examining microelectronics and employment. Although Canada may be seen as riding on the economic coattails of the U.S., Canada is often ahead of the U.S. in anticipating the future and acting in a collective way that implies more thoughtful analysis and social cohesion. The task force received input from all sectors of the work force, and the results of their cooperative effort are well organized into an extremely readable report on triggering technologies, microelectronics and work, industrial relations, quality of working environment and work (health and safety, and women), and training and education.

Several articles in the monthly magazines were of interest. First is Strassman's article in *Technology Review*: "The Office of the Future: Information Management for the New Age." This was written in 1980, which seems a long time ago in this electronic age, but Strassman was looking into the future and warning all of us that we must not leap headlong into the age of information, but look carefully at what it has to offer, assess our needs, learn to think in new ways, and plan carefully. He gives a good overview of the transition from industrial to information society and economy.

Datamation is a good magazine for keeping its ear to the ground in regard to future trends. In the September 1982 issue are two good articles. One is "At the Mercy of Machines" by Engelbert Kirchner, in which there is a good overview of the sectors of the work force involved in working with computers or computerized equipment, as well as the social, labor, and political dilemmas that accompany this situation. The other is "Wanna Bet?" It's *Datamation*'s survey of some office automation "soothsayers" about what exactly is going on in the area of office automation. It surveys such people as Amy Wohl (president of Advanced Office Concepts), a prolific and extremely readable analyst in the field, Ulric Weil of Morgan Stanley, and Bruce Hasenyager (vice president for information systems at Kidder Peabody), who says most eloquently:

> The technology of the automated office will amplify the behavior of the people working there. It will allow good managers to manage better, insightful professionals to contribute more, good support staff to support more, and effective teams to synergize more easily. It will also allow confused managers to obfuscate situations more thoroughly, bad leaders to charge off more rapidly in the wrong direction, fools to make their foolishness more quickly and more broadly known, boors to be more boorish, and bores to be more boring. In addition to the pleasures of broader spans of control and crisper decision-making, we will have the pains of information addiction and electronic junk mail (Klee, p. 165).

Working Woman is a relatively new magazine, and is hard to find in libraries (but easy to find on airplanes). The November 1982 issue has a good article by Joanne Tangorra on telecommuting, which gives some interesting information on the use of telecommuting in industry—an area where telecommuting is still not seen much, due to a seeming fear of loss of control over workers and invasion of company proprietary information through use of public means of data transmission. However, some industries are doing pilot experiments, and Tangorra gives good interesting descriptions, as well as how the opportunity to telecommute is being experienced by women workers, from word processor operators to managers. One woman sums up the opportunities inherent in the ability to telecommute:

> There's a small but real career path for nonprofessional women to move up out of the support staff—from word processing to managing systems to sales positions with vendors of automated office equipment. This revolution is not as prone to sex barriers, and women can be among the innovators. (Tangorra, p. 54)

Business Week does a good job of keeping up with everything affecting business. I include one article as another good source on what industry is doing with telecommuting, and the response of organized labor to the increased incidence of telecommuting. It is called "If Home Is Where the Worker Is," and is found in the May 3, 1982, issue.

Finally, no survey of literature referring to the information society can neglect three important books. It is hard to believe that *Future Shock* was written over 10 years ago, but reassuring to find that Toffler has made every effort to keep up (in a time when it's hard to know when the right time has come to say that something significant has happened), and published *The Third Wave* in 1980. And second on the *New York Times* Best Seller List right now is John Naisbitt's *Megatrends*, subtitled "Ten New Directions Transforming our Lives." Naisbitt uses the technique of content analysis to survey the changing content of our national newspapers, and he keeps track of trends, fads, and real changes by this technique. As one subject demands more physical space (column inches) in a newspaper, other subjects are shunted to the back pages and eventually out of the public eye. Naisbitt's analysis of high tech and high touch is especially relevant to this examination of telecommuting and its impact on our home lives.

Methods

In order to gather the preliminary data presented in this paper, I decided to limit and tailor my sample in the following ways: I collected information from one work site only, Stanford University, and this limits variables existing from one worksite to another, to some extent. I therefore did not seek to compare telecommuting at various places of employment. I wanted to obtain responses from telecommuters only, and this limits variables existing between telecommuters and nontelecommuters. I sought as wide a selection of occupations as possible, and this avoids a collection of information solely from computer professionals. Future research may well take these other variables into account, but my sample sufficed for my purpose: I wanted to know how it is for people to experience telecommuting and what it is like for them to work at home as compared to working at the office.

I designed an 18-item questionnaire, which I sent via electronic mail to 15 men and 15 women employees at Stanford who have access to the central computer; I knew that most of them were telecommuters in the

293

sense that they often work at home instead of in their offices. I also assumed that the aforementioned negative aspects of telecommuting are not perceived so negatively by Stanford telecommuters. I tried to select survey recipients to maximize the number of different professions represented in the response. Included were the professions of writer, manager, university officer, attorney, computer programmer, assistant professor, personnel director, etc. The electronic mail versions of the questionnaire were followed by paper copies, in case the respondents preferred to write down their answers instead of keying them into the computer. Participation was voluntary, and the returned questionnaires numbered 12 from the men, and 10 from the women, or a total of 22 (73%).

The questionnaire is attached as an appendix. Analysis of the responses was done by compiling the answers to each question and making generalizations from their collected concerns. Several of the respondents expressed interest in the results, and copies of the report will be distributed to them.

The Study

Of the 22 responses to the questionnaire, the occupations represented by the respondents included manager, technical writer, director, university officer (public affairs), university officer (Provost's Office), technical/managerial consultant, university officer (internal audit), documentation coordinator, attorney, accounting supervisor, executive assistant, office manager, publications assistant, manager of technical/professional staff, researcher/evaluator, research assistant (Ph.D. candidate), consultant, assistant professor, social researcher, financial officer, and personnel manager. One of the respondents said he was once a telecommuter for another employer, but did not telecommute at Stanford. His responses have not been included in the numerical compilation, but his attitudes and experiences with telecommuting have been included in the commentary. Another respondent is a former Stanford employee who is now on consultant status with the university, so his relationship to Stanford is somewhat different from the others, and this is reflected in the slightly different point of view of his responses.

All of the telecommuters who responded use their own personal computer equipment at home or have the university pay for the rental of the equipment to them. No one has to work at home, although it is a very common practice at the university. (To be more accurate, it is a matter of limited choice for many people: if those around you are working at home, beyond the normal number of business hours, and they need your input on their work, they are slowed down unless you are keeping up with them. Although all telecommuters see themselves as voluntary telecommuters, there is a subtle, and sometimes not so subtle, pressure to expand the capacity to work by this means.)

To give some sort of scale to the following, consider that two years ago Stanford's community of about 20,000 people had 400 computer professionals (people who use a computer as part of their jobs), and about 4,000 more people (faculty, students, and staff) who used a computer as part of their work. Thus about 20% of the university population was using computers to some extent. After the introduction of electronic mail in the administrative sector in 1980/81, the use of that computer system went up steeply, and student demand for computing facilities also increased rapidly. Now it is estimated that about 40% of the Stanford community is using computers for some part of their work.

According to the surveys returned, 21 respondents replied that they do Stanford work at home using a computer. One commented, "I do a great deal of it. Using a computer at my home as an adjunct to my work in the office at Stanford has become utterly essential in the performance of my duties."

When asked if anyone else in the home worked for an employer in this way, 2 women and 4 men responded "Yes" (total 6), and 8 women and 7 men responded "No" (total 15). It was much more common, then, for our telecommuters to be the only ones in their households to be using computer equipment at home for work.

Question 4 asked about whether people worked away from the office because of travel demands. Fourteen people (8 women and 6 men) said that they did not. Eight people replied that they did, although not always with a computer. Of these 2 were women and 6 were men. One respondent commented:

Frequently. I often travel with a portable computer terminal. I use electronic mail to send frequent dispatches back to Stanford as well as to receive much essential information from Stanford. The Stanford electronic mail system is a principal not a peripheral means of communication with Stanford while I am away from the campus. (Witness: This questionnaire is being filled out on a microcomputer in Washington, D.C., and will be entered into electronic mail by file transfer, and sent to you.)

Another traveling worker commented that he was finding it "pretty inconvenient to carry a bulky 'portable' terminal when travelling." One further person to whom the questionnaire was sent replied from New York City that she had received the questionnaire, but would be too busy with other obligations to respond to it right away.

Questions about the impact of using computers in the home follow. All but two of the respondents claimed that they had had to make space accommodations in their homes to have the computer equipment there. People chose a variety of rooms to house their equipment: the living room, the bedroom, the family room, the guest room were all used, and one person chose to move the terminal around, not having chosen a permanent place to put it. Eight men and 5 women put the equipment in what they identified as studies or offices, or space in a larger room used as an office/ work area. Eleven men and 7 women said they have offices or studies at home, and of these, 8 men and 1 woman claimed that these rooms were for their own use only. Respondents replied that they had had these rooms as part of their households from six months to 14 years, or an average of 4–5 years. One person, who did not have an office or study, commented:

I feel strongly that work and home life are separate. My home needs to be instant relaxation for me. I want it to be a place to relax, with good vibrations, and have had it this way ever since graduate school days. I feel like my home has been invaded with the terminal in the living room. I have a small house, and telecommuting has brought work and the pressure of work into my house in a way I resent. Even so, I choose it because it makes work more bearable. It has destroyed a relaxed quality of my house, which should be a refuge away from work. I can't remedy this without getting the salary and promotion that would enable me to buy a house big enough to have a study. I'd need a bigger place to live in to make it (telecommuting) acceptable.

When asked whether their Stanford work at home was done mostly during, outside of, or in addition to normal business hours, most people (15) responded that it was a combination of these, and many of them were doing all three. The common answer was "outside of, and in addition to." Some people responded that they worked at home sometimes during normal business hours (1/2 day to 2 full days), as well as in addition to these hours. Many indicated a flexibility as to choice—they could mostly work where they wanted when they needed to, but they all worked more than normal business hours. When asked whether they worked entirely at home or, if only part of the time, what percent, there was no one who worked entirely at home. Most people spent about 10–20% of their total work time working at home, with a few up around 50%.

It is interesting to know what kind of work people prefer to do at home, or at least reserve for work at home. The most popular use of the computer at home was for electronic mail (reading, writing, replying, distributing information), with 17 people voting for this one. Writing and "think" work came in second (14 people), which includes word processing, text editing, composing of minutes, memos, reports, letters, documents of all sorts, and issuing commands that cause the printer on campus to print documents in whatever format is chosen. One respondent said,

I am a heavy user of electronic mail at home. I also use my home computer to write a variety of important documents. Using electronic mail as a link between our office microcomputer and my home computer, I work at home on the same items I work on at the office. Because use of electronic mail with Washington and other institutions is important to my work, I frequently send mail back East late at night, and I generally check mail early in the morning at home before going to the office.

Another respondent thriftily replied that it was useful to take "advantage of cheaper evening and weekend rates," which was easier to do from home than the office. Other people replied that they use the computer at home for programming and software maintenance (6) and data or statistical analysis (3).

What are the advantages of working at the office as opposed to working at home? This question and the obverse were asked. Most people claimed the people component was the advantage to working in the office. From managing and directing, down to just plain socializing, the office was the best place (13 people). This included meeting people, the social environment, participating in meetings, touching base with colleagues, planning, scheduling, and resolving problems. The second most popular advantage to being at the office was the access to support staff and other resources (equipment, files, source documents, tools, phones, etc.), which netted 10 votes. A third preference had to do with a discipline factor: 5 people remarked upon the need to segregate work and personal life, to contain stress to the workplace, to have a feeling that the work period is clearly defined, making it easier to stick to work and giving a feeling of a more professional atmosphere. Two people claimed they ate less at the office, and one person remarked that it was nice to have some place to *go* to for work.

The advantages of working at home are, for the majority of the respondents (19), fewer distractions and interruptions, control over distractions and interruptions, relative quietness, ability to concentrate, think, and work longer, and less stress. Three mentioned the ease of access from home at night and on weekends, and the reduced rates in effect. Two others mentioned that it is more comfortable to work at home, and that often home is heated at nights and on weekends when the office is not. Other mentions were the reduced requirements on dressing for work and time to commute.

To go further with the effects of telecommuting on the home, respondents were asked what effects their working at home had on the others at home. More positive effects were noted than negative. The most positive effect noted was that the presence in the home of the worker was perceived as positive by the others. Five people reported they could be at home when needed, their being there was more appreciated (and although they were working, they were not seen in such a negative light as when they went back at night to work, thus leaving family again). Three people reported that the family interest in computing was promoted by this activity, with a special remark on computer literacy in children. And three people reported that this was an excellent way for the children to develop appropriate role models, especially in seeing their mothers as doing interesting and responsible work. Related to this, two others reported that the work promoted an understanding of their jobs among people at home. Two reported that a positive aspect is that people can work together at home and share ideas in their work. Other positive aspects were the social flexibility (can meet spouse for lunch), can be there when the kids get home, can work chores such as laundry, shopping, and cooking into the work day.

Seven people reported no effects, positive or negative. The few mentions of negative effects were single responses having to do with noise from a home printer, spending more time working, taking away from relaxation time with family, irritating spouse, and sometimes being incommunicative due to concentration on work.

Of particular interest to employers was the question about perceived benefit to the employer of having people working at home. The advantages are many to the employer: all agreed that the university gets more work out of them. Seven reported getting more work done, and five reported increased productivity. One person said, ''It's a goldmine to the employer!

My productivity is orders of magnitude higher by having and using my home computer extensively—and this is all in addition to my full-time work at the office. I did relatively little work at home in the yellow pad and pencil days, but now do a great deal." Another said, "Despite any plans, the net effect of having a terminal at home is that more work gets done." This person also worked in industry, and referred to this past employer: "_____Company is especially backward in this respect. Policy there is that you get a terminal at home only if you are on a critical project or if you promise to do some special work on your own time. The reality is that people like to work more without being asked." Four people reported that telecommuting can extend the work time in a convenient way, and that work can go on beyond normal business hours. Three people said that they could think better, and related to that were the enhanced creativity, the increased efficiency, and increased effectiveness reported by 5 people. Also related to creativity was the report that electronic mail allowed one person to disseminate creative ideas quickly to colleagues. Two others reported the ability to respond to crises and emergencies quickly, without unnecessary delay, and two more reported the ability to meet deadlines better.

There were several other notable quotations in connection with the benefit to the employer:

I am really able to be more creative and more productive—as I said, I do better thinking at home. So if my employer wants my ideas, (s)he should send me home.

Increased productivity [is a benefit] because flexibility promotes good mental health. People work better in different environments, even the same person needs variation.

[Working at home gets my employer] more work and efficiency—two times more productivity, and consider that we already have electronic mail in our offices to make our work more efficient!

The last substance question asked for an opinion as to where the respondents thought they could get more work done. Three women and 2 men thought they could get more done at home. Four women and two men opted for the office. The rest preferred a combination, depending upon what they were expected or needed to do. There was a consensus that concentrated work, like thinking, planning, and writing, was more effectively done at home, while people work (managing, meeting, problem solving) was best done on a face-to-face basis at the office.

Summary and Conclusions

This has been a preliminary inquiry into the impact of telecommuting on home life. Limited to a small sample of relatively experienced telecommuters working for Stanford University, some very general information has been gathered about their work in the home and the effect of that work upon the home and the people they share their homes with. Much more extensive inquiry and more sophisticated techniques for gathering further information immediately suggest themselves, and it is hoped that this work will generate further study.

We have learned that our telecommuter sample likes to have flexibility in work, the ability to work at home and at the office, with certain kinds of work being suitable to each environment. In general, there are more benefits to being able to work at home, and one would suspect that this may only be true if the ability to work at the office is there, too, since more people reported a preference for working at the office, and not one respondent was restricted to work in the home.

Employers considering the benefits of telecommuting should take special note of the resounding vote that the employer benefits when people are allowed to work at home using computers. Employers might also take into consideration that workers may wish flexibility more than anything, and the ability to measure the increase in productivity that may be released by certain measures toward flexibility is a worthwhile project to pursue.

Finally, this sample—although it comes from an extremely sophisticated population of information workers, from whom it might be expected that primary concern would be directed toward more technical and analytic matters—makes a strong and lucid declaration about the need for contact with other people in the work situation, for face-to-face contact, for socializing, for being together with others. John Naisbitt refers to this as "high touch." He says: "What happens is that whenever new technology is introduced into society, there must be a counterbalancing human response—that is, high touch—or the technology is rejected. The more high tech, the more high touch."

I think it is fitting to conclude this study with some further thoughts from Naisbitt:

> Technology and our human potential are the two great challenges and adventures facing humankind today. The great lesson we must learn from the principle of high tech/high touch is a modern version of the ancient Greek ideal—balance.
>
> We must learn to balance the material wonders of technology with the spiritual demands of our human nature. (Naisbitt, p. 40)

Bibliography

Business Week (1982). "If Home Is Where the Worker Is," p. 66, May 3.

Kirchner, Engelbert (1982). "At the Mercy of Machines," *Datamation*, pp. 252–261, September.

Klee, K. (1982). "Wanna Bet? Datamation asks some office automation soothsayers to put their money where their mouths are," *Datamation*, pp. 164–165, September.

Labour Canada/Travail Canada (1982) *In the Chips: Opportunities, People, Partnerships.* Report of the Labour Canada Task Force on Micro-Electronics and Employment, Ottawa.

McClintock, C.C. (1981). "Working Alone Together: Managing Telecommuting," *National Telecommunications Conference Record,* Institute of Electrical and Electronics Engineers (IEEE), Vol. 9, A821–A824.

Naisbitt, John (1982). *Megatrends,* Warner Books, Inc. New York, N.Y.

Strassman, Paul (1980). "The Office of the Future: Information Management for the New Age," *Technology Review, pp. 55-65, December/January.*

Tangorra, Joanne (1982). "Telecommuting," *Working Woman*, pp. 52–54, November.

Toffler, Alvin (1970). *Future Shock.* Random House, Inc., New York, N.Y.

Toffler, Alvin (1980). *The Third Wave.* Bantam Books, New York, N.Y.

Appendix
Questionnaire Format

Dear   :

I am doing a social psychology research project on the subject of telecommuting, or using a computer to work for an employer from home or some other non-central site.

Anthropologists tell us that work originally was done in the home, went out into the larger community, and now seems to be coming back with the tools available through present technology. I am particularly interested in the effects on homelife with the introduction of paid work back into the home. I am further interested in comparing the viewpoints of both men and women who work as telecommuters, whether part of the time or all of the time.

If you would be willing to furnish some information to me, kindly respond to the following questions and send your answers back to me, preferably within the next week. Your answers can be sent back online, or by paper copy (which is being printed to you), to Pine 127.

Thank you very much.

Jane Kingston (home 856-3369, office 497-4807)

1. Given the definition of telecommuting at Stanford as working for Stanford at home (part of the time or full time) using a computer either connected to a Stanford computer or compatible with a Stanford computer by some other means (floppy disk, e.g.), do you consider yourself a telecommuter?
2. Do you do Stanford work at home using a computer?
3. Does anyone else in your home work for an employer this way?
4. When you work away from your office, is it ever because you are traveling?
5. Have you made space accommodations to have computer equipment in your home?
6. Which room is your computer equipment in?
7. Do you have an office or study at home?
8. Is this office or study for your own use only?
9. If you have an office or study or other work area at home, how long have you had this as a part of your household?
10. Is your Stanford work at home done mostly during, outside, or in addition to normal business hours?
11. Do you work entirely at home, or part time? (What percent?)
12. What kind of work do you do at home using a computer?
13. How is working at the office better than working at home for you?
14. How is working at home better than working at the office for you?
15. What effects (positive and negative) has your working at home had on the people you live with?
16. What do you think the advantages to your employer are to your being able to work at home?
17. Where can you get more work done—at home or at your office?
18. What is your occupation or professional identification?

300

Work/Family Policies:
An Innovation Theory Approach

by

Lillian Little

"Firms are disrupted by wave of pregnancy at the manager level" read a headline in the Wall Street Journal on July 20, 1981. One may wonder, if an outbreak of pregnancy disrupted firms in the summer of '81, how are those firms faring now, with the consequent wave of new parenthood. The answer for most firms would probably be "not very well."

Traditionally the thinking has been that problems associated with combining work and family should be the burden of the individual who chooses to do so. But that thinking is changing—out of necessity—simply because so many employees nowadays do combine work and family. And the bottom line is that outcomes arising from work/family conflict will be felt by the organization as well as the individual. For example, absenteeism, work time spent on family business (Olmsted, 1981), lower performance, overqualified job incumbents (U.S. Commission on Civil Rights, 1981), and lower job satisfaction (Pleck, Staines & Long, 1980) have been cited as problems resulting from work/family conflict. If anticipated or experienced conflict is great enough for one spouse to leave work permanently, the employer pays dearly; a middle manager is expensive to replace, and even a low-level clerk who departs will cost the firm an estimated $1,500 (Saxe, 1982). And the situation is no longer uniquely a women's issue: ". . . men in dual-career families are just as 'non traditional' in technical and managerial roles as women are" (Bailyn, 1983, p. 2). Additionally, a 1981 Catalyst study found 83.1% of polled Fortune 1300 companies agreeing with the statement "Among two-career couples in our company, men are increasingly feeling the need to share parenting responsibilities." That same study found, among two-career couples of all ages, both men and women value family significantly higher than career. So, in a crunch, the organization, rather than the family, will suffer.

Of course work/family conflict costs the individual and society as well. A 1978 national survey of working women found 29% of lower-level employees and 36% of professional, managerial, and technical employees reporting child care as a major problem (U.S. Commission on Civil Rights, 1981). Moreover, as of 1975, an estimated 32,000 *preschoolers* were

Lillian Little is an assistant professor of management at the School of Management, Suffolk University, Boston, Massachusetts.

caring for themselves and recent census data report that at least 2 million 7–13 year olds are left with no supervision (U.S. Commission on Civil Rights, 1981). Lower satisfaction with family life and life in general has also been reported as an outcome of work/family conflict (Pleck, et al., 1980). But perhaps the most devastating outcome is all the young couples denying themselves a family because under the circumstances they can't manage two careers and family responsibilities simultaneously.

Where did this relatively new issue of work/family problems come from and what does the future hold? As of 1980, according to the Department of Labor, 47% of all women with preschool children were in the work force (Christie, 1981). In fact, in the 1970s women with preschoolers became the segment with the fastest growing participation rate (Olmsted, 1981). Economic pressures are certainly primary motivators behind this trend; inflation in general, but housing costs specifically, have forced many reluctant mothers into the marketplace. The frustration of not being able to put education to use is another motivator, as well as fear of straying from the fast-track career path. The increase of the single parent is still another factor that has aggravated work/family conflict.

None of these trends appear to be reversing. Although inflation has slowed down in recent months, mortgage rates may never be 8.5% again; nor will house prices come down substantially, if at all. As far as educational trends go, "women now represent 52% of undergraduates, 15% of engineering students, 33% of MBA candidates, and almost 50% of law school students" (Catalyst, 1983, p. 1) Certainly the women trained in the professions today will not be content to stay home and bake cookies tomorrow. And, with all those other "baby-boomers" to contend with, career paths will probably not become less treacherous. To compound the problem, it has been recognized that the brunt and stresses of establishing a career and a family occur simultaneously in one's life (Bailyn, 1983). And finally, even a casual observer would have to agree that the single-parent family has become a typical feature of American life.

As can be seen from the discussion above, the problems are not trivial, nor are their sources temporary. And yet solutions, so far, have been hard to come by.

Although, in acknowledging the political "gender gap," a Democratic aid has stated "issues like child care could be politically sexy in '84" (Friedan, 1983, p. 36), political/legal action cannot be counted on to solve such problems. Solutions are found where the problem exists—in the private sector.

In fact, in a 1981 study of the Fortune 1300 (Catalyst, 1981), 372 companies responded to the statement: "Companies are concerned about two-career family problems because such issues could affect recruiting, employee morale, productivity and ultimately corporate profits" (p. 11); seventy-six percent agreed, 9% disagreed, and 15% were uncertain. Yet when comparing "corporations that have practice" and "corporations that favor practice" (Table 1) against each other and against the 76% who foresee a problem, gaps are immediately apparent.

Table 1

Comparison of companies that have and companies that favor selected work/family policies

	Corporations that have practice	Corporations that favor practice
Flexitime	37%	73%
Flexible work places	8%	42%
On-site child care	1%	20%

N = 355-368
Source: *Corporations and Two-Career Families: Directions for the Future,* Catalyst Career and Family Center, New York, 1981.

The first gap, between the perception of the problem and belief that a particular practice will serve as a remedy, may be due to lack of knowledge of the practice or perhaps believing another practice will serve as a better remedy. The second gap, between favoring the practice and operationalizing it, may be a result of the perception of too many obstacles in the path, preventing adoption of a favored practice. In either case, the issues, placed in an innovation theory context, can be analyzed and channeled in such a way that organizations may be shown the connection between remedying a present or anticipated dip in corporate profits and a specific work/family policy. In the same way, innovation theory may help translate a favored practice to an operationalized practice.

Following brief definitions of six work/family policies, the remainder of this paper will discuss how innovation theory can facilitate both diffusion and adoption of such policies.

Flexitime refers to a scheduling system whereby employees choose, within some constraints, when they arrive at work and when they leave work.

Permanent part-time work is long term but consists of a less than 35-hour week.

Job sharing is the combination of two people fulfilling the requirements of one job.

On-site daycare consists of child care located at, or near, the work site.

Flexible work places is defined as the ability of employees to work at home at least part of the time.

Task contracting refers to payment for work done rather than for hours worked.

Innovation Theory

Innovation has been almost universally defined as "the earliness or extent of use by a given organization of a new idea, where new means only new to the adapting agent, and not necessarily to the world in general" (Downs and Mohr, 1979, p. 385; Rogers and Shoemaker, 1971; Zaltman, Duncan and Holbek, 1973). This definition fits work/family policies since none of them are new to American organizations at large, and it seems a safe bet that no one American organization has incorporated *all* of the policies discussed in the paper.

Most innovation theorists have divided the innovation process into two stages: diffusion and adoption (Downs and Mohr, 1979). Some refined the two stages by adding substages to the process. The Zaltman, Duncan, and Holbek model (1979) (see Table 2) was chosen for this paper because each of the substages of the innovation process is associated with one or more attributes of the innovation.

Innovation attributes are discussed widely in the literature and are considered to be, along with organizational characteristics, characteristics of the change agent, partial predictors of whether an organization will adopt a specific innovation. The remainder of this paper will explain how attributes of the innovation and the organization have kept work/family policies from being widely accepted and adopted. Concurrently, methods will be explored by which those same attributes may be utilized in order to promote further adoption.

Table 2
Stages of Innovation Adoption Process

I. Initiation stage
  1. Knowledge-awareness
  2. Formation of attitudes toward innovation
  3. Decision
II. Implementation stage
  1. Initial implementation
  2. Continued-sustained implementation

Source: Zaltman, Duncan, and Holbek, 1979, p. 158

During "knowledge-awareness," the first substage of the "initiation" stage, **communicability** is said to be an outstanding innovation attribute (Rogers and Shoemaker, 1971). Communicability has been a problem for work/family innovations on two levels. First, the dissemination of information describing the policies has been negligible, especially the more radical policies, such as flexible workplaces. Second, even if the concept of the policy is known, the benefits of adopting such a policy probably are not known or understood. This problem is aggravated by the fact that work/family benefits to the employer are so indirect. For example, job sharing may increase productivity as much as (if not more than) replacing a human being with a robot, but the relationship in the former case is more difficult to ascertain. And, as a result, one organization cannot easily look to another to determine whether an innovation is worthy. Rogers and Shoemaker (1971) have noted that this is a problem for most organizations. The remedy is obvious—disseminate the information, description, benefits, *and* problems associated with each policy. (Although there may be a temptation to play down the problems, communication theory suggests that intelligent audiences are suspicious of one-sided stories.) Additionally, measurements linking work/family policies to benefits must be shown to be valid and reliable, thus providing a more direct connection between the two.

A number of innovation attributes are relevant to the attitude-formation substage. One of them is **cost**. (Cost is a salient attribute of the decision stage as well.) As a matter of fact, Downs and Mohr (1979) have suggested that all attributes of innovations can be reduced to a matter of cost. They also make the important point that cost is relative; a successful organization with abundant slack resources will perceive a given policy as less costly than will a less successful company with less money to spend. Cost undoubtedly has prevented many organizations from adopting work/family policies, but the perceived cost is often unrealistic. For example, it is not unheard of for organizations to form a negative attitude towards flexitime because they think the cost of paperwork and coordination will be astounding. Obviously costs cannot be neglected, but the potential innovator needs to be shown what the costs are likely to be and how the organization can minimize those costs.

A more sophisticated attribute than cost is **return on investment**, because it weighs benefits against costs. In fact, many studies have concluded that diffusion is faster for innovations with higher profitability (Griliches, 1957; Mansfield, 1968). Zaltman et al. (1973) cite (slow or low) return on investment of "special significance among organizations with particularly scarce resources" (p. 35). The problem for work/family policies, as alluded to in the discussion of communicability, is the indirect relationship of costs to benefits. For example, if the admittedly costly policy of on-site day care is adopted and anxiety levels of parents/employees decreases, how does that affect productivity? Many organizations are even primitive in their accounting for economic gains due to decreased absenteeism and turnover. Three possible solutions are open: show organizations what is known about the relationships between specific costs and benefits (and how long it should take to recover costs); research the more abstract relationships (i.e., reduced parental anxiety and increased productivity); and help organizations minimize initial costs until benefits are assessed (i.e., start flexible workplaces with employees who don't need expensive computer terminals to work at home).

Another attribute important in the attitude-formation stage is **risk and uncertainty**. This is particularly relevant to firms who are among the first adopters of an innovation, since they have few, if any, models to check for problems and benefits. In terms of work/family policies, task contracting would involve more risk and uncertainty than flexitime simply because far fewer organizations have adopted task contracting than have adapted flexitime. Risk and uncertainty is intimately related to "trialability (Rogers and Shoemaker, 1971). In other words, the more an innovation can be tried on a trial basis the less risk and uncertainty there will be. Some work/family policies, such as on-site day care, have high start-up costs and consequently do not lend themselves to trialability. Moreover, if a day-care center is established and later withdrawn, there may be a high level of employee resentment. However other policies such as task contracting can fairly easily be done on a small, trial basis before a long-term commitment is made. Permanent part-time work can be tried as long as the employee is fully aware of the trial status.

Compatibility, as defined by Rogers and Shoemaker (1971), refers to "the degree to which an innovation is perceived as being consistent with the existing values, past experiences, and needs of receivers. . . Adoption of an incompatible innovation often requires the prior adoption of a new value system'' (p. 22). At least one research team has hypothesized that incompatibility will hamper innovation adoption (Nathanson and Morlock, 1980). Compatibility is easily one of the most important innovation attributes concerning work/family policies. The simple point is that most policy makers do not have to deal with child-care issues in their personal life because theirs is a traditional family unit—husband works, wife stays home with children. It would be unfair to say that all policy makers who are part of traditional households are insensitive to the problems of non-traditional households. But there are, undoubtedly, many corporate executives who feel, on an emotional level, that mothers should be home with their children and that work/family policies are unneeded and possibly harmful to family structure. In time, as men and women who personally face work/family problems themselves climb the corporate ladder and become executives, the issue of compatibility will solve itself. In the meantime, because attitudes are not easy to change directly, the best that can be done is to explain the economic net benefits of work/family policies, appealing on a cognitive level without attacking the affective element.

Complexity, the degree to which an innovation is perceived as relatively difficult to understand and use, is negatively related to its rate of adoption. Although none of the work/family policies are inherently difficult to understand or to use (perhaps with the exception of task contracting), the key to complexity lies in the perception of potential adopters. It is natural for any idea that has no precedent in one's own experience (i.e., on-site day care) to be perceived as more complex than it really is. Precedents can be created, either by demonstrating what other organizations (particularly those in the industry or geographic area relevant to the potential adopting organization) have done, or by suggesting that the potential adopter start with relatively simple policies, such as flexitime. Once the logistically easier policies have been shown to be feasible, a precedent, internal to the organization, will effectively be set, paving the way for more radical policies in the future.

Relative advantage, the degree to which an innovation is perceived as being better than the idea it supersedes, is a relevant innovation attribute of the decision substage. Rogers and Shoemaker (1971) make the point that a crisis situation emphasizes the relative advantage of an innovation. As discussed in the introduction of this paper, a sizable percentage of polled organizations view two-career-family problems as having the potential for affecting corporate profits, yet it is doubtful that any one organization has experienced a crisis situation so far. And while most top management teams pride themselves on their ability to anticipate trends before a crisis is imminent, few organizations seem to have taken heed of the two-career-couple trends. Perhaps the trends need to be made more explicit—showing what the future demographics are likely to look like *and* the organizational impact those demographics are likely to have if work/family policies are not planned. Another relevant point made by Rogers and Shoemaker concerning relative advantage is that if rewards are not immediate, innovation adoption will be delayed. The problem again for work/family policies is the indirect nature of benefits. One strategy to remedy this problem may be to emphasize the more immediate benefits, such as decreased absenteeism associated with flexitime, while also pointing out the benefits likely to accrue in the longer term.

An innovation characteristic associated with the initial implementation stage is **publicness versus privateness**, which refers to whether the innovation is available to all members and whether those members opposing its implementation must accept it. This is one characteristic whereby work/ family policies have a definite advantage: there are actually very few, if any, jobs that couldn't fit into flexitime, permanent part-time, flexible workplaces, or task contracting policies. And of course the ability to take advantage of on-site day care is virtually unrelated to one's position in the organization, while at the same time no employee is forced to incorporate any work/family policy into his or her work style.

The last innovation attribute to be discussed, **susceptibility to successive modification**, becomes salient in the sustained implementation substage. This attribute involves the ability of the innovation to be adapted to improvements. In this case, some work/family policies have an advantage over others. For example, it is relatively easy to modify flexitime or flexible workplace policy and considerably more difficult to alter a task contracting policy. Modification of permanent part-time and on-site daycare policies may be more contingent upon the individual situation.

As the discussion above indicates, both the parameters and the presentation of work/family policies may be designed to make them more acceptable, and therefore adoptable, to organizations. However, because of the assumption that the probability of a given firm adopting a specific innovation is positively related to the proportion of firms in an industry that have already adopted the innovation (Jensen, 1982), it would be unwise to neglect organizational characteristics relating to the propensity to adopt. In other words, it makes the most sense to attempt to "market" work/family policies to those organizations that, due to their characteristics, are likely to be receptive. And as the receptive organizations adopt work/family policies, the remaining organizations will become more receptive—the innovation will become visible and popular. Organizational characteristics will be described in order of hypothesized importance for work/family policy innovations.

Zaltman, et al. (1973) suggest that "the impetus to innovation arises when organizational decision makers perceive that the organization's present course of action is unsatisfactory" (p. 55). If that is the case, then it would seem most plausible to try to initiate work/family policies in organizations that already suspect that either presently or down the road they may have problems in recruitment, for example, if they do not have established work/family policies.

According to Nathanson and Morlock (1980), the adoption of social innovations in particular (such as work/family policies) is facilitated by the "presence in an organization of influential individuals ideologically committed to social change" (p. 328). In this instance, those "influential individuals" may indeed be people facing work/family problems themselves. Or they may simply be individuals who are sensitive to the issue.

Admittedly, identifying organizations where such people are influential is not easy.

An obvious organizational factor that promotes innovation adoption is **organizational wealth** or **slack resources**. According to Downs and Mohr (1979), this is particularly important if the innovation is costly (e.g., on-site day care). Wealthy companies (in terms of sales) are not difficult to pinpoint, but wealth alone is not an indication of slack resources. In fact, if there is any indicator of slack resources it may be the overall health of the economy; the current recession has undoubtedly put a damper on at least some work/family policies.

Not surprisingly, **involvement in professional associations**, has been cited as a predictor of innovation adoption (Aiken and Hage, 1971). Current information is exchanged at professional meetings, and since work/family policy information diffusion appears to be a major problem, attendance at meetings by organizational members could be vital. For those interested in disseminating such information, speaking at professional meetings is obviously very helpful.

Another commonly cited characteristic facilitating innovation adoption is organizational **size** (Jensen, 1982; Moch and Morse, 1977). Baldridge and Burnham (1975) suggest that one reason size correlates to innovation adoption is that "increased size produces critical masses for certain problems that stimulate the adoption of innovations to handle them" (p. 170). Since women still carry most of the child-care responsibilities, a critical mass of female employees, rather than size itself, may be the important factor for work/family innovations.

A significant number of researchers have found innovation adoption to be associated with **decentralization** of decision-making. However, Downs and Mohr (1979) suggest that decentralization only has an impact if there is heterogeneity in values and information throughout the organization. In a similar vein, Moch and Morse (1977) found that decentralization is only relevant when the innovation is compatible with lower-level organization members. In terms of work/family policies, then, decentralization is critical when large numbers of women are concentrated in low-end jobs and upper management is rather unsympathetic to work/family problems.

Innovation diffusion and adoption theory is not a panacea; however, there is no reason why its use shouldn't facilitate a faster dissemination of work/family policy information as well as streamline the decision to adopt such policies.

References

Aiken, M., and Hage, J. The Organic Organization and Innovation. *Sociology*, 1971, *5*, 63–82.

Bailyn, L. Work and Family: The Context of Careers. Working Paper 1406-83, Alfred P. Sloan School of Management, M.I.T., February 1983.

Baldridge, J.V., and Burnham, R.H. Organizational Innovation: Individual, Organizational, and Environmental Impacts. *Administrative Science Quarterly*, 1975, *20*, 165–176.

Catalyst Career and Family Center. *Corporations and Two Career Families: Directions for the Future*, New York: Catalyst, 1981.

Catalyst. *Why Should Companies Think About Women?* New York: Catalyst 1983.

Christie, C.M. Who's Watching the Children? *New England Business*, October 5, 1981, pp. 21–24.

Downs, G., and Mohr L. Toward a Theory of Innovation. *Administration & Society*, 1979, *10*, 379–408.

Friedan, B. Twenty Years After the Feminine Mystique. *New York Times Magazine*, February 27, 1983, pp. 35–36, 42–57.

Griliches, Z. Hybrid Corn: An Exploration in the Economics of Technological Change. *Econometrica*, 1957, *25*, 501–522.

Handy, C. The Changing Shape of Work. *Organizational Dynamics*, Autumn 1980, pp. 26–34.

Hovland, C.I., Janis, I.L., and Kelly, N.H. *Communication and Persuasion*. New Haven: Yale University Press, 1953.

Jensen, R. Adoption and Diffusion of an Innovation of Uncertain Profitability. *Journal of Economic Theory*, 1982, *27*, 182–193.

Mansfield, E. *The Economics of Technological Change*. New York: Norton, 1968.

Moch, M., and Morse, E. Size, Centralization and Organizational Adoption of Innovations. *American Sociological Review*, 1977, *42*, 716–725.

Nathanson, C., and Morlock, L. Control Structure, Values, and Innovation: A Comparative Study of Hospitals. *Journal of Health and Social Behavior*, 1980, *21*, 315–333.

Olmsted, B. Alternative Work Time: A New Tool for Managing. *American Banker*, October 5, 1981, pp. 22–23; 34–35.

Pleck, J.H., Staines, G.L., and Lang, L. Conflicts Between Work and Family Life. *Monthly Labor Review*, March 1980, pp. 29–32.

Rogers, F. and Shoemaker, F. *Communication of Innovation*. New York: The Free Press, 1971.

Saxe, M.G. *New Work Schedules for a Changing Society*. Paper presented at "The Changing Workforce" conference, sponsored by Associated Industries of Massachusetts, Dedham, Massachusetts, March, 1982.

U.S. Commission on Civil Rights. *Child Care and Equal Opportunity for Women*. 1981. (Clearing House Publication No. 67).

Wood, W., Eagly, A.H., and Chaiken, S. *Casual Inferences about Communicators and their Effect on Opinion Change*. Paper presented at the annual meeting of the Eastern Psychological Association, Boston, 1977.

Zaltman, G., Duncan, R., and Holbek, J. *Innovations and Organizations*. New York: John Wiley & Sons, 1973.

Work, Leisure, and Culture

by

Vukan Kuic

Throughout the ages, it has been held that leisure is the basis of culture. This view can be found in the Old Testament and in Plato, Burke, Marx, Veblen, and T.S. Eliot. Whether they were glad for it or sad, people seem to have always taken it for granted that in order to have culture one must first have leisure. Applicable to society as well as to individuals, this rule was put concisely by Dr. Johnson as follows: "All intellectual improvement arises from leisure; all leisure arises from one working for another."

This historical theory of leisure as the necessary basis of culture appears at present, for the first time in all history, to be undergoing an actual empirical test. In the more advanced industrial societies, as years of formal education are prolonged, hours and strain of work reduced, vacations guaranteed, and the age of retirement lowered, leisure time has been distributed to very large numbers of people. In fact, in these societies leisure seems to have become a problem. On the one hand, more leisure time for everyone has led to larger sales of books and records (including classics), attendance at plays and concerts, museums and galleries, travel abroad, purchase of objects of art, etc., all of which may be taken as indices of cultural developments. But on the other hand, much of this new free time is also being spectacularly wasted in activities that, far from leading to cultural development, often destroy the very possibility of intellectual, moral, or spiritual improvement.

In modern experience, work, leisure, and culture are no longer embedded in the division of society into the working mass and a culture-bearing leisure class, so we are able to consider their relations much more objectively. While old practices unfortunately continue in many places throughout the world, under modern conditions for a society to enjoy freedom from work no longer requires "one to work for another." This in itself removes many reasons for taking sides and clears the ground for an impartial consideration of how culture is acquired and whether it necessarily

Vukan Kuic is a professor of government and international studies at the University of South Carolina, Columbia, South Carolina. This article, which is excerpted from a paper that appeared in The Review of Politics, *Vol. 43 (July 1981), No. 3, pp. 436–465, is reprinted by permission.*

310

transcends social utility. We no longer have to contend with empirical evidence of a society functionally divided into those who work and have no leisure and those who have both culture and leisure. Thus, while up to now most interpretations of culture have more or less depended on ideological positions, today we have an opportunity to develop a genuinely philosophical theory of culture.

While this, of course, cannot be done in these few pages, answering the above questions may give such a theory a good start. How is culture acquired? Today, with no culture-bearing leisure class obstructing our view, it has become quite clear that mere freedom from work, that is, just having free time on our hands, is not enough. Experience has taught post-industrial man that in order to develop that special quality which "arises from the interest in and acquaintance with what is generally regarded as excellent in arts, letters, manners, scholarly pursuits, etc.," one must invest much time and effort doing things closely resembling work, which in fact may be a species of work, namely rational, socially useful activities. Let us briefly consider first a person and then a society possessed of culture.

As far as individuals are concerned, we all know what pain and drudgery it often takes merely to develop no more than an initial taste for the best, say, in some scholarly pursuit. To become then an expert even in a single scholarly discipline requires, of course, not just additional effort, but a higher kind of effort. Still, an expert is not necessarily a cultured person, unless he is acquainted with the best in all arts, letters, and manners, which means in practice that we can never stop acquiring culture. Indeed, culture, in order to be maintained, needs to be cultivated, not unlike the crops in the field, by continuous efforts whose kinship with work is unmistakable. In fact, what we call intellectual work is work, and the moment a person ceases to be seriously interested in it, his or her claim to possession of culture necessarily begins to lose validity. Leisure resting on culture may be carefree enjoyment of life, but culture itself is the product of hard work.

This essential connection between culture and work can be seen even more clearly when we consider that culture, after all, is a social quality that represents the sum total of achievements not only in all scholarly pursuits but also in all arts, letters, manners, and a few other things. This has been well stated by T.S. Eliot in his *Notes Towards the Definition of Culture*, in which he actually complains repeatedly against the decline of culture in modern times due to the subordination of objective standards of excellence to social considerations. Eliot maintains that the only way culture could be preserved is by a specialized social class enjoying, among its other privileges, full freedom from work. Yet Eliot has no doubts whatsoever that culture as such belongs to society. It is true, he explains, that there are three senses of *culture*, depending on whether we have in mind the development of an *individual*, of a *group* or *class*, or of a *whole society*. Thus it makes sense to speak of culture in relation to an individual, and it makes sense also to speak of culture in relation to a social class. But the primary meaning of "culture" clearly pertains to society, for the simple reason that culture consists of many perfections.

Eliot writes:

> And if we do not find culture in any one of these perfections alone, so we must
> not expect any one person to be accomplished in all of them; we shall come to
> infer that the (wholly) cultured individual is a phantasm; and we shall look for
> culture, not in any individual or any one group of individuals, but more and
> more widely, and we are driven in the end to find it in the pattern of society
> as a whole.[1]

Thus no matter how one looks at it, culture always retains the character
of a social enterprise pervading the whole life of society. Long before
C.P. Snow alerted us to the problem of "two cultures," Eliot saw that
culture is all of one piece and that any divisions in it endanger not only
culture but also society. Such cultural disintegration, according to Eliot,
may occur both vertically, as for instance through alienation between
science and humanities (or between science and politics, or philosophy,
or religion), and horizontally, that is, through alienation between various
classes of society. "Cultural disintegration," he writes,

> is present when two or more strata so separate that these become in effect
> distinct cultures; and also when culture at the upper group level breaks into
> fragments each of which represents one cultural activity alone. If I am not
> mistaken, some disintegration of the classes in which culture is, or should be,
> most highly developed, has already taken place in western society [1949]—as
> well as some cultural separation between one level of society and another.[2]

In fact, despite his rejection in principle of the anthropological usage
of the term *culture*, Eliot goes so far as to specifically declare that "culture
is not merely the sum of several activities, but *a way of life*."[3] Too broad
to be a definition strictly speaking, this usage serves nevertheless to con-
firm the fact that, rather than on leisure, culture depends on socially useful
activities, including science and politics as well as the mode of production
of the necessities of life. But Eliot puts it also in another way, which
considerably narrows the meaning of culture and could well pass for a
definition. "Culture," he suggests, "may even be described simply as
that which makes life worth living."[4] Notice that as far as its dependence
on work is concerned, this changes nothing. The difference lies in the
grasping of the purpose of all that work. Thus, seeing culture as that which
makes life worth living, rather than just a way of life, we recognize, as
is Eliot's intention, that culture allows us to transcend temporal social
experience. In other words, remaining itself firmly grounded in work,
culture enables us to break the fetters of the processes of work to enjoy
true leisure.

I agree with Eliot on the transcendent nature of culture. But I have
cited him primarily to show that he also fully recognizes the essential
connections linking culture with work and society. What I want to do
now is to show how this transcendent nature of culture is necessarily
recognized even by a writer who apparently wants to keep it tied to the
standard of social utility. For instance, in *To Hell with Culture*, Herbert
Read declares categorically that if it is not for everybody, it is not culture.
The Greeks, he reminds us, did not have a word for culture, because it
never occurred to them that culture could be something separate from

their way of life. It was the Romans, the first large-scale capitalists, who first made "culture" into a distinct, salable commodity. In the Middle Ages, during which the term *fine arts* was unknown, culture once again became that spontaneous, un-self-conscious integration of art and work that we find in the production of its famous craftsmen. But at the beginning of the sixteenth century, with the rise of modern capitalism, this situation is changed again, and by the nineteenth century, when things really began to be made by machines, the divorce between culture and work is completed. For Read, this was also the end of true culture, and he suggests that we stop using the word. "The whole of our capitalist culture is one immense veneer," he writes, "a surface refinement hiding the cheapness and shoddiness at the heart of things. To hell with such culture! To the rubbish-heap and furnace with it all."[5]

In Read's view, then, the social order is decisive for culture, and he sets down three conditions for the restoration of culture to its proper place in society. First, all production should be for use, none for profit; second, each should give according to his ability and each receive according to his needs; and third, the workers in each industry should collectively own and control that industry. Read calls this "democracy" and contends that when it is achieved all workers would become artists, because "the artist is not a special kind of man, but every man is a special kind of artist." It all depends on how society is organized. As he puts it:

> When once a democratic society is established, it will inevitably lead to the creation of new values in art, literature, music and science. In some distant time men will call these new values the Democratic Civilization, or the Culture of Democracy, and I believe that it will be the greatest and the most permanent culture ever created by man.[6]

These statements, along with the title of his essay, leave no doubt as to Read's ideological position. He is a radical democrat for whom questions of social justice are of a higher order than any consideration of aesthetic standards. For him, society comes first, culture second. Indeed, he holds that culture which does not serve society does not deserve the name. And yet, for all his preoccupation with social utility and justice, for all his hostility to the traditional notion of culture as something rather elevated and accessible only to a few, Read cannot bring himself to deny that culture, in order to be true to its own nature, must ultimately transcend temporal social experience. Thus, while on one page he places culture in bondage to democratic social order, on the very next page he recognizes and eloquently expounds on its transcendental character, without even noticing that he has changed positions. True culture, Read insists, must be democratic, but

> Certain types of art are archetypal! That is to say, though they may have a limited range—indeed, by the nature of things, must have this limited range—they are formally perfect. A song by Shakespeare or Blake, a melody by Bach or Mozart, a Persian carpet or a Greek vase—such "forms," in the words of Keats, "tease us out of thought as doth eternity." They tease us out of our human preoccupations—the theme of epic and drama and novel—and for a few brief seconds hold us suspended in a timeless existence. Such rare moments are beyond daily reality, supersocial and in a sense superhuman.[7]

True, Read sees these forms only as the "glittering pinnacles" of the otherwise solid body of culture consisting over and above arts, letters, and manners also of human love, labor, and brotherhood. He thus keeps culture well rooted in society. But despite his emphasis on the importance of democratic social forms for the development of culture, Read's interpretation does not seem to me all that different from Eliot's with regard to what may be called the substance of true culture. Even though his preferences may have run in the direction of aristocratic social forms, Eliot never denied the essentially social nature of culture. But what is truly remarkable is that approaching the question of culture from two opposite political points of view, they end in perfect agreement on the objective standards by which to judge its quality. If it is culture that provides those rare moments beyond daily reality, "supersocial and in some sense superhuman," as Read says, then it is indeed culture that makes "life worth living," as Eliot contends. And neither of them has any reason then not to accept Aristotle's description of a life of leisure (based on intellectual and moral achievement): "A man will live thus, not to the extent that he is a man, but to the extent that a divine principle dwells within him."[8]

The dictionary defines culture as that which is excellent in arts, letters, manners, and scholarly pursuits, and both Eliot and Read tell us that this excellence consists in achievements that transcend ordinary social and temporal boundaries, making culture the common heritage of mankind. What I am concerned with here, however, is to make sure that in praise of culture we do not forget its humble but indispensable source, which is work in its broadest sense understood as a social enterprise. Both individuals and society must invest much time and effort in order to attain what makes life worth living. Yet I do not want to be dogmatic either about the transcendent nature of culture or about its requirement of almost superhuman effort. As I see it, a vase does not have to be Greek and a song does not have to be by Blake in order to "tease us out of our human preoccupations" and give us a glimpse of eternity. The anthropologists are not entirely wrong when they include decorative pottery along with cave paintings in their concept of culture. For it is not only that some of these things have timeless beauty. A more general reason for including them in the notion of culture is that they testify to even the primitive man's interest in doing something that is not absolutely necessary and yet makes life worth living. Thus, while we must continue to defend standards of excellence in order to save culture, we should also recognize not only that there are degrees of excellence but also that societies reach the "glittering pinnacles" of culture by way of lesser achievements.

Culture, in my view, is never far from work. Clearly, excellence in arts, letters, even manners, not to mention scholarly pursuits, requires much both individual and social effort. Moreover, most artists, writers, and scholars, when "doing their thing," consider themselves working, and today society seldom challenges them. But even though they cannot be neatly separated in practice, there is a difference in principle between culture and work. We have defined work as consisting in *rational, socially useful activities*. I suggest that culture consists in *rational activities that transcend social utility*. Without culture so conceived and practiced, I do not think that a society, or an individual, can have true leisure. For it is the enjoyment of products not of work but of culture that affords us, in Read's words, those "rare moments beyond daily reality, supersocial and in a sense superhuman."

Conclusions

Trying to combine the lessons of modern social experience with the legacy of ancient wisdom, I have argued in the preceding that, contrary to the prevailing opinion, it is not freedom from work but rather the development of a work-based culture that makes meaningful leisure possible. Thus, if we take the contemporary understanding of what work can do for society, which is unsurpassed in history, and set it alongside the classical insight into what man can expect of leisure, we can see that if we are to have the best of both these worlds, we need to rethink our understanding of culture.

Now this overall thesis may be construed in two ways. It can be presented as a dialectical synthesis of old and new thoughts made possible by exposing errors and illusions both old and new. Or in a more irenic approach, it can be seen as a refinement of a rather vague understanding of work among the ancient philosophers and of leisure among modern social thinkers. I prefer the latter approach, because it reveals a certain basic continuity in our civilization. For instance, even though he sharply distinguishes it from work, Plato does not see politics as something transcending society. On the contrary, for him politics is the sociotemporal means, or prerequisite, for transcendent philosophical contemplation. But is it not true also that, even though he sees in work the expression of man's essential nature, Marx, too, looks forward to that revolutionary leap from necessity to freedom, which would turn work itself into a kind of leisure activity? In other words, despite all their differences, Plato and Marx may well have wanted to say the same thing, namely, that political activity is the single key to, on the one hand, social justice, and, on the other hand, a kind of eternal life for the individual. With the much broader concept of culture in place of politics, this is roughly also my thesis about the relation between work and leisure, which I find at the heart of Western civilization. It supports the conception of the good life as one in which, as Paul Weiss put it, a rich leisure gives direction and meaning to all else we do.[9]

As I see it, then, this not-so-new concept of culture, which does justice both to our work and to our leisure, is today needed primarily in order to repair the semantic and ideological rift between the modern work ethic and the classical respect for high culture. It is not impossible that the people who today urge the abandonment of the work ethic, so that we may enjoy our plenty without feeling guilty, do so in part at least because they see high culture as an embodiment of past social injustices. But dumping at the same time both the work ethic and the ideal of a transcendent culture is, in my opinion, positively the worst thing we could do today.

It is not only that the abandonment of the work ethic would eliminate among the vast majority of mankind any chance they have of catching up with the advanced industrial societies and, under *their* conditions, could even doom them to extinction. Nor is it that in order to prevent the increasingly damaging effects to the global environment of present-day technology, advanced societies need to replace the profit motive in their scientific work with ethical considerations. These are two very good reasons for sticking to the belief that there will always be work to be done and that what is worth doing is worth doing well. And yet, the huge technical-scientific work envisaged in this realistic scenario does not come even close to the requirements of future social work that needs to be done to assure not the flourishing but the very survival of our civilization. For if it ever was true that, as Aristotle said, the political society comes into being for the sake of life, this is true of the world today. Even just to produce the necessities of life without depleting irreplaceable resources, not to mention their equitable distribution, what the world obviously needs now is an almost superhuman effort at reorganizing politics at all levels, from local to some sort of world government. If the quality of life is our concern, we need a new society even more than we need a new technology, and we shall never get it without the work ethic.

Notice that this means, in effect, that we need our social sciences also inspired by ethical rather than profit and power motives. Is not part of our present troubles that our jurisprudence and economics, psychology and sociology, and most importantly our political science have proven themselves so sorely inadequate? But fortunately, there are indications that this situation may be improving. The current interest in future studies shows a great promise in helping to restore political science to its former place of relevance and prominence among social studies. For in one way or another, all future studies address the same questions that both Aristotle long ago and Lenin in our time recognized as quintessential questions of politics. The ancient philosopher and the modern activist may not have much else in common, but they fully agree that political knowledge should enable us to give an answer not only to, What is to be done? but also to, What is good for man? Thus, quite apart from all the technical scientific work needed to keep this world fit to live in, it is because of the concomitant but incomparably harder social scientific work ahead that we must not even think of letting go of the work ethic.

Taking work seriously, however, may well be of greatest importance in the realm of culture. For even though cultural activities, by definition, transcend social utility, they are subject to standards in the upholding of which the presence of an attitude akin to the work ethic is crucial. The clearest example of this is found in theoretical sciences such as mathematics. In mathematics, Aristotle said, there is no goodness, meaning that numbers cannot be judged by moral standards. Yet everybody knows well that sloth is not conducive to mathematical inquiry. Or consider Descartes's famous rules of the scientific method. While they may have little to do with scientific knowledge as such, following them is certainly recommended as the best approach to science. Indeed, without being clear and distinct, patient, persistent, and thorough, we are bound to do worse in our intellectual endeavors than in our social activities, where we mostly have to get by on good will anyway.

But, one may object, theoretical science alone is not what makes a culture. In fact, most premodern cultures are distinguished by other kinds of interests and achievements, especially in religion and art, and we might be better off ourselves if we followed their example. This is a familiar enough criticism of the allegedly narrow, one-dimensional Western scientific culture, and viewing certain contemporary social attitudes and practices, it must be admitted that it is well founded. But does it follow that, in a culture dedicated to religious and artistic value, the work ethic would be out of place and in the way of the enjoyment of leisure? I do not think so. Leaving again religion aside to make it simpler, let us grant that a work-obsessed scientific culture would not be conducive to leisure. But would meaningful leisure be possible in an artistic culture in which art was not taken seriously? A frivolous culture is not inconceivable, and all of us could find our favorite example from history. The real question, however, is, Could such a nonscientific, artistic culture lead us to experience a reality that is supersocial, even superhuman? And since no one seems to defend such a position seriously, we must conclude that the work ethic is not alien to great art either.

Notes

1. T.S. Eliot, *Notes Towards the Definition of Culture* (New York, 1949), p. 21.
2. *Ibid.*, pp. 24–25.
3. *Ibid.*, p. 40.
4. *Ibid.*, p. 26.
5. Herbert Read, *To Hell with Culture* (New York, 1963), p. 30.
6. *Ibid.*, p. 34.
7. *Ibid.*, p. 35.
8. *Ethics* 10.7.1177b.
9. "A Philosophical Definition of Leisure," in James C. Charlesworth, *Leisure in America: Blessing or Curse?* (Philadelphia, 1964), p. 29.

Additional Reading

An Overview of Work Issues:
A Selected Bibliography from
FUTURE SURVEY

by

Michael Marien

FUTURE SURVEY is an abstract journal of books, reports, and articles concerning trends, forecasts, and ideas about the future, published monthly since 1979 by the World Future Society.

Abstracting can be seen as an effort to miniaturize units of information so that they can be more readily seen, and grasped in relation to other units of information. The abstracts that follow are a further step in miniaturization—essentially abstracts of abstracts—enabling an overview of what has been published in the past three to four years on issues related to work, largely in the United States but also in other developed and developing countries.

The 120 items are selected from about 200 longer abstracts of work-related literature published in the three *Future Survey Annuals* and in monthly issues since June 1982 (the last issue incorporated in an Annual). Item numbers of the longer abstracts in FS/FSA are at the end of each brief abstract provided here: numbers 001–1603 are in *Future Survey Annual 1979*, numbers 1604–3090 are in *Future Survey Annual 1980–81*, and numbers 3091–4457 are in *Future Survey Annual 1981–82*. Numbers referring to monthly issues of FUTURE SURVEY (e.g., FS 5:4, #83–244) reflect items not yet incorporated in an Annual.

Items are arranged in eight categories: I. GENERAL PERSPECTIVES: changes in work, productivity, work and the environment; II. TECHNOLOGY AND WORK: microelectronics in general, robots in factories, information processing in offices; III. UNEMPLOYMENT: global scarcity of jobs, full employment plans, job creation, changes in career patterns, worksharing; IV. DISCOVERING THE INFORMAL ECONOMY: potential for dealing with the unemployment problem, self-help and volunteerism, off-the-books employment in the underground economy, household work; V. SPECIAL GROUPS IN THE WORK FORCE: women, blacks, illegal immigrants/temporary workers, youth; VI. WELFARE, RETIREMENT, SECURITY: older workers, Social Security problems, disability, guaranteed annual income; VII. INDUSTRIAL RELATIONS: trade unions worldwide, ending adversarial relationships; VIII: NEW WORK ARRANGEMENTS: the Japanese challenge, making organizations human, flextime, worker participation, worker's co-ops.

Michael Marien is editor of Future Survey, *a monthly publication of the World Future Society. The views expressed herein are his own and do not necessarily reflect those of the Society.*

I. GENERAL PERSPECTIVES

1. **Working in the Twenty-First Century.** Edited by C. Stewart Sheppard (U of Virginia) and Donald C. Carroll (U of Pennsylvania). NY: Wiley-Interscience, Jan 1980/235p/$18.95. (Essays from a 1979 conference in Richmond sponsored by Philip Morris, Inc. Topics include the effects of dwindling resources and new technologies, labor relations, work force trends, lifestyles, longshot forces for change.)
[2491]

2. **The New International Division of Labor.** Folker Fröbel *et al.* (Max Planck Institute, Starnberg). NY: Cambridge U Press, Feb 1980/c500p/$39.95. (On the profound structural change caused by large reservoirs of cheap labor in LDCs, relocation of production to new industrial sites, and accelerating rationalization measures at traditional sites.)
[1657]

3. **The Changing Character of Work: Attitudes, Trends, Emerging Patterns for the 1980s.** The New York Times Information Service. Parsippany NJ: NYT Information Service, Sept 1979/$250.00. (Offers over 1,500 summaries from the NYT Information Bank, a data base of items compiled from 63 periodicals.)
[953]

4. **The Third Wave.** Alvin Toffler, NY: William Morrow & Co, Mar 1980/544p/$14.95; Bantam, 1981/$3.95pb. (On the rise of a new Third Wave civilization, characterized by smaller and more human-scale industries, demassified manufacture, more people working at home in the "electronic cottage," the demassification of time (ending the 9 to 5 workday), and the shift from consumers to prosumers—people who consume what they produce, enabled by new self-help methods.)
[2274]

5. **Seven Tomorrows: Toward a Voluntary History.** Paul Hawken, James Ogilvy, and Peter Schwartz (SRI International). NY: Bantam Books, Feb 1982/235p/$6.95pb./ (Seven possible futures exploring the optimistic and pessimistic extremes of five driving trends: energy, climate, food, the economy, and values. Each scenario is accompanied by a chart showing businesses and occupations that are growing or contracting for the seven different conditions.)
[3695]

6. **"Careers With a Future: Where the Jobs Will Be in the 1990s,"** Marvin Cetron and Thomas O'Toole, *The Futurist*, XVI:3, June 1982, 11–19. (Authors of *Encounters with the Future* [McGraw-Hill, 1982/320p/$12.95] forecast increasingly important occupations by 1990, implicitly assuming a probable technologically-oriented US.) [3905]

7. **The American Economy: Employment, Productivity, and Inflation.** Panel 2, President's Commission for a National Agenda for the Eighties. Washington: USGPO, Jan 1981/$3.75. (Recommends policies to restore productivity growth, use more fully the talents and energies of the American people, and bring us closer to full employment.)
[3697]

8. **Work Decisions in the 1980s.** Eli Ginzberg (Columbia U) *et al.* Boston MA: Auburn House, 1982/137p/$19.95. (Essays on early retirement, productivity slowdown and unemployment, birth rate fluctuations and labor force participation, and implications of changing the length of the workweek.) [FS 5:4; #83–244]

9. **Good Jobs, Bad Jobs, No Jobs.** Eli Ginzberg (Columbia U). Cambridge MA: Harvard U Press, Oct. 1979/224p/$15.00. (Advocates changes in manpower policies, equity in the job market, job creation, etc.) [977]

10. **Work in America: The Decade Ahead.** Edited by Clark Kerr and Jerome M. Rosow. NY: Van Nostrand Reinhold, Work in America Institute Series, July 1979/352p/$15.95. (Essays on work and values, reindustrialization, women and minorities, changing attitudes toward work, impacts of new technology, and public policy and the quality of work life.) [954]

11. **Work in America Institute Studies in Productivity.** 30 Volumes. Scarsdale NY: Work in America Institute, 1979–1983/$35 per volume; also available from Pergamon Press, Elmsford NY. 1) Mid-Career Perspectives; 2) Productivity and the Quality of Working Life; 3) Trends in Product Quality and Worker Attitude; 4) Managerial Productivity; 5) Worker Alienation; 6) Human Resource Accounting; 7) New Patterns of Work; 8) Occupational Stress and Productivity; 9) Redesigning Work; 10) Jobs and the Environment; 11) Changing Attitudes Toward Work; 12) Women in Management; 13) The Implications of Work-Family Relationships for Productivity; 14) Performance Evaluation for Professional Personnel; 15) Managerial Compensation; 16) Productivity Measurement; 17) Controlling Absenteeism and Turnover; 18) The Impact of New Technology: People and Organizations in Manufacturing; 19) The Impact of New Technology in the Service Industries; 20) Cost-Effective Pension Planning; 21) Innovative Work Practices; 22) Designing Cost-Effective Employee Health Plans; 23) White-Collar Productivity; 24) Sharing the Gains of Productivity; 25) People and Productivity in Japan; 26) Quality Circles; 27) Training for New Technology; 28) Participative Management; 29) Management Development Strategies; 30) Labor-Management Cooperation for Productivity. [3888]

12. **Making America Work: Productivity and Responsibility.** James O'Toole (USC). NY: Continuum Publishing Co, Sept 1981/216p/$14.95. (Principal author of the HEW Special Task Force Report, *Work in America* (MIT Press, 1973) argues that managers must increase the responsibility of workers. Concluding chapter describes noninflationary strategies for reducing unemployment and utilizing human resources.) [3879]

13. **Productivity: The New Economic Context.** Kathleen Newland. Worldwatch Paper 49. Washington: Worldwatch Institute, June 1982/ 47p/$2.00. (On the array of conflicting influences that will shape productivity, broadly viewed. Positive forces include new technology,

innovations in organization of work, demographic change, etc; negative influences include sustainable economic advance, greater attention to externalities, engineered recession, and reduced effort to develop human capital.) [FS 4:10, #82–824]

14. **"Why Is U.S. Productivity Slowing Down?"** Campbell R. McConnell (U of Nebraska), *Harvard Business Review*, 57:2, March-April 1979, 36–60. (Analyzes five disparate explanations of US productivity decline: the mainstream position of neoclassical economists, the war economy argument of Seymour Melman, the neo-Marxist view of alienated workers, the doomsday stance of the Club of Rome and others, and the libertarian view of misguided government policies.) [962]

15. **The Productivity Challenge: How to Make it Work for America and You.** Michael LeBoeuf (U of New Orleans). NY: McGraw-Hill, Nov 1982/273p/$12.95. (A popular guide to the interlocking pieces of the productivity puzzle: a lack of national commitment, lack of incentives, aging plant and equipment, foreign competition, the R&D slump, changing composition of the work force, the decline of public education, inept management, and counterproductive values.) [FS 5:2, #83–064]

16. **Jobs for Tomorrow: The Potential for Substituting Manpower for Energy.** Walter R. Stahel and Genevieve Reday-Mulvey. NY: Vantage Press, 1981/116p/$12.50. (Based on a 1977 report prepared for the Commission of the European Communities, on reversing the historical trend of machine-for-manpower substitution in certain sectors.) [3886]

17. **Fear at Work: Job Blackmail, Labor and the Environment.** Richard Kazis and Richard R. Grossman (Environmentalists for Full Employment). NY: Pilgrim Press, Oct 1982/306p/$10.95pb. Brief versions in *Environment*, Nov 1982, and *The New York Times* 15 Jan 1983, p23. (Argues that jobs and environmental quality are not mutually exclusive, and that many business and government leaders distort national investment priorities by unfounded claims that environmental regulations kill the economy.) [FS 5:2, #83–087]

18. **"The Manpower Quality Decline: An Ecological Perspective,"** Bernard Rimland and Gerald E. Larson (Navy Personnel R&D Center, San Diego), *Armed Forces and Society*, 8:1, Fall 1981, 21–78. (Heavily-documented argument that the quality decline of recent military recruits is due to ecological changes in the past few decades: pre- and post-natal medical interventions, nuclear fallout, increased maternal smoking, the increase in bottle feeding, lead and other toxic metals in the blood, and increased intake of food additives and sugar.) [3903]

19. **Labor and Employment Policy.** Edited by Charles Bulmer and John L. Carmichael, Jr (U of Alabama-Birmingham). *Policy Studies Journal*, 8:3, Winter 1979. (Essays on full employment as a policy issue, equal employment opportunity, occupational safety and health, labor law reform, and public employee unions.) [2460]

20. **Cities in Transition: Changing Job Structures in Atlanta, Denver, Buffalo, Phoenix, Columbus, Nashville, and Charlotte.** Thomas M. Stanback, Jr (NYU) and Thierry J. Noyelle (Columbia U). Conservation of Human Resources Series #15. Totowa NJ: Allanheld, Osmun, 1982/198p/$28.95. (Analyzes the growth of service-related activities and the white-collarization of labor.) [FS 5:4, #83–267]

21. **Human Economy: A Bibliography. Vol 1—Books.** Compiled by John Applegath (Director, Human Economy Center). Amherst MA: The Human Economy Center (PO Box 551), June 1981/77p/$12.00 libraries; $7.50 individuals. (About 1,000 items on human scale economic arrangements and a more conserving mode of life, with such categories as cooperation, the household economy, productivity, self-sufficiency, small business, technology, and values.) [3792]

II. TECHNOLOGY AND WORK

22. **The Mechanization of Work.** *A Scientific American* Book. San Francisco: W.H. Freeman, Nov 1982/119p(8½ x 11")/$19.95; 9.95pb. Reprinted from *Scientific American*, 247:3, Sept 1982/66–204. (Essays on the displacement of the labor force from the production of goods, and the mechanization of mining, design and manufacturing, commerce, office work, and women's work. Concluding essay by Wassily Leontief argues that work and income must be equitably shared.) [FS 5:2, #83–088]

23. **Microelectronics and Society: For Better or For Worse.** Edited by Gunter Friedrichs and Adam Schaff. A Report to the Club of Rome. Elmsford NY: Pergamon, Feb 1982/353p/$15.00pb. (Essays on microelectronic technology and its impacts, the worker and the workplace, a Third World perspective, and the need to distribute work by promoting reduced working hours and continuing education as a form of universal occupation.) [FS 4:11, #82–889]

24. **Microelectronics, Productivity, and Employment.** Organization for Economic Cooperation and Development. Paris: OECD, June 1981/290p/$18.00. (Examines the impact of information technologies on productivity, growth, employment, industrial structures, and adjustment policies.) [not in FS]

25. **Futuribles,** No 36, Sept 1980, 3–88. (Nine articles on the impact of microelectronics on employment, including "La microelectronique contre l'emploi," and "L'Informatique, creatrice d'emplois".) [not in FS]

26. **Microelectronics at Work: Productivity and Jobs in the World Economy.** Colin Norman. Worldwatch Paper 39. Washington: Worldwatch Institute, Oct 1980/63p/$2.00. (On productivity improvements in factories and offices, alterations in the content of many jobs, and policies to deal with technological unemployment.) [2456]

27. **Women and the Chip: Case Studies of the Effects of Informatics on Employment in Canada.** Heather Menzies. Toronto: Institute for Research on Public Policy, April 1981/130p/$6.95. (Warns that the

automation of all phases of information manipulation will render obsolete many jobs in the service sector traditionally held by women; unless occupational mobility policies are implemented, women risk massive unemployment.) [3908]

28. **The Future With Microelectronics: Forecasting the Effects of Information Technology.** Iann Barron (Immos Co) and Ray Curnow (SPRU, U of Sussex). London: Frances Pinter (dist in US by Nichols Publishing Co), Fall 1979/243p/$17.50. (A study sponsored by the UK Dept of Industry, warning of impacts on employment in the information occupations which account for 65% of the UK labor force.) [2849]

29. **"Quantifying the Employment Effects of Micro-Electronics,"** J.D. Whitley and R.A. Wilson (U of Warwick), *Futures*, 14:6, Dec 1982, 486–495. (Views the fear of mass unemployment due to microelectronics as exaggerated due to inadequate attention to potential offsetting factors; still, many people may lose their jobs in the short-run.) [FS 5:2, #83–090]

30. **The Socio-Economic Impact of Microelectronics.** Edited by Jan Berting (Erasmus U) *et al*. Elmsford NY: Pergamon, 1980/200p/ $54.00. (Essays on economic and political consequences in socialist and developing countries, industrial relations and work organization, and participative design.) [4303]

31. **The Microelectronics Revolution: The Complete Guide to the New Technology and Its Impact on Society.** Edited by Tom Forester. Cambridge MA: MIT Press, Feb 1981/608p/$25.00;$12.50pb. (Essays on automation in factories and offices, consequences for employment and industrial relations, and the problems of an information society.) [4300]

32. **Exploratory Workshop on the Societal Impacts of Robotics.** U.S. Congress, Office of Technology Assessment. Washington: USGPO, March 1982/$6.00. (On the growing use of robots, productivity, labor issues, education and training, and international competition.) [3913]

33. **"Industrial Robots on the Line,"** Robert Ayres and Steve Miller (Carnegie-Mellon U), *Technology Review*, 85:4, May-June 1982, 34–46. (On the factory of the future and how private industry has done very little to prepare workers whose jobs may be eliminated or substantially changed by using robots.) [3914]

34. **"The Electronic Office: How It Will Change the Way You Work,"** Marvin Kornbluh (Congressional Reference Service), *The Futurist*, XVI:3, June 1982, 37–42. (On the potential for large productivity gains in such office functions as typing, editing, filing, scheduling, accounting, copying, and mailing.) [3917]

35. **The Office of the Future: Communication and Computers.** R.P. Uhlig, D.J. Farber, and J.H. Bair. NY: Elsevier North-Holland, 1979/ 380p/$35.00. (On future communication tools to support knowledge workers, factors making it feasible to place these tools in offices, and the impact on workers and organizations.) [2865]

36. **"Teleworking: Working Closer to Home,"** Jack Nilles (USC), *Technology Review*, 85:3, April 1982, 56–62. (If the information sector continues to grow, there may be as many as 10 million tele-commuters working at home by 1990; many workers complain of isolation, though, and there may be greater emphasis on local work centers.) [3918]

III. UNEMPLOYMENT

37. **The Lean Years: Politics in the Age of Scarcity.** Richard J. Barnet (Institute for Policy Studies). NY: Simon & Schuster, May 1980/ 349p/$12.95. Excerpts in *The New Yorker*, March 24, March 31, and April 7, 1980. (A global inventory of five critical resource systems: energy, nonfuel minerals, food, water, and human skill—all increasingly integrated into global systems of control. Almost a billion people cannot find enough work at adequate wages, while the global division of labor results in the Global Factory.) [1618]

38. **"A New World Employment Plan: A Proposal,"** Jan Tinbergen *et al*, *IFDA Dossier 21*, Jan-Feb 1981, 35–54. (A proposal for a large-scale international operation to stimulate the economies of and raise employment in all countries, by attempting an optimal international division of labor.) [3192]

39. **Unemployment in Western Countries.** Edited by Edmond Malin-vaud and Jean-Paul Fitoussi. NY: St. Martin's, Oct 1980/c560p/$40.00. (Proceedings of an International Economic Association conference on the structural redeployment of labor, the absorption of unemployment from technological progress, and alternative solutions to unemployment.) [2459]

40. **Measuring Underemployment: Demographic Indicators for the United States.** Clifford C. Clogg (Penn State U). NY: Academic Press, Dec 1979/288p/$21.50. (Criticizes inaccuracies of the conventional unemployment measure and proposes a three-dimensional scheme utilizing time, income, and skill utilization.) [2461]

41. **Employing the Unemployed.** Edited by Eli Ginzberg (Columbia U). NY: Basic Books, June 1980/$15.00. (On youth and minority programs, the supported work experiment, public service employment, and encouraging more direct involvement by private industry.) [2465]

42. **"Full Employment: Planning From the Bottom Up,"** Bertram Gross and Stanley Moses (CUNY-Hunter College), *The Nation*, April 10, 1982, 424–425. (On a proposal for locally-based national planning, championed by Rep. John Conyers, by which people in neighborhoods and local governments could formulate their own full employment goals and the means to meet them. Moses was the editor of *Planning for Full Employment, The ANNALS of the American Academy of Political and Social Science*, Vol 418, March 1975.) [FS 4:10, #82–817]

43. **Managing Human Resources: The Art of Full Employment.** David Stern (U of California-Berkeley). Boston MA: Auburn House, Jan 1982/200p/$19.95. (Argues that sustaining a sufficient quantity of employment becomes more feasible as the quality of worklife improves, with major benefits for both employers and employees.)

[3885]

44. **"Who Creates Jobs?"** David L. Birch (MIT), *The Public Interest,* No 65, Fall 1981, 1–14. (Examined data on 5.6 million establishments over a 7-year period, finding that job-replacing firms tend to be small, young, and overwhelmingly providers of services, while large companies are the least likely to create jobs.)

[3887]

45. **Innovation and Employment.** David Foster (Surrey, UK). Elmsford NY: Pergamon, Feb 1980/193p/$22.00;$11.00. (Opposes artificial job creation, and supports encouraging the self-employed in technical and professional enterprise and owners of small businesses—the self-starters who get things going.)

[2479]

46. **Flexible Life Scheduling: Breaking the Education-Work-Retirement Lockstep.** Fred Best (California Employment Development Dept). NY: Praeger, 1980/267p. Brief version in *The Wharton Magazine,* 5:2, Winter 1980–81, 13–21. (On ways to allow persons in mid-life to reduce or temporarily leave their jobs, and thus share their work with others: incentives for voluntary time-income tradeoffs, redefining the standard workweek, sabbatical leaves, extended leaves of absence without pay.)

[3873]

47. **Working Free: Practical Alternatives to the 9 to 5 Job.** John Applegath (Human Economy Center). NY: AMACOM, May 1982/207p/$13.95. (Argues for more part-time work, free-lancing, working at home, and portable skills; and for a rational distribution of work that would guarantee to all the equivalent of nine months of full-time work per year.)

[3874]

48. **"Creative Crisis: New Patterns of Growth and Employment,"** Michel Godet (Auguste Comte Institute, Paris), *Long Range Planning,* 14:5, Oct 1981, 12–19. (Warns of increasing unemployment and the necessity to share work in a more flexible manner involving part-time work, retirement on request, work at home, and protecting informal activities.)

[3190]

49. **Sharing the Work: An Analysis of the Issues of Worksharing and Jobsharing.** Noah Meltz *et al* (U of Toronto). Toronto: U of Toronto Press, Fall 1980/c100p/$7.50pb. (On spreading available opportunities among more people through worksharing—shortening the workweek to prevent layoffs—and jobsharing, or converting full-time jobs into part-time positions.)

[2497]

50. **Job Sharing: A New Pattern for Quality of Work and Life.** Gretl S. Meier (New Ways to Work, San Francisco). Kalamazoo MI: W.E. Upjohn Institute for Employment Research, Feb 1979/187p/$4.50pb. (Draws on information from a survey of several hundred job sharers and selected interviews with partners and supervisors.)

[979]

51. **"Leisure Sharing: Its Time Has Come,"** James R. Mills (California State Senate), *State Government*, 52:2, Spring 1979, 75–79. (Rather than work sharing, which redistributes available work, Mills has introduced two bills to promote leisure sharing—a process where the desire for reduced worktime among the employed is matched with the desire of the unemployed to reduce involuntary idleness.) [981]

IV. DISCOVERING THE INFORMAL ECONOMY

52. **"Development of the Informal Economy: A Strategy for Resolving the Crisis of the Welfare State,"** Rolf G. Heinze (U of Paderborn) and Thomas Olk (U of Oldenburg), *Futures*, 14:3, June 1982, 189–204 (translated from the German by Julie Owens). (The crisis of structural unemployment has opened up possibilities for the informal sector, which is not recognized by classical economics; outlines three sociopolitical strategies, including a complementary network model with voluntary contraction of both private market and state activity in certain areas.) [FS 5:2, #83–091]

53. **"Towards the Dual Economy and Emancipation from Employment,"** Denis Pym (London Business School), *Futures*, 12:3, June 1980, 223–237. (Universal employment is a dubious privilege that we cannot afford, and a policy of gradual withdrawal from the employment economy is necessary, in favor of the growing informal economy.) [2478]

54. **The Redistribution of Work.** James Robertson and Alison Pritchard. Turning Point Paper No 1. Ironbridge, Shropshire UK: Turning Point (9 New Road), Feb 1981/40p/£1.00. (We must distinguish between organized work, gift work for ourselves and others, and pocket money work which fills the gap between the first two kinds; opportunities to do all three types of work should be shared more widely, as part of a worldwide shift towards greater self-sufficiency at national as well as local and household levels.) [3870]

55. **"Work,"** Willis Harman (Institute for Noetic Sciences, San Francisco), in *Millennium*, edited by Alberto Villoldo and Ken Dychtwald (Los Angeles:/ J.P. Tarcher, 1981), 171–186. (Full employment will no longer be needed from a production standpoint, but full participation is essential from a social standpoint; this situation can be addressed by enhancement income maintenance or by decentralizing production.) [3871]

56. **Helping Ourselves: Local Solutions to Global Problems.** Bruce Stokes (Worldwatch Institute). NY: W.W. Norton, April 1981/160p/ $12.95;$4.95pb. Short version in *The Futurist*, Aug 1981, 44–51. (Dependency has no place in a humanistic world; to mold more democratic and self-reliant societies we need worker participation, the consumer as energy conserver and energy producer, self-help housing, home and community gardening, responsibility for one's own health, and family planning.) [3741]

57. **Volunteerism in the Eighties: Fundamental Issues in Voluntary Action.** Edited by John D. Harman (St. John Fisher College, Rochester NY). Washington: University Press of America, Aug 1982/292p/ $24.00;$11.50pb. (Essays from a 1980 conference on such topics as voluntary organizations, neighborhood government, government funding and the voluntary sector, and prospects for developing volunteerism.) [FS 5:2, #83–094]

58. **Informal Institutions: Alternative Systems in the Corporate State.** Edited by Stuart Henry (Middlesex Polytechnic, UK). NY: St. Martin's, May 1981/c240p/$22.50. (Essays on informal income and work, non-monetary exchange, informal human services, the revival of self-help, and alternative futures for the informal economy.) [3785]

59. **The Future of Work.** Vanier Institute of the Family. Ottawa: VIF (151 Slater), 1981/70p/$3.50pb. (Proceedings of a 1980 seminar on such issues as providing enough job-work, making this work more satisfying, how to make work without jobs more respectable, encouraging the informal economy, and whether income entitlements should depend on jobs.) [FS 5:2, #82–093]

60. **A Bibliography on Material Pertinent to the Informal Economy.** The Canadian Network on the Informal Economy. Ottawa: Vanier Institute of the Family, Sept 1982/54p mimeo/$2.00. (Annotations of about 75 Canadian and 100 non-Canadian books, reports, and articles; about 10% of the items are French language.) [FS 5:2, #83–092]

61. **"Les modes d'évaluation de l'économie occulte,"** Werner W. Pommerehne and Bruno S. Frey, *Futuribles*, No 50, Dec 1981, 3–32. (Compares different methods and estimates of the informal economy in the US and European nations.) [not in FS]

62. **Beating the System: The Underground Economy.** Carl P. Simon (U of Michigan) and Ann D. Witte (U of North Carolina). Boston MA: Auburn House, Nov 1981/200p/$21.95;$12.95pb. (Estimates hidden economic activities at about one-tenth the reported national income, and growing by about 10% per year.) [3787]

63. **"The Subterranean Economy Five Years Later,"** Peter M. Gutmann (CUNY-Baruch College), *Across the Board: The Conference Board Magazine*, XX:2, Feb 1983, 24–31. (In late 1977, Gutmann estimated the US underground economy at slightly over 10% of official GNP; this off-the-books employment overstates the present 10.8% unemployment rate by at least 2.5%.) [FS 5:4, #83–243]

64. **Shadow Work.** Ivan Illich. Salem NH: Marion Boyars, March 1981/ 152p/$5.95pb. (On the rise of the shadow economy: economic activities that are not in the monetized sector and do not exist in pre-industrial societies—a form of unpaid work which an industrial society demands as a necessary complement to producing goods and services. This unpaid servitude, comprising most housework done by women, commuting, forced consumption, etc., does not contribute to subsistence, but ravages it.) [3872]

65. **Homemakers: The Forgotten Workers.** Rae André (General Motors Institute). Chicago: U of Chicago Press, April 1981/352p/$15.00. (On the quality of life among the 35 million American women whose main occupation is homemaking, and what can be done about solving their problems through legislation and attitude change.) [3893]

66. **Women and Household Labor.** Edited by Sarah Fenstermaker Berk (U of California-Santa Barbara). Beverly Hills CA: Sage Publications, Jan 1980/296p/$20.00;$9.95pb. (Essays on such topics as household technology, an agenda for social research in the new home economics, satisfaction with housework, and sexual equality in wage and household work.) [2476]

V. SPECIAL GROUPS IN THE WORK FORCE

67. **Women, Men, and the Division of Labor.** Kathleen Newland. Worldwatch Paper 37. Washington: Worldwatch Institute, May 1980/ 43p/$2.00. (Paid employment is dominated by men, while women's work is concentrated in the lower status, unpaid, and officially unmeasured household sector. This division is breaking down worldwide, but if women are to take full advantage of the formal labor market, men must increase their share of the essential work that goes on outside of it.) [2475]

68. **Women Returning to Work: Policies in Five Countries.** Alice M. Yohalem (Columbia U). Totawa NJ: Allenheld, Osmun, March 1980/ c256p/$25.00. (Since WWII, the growing propensity of adult women to reenter or belatedly enter the labor force has been a major force; responses to these pressures are examined in Germany, France, Sweden, the UK, and the US.) [2474]

69. **Equal Employment Policy for Women: Strategies for Implementation in the United States, Canada and Western Europe.** Ronnie Steinberg Ratner (SUNY-Albany). Philadelphia: Temple U Press, Feb 1980/520p/$25.00. (Equal employment policy encompasses the goals of equal pay and equal opportunity; despite gains in policy development, pervasive sex discrimination in the workplace still persists.) [2472]

70. **Manual on Pay Equity: Raising Wages for Women's Work.** Edited by Joy Ann Grune. Washington: Conference on Alternative State and Local Policies, May 1980/230p/$9.95. (Reviews the movement for equal pay for work of comparable value, with attention to legislative initiatives, litigation, organizing campaigns, and recent research.) [2473]

71. **U.S. Women at Work.** Linda J. Waite (Rand Corp). *Population Bulletin*, 36:2, May 1981/43p/$2.00. (The surge in women's employment—from 20% of the 1950 labor force to 43% of the 1980 labor force—is linked to more delayed marriage, more divorce, better education, lower fertility, and changed attitudes about women's place.) [3890]

72. **The Black Underclass: Poverty, Unemployment, and Entrapment of Ghetto Youth.** Douglas G. Glascow (Howard U). San Francisco: Jossey-Bass, March 1980/$13.95. (The problem of a permanent black underclass worsens steadily, as it absorbs ever-greater numbers of young blacks who lack education and salable skills. Proposals are made to expand inner-city employment opportunities, develop neighborhood training and counseling agencies, etc.) [2468]

73. **The State Against Blacks.** Walter E. Williams (George Mason U). NY: McGraw-Hill/New Press, Oct 1982/183p/$14.95. (Argues that many of the economic handicaps faced by blacks are due to Federal, state, and local laws that impede employment and advancement.) [FS 5:4, #83-245]

74. **International Migration: The Search for Work.** Kathleen Newland. Worldwatch Paper 33. Washington: Worldwatch Institute, Nov 1979/31p/$2.00. (Voluntary migration of workers has become a central characteristic of the global economic system, and may become a high priority problem at domestic and international levels as the global labor force grows by nearly a billion people by 2000—the vast majority coming from poor countries.) [1638]

75. **The Border That Joins: Mexican Migrants and U.S. Responsibility.** Edited by Peter G. Brown and Henry Shue (U of Maryland). Totowa NJ: Rowman and Littlefield, 1982/c288p/$26.50. (On whether the US should create temporary worker programs, how many workers should be permitted to come and for how long, and the benefits and protections that should be granted.) [FS 5:4, #83-249]

76. **"Temporary" Alien Workers in the United States: Designing Policy from Fact and Opinion.** Sidney Weintraub and Stanley R. Ross (U of Texas-Austin). Boulder CO: Westview, April 1982/124p/ $16.00. (Brings together current knowledge about temporary workers in the US, how they affect the US labor market, and the desirability of some system to identify temporary workers in the US.) [FS 5:4, #83-250]

77. **Giving Youth a Better Chance: Options for Education, Work, and Service.** Carnegie Council on Policy Studies in Higher Education. San Francisco: Jossey-Bass, Dec 1979/$13.95. (Advocates more and better choices for youth, and less segregation of young from old, race from race, education from work and service, and youth from employment. Many recommendations are made, including nonprofit job corporations to prepare and place students, new and better apprenticeship programs, and a multifaceted voluntary youth service.) [1210]

78. **The Transition of Youth to Adulthood: A Bridge Too Long.** The National Commission on Youth. Boulder CO: Westview, July 1980/ 228p/$25.75;$11.00pb. (Recommendations for a national youth service and ways to build new linkages between family, school, the private sector, voluntary agencies, and government.) [2746]

79. **"Youth Unemployment,"** Eli Ginzberg (Columbia U), *Scientific American*, May 1980, 43–49. (Teenage unemployment has risen from 11% in 1955 to more than 16% in 1978, and minority unemployment is much higher; if Americans want to cease paying the high costs of this unemployment, they must focus on remedying it.)   [2466]

80. **National Service: Social, Economic and Military Impacts.** Edited by Michael W. Sherraden (Washington U) and Donald J. Eberly (Selective Service System). Elmsford NY: Pergamon, May 1982/240p/$25.00. (On the history of national service proposals, why a voluntary system of service is needed in postindustrial America, how national service might work in a 3- to 5-year developmental stage, and six possible futures for national service in the far future.)
                                        [FS 4:8, #82-639]

81. **The Youth Labor Force, 1945–1995: A Cross-National Analysis.** Beatrice G. Reubens *et al.* (Columbia U). Totowa NJ: Allanheld, Osmun, 1982/412p/$48.50. (Projects youth labor force trends through 1995 in the US, Canada, France, West Germany, Italy, The Netherlands, Sweden, Switzerland, the UK, New Zealand, Australia, and Japan.)   [FS 5:4, #83-249]

82. **Children at Work.** Edited by Elias Mendelievich. Washington: International Labor Office, 1980/$18.55;$12.85pb. (Examines the problems of child labor in various parts of the world, and advocates possible solutions. The ILO estimates at least 52 million child workers less than 15 years old in the world today.)   [2469]

83. **Earning and Learning: Youth Employment Policies and Programs.** Ray C. Rist (US General Accounting Office). Beverly Hills CA: Sage Publications, Dec 1981/256p/$20.00;$9.95pb. (Evaluates the results of 16 projects to improve school-to-work transitions, and such strategies as youth-oriented projects and expanded private sector involvement.)   [3899]

84. **Horatio Alger, Farewell: The End of the American Dream.** Celeste MacLeod (Berkeley Support Services). NY: Seaview Books, Dec 1980/310p/$12.95; P.E.I. Books, $7.50pb. (On the shrinking of opportunity for youth, their migration in search of work, providing services for the new migrants, and creating different kinds of jobs for youth.)   [3900]

85. **Underemployed Ph.D.'s.** Lewis C. Solmon (UCLA) *et al.* Lexington MA: Lexington Books, 1981/368p/$33.95. (On policy options for dealing with the present and future oversupply of Ph.D.'s, with emphasis on jobs outside of academe.)   [3895]

VI. WELFARE, RETIREMENT, SECURITY

86. **Early Retirement: Boon or Bane?** Dean Morse and Susan H. Grey (Columbia U). Totawa NJ: Allenheld, Osmun, 1980/c180p/$23.00. (Explores the nature of early retirement decisions, consequences for workers and families, and implications for policy issues such as mandatory retirement and Social Security reform.)   [2470]

87. **The Future of Older Workers in America: New Options for an Extended Working Life.** Work in America Institute. Scarsdale NY: Work in America Institute, Fall 1980/135p/$9.95pb. (Some 46% of retirees say that they would like to be working; this report discusses age-neutral personnel policies and the role of unions and government.) [2498]

88. **Young Programs for Old Workers.** Beverly Jacobson. Scarsdale NY: Work in America Institute, Fall 1980/124p/$16.95; $25 per set with above title. (Presents 70 case histories of innovative work arrangements for older workers such as part-time jobs, phased retirement, job redesign, and second careers.) [2499]

89. **Reforming Retirement Policies.** Committee for Economic Development. NY: CED, Sept 1981/66p/$6.50;$5.00pb. (A new strategy for retirement policy should have the goal of assuring a minimum level of retirement income for all workers and their families; policymakers should encourage working beyond the traditional retirement age, and changes in job design and work schedules.) [3842]

90. **World Crisis in Social Security.** Edited by Jean-Jacques Rosa. San Francisco: Institute for Contemporary Studies, 1982/300p/$9.95pb. (Scholars from European nations, the US, and Japan look at the major problems in the social security programs of their nations. Most programs are beset with severe financing difficulties and are being attacked for their unfairness.) [FS 5:2, #83-075]

91. **Economic and Social Security: Social Insurance and Other Approaches.** 5th Edition. C. Arthur Williams, Jr., John G. Turnbull, and Earl F. Cheit. NY: John Wiley/Ronald Press, March 1982/608p/$23.95. (Includes consideration of employee benefit plans, worker's compensation, social disability insurance, unemployment insurance, the welfare system, income maintenance, and other plans.) [FS 5:2, #83-084]

92. **Disability and Work: The Economics of American Policy.** Richard V. Burkhauser (Vanderbilt U) and Robert H. Haveman (U of Wisconsin). Baltimore: Johns Hopkins U Press, July 1982/160p/$14.00. (A review of the US disability network, its efforts to protect and compensate the handicapped, the skyrocketing costs of the system, and Federal programs for the disabled.) [FS 5:2, #83-085]

93. **A Guaranteed Annual Income: Evidence from a Social Experiment.** Edited by Philip K. Robins (SRI International) et al. NY: Academic Press, Dec 1980/346p/$28.00. (Reports on findings of the largest of four major income maintenance experiments conducted in the US, each testing several versions of a negative income tax.) [3836]

94. **Work and Welfare: The Unholy Alliance.** David Macarov (Hebrew U., Jerusalem). Beverly Hills CA: Sage Publications, Feb 1980/250p/$18.00;$8.95pb. (Proposes that the system of welfare should be divorced from the restrictive boundaries of the work ethic which have dominated it for so long, and instead provide people with a guaranteed means of survival and the option to work if desired.) [2477]

VII. INDUSTRIAL RELATIONS

95. **Towards Industrial Democracy: Europe, Japan, and the United States.** Edited by Benjamin C. Roberts (London School of Economics). Totawa NJ: Allenheld, Osmun, 1979/c300p/$23.00. (Compares the effects of different labor participation and collective bargaining methods on labor-management relations and decision-making.) [973]

96. **World Labor Rights and Their Protection.** James Avery Joyce. NY: St. Martin's, 1980/c200p/$22.50. (Examines mechanisms for protecting workers as individuals and as members of trade unions, and instances where worker's rights have been abused.) [2484]

97. **Challenge to Power: Trade Unions and Industrial Relations in Capitalist Countries.** Klaus von Beyme (U of Heidelberg). Beverly Hills CA: Sage Publications, 1980/407p/$20.00;$9.95pb. (A comparative view of trade unions and their changing functions in highly industrialized societies, with a proposal for a method of constructive conflict.) [2485]

98. **International Handbook of Industrial Relations.** Edited by Albert A. Blum (Illinois Institute of Technology). Westport CT: Greenwood Press, May 1981/698p/$45.00. (Essays on industrial relations in 27 nations and regions of the industrialized world, with an emphasis on the increasing role of government in each country.) [3920]

99. **Unions in Postindustrial Society.** John Schmidman (Penn State U). University Park PA: Penn State U Press, 1979/192p/$12.00. (The labor movement can adapt to an economy in which fewer workers produce an ever-larger share of manufactured goods, if they maintain flexibility and meet the needs of well-educated employees.) [967]

100. **Unfinished Business: An Agenda for Labor, Management, and the Public.** Edited by Abraham J. Siegel (MIT) and David B. Lipsky (Cornell U). Cambridge MA: MIT Press, 1978/178p/$9.95. (Contributions by the seven US Secretaries of Labor who have held office since the 1960s, with commentary by major figures from management and labor. Topics include collective bargaining and labor law.) [970]

101. **"The Future of the American Labor Movement,"** John T. Dunlop (Harvard U), in *The Third Century: America as a Post-Industrial Society.* Edited by Seymour Martin Lipset. Stanford CA: Hoover Institution Press, 1979/471p/$14.95; U of Chicago Press, 1980/ $7.95pb. (On six strategic issues that will confront the labor movement in the next few decades: worker attitudes, union growth, participation in management, productivity, collective bargaining, and international aspects.) [2247]

102. **"The New Industrial Relations"** (Special Report), *Business Week,* 11 May 1981, 84–98. (Changed social values, high educational levels, and economic strains are resulting in a new industrial relations system aimed at ending the adversarial relationship.) [3924]

VIII. NEW WORK ARRANGEMENTS

103. **Theory Z: How American Business Can Meet the Japanese Challenge.** William Ouchi (UCLA). Reading MA: Addison-Wesley, April 1981/192p/$10.95; NY: Avon, 1982/$2.95pb. (Best-seller on how Japanese organizations are typified by life-time employment, slow promotion, and employee participation in decision-making.)
[3928]

104. **Work and People: An Economic Evaluation of Job Enrichment.** Henri Savall (Lyon, France). NY: Oxford U Press, 1981/224p/$45.00. (Case histories and strategies of change on how workers can share in creating new forms of work organization.) [3927]

105. **Making Organizations Humane and Productive.** Edited by H. Meltzer and Walter R. Nord (Washington U). NY: Wiley-Interscience, 1981/512p/$27.95. (The 28 essays consider such topics as managerial processes, women in organizations, realities of aging, modernizing unions, work redesign, and humanizing technology.)
[3930]

106. **New Work Schedules in Practice: Managing Time in a Changing Society.** Stanley D. Nollen (Georgetown U). Work in America Institute Series. NY: Van Nostrand Reinhold, 1981/215p/$18.95. (On flexible schedules and compressed workweeks, now enjoyed by 10 million US workers, and how they benefit workers, management, and communities.) [3875]

107. **Flexible Working Hours: An Innovation in the Quality of Work Life.** Simcha Ronen (NYU). NY: McGraw-Hill, Jan 1981/352p/ $14.95. (On flextime in the US and abroad, and the impact on employees, employers, and society.) [2496]

108. **"How to Forecast Your Own Working Future,"** James O'Toole (USC), *The Futurist*, XVI:1, Feb 1982, 5–11. (Sketches four scenarios of the industrial workplace in 1995: the meritocratic workplace, the behaviorist workplace, the entitlementarian workplace, and the humanistic workplace.) [3880]

109. **Workplace Democracy and Social Change.** Edited by Frank Lindenfeld and Joyce Rothschild-Whitt. Boston MA: Porter Sargent, Jan 1983/456p/$20.00;$12.00pb. (Anthology on such topics as collectivist organizations, worker ownership, the rewards of participation, participation in a conventional corporation, and the labor movement and worker management.) [FS 5:2, #83-096]

110. **Workplace Democracy: An Inquiry Into Employee Participation in Canadian Work Organizations.** Donald V. Nightingale (Queens U). Toronto: U of Toronto Press, May 1982/c312p/$30.00;$14.95. (Examines 20 industrial organizations—10 permitting some form of participation and 10 following conventional hierarchical design— finding greater productivity where employees participate in decisions related to their work.) [FS 5:2, #83-097]

111. **Worker Participation: Productivity and the Quality of Work Life.** Bruce Stokes. Worldwatch Paper 25. Washington: Worldwatch Institute, Dec 1978/48p/$2.00. (There is an untapped reserve of human energies and resources that could be utilized through participatory organizational forms, and instances of labor-management cooperation in the US and Europe are described.) [990]

112. **Working Together: Participation from Shopfloor to Boardroom.** William Mares and John Simmons. NY: Knopf, Jan 1983/304p/ $15.00. (Shows how pioneering US companies are decentralizing their decision-making, listening to employees, delegating responsibility, and enabling workers to become part-owners.)
[FS 5:2, #83-098]

113. **Guide to New Work Innovations in America.** Edited by R. Zager and M.P. Rosow (Work in America Institute). Elmsford NY: Pergamon, Fall 1982/300p/$25.00. (Offers 12 case studies of organizations using work innovations to increase productivity and encourage employee participation in decision-making.) [FS 5:2, #83-099]

114. **The Case for Workers' Co-ops.** Robert Oakeshott. Boston: Routledge & Kegan Paul, Dec 1978/$21.00. (On the historical and contemporary experience in the UK, France, and Italy, arguing that attempts at true worker's co-ops have rarely been made.) [986]

115. **Revolt From the Center.** Niels I. Meyer *et al.* Salem NH: Marion Boyars, July 1981/190p/$7.95pb. (A 1978 Danish best-seller depicting a humane, ecologically sustainable society of the 21st century in which the bulk of the economy would be run as cooperative enterprises with all employees receiving the same wage, and where there is guaranteed work for all who want it.) [3733]

ADDENDA

116. **Automation and the Workplace: Selected Labor, Education and Training Issues.** U.S. Congress, Office of Technology Assessment, Washington: USGPO, March 1983/$4.50. S/N 052-003-00900-5. (Preliminary component of a larger OTA assessment on computerized workplaces, due for completion in late 1983. Also see "Automation et Emploi," *Futuribles,* No 64, March 1983, 73–88.)
[FS 5:7, #83–489]

117. **Emerging Careers: New Occupations for the Year 2000 and Beyond.** S. Norman Feingold (National Career & Counseling Service, Washington) and Norma Reno Miller. Garrett Park MD: Garrett Park Press, Spring 1983/176p/$11.95. (Also see *Jobs for the 21st Century.* Robert V. Weinstein. NY: Macmillan, June 1982/192p/ $6.95pb.) [FS 5:7, #83–470]

118. **Employment, Economics and Technology: The Impact of Technical Change on the Labor Market.** Charles Cooper and John Clark (Science Policy Research Unit, U of Sussex). NY: St. Martin's, Sept 1982/c180p/$25.00. [FS 5:7, #83–492]

119. **Full Employment and Public Policy: The United States and Sweden.** Helen Ginsberg (CUNY-Brooklyn College). Lexington MA: Lexington Books, March 1983/235p/$24.95.   [FS 5:7, #83–476]
120. **Sleepers, Wake! Technology and the Future of Work.** Barry Jones (Australian Shadow Minister for Science and Technology). NY: Oxford U Press, Feb 1983/285p/$24.95;$9.95pb.

[FS 5:7, #83–483]